lonely planet

Lincolnshire

KT-556-938

discover libraries

This book should be returned on or before the due date.

Contents

CALA SANT VICENÇ P116

PALMA DE MALLORCA P49

STUART BLACK/GETTY IMAGES ©

HOLGER LEUE/GETTY IMAGES ©

Contents

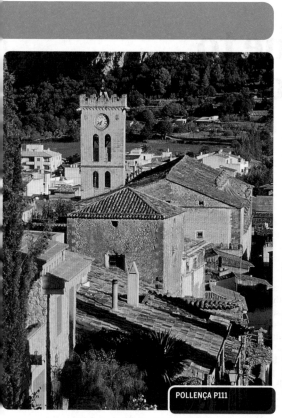

POLLENÇA P111

Welcome to Mallorca

The ever-popular star of the Mediterranean, Mallorca has a big sunny personality thanks to its ravishing beaches, remote mountains and soulful hill towns.

Lyrical Landscapes

For Miró it was the pure Mediterranean light. For hikers and cyclists it is the Serra de Tramuntana's formidable limestone spires and bluffs reigning over the island's west coast. For others it is as fleeting as the almond blossom snowing on meadows in spring, or the interior's vineyards in their autumn mantle of gold. Wherever your journey takes you, Mallorca never fails to seduce. Cars conga along the coast in single file for views so enticing they make resort postcards look like poor imitations. But even in the tourist swarms of mid-August, you can find your own muse – trek to hilltop monasteries, pedal through honey-stone villages and engrave Mallorca's landscapes to memory.

Return to Tradition

Mallorca's culture has taken a back seat to its beaches for decades, but the tides are changing. Up and down the island, locals are embracing their roots and revamping the island's old manor houses, country estates and long-abandoned *fincas* (farmhouses) into refined rural retreats. Spend silent moments among the olive, carob and almond groves and you'll soon fall for the quiet charm of Mallorca's hinterland. Summer is one long party and village *festes* (festivals) offer a genuine slice of island life.

Coastal Living

There are many reasons why Mallorca tops Europe's summer-holiday charts, but one ranks above all others: the island's beautiful coast. Beyond the built-up resorts, coves braid the island like a string of pearls – each one a reminder of why the island's beaches have never lost their appeal. Go west for cliff-sculpted drama and sapphire seas, or head north for hikes to pine-flecked bays and breezes that carry kitesurfers, windsurfers and sailors across turquoise waters. Scope out deserted coves in the east, or dive off bone-white beaches in the south. With a room overlooking the bright-blue sea, sundown beach strolls to the backbeat of cicadas, and seafood at restaurants open to the stars, you'll soon click into the laid-back groove of coastal living.

Mediterranean Flavours

Eating out in Palma has never been more exciting, with chefs – inspired as much by their Mallorquin grandmothers as Mediterranean nouvelle cuisine – adding a pinch of creativity and spice to the city's food scene. Inland restaurants plate up hearty dishes, such as suckling pig spit-roast to perfection, paired with local wines. On the coast, bistros keep flavours clean, bright and simple, serving the catch of the day with big sea views.

Why I Love Mallorca

By Kerry Christiani, Author

No island holds such a special place for me as Mallorca. Time and again it draws me back to hike the Tramuntana's heights and the coastal trails combing Formentor and Cap des Pinar. It was here, in the backstreets of Pollença, that I perfected my Spanish, and here that I met my now-husband one hazy summer in Platja de Muro 14 years ago. Every time I return, I fall in love with the island all over again – be it on a clifftop walk in spring when the rosemary is in bloom or during a monastery stay in the wood-smoke-scented depths of winter.

For more about our author, see page 232

Above: Cala Sant Vicenç (p116)

Mallorca

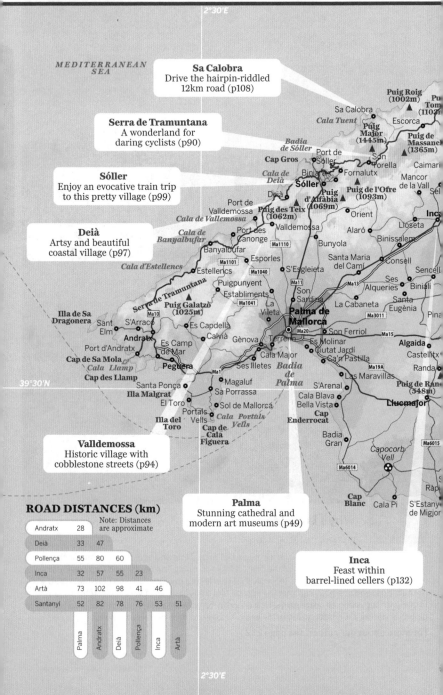

MEDITERRANEAN SEA

Sa Calobra
Drive the hairpin-riddled
12km road (p108)

Serra de Tramuntana
A wonderland for
daring cyclists (p90)

Sóller
Enjoy an evocative train trip
to this pretty village (p99)

Deià
Artsy and beautiful
coastal village (p97)

Valldemossa
Historic village with
cobblestone streets (p94)

Palma
Stunning cathedral and
modern art museums (p49)

Inca
Feast within
barrel-lined cellers (p132)

ROAD DISTANCES (km)

Note: Distances are approximate

	Palma	Andratx	Deià	Pollença	Inca	Artà
Andratx	28					
Deià	33	47				
Pollença	55	80	60			
Inca	32	57	55	23		
Artà	73	102	98	41	46	
Santanyí	52	82	78	76	53	51

2°30'E

39°30'N

Cap de Formentor
Breathtaking peninsula high above the Med (p119)

Platja des Coll Baix
Isolated and near-perfect wilderness beach (p124)

Pollença
Pilgrimage town with medieval streets (p111)

Cala Ratjada
Unspoiled east coast beaches (p147)

Artà
Castle lookout and great food (p143)

Parc Natural de S'Albufera
Best birdwatching in the Mediterranean (p126)

Illa de Cabrera
Pristine archipelago with stunning coves (p162)

0 — 20 km
0 — 10 miles

3°E

3°30'E

Cala Figuera
Cap de Formentor
Illot del Colomer
Cases Velles
Ma2210 **Moll des Patronet**

Cala Sant Vicenç
Ca'n Es Faro
Vall de Bóquer
Serra de Tramuntana
Pollença
Port de Pollença
Badia de Pollença
10
Sa Marina
Bonaire
Cap des Pinar
Ma2200
Alcúdia
Mal Pas
Platja des Coll Baix

Cova de Sant Martí
Port d'Alcúdia
Alcanada
Badia d'Alcúdia
Cap Ferrutx
Platges de Mallorca
Talaia Moreia (432m)
Cala Fosca
S'Arenal et des Verger
Parc Natural de S'Albufera
Son Serra de Marina
Colònia de Sant Pere
Es Caló
Betlem
Cala Matzoc
nibona
Campanet
Ca'n Picafort
Cala Mesquida
Moscari
Sa Pobla
Ma3410
Finca Pública de Son Real
S'Estanyol
Pare Natural de la Península de Llevant
Cala Agulla
a13A
Puig de Santa Magdalena (307m)
Muro
Santa Margalida
Son Morell Vell
Cala Ratjada
Punta de Capdepera
Llubí
Ma12
Capdepera
Son Moll
Ses Pastoras
Artà
Ma3551
Maria de la Salut
Son Doblons
Son Figuera
Ma4041
Font de Sa Cala
Coves d'Artà
Costitx
Ariany
Ma15
Son Servera
Ma4040
Canyamel
berts
Sineu
Petra
Sant Llorenç d'es Cardassa
Cala Bona
Costa de los Pinos
Lloret de Vistalegre
Sant Joan
Ma4030
Son Moro
Badia de Son Servera
Montuïri
Els Calderers
Son Carrio
S'Illot
Cala Millor
Ma3220
Ma5017
Vilafranca de Bonany
Manacor
Ma4020
Coves dels Hams
Cala Moreia
Cala Moranda
Porreres
Ma4015
Porto Cristo
Coves del Drac
Porto Cristo Novo
Ma5020
Ma14
Cala Romàntica
Cova del Pilar
Cala Varques
Cala Sequer
Felanitx
Ma4010
Cales de Mallorca
Cala Murada
Campos
Ma5120
Ca'n Roig
Ca's Concos des Cavallers
Portocolom
Sa Punta
MEDITERRANEAN SEA
Ma6030
S'Horta
Calonge
Caló d'en Marçal
Ma19
Ma14
S'Alqueria Blanca
Cala Mitjana
Ses Salines
Santanyí
Cala d'Or
Portopetro
Colònia de Sant Jordi
Llombards
Cala Figuera
Cala Mondragó
Cova de Sa Plana
Cala Santanyí
Cala Llombards
Ma6110
Caló des Màrmols
Cala en Tugores
Reserva Marina del Migjorn de Mallorca
Cap de Ses Salines
Illa des Conills
Illa de Cabrera

39°30'N

ELEVATION

1000m
700m
500m
300m
200m
100m
0

3°E

3°30'E

Mallorca's
Top 17

Palma Catedral

1 Resembling a vast ship moored at the city's edge, Palma Catedral (p49) dominates the skyline and is the island's architectural tour de force. On the seaward side, the flying buttresses are extraordinary. A kaleidoscope of stained-glass windows and an intriguing flight of fancy by Gaudí inhabit the interior, alongside an inventive rendering of a biblical parable by contemporary artist Miquel Barceló. You'll find yourself returning here, either to get your bearings, or simply to admire it from every angle.

The Road to Sa Calobra

2 Even local drivers say three Hail Marys before braving the helter-skelter of a road to Sa Calobra (p108). It translates as 'The Snake' and slither it does, for all 12 brake-screeching, hair-raising, wow-look-at-the-view-over-the-cliff kilometres. But if you think the looping hairpin bends are tough by car, spare a thought for the mountain bikers that slog it up here. Drivers teeter perilously close to the edge to glimpse a ravine that scythes through the wild, bare peaks of the Tramuntana to reach a sea of deepest blue.

Platja des Coll Baix

3 Isolated coves remote from roads are Mallorca's forte, but few can rival the Platja des Coll Baix (p124). Accessible only on foot through fragrant woods or by sea, this hidden beach on the pine-draped headland of Cap des Pinar is a stunning white crescent, backed by cliffs and pummeled by sea that shimmers unfathomable shades of cobalt blue and turquoise. Here the soundtrack is an increasingly rare one – water lapping against the shore, the trill of birdsong and (if you time it right) complete silence.

The Village of Deià

4 The mountains of Serra de Tramuntana rise like an amphitheatre above Deià (p97), a real bird's nest of a village perched high above the iridescent Mediterranean. Mallorca has countless pretty towns, but none surpass this beauty: its gold-stone buildings climb a pyramid-shaped hill and glow like warm honey as day fades to dusk. It has long been the muse of artists and writers, not least the poet Robert Graves. Head to nearby Son Marroig, once the romantic abode of an Austrian archduke, to see the Mediterranean turn to flame at sunset.

HOLGER LEUE/GETTY IMAGES ©

SEBASTIA TORRENS/GETTY IMAGES ©

Taking the Slow Train to Sóller

5 Palma and Sóller rank highly as attractions in their own right, but the antique wooden train (p77) that rattles between them is like rewinding 100 years. Scenes of rural Mallorca flash past like film stills as the train zips through fertile valleys and climbs languidly into the foothills of the Serra de Tramuntana. Travelling through tunnels and across narrow valleys before emerging high above pretty Sóller, this memorable ride is a poignant reminder that it is the journey itself that matters.

Touring the Coast of Cap de Formentor

6 The narrow, precipitous peninsula of Cap de Formentor (p119) is one of the most dramatic mountain ranges in southern Europe. Here, peaks thrust upwards like the jagged ramparts of some epic Mediterranean fortress, while forests of Aleppo pines add light and shadow to austere rocky outcrops that drop abruptly to some of the most beautiful and isolated beaches and coves on the island. However you travel the road running its length, prepare for drama and photo-ops on every sweeping bend.

Birdwatching in Parc Natural de S'Albufera

7 Twitchers flock to Parc Natural de S'Albufera (p126), a tranquil nature park and one of the Mediterranean's premier sites for birdwatching, as the home of 300 bird species, including 64 who breed here. The trails that wind amid the wetlands of this protected area are best explored on foot or by bike. Look out for herons, osprey and egrets from the observation decks discreetly tucked between the reeds, and bring binoculars for the best chances of spotting waterbirds in the marshes. Above: Common terns feeding

DAVID TOMLINSON/GETTY IMAGES ©

The Pollença Sanctuaries

8 Of all the towns of the Mallorcan interior, it is Pollença that rises above the rest. Its two hilltop sanctuaries and pilgrimage points look down on a medieval roofscape of stone and terracotta. Climb the 365 steps of the Calvari (p111) or walk through woods of holm oak and pine to Santuari de la Mare de Déu des Puig (p118) for spirit-lifting views. At ground level, wander the town's tangle of lanes, mooch around its Sunday market and watch the world go leisurely by from a front-row cafe on the Plaça Major. Above: View of Pollença from the Calvari

Water Sports

9 One look at Mallorca's unfathomably blue sea has water-sports enthusiasts itching to slip into a wetsuit or leap on a board. Scuba divers are in their underwater element in Formentor's caverns and around the southern islands – Illa de Sa Dragonera (p89) and Illa de Cabrera (p163), with wrecks, cave drops and water swirling with rays, octopuses and barracuda. Coasteering, kayaking and – deep breath now – cliff jumping lure adventure seekers north. Kitesurfers go with the winds off the Badia de Pollença. Top right: Illa de Sa Dragonera

Eating at a Celler in Inca

10 A suckling pig turns slowly on a spit, the burble of animated conversation rises above the clamour of pans and the chink of glasses, waiters bustle between tables, bringing generous helpings of *conill amb ceba* (rabbit with onions), *frit Mallorquí* (a lamb offal fry-up) and *llom amb col* (tender pork loin in cabbage parcels). You eat heartily and drink deep of local wine below the beams and next to giant barrels in Inca's *celler* restaurants (p133) – this is Mallorcan dining at its most authentic.

Palma's Art Trail

11 The crisp Mediterranean light drew some of Europe's most respected painters throughout the 20th century, but two in particular – Joan Miró and Mallorquin Miquel Barceló – will be forever associated with the island. Miró's former home, the Fundació Pilar I Joan Miró (p81), contains a fine range of his works, while Barceló adorned Palma's cathedral (p49) with flair and distinction. Elsewhere, works by Picasso and Dalí can be found in Palma's galleries, Es Baluard (p60), Palau March (p51) or the Museu Fundació Juan March (p55).
Below: Es Baluard

Cruising to Illa de Cabrera

12 The only national park in the Balearics, Parc Nacional Marítim-Terrestre de l'Arxipèlag de Cabrera (p163) is a special place and Illa de Cabrera is the jewel in its crown. The largest of 19 uninhabited islands that make up the marine park, Cabrera is blissfully peaceful – its wild headlands and secluded beaches are protected by laws that limit the number of daily visitors to sustainable levels. Boat excursions to the island from Colònia de Sant Jordi stop off at Sa Cova Blava, an exquisitely blue marine cave of rare beauty.

11

12

Cala Ratjada's Beaches

13 Amid the overdevelopment that blights so much of eastern Mallorca, there are beautiful bays and half-moon coves that serve as reminders of why people have always come here in search of the perfect stretch of sand. The beaches within striking distance of Cala Ratjada – particularly Cala Agulla (p147), Cala Mesquida (p151) and those of the Parc Natural de la Península de Llevant – are some of the best on the island, with pearly white sand and turquoise waters set against a backdrop of pine trees and sand dunes. Below: Cala Mesquida

Valldemossa

14 In any poll of the prettiest villages in the Balearics, Valldemossa (p94) is sure to make the grade. Draped around the eastern foothills of the Serra de Tramuntana, the village has the usual cobblestone lanes, flowerpots and pretty church. But Valldemossa is given added cachet by having its very own saint and a former royal monastery which once housed Frédéric Chopin and George Sand; their stay bequeathed to the town one of Mallorca's most uplifting music festivals, Festival Chopin.

HOLGER LEUE/GETTY IMAGES ©

HOLGER LEUE/GETTY IMAGES ©

Cycling the Serra de Tramuntana

15 British Olympian Bradley Wiggins once called Mallorca a 'Scalextric set for cyclists', and never is this truer than in the Serra de Tramuntana (p109), where road and track racing professionals like to limber up for the Tour de France. This wild mountainscape of pockmarked limestone peaks, serpentine roads and cliffs that sheer down to the Mediterranean is a cycling wonderland, offering the most challenging terrain of this bikeable island. Among the top rides are the 55km loop from Pollença to Monestir de Lluc (p109) and, for the fast and fit, the 12km ascent from Sa Calobra.

Staying on a Farm

16 Light years away from the busy coastal resorts, Mallorca's hinterland is sprinkled with *fincas* (farm-stays; p167) where it is often peaceful enough to hear an olive hit the ground. Whether endearingly rustic or revamped in boutique-chic style, these properties take you that bit closer to the spirit of rural Mallorca. Days unfold unhurriedly here, with lazy mornings by the pool, strolls through olive groves and citrus orchards, and dinners under the stars to the drone of cicadas. Top right: Agroturisme Monnàber Vell (p177)

Medieval Artà

17 Set back from eastern Mallorca's busy summer coast, Artà (p143) has enduring year-round charms. Its stone buildings line narrow medieval streets that gently climb up a hillside before ascending steeply to one of the island's most unusual church-castle complexes. The far-reaching views here are compelling, while back in town fine restaurants, hotels and an agreeably sleepy air make it an ideal base for your exploration of the island, including nearby Parc Natural de la Península de Llevant.

Need to Know

For more information, see Survival Guide (p208)

Currency
Euro (€)

Language
Spanish and Mallorquin (a dialect of Catalan)

Visas
Generally not required for stays of up to 90 days (or not at all for members of EU or Schengen countries). Some nationalities will need a Schengen visa.

Money
ATMs are widely available in towns and resorts. Credit cards are accepted in most hotels, restaurants and shops.

Mobile Phones
Local SIM cards are widely available and can be used in European and Australian mobile phones. Other phones may need to be set to roaming.

Time
Central European Time (GMT/UTC plus one hour)

When to Go

Dry climate
Warm to hot summers, mild winters

Pollença
GO Mar–Oct

Sóller
GO Apr–Jun & Sep–Oct

Cala Ratjada
GO May–Sep

Palma de Mallorca
GO year-round

Cala d'Or
GO May–Sep

High Season
(Jul–Aug)

⇒ Clear skies, sunny days and warm seas.

⇒ Temperatures soar as do room rates. Book well ahead or try for a last-minute deal online.

⇒ Fiesta time! The island's towns host high-spirited parties, parades and music festivals.

Shoulder
(Easter–Jun, Sep & Oct)

⇒ Most hotels and restaurants open at Easter and stay open until October.

⇒ Days are often still mild and crowds are few.

⇒ Ideal season for hiking, climbing, mountain biking and canyoning.

Low Season
(Nov–Easter)

⇒ Many hotels and restaurants close. Palma is the exception.

⇒ Pack layers for cooler-than-expected evening temperatures.

⇒ You'll have the island's trails, beaches and sights all to yourself.

Useful Websites

Consell de Mallorca (www.info-mallorca.net) Excellent website from the island's regional tourist authorities.

LonelyPlanet (www.lonelyplanet.com/mallorca) Destination information, hotel bookings, traveller forums and more.

Top Fincas (www.topfincas.com) Directory and booking service for Mallorca's rural properties.

ABC Mallorca (www.abc-mallorca.com) Lifestyle portal for both residents and tourists.

See Mallorca (www.see mallorca.com) News, upcoming events and listings.

Important Numbers

There are no area codes in Spain.

International access code	📞0
Spain's country code	📞34
International directory enquiries	📞11825
Emergency	📞112
Policía Nacional	📞91

Exchange Rates

Australia	A$1	€0.66
Canada	C$1	€0.66
Japan	¥100	€0.70
New Zealand	NZ$1	€0.61
UK	UK£1	€1.21
USA	US$1	€0.72

For current exchange rates see www.xe.com.

Daily Costs

Budget: Less than €100

➡ Basic digs in a hostel or guesthouse: €45–60

➡ Hotel breakfast, three-course *menú del día* lunch: €15–20

➡ Bus ticket to nearby towns and beaches: €2–5

Midrange: €100–250

➡ Double room in midrange hotel: €75–150

➡ Cafe lunch, dinner at a tapas bar: €30–40

➡ Car rental: from €30 per day

Top End: More than €250

➡ Double room in top-end hotel: €150 and up

➡ Sit-down lunch and dinner at first-rate restaurant: €80–100

➡ Boat tour or guided activity: around €50

Opening Hours

Opening hours vary throughout the year. We've provided high-season opening hours; hours will generally decrease in the shoulder and low seasons. Most resort restaurants and hotels close from mid-October to Easter.

Banks 8.30am–2pm Monday to Friday; some also 4–7pm Thursday and 9am–1pm Saturday

Bars 7pm–3am

Cafes 11am–1am

Clubs midnight–6am

Post offices 8.30am–9.30pm Monday to Friday, 8.30am–2pm Saturday

Restaurants lunch 1–3.30pm, dinner 7.30–11pm

Shops 10am–2pm & 4.30–7.30pm Monday to Saturday; supermarkets and department stores 10am–9pm Monday to Saturday

Arriving in Mallorca

Palma de Mallorca Airport (PMI) Bus 1 runs every 15 minutes from the airport (ground floor of Arrivals) to Plaça d'Espanya in central Palma (€3, 15 minutes); buy tickets from the driver. A taxi for the same 15-minute journey from the centre will set you back between €18 and €22. Some hotels can arrange transfers.

Ferry Port, Palma Bus 1 (the airport bus) runs every 15 minutes from the ferry port (Estació Marítima) to Plaça d'Espanya. Tickets cost €1.50 and the journey takes 10 to 15 minutes. Expect to pay €10 to €12 for a taxi to the city centre.

Getting Around

Transport in Mallorca is reasonably priced, though buses and trains do not cover every corner of the island, and services slow to a trickle in the low season. For timetables throughout the island, head to Transport de les Illes Balears (www.tib.org).

Train Modestly priced and fairly frequent but limited in scope – one line to Sóller in the west, one to Inca, where the line splits to serve Sa Pobla and Manacor.

Car Great for exploring the island's remoter beaches, hill towns and mountains at your own pace. Cars can be hired in every town or resort. Drive on the right.

Bus The island's buses cover major towns and many villages. You'll be limited to a handful of services in low season, while some (for instance to beaches) stop entirely.

For much more on **getting around**, see p215

First Time Mallorca

For more information, see Survival Guide (p208)

Checklist

⇒ Ensure that your passport is valid for at least six months after your arrival

⇒ Make advance bookings for accommodation, restaurants, travel and tours

⇒ Inform your credit-/debit-card company that you'll be travelling abroad

⇒ Arrange comprehensive travel insurance (p209)

⇒ Verify what you need to hire a car (including excess insurance; p217)

What to Pack

⇒ Travel adapter plug

⇒ High factor sun cream

⇒ Mosquito/insect repellent

⇒ Flip flops

⇒ Hiking boots for Tramuntana trails

⇒ Mobile (cell) phone charger

⇒ Sunhat and sunglasses

⇒ Beach towel and swimmers

⇒ Waterproof coin holder/dry bag

⇒ Phrasebook

⇒ A sociable nature – the Mallorquins love a good chinwag

Top Tips for Your Trip

⇒ Mallorca is a tale of two islands – detour off the well-trodden trail for a spell and you will find peaceful countryside, restful *fincas* (farms) and uncrowded beaches.

⇒ Get high: the best views and photo ops are from the monasteries, forts and castles that crown Mallorca's hillsides. Time it right and you'll catch a fiery sunset.

⇒ Allow ample time to get from A to B. Looking at a map of Mallorca is deceptive. Yes, it is an island and fairly compact, but those twisting mountain roads bump up journey times.

⇒ Walk. Whether it's pilgrim-style to a monastery, through the back alleys of a cobbled old town or to a hidden bay – many of Mallorca's most alluring sights can only be seen on foot.

What to Wear

Mallorca is a laid-back island and most people find they over-pack, especially for beach and poolside holidays that require little more than bathing suits and a couple of changes of shorts and T-shirts. Going out is a casual affair and ties and jackets are not required, even in the smartest restaurants.

Summers are hot, but layers are advisable for the rest of the year when the weather is patchier and evenings are cool. Forget wearing high heels on the cobbled streets of Mallorca's hill towns – flats it is.

Sleeping

Reserving a room is always a good idea – book well in advance (at least two months) if you are travelling in the peak months of July and August when beds are like gold dust.

⇒ **Hotels** These range from family resort hotels beside the sea to converted manors with boutique-chic interiors inland.

⇒ **Hostal** A small no-frills budget hotel, usually family run.

⇒ **Fincas** Farm-stays in rural, peaceful areas.

Money

Cash is king for small purchases in Mallorca, and spare change is handy for coffee pit stops and spontaneous market buys. Avoid taking more money to the beach than you need for ice cream, drinks and sunbed and parasol hire (€10 to €15 per day).

Credit and debit cards are generally accepted in hotels, with the exception of some rural B&Bs. Small, family-run restaurants and cafes might insist on cash – check before ordering to be on the safe side.

ATMs are plentiful in resorts and towns but not in rural areas. You should be able to withdraw money with your bank card, though transaction fees sometimes apply.

For more information, see p210.

Bargaining

Hone your haggling skills for the island's markets; elsewhere be prepared to pay the stated price.

Tipping

➡ **Hotels** Discretionary. As a rule, tip bellboys around €1 per bag and room cleaners €2 per day in fancier hotels.

➡ **Cafes and bars** Not expected, but you can reward good service by rounding the bill to the nearest euro or two.

➡ **Restaurants** Service charge is included in restaurant bills, but most diners leave an extra tip of around 5% to show their satisfaction.

➡ **Taxis** Not necessary, but feel free to leave a modest tip, especially for longer journeys.

Language

Travelling in Mallorca without speaking a single word of Spanish or Mallorquin is entirely possible, but picking up a smattering of these languages will go along way to winning the affection of the locals. English is widely spoken in the beach resorts and in major towns, but in the rural hinterland and small villages you'll find it handy to have a grasp of a few basic phrases, plus it's part of the fun!

① **What time does it open/close?**
¿A qué hora abren/cierran? a ke o·ra ab·ren/thye·ran

The Spanish tend to observe the siesta (midday break), so opening times may surprise you.

② **Are these complimentary?**
¿Son gratis? son gra·tees

Tapas (bar snacks) are available pretty much around the clock at Spanish bars. You'll find they're free in some places.

③ **When is admission free?**
¿Cuándo es la entrada gratuita?
kwan·do es la en·tra·da gra·twee·ta

Many museums and galleries in Spain have admission-free times, so check before buying tickets.

④ **Where can we go (salsa) dancing?**
¿Dónde podemos ir a bailar (salsa)?
don·de po·de·mos eer a bai·lar (sal·sa)

Flamenco may be the authentic viewing experience in Spain, but to actively enjoy the music you'll want to do some dancing.

⑤ **How do you say this in (Catalan/Galician/Basque)?**
¿Cómo se dice ésto en (catalán/gallego/euskera)?
ko·mo se dee·the es·to en (ka·ta·lan/ga·lye·go/e·oos·ke·ra)

Spain has four official languages, and people in these regions will appreciate it if you try to use their local language.

Etiquette

➡ **Greetings** Shake hands if meeting for the first time and say 'bon dia' (good day) or 'bona tarda' (good evening). In more casual situations, greet with two kisses – offer your right cheek first.

➡ **Socialising** Mallorquins, like all Spanish, are a chatty, sociable lot. Don't be shy – try to join in their rapid-fire conversations if you can get a word in edgeways. Be prepared for people to stand quite close to you when speaking.

➡ **Eating and drinking** If you are invited to a Mallorquin home, take a small gift of wine, flowers or chocolate. Wait for your host to say 'bon profit!' (enjoy your meal) before getting stuck in. Dunking bread in soup is a no-no, but otherwise meals here are fairly relaxed affairs. Join in a toast by raising your glass and saying 'salut!'

If You Like...

Scenic Drives & Rides

Mallorca's precipitous coastlines and hairpin-riddled mountains call for slow touring. Slip behind the wheel for gear-crunching drives (and heart-pumping bike rides) never to be forgotten.

Andratx to Monestir de Lluc Mallorca's drive among drives cuts across the spectacularly rugged Serra de Tramuntana high above the Mediterranean. (p93)

Sa Calobra 'The Snake' sounds like a fairground attraction and indeed this is a rollercoaster of a road to a once isolated cove. (p108)

Cap de Formentor Eighteen kilometres of precipice-hugging, sea-gazing gorgeousness. (p119)

Artà to Ermita de Betlem A 7km route with pine forests, fine views and a soulful hermitage. (p127)

Sóller to Alaró Meander through mountainous foothills, olive groves and sleepy rural hamlets. (p106)

Beach Beauties

Coves with bluer-than-blue water, silky sands fringed by pines and dunes, and cliff-flanked bays only reached on foot – Mallorca has a beach for every mood and moment.

Platja des Coll Baix Draw breath as you rock-hop down to this perfect crescent washed by cobalt blue water. (p124)

Platja des Trenc Stretch out on this vast southern ribbon of sand. (p158)

Platja de Muro Powder-soft sand, dunes and kid-perfect shallow, crystalline waters. (p126)

East Coast Hop from one glorious white-sand cove to another. Calas Torta (p151), Agulla (p147), Matzoc (p151) and Mitjana (p151) top our list.

Cap de Formentor Cliff-backed seclusion on a string of coves reached on foot. (p117)

Cala Tuent Sa Calobra's quiet sister is watched over by 1445m Puig Major. (p108)

Cultural Highs

Break from the beach to discover Mallorca's cultured side, with a mooch around cathedrals, galleries and artsy hill towns.

Catedral Sing a stained-glass rainbow in this Gothic wonder moored on Palma's seafront. (p49)

Museu Fundació Juan March Picasso, Miró, Dalí, Juan Gris and Mallorquin native Miquel Barceló. (p55)

Real Cartuja de Valldemossa A Carthusian monastery and the former residence of royals and Chopin. (p94)

Ses Païsses Piece together the puzzle of Mallorca's Bronze Age *talayots* (watchtowers). (p143)

Pol·lentia Sprawling Roman ruins with an eye-catching theatre amid the trees. (p120)

Fundació Pilar i Joan Miró Miró's former home filled with his works and spirit. (p81)

Family Adventures

Mallorca's energy-burning activities, beautiful beaches, and romps around castles, aquariums and water parks are surefire kid-pleasers.

IF YOU LIKE... PERSONAL PILGRIMAGES

Walk in silent wonder through the cloister of Monestir de Lluc (p109), or spend the night at spirit-lifting Santuari de la Mare de Déu des Puig (p168) above Pollença.

Palma Aquarium Dip your toes into Mallorca's underwater world. Shark sleepovers notch up the fear factor. (p79)

Coves del Drac Spelunk the stalactite-encrusted depths of Mallorca's most magical caves. (p151)

Castell d'Alaró Play king of the castle at this impossibly perched medieval fortress. (p107)

Aqualand Race the spaghetti-like slides and white-knuckle flumes at one of Europe's biggest water parks. (p79)

Parc Natural de S'Albufera Gentle strolls in bird-rich wetlands. (p126)

North Coast Caving, cliff-jumping, coasteering and scuba diving will keep older kids as busy as bees. (p110)

Coastal Walks

The lure of the sea is palpable as you stride along cliffs, hop between coves and trace Mallorca's coastal contours from a mountaintop.

Ruta de Pedra en Sec The queen of coastal walks is a mind-blowing multiday traverse of the Serra de Tramuntana. (p90)

Ermita de la Victòria to Penya Rotja Survey the entire north coast from this pine-cloaked peninsula. (p125)

Cap de Formentor The jaw-dropping northern finale of the Tramuntana. (p119)

Parc Natural de la Península de Llevant Quiet trails link beaches and pine valleys. (p145)

Cap de Ses Salines to Colònia de Sant Jordi A rocky trail with bountiful swimming spots and bewitching sea views. (p160)

Finca Can Roig to Cala Magraner Traipse to four pretty, little-visited coves. (p153)

(Above) Cap de Formentor, p119
(Below) Palma Aquarium, p79

Month by Month

January

Winter wraps the island in a blanket of calm, with some mild, some chilly days. Beach resorts are still in hibernation, with many hotels and restaurants closed; Palma is a notable exception.

✷ Three Kings

The *tres reis* (three kings) rock up on 5 January, the eve of Epiphany, bearing gifts of gold, frankincense and myrrh. They are the stars of a flamboyant parade in Palma.

✷ Festes de Sant Antoni Abat

The Festes de Sant Antoni Abat (16 and 17 January) are celebrated with concerts, prancing demons, huge pyres and fireworks, and parading farm animals get a blessing. It's celebrat-ed with particular gusto in Sa Pobla and Artà.

✷ Sant Sebastià

Palma pulls out the party stops on the eve of the feast day of its patron saint (20 January), with live music, fireworks and revelry in city squares.

February

Almond trees in bloom cast flurries of white blossom across the countryside. High-spirited carnivals shake the island out of its winter slumber for pre-Lenten feasting and parading. Many places are still closed.

✷ Carnivals

The pre-Lenten season kicks off with parades across the island. In Palma a children's procession, Sa Rueta, is followed by the grown-ups' version, Sa Rua, with pumping music, fancy dress and colourful floats.

March

A glorious month, with solemn Easter celebrations, wildflowers flourishing and fantastic birdwatching in the Parc Natural de S'Albufera.

✷ Semana Santa

Follow the Semana Santa (Holy Week) processions around the island. Begin in Palma on Holy Thursday evening, then head to Pollença for its moving Good Friday Davallament (bringing down). On Easter Sunday, head to Montuïri's S'Encuentro.

April

Mallorcan hotels and restaurants dust off the cobwebs, and resorts start to fill. Milder days make this a brilliant month for hiking and mountain biking.

🍷 Fira del Vi

Pollença pops a cork on regional wines at its Fira del Vi (Wine Fair) in the Convent de Sant Domingo in late April.

May

Coastal Mallorca has a real spring in its step as resorts come to life.

Sa Fira

Since 1318, Sineu has been the setting for Sa Fira, the island's largest and most authentic livestock and produce market, held on May's first Sunday.

Es Firó

On the second weekend of May, Sóller stages Es Firó, where the town's heroic defenders, led by the so-called Valiant Women, fight off Muslim pirates as in 1561, amid much merriment.

Corpus Christi

Corpus Christi (on the Thursday of the ninth week after Easter) is a major celebration in Palma. The weeks leading up to it are marked by concerts in the city's baroque courtyards.

June

Mallorca moves into top gear. Patron saints' festivals, where religious tradition mixes with good old-fashioned pagan partying, are the excuse for many a knees-up.

Nit de Sant Joan

The feast day of St John (24 June) is preceded the night before by fiery partying on the Nit de Sant Joan. In Palma, there's *correfoc* (fire running), concerts and partying on the beaches until dawn.

July

There's little to interrupt the lazy days on the beach and long liquid nights.

Festa de la Verge del Carme

On 16 July, many coastal towns stage processions for the Festa de la Verge del Carme, the patron saint of fishers and sailors.

Festa de Sant Jaume

July 25 sees *cossiers* do traditional dances in the streets of Algaida for the Festa de Sant Jaume. Six men and one woman dance alongside a demon, who ultimately comes unstuck.

August

The weather god cranks up the heat, festivals are in full swing and the hotels (and beaches) are full to bursting point.

Festes de la Patrona

One of Pollença's most colourful festivals culminates in a staged battle between townsfolk and a motley band of invading Moorish pirates during the week-long Festes de la Patrona.

Festival Chopin

Valldemossa pays tribute to one-time resident, composer Frédéric Chopin at the stately Real Cartuja de Valldemossa, with top-notch classical concerts devoted mostly to Chopin throughout August.

Mallorca Jazz Festival

Sa Pobla is an unlikely setting for one of the Mediterranean's most celebrated jazz festivals. It swings with some of the genre's big names every August.

September

September is like the joyous last drink before the hangover. Autumn is good for migrating birds in the Parc Natural de S'Albufera, coastal hikes, bike rides and water-based activities.

Festes de la Verema

Mallorca's vine-cloaked interior celebrates the grape harvest with the Festes de la Verema in late September. Binissalem gets stuck into a big juicy mess of a grape fight.

October

Last drinks! People bid tearful farewells to new-found friends at resorts across the island.

Alcúdia Fair

Concerts, produce markets, music and parades come to Alcúdia on the first weekend in October.

November

As the weather turns chilly, most places close for the winter. Autumnal markets spring up selling wine, just-harvested olives and mushrooms.

December

Christmas brings a twinkling market to Palma's Plaça Major, and locals ring in the New Year across the island with grape gobbling and fireworks.

Itineraries

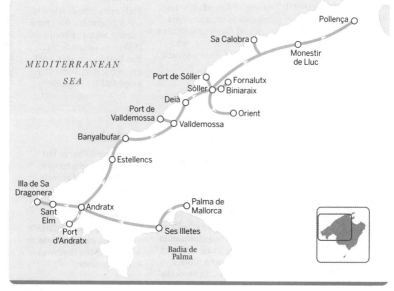

The West Coast

Warm up with a day or two in sea-splashed **Palma**, exploring its colossal cathedral, soulful alleyways and impressive portfolio of galleries and palaces. Drift southwest to beach belle **Ses Illetes**, harbourside **Port d'Andratx** and enticingly low-key **Sant Elm**; from the latter, hop to offshore **Illa de Sa Dragonera**. Marvel at cliff-edge and mountain views on the dramatic road unfurling northeast from **Andratx**. Slow the pace in alley-woven **Estellencs** and **Banyalbufar**, before overnighting in hill-town stunner, **Valldemossa**, one-time abode of Chopin. Peer through an archduke's rose-tinted specs at romantically perched mansions Miramar and Son Marroig. Just north, **Deià** twirls artistically up a hillside and begs to be photographed. Cool off in Cala de Deià, then swing north to valley-cupped **Sóller** for backstreet strolls, Modernista treasures, Picasso and Miró. Time permitting, detour to charming hill-toppers **Orient**, **Biniaraix** or **Fornalutx**, or board a rickety vintage tram down to **Port de Sóller**. As the Ma10 weaves inland, take the hair-raising road down to **Sa Calobra** en route to pilgrims' respite **Monestir de Lluc**. See the wild peaks of the Tramuntana unfurl in all their brooding splendour as you descend to the quintessentially Mallorcan town of **Pollença**.

MEDITERRANEAN SEA

Cala Figuera
Cap de Formentor
Cala Sant Vicenç
Port de Pollença
Badia de Pollença
Cap des Pinar
Pollença
Alcúdia
Port d'Alcúdia
Badia d'Alcúdia
Parc Natural de S'Albufera
Artà

Badia d'Alcúdia
Parc Natural de la Península de Llevant
Cala Ratjada
Artà
Capdepera
Sineu
Petra
Platja de Canyamel
Els Calderers
Porto Cristo
Santuari de Sant Salvador
MEDITERRANEAN SEA
Ses Salines
Colònia de Sant Jordi
Parc Nacional Marítim-Terrestre de l'Arxipèlag de Cabrera

The Northeast

1 WEEK

Idle away a couple of days in remarkably pretty **Pollença**, wandering its rabbit warren of lanes, soaking up life on the square and climbing the 365 spirit-lifting steps to the Calvari; try to time your visit to catch Sunday's vivacious market. From Pollença, drive to cliff-embraced **Cala Sant Vicenç** for dips in turquoise coves and an ultra-fresh fish lunch. Ooh and aah along the vertiginous coastal road to lighthouse-tipped **Cap de Formentor** and back again; allow time to hike down down to the cove of **Cala Figuera**. If you're a water-sports fan or have family in tow, spend a night or two in **Port de Pollença** or **Port d'Alcúdia**. Otherwise, make for medieval-walled **Alcúdia**. Tiptoe east to little-known **Cap des Pinar**, a pine-fringed peninsula of exceptional beauty, for coastal hikes and to enjoy the hush on the simply stunning Platja des Coll Baix. As you continue east, engage in a spot of birdwatching in the wetlands of **Parc Natural de S'Albufera**, then make for laid-back **Artà** for scintillating fortress views and forays into Mallorca's prehistoric past.

The East & South

10 DAYS

Linger in fortress-topped **Artà** for a day, then tour the remote coastal loveliness of wind-sculpted **Parc Natural de la Península de Llevant**, a jewel-box of pristine coves and quiet trails. Moving on from Artà, squeeze in a visit to **Capdepera**, a town absorbed wholly by its castle. Earmark a couple of nights in the vicinity of **Cala Ratjada**, hopscotching along the east coast to beguiling half-moon bays like Cala Mesquida, Cala Agulla and Cala Matzoc. Inching south from Cala Ratjada, devote time for the Coves d'Artà and medieval Torre de Canyamel around **Platja de Canyamel**. Away to the south, ponder the glittering depths of Coves del Drac in **Porto Cristo**, then point your compass inland to vine-streaked **Petra** and **Sineu**, stopping off at wineries along the way. As you wend your way back to the coast, visit handsome Mallorcan estate **Els Calderers**, ascend hilltop hermitage **Santuari de Sant Salvador** for heavenly views, then head for artsy **Ses Salines**, detouring via pretty beaches for a quick swim. Wrap up your trip in **Colònia de Sant Jordi**, springboarding to the island-speckled **Parc Nacional Marítim-Terrestre de l'Arxipèlag de Cabrera**.

Off the Beaten Track: Mallorca

MEDITERRANEAN SEA

SA FORADADA

This finger of rock juts out into the Med at the base of Son Marroig. Wander through sheep-dotted olive groves down to the sea and linger for a watercolour sunset. (p97)

BANYALBUFAR

So you've swooned over Deià and visited Valldemossa, but what about Banyalbufar? Centuries-old farming terraces form steps down to the wave-lashed coast – this speck of a village is postcard stuff. (p91)

Sa Calobra O

Cap Gros

O Sóller

PUIG D'ALARÓ ▲

Deià O

O Valldemossa

◉ SA

BANYALBUFAR O **FORADADA**

ILLA DE SA DRAGONERA

O Andratx

O Peguera

Cap des Llamp

Palma de O Mallorca

Badia de Palma

Llucmajor O

Cap Enderrocat

Cap de Cala Figuera

Cap Blanc

ILLA DE SA DRAGONERA

This rippled island reposes like a slumbering dragon off the island's westernmost tip. Trails thread through this nature reserve to quiet capes, far from the beach resort swarms. (p89)

PUIG D'ALARÓ

Even in summer those who make it to the top of the rock are few and far between. It's a stiff two-hour climb to the enigmatic remains of a Moorish castle. Or cheat by driving part way. (p107)

0 — 20 km
0 — 10 miles

FUMAT

Give the Formentor crowds the slip and take a brisk hike up to Fumat, a 334m crag with 360-degree views reaching from the tip of the headland to the Tramuntana. On the trail you may meet the odd sunbathing goat. (p120)

SANTUARI DE LA MARE DE DÉU DES PUIG

Silence blankets the courtyards and chapel of this former nunnery, high above Pollença. It's hard to drag yourself away from the views that embrace the full sweep of the north coast. (p118)

CALES DE MALLORCA

Walking is the only way to reach the tiny coves that dot the coastline north of Cales de Mallorca, but chances are you'll have their iridescent waters all to yourself. (p153)

PLATJA DES TRENC

This 3km ribbon of frost-white, dune-backed sand hems Mallorca's southern coast and is lapped by aquamarine water. Even in August, there's space to breathe and go nude if you dare. (p158)

Cap de Formentor
FUMAT
Pollença
Badia de Pollença
Cap des Pinar
SANTUARI DE LA MARE DE DÉU DES PUIG
Parc Natural de S'Albufera
Badia d'Alcúdia
Parc Natural de la Península de Llevant
Finca Pública de Son Real
Santa Margalida
Cala Ratjada
Artà
Manacor
Felanitx
CALES DE MALLORCA
Portocolom
PLATJA DES TRENC
Parc Natural de Mondragó
Cala d'Or
Cap de Ses Salines
Illa des Conills
Illa de Cabrera
MEDITERRANEAN SEA

Eat & Drink Like a Local

Hungry? Good. Mallorquins love nothing more than to see visitors to their island well fed. Whether it's sizzling-from-the-spit suckling pig in Inca's vaulted *cellers* (cellars), Med-fresh fish on a terrace with big sea views or new-wave Balearic cuisine in Palma – loosen a belt notch and get stuck in!

The Year in Food

Best in Spring

Sprigs of wild rosemary and thyme add flavour to *anyell de llet* (suckling lamb). *Espàrrecs* (asparagus) and *caracoles* (snails) pop up on many menus.

Best in Summer

You can pick *fonoll marí* (samphire), a coastal plant that's marinated and used in salads. Markets and menus fill with a bounty of fresh fruit, veg and fish.

Best in Autumn

Join locals to comb the hills for *esclata-sang*, a mushroom of the milk-fungus family. The island's grape harvest and festivals in late September are great fun, especially the grape-throwing festival in Binissalem.

Best in Winter

Menus go meaty with *sobrassada* (paprika-flavoured cured pork sausage), *llom amb col* (pork wrapped in cabbage with pine nuts and raisins) and *lechona asada* (roast suckling pig).

Food Experiences

Meals of a Lifetime

➡ **Simply Fosh** (p66) The star of Palma's gastro scene, this slinky restaurant lodged in a 17th-century convent refectory has Marc Fosh at the helm. The food? Mediterranean with a light creative touch.

➡ **Es Verger** (p107) This rustic bolthole perched high above fertile plains, close to Castell d'Alaró, is at the end of a long, winding road with many a heart-stopping turn. The highlight of the menu is lamb slow-cooked in its own juices in a wood fire.

➡ **Es Racó d'es Teix** (p99) Josef Sauerschell's gourmet haunt in Deià twinkles with one Michelin star. The mountain views are sublime, the concise menu plays up regional flavours – all beautifully cooked and presented with flair.

➡ **Béns d'Avall** (p103) Could the setting be any dreamier? The sea is a glittering expanse from this cliff-hugging restaurant. Top points for romance and seafood expertly cooked.

➡ **Celler Ca'n Amer** (p133) No visit to the interior is complete without eating in one of Inca's barrel-lined *cellers*. Keep it hearty with mains like suckling pig roast to crackling perfection.

Cheap Treats

You can eat on the hoof often with change from a €5 note by popping into a *forn* or *confiteria* (pastry shop) for crispy, sugar-topped *ensaïmades* (a croissant-like pastry dusted with icing sugar, and sometimes filled with cream) pastries, *empanades* (pasties with savoury fillings) and the larger version, *cocarrois*.

Tapas and *pintxos* (mini tapas; often bite-sized breads with various toppings) are a great way to stave off hunger and absorb local life. Hit Palma's Ruta Martiana on a Tuesday or Wednesday evening when a drink and a tapa cost as little as €2.

Dare to Try

➡ **Caracoles** Dig into snails cooked in a garlicky, herby broth or served in a rich stew.

➡ **Arròs brut** The name 'dirty rice' is offputting, but trust us this soupy wonder, with pork, rabbit and vegetables, is delicious.

➡ **Botifarró** Cured blood sausage (not unlike British black pudding) – surprisingly tasty.

➡ **Percebes** Goose barnacles – clawlike, filter-feeding crustaceans that cling to rocks – look ghastly but taste divine. Perfect finger food.

➡ **Frit Mallorquí** A flavoursome lamb offal and veg fry-up, born out of a desperate need for protein during time of poverty.

Cooking Courses

Mallorca's fledgling cooking-course scene is just starting to spread its wings, with restaurants and *fincas* (farms) occasionally offering the odd class where you can roll up your sleeves and learn the basics. Cooking Holidays Mallorca (☑971 64 82 03; www.cookingholidays mallorca.com; Avinguda Llonga, Cala d'Or) holds courses at the Yacht Club Cala d'Or, covering everything from one-day tapas classes to seven-night gourmet breaks. You can learn to make tapas or prepare paella at three-hour courses run by Mallorca Cuisine (☑971 61 67 19; www. mallorcacuisine.com; Sa Mola Gran 8, Galilea), northwest of Palma. It also organises winery and market visits. See the websites for dates and prices.

Local Specialities

You might think of Mallorca's coastline and expect to find nothing but fish on menus, yet traditional dishes are surprisingly gutsy and meat-focused, especially in the rural interior. Pork is a popular ingredient and is found in countless sausages, stews, soups and even some vegetable dishes and desserts. The centuries of hunger Mallorquins endured taught them to appreciate every part of the pig; even today, they use everything but the oink.

It's true that much of the fish eaten on Mallorca is flown in from elsewhere, but many species still fill the waters near the island. *Besugo* (sea bream) and *rape* (monkfish) are some of the most common fish caught here. Especially appreciated is *cap roig*, an ugly red fish found around the Illa de Cabrera.

Although you'll find fish and seafood cooked in a variety of sauces, this is largely a nod to foreign tastes. Mallorquins long ago learned that fresh seafood is best served grilled with just a bit of salt and lemon. Another delicious way to eat it is 'a la sal' (baked in a salt crust).

Paella may have its origins just across the water in Valencia on the mainland, but this and other rice dishes have been taken to heart by Mallorquins to the extent that some of Spain's best paellas are found on the island.

TAKE IT HOME

For a lingering taste of Mallorca, save room to take home hand-harvested salt from des Trenc, fig bread, *sobrassada* (paprika-flavoured cured pork sausage), olives, almonds, wine, Hierbas liqueur and tangy orange preserves from Sóller – a burst of island sunshine when summer is long gone. Here's where you'll find them:

➡ Enseñat (p116)

➡ Típika (p75)

➡ Flor de Sal d'es Trenc (p122)

➡ Fet a Sóller (p103)

➡ Tramuntana Gourmet (p105)

➡ Cassai Gourmet (p161)

➡ Colmado Santo Domingo (p75)

➡ Malvasia de Banyalbufar (p92)

Vegetarians & Vegans

There has been a rise in restaurants and cafes dishing up vegetarian and vegan fare in recent years. They make the most of the island's fava broad beans, peppers, aubergines, artichokes, cauliflowers and asparagus. Figs, apricots and oranges (especially around Sóller) are abundant.

If you want something light, try *trempó*, a refreshing Mallorcan salad made of chopped tomatoes, peppers and onions, drizzled in olive oil. *Pa amb oli* is another good option, as is tumbet. Spanish gazpacho (cold, garlicky tomato soup) and tortillas, thick omlettes made with potatoes or vegies, are popular too.

It's worth bearing in mind that many traditional vegie dishes are prepared with salted pork, meat broth or lard. For meat-free meals be sure to stress that you are a vegetarian. *Soy vegetariano/a* (I'm a vegetarian) or *no como carne* (I don't eat meat) should do the trick.

Mallorcan Wine

Mallorca has been making wine since Roman times but only in recent years has it been toasted for its quality. Just over 30 cellars, with 2500 hectares between them, make up the island's moderate production, most of which is enjoyed in Mallorca's restaurants and hotels. The wineries are huddled in the island's two DOs (Denominaciones de Orígen), Binissalem and an area in the interior of the island that includes towns such as Manacor, Felanitx and Llucmajor, where growing conditions are ideal. International varieties like cabernet sauvignon are planted alongside native varieties, like Manto Negro, Fogoneu and Callet. Local white varieties include Prensal Blanc and Girò Blanc, which are blended with Catalan grapes like Parellada, Macabeo and moscatel or with international varieties like chardonnay.

PRICE INDICATORS

The price categories used in this guide relate to an average main course.

CATEGORY	PRICE
€ budget	<€15
€€ midrange	€15-25
€€€ top end	>€25

Wine production also takes place on the seaward slopes of the Serra de Tramuntana, particularly around Banyalbufar where the Malvasia grape is enjoying a revival.

Tourist offices across the wine country generally have a list of local wineries and their opening hours.

How to Eat & Drink

Stopping to sit down and slowly savour a meal is one of the best things about Mallorca, where eating is not just a functional pastime but one of life's great pleasures. Mallorquins eat late, no matter what the meal, although the large foreign population on the island means that restaurants tend to open an hour or more earlier than they do on the mainland.

Menu Decoder

➡ **Arròs bogavante** Moist, juicy lobster rice.

➡ **Arròs brut** Literally 'dirty rice', a soupy dish made with pork, rabbit and vegetables.

➡ **Arròs negre** A rice dish, cooked in and coloured by squid ink, and sometimes served with shellfish. A regional take on paella.

➡ **Botifarra** This flavourful pork sausage and *botiffarón* (a larger version of botifarra) are some of the best island sausages.

➡ **Cocas de patata** A breadlike pastry dusted with sugar and particularly famous in Valldemossa.

➡ **Conill amb ceba** Rabbit with onions.

➡ **Ensaïmada** The Mallorcan pastry par excellence is a round bun made with a spiral of sweet dough, topped with powdered sugar and sometimes filled with cream, chocolate or *cabell d'àngel* (pumpkin paste).

➡ **Gató Mallorquí** A dense almond cake.

➡ **Lechona** Suckling pig, often roasted on an open spit.

➡ **Llom amb col** Pork loin wrapped in cabbage, flavoured with garlic, tomatoes, *sobrassada*, parsley, sultanas and pine nuts.

➡ **Marisquada** A heaped tray of steamed shellfish – plan to share.

➡ **Pa amb oli** Literally bread with oil. Traditional *pa moreno* (rye bread) usually topped with chopped tomatoes, as well as variety of other toppings. Some are a meal in themselves.

➡ **Sobrassada** Tangy cured pork sausage flavoured with paprika and sea salt.

➡ **Suquet** Stew cooked in rich fish stock and filled with fish and/or seafood.

➡ **Tumbet** A kind of vegetable ratatouille made with aubergines, courgettes, potatoes, garlic and tomatoes. Mop up with crusty bread.

When to Eat

Most Mallorquins kick-start the day with a shot of *cafè* (black coffee), but they might head out to *esmorzar* (breakfast) around midmorning. This is the ideal time to try a sugary *ensaïmada* (Mallorcan pastry) and wash it down with a *cafè amb llet* (espresso with milk) or a *suc de taronja natural* (freshly squeezed orange juice).

Lunch is the biggest meal of the day. On Sundays, the midday family meal may last until late afternoon. Social dinners are equally drawn out, with each step from appetisers to postdinner drinks being relished to the fullest. Even when not ordering a *menú* (set menu), Mallorquins generally order two courses and a dessert when they go out for lunch.

Mallorquins' stomachs start growling by 7pm or so. This is a great time to stop for tapas. An import from the mainland, tapas aren't as widespread here as in other Spanish cities, but many bars and cafes will have a small selection of snacky things to choose from. Olives or a dish of almonds are the ideal accompaniment to a *caña* (beer).

For most Mallorquins, the appropriate dinner time is around 9pm. A meal usually begins with *pa moreno* and perhaps a *pica pica,* when many small appetisers are put out for everyone to share. Next comes the *primer plato,* which may be a salad, pasta, grilled-vegetable plate or something more creative. Desserts are most often a simple *gelat* (ice cream), flan or fruit.

Where to Eat

➡ **Celler** A country wine-cellar-turned-restaurant, with a solid menu of traditional home cooking, a local crowd and relaxed feel.

➡ **Cafe** Takes you through from morning coffee to evening tapas and drinks.Great for light bites like salads and *pa amb oli.*

➡ **Chiringuito** Beach shack serving drinks, snacks and sometimes tapas and seafood.

LUNCHTIME SAVER: MENÚ DEL DÍA

Save by following the lead of locals and making lunch your main meal of the day. The best value is the *menú del día,* a fixed-price lunch menu that offers several options each for *primeros* (starters), *segundos* (mains) and *postres* (desserts), bread and a drink (including wine or beer) for roughly €10 to €15.

➡ **Confiteria** A pastry shop, alternatively called a *forn* or a *pastelería.* Find the best *ensaïmades* here.

➡ **Gelateria** Ice-cream parlour, often with Italian-style gelato (made with milk and fresh fruit).

➡ **Marisquería** Specialises in seafood. Sometimes called a *restaurant de marisc.*

➡ **Restaurant** From simple to gourmet. Anything with ca'n or ca's in its name serves traditional fare in a family-style atmosphere.

➡ **Tabernas** Rustic taverns serving tapas or meals. *Tascas* work to a similar concept.

Dining Tips

English menus are a given in coastal resorts, but not necessarily elsewhere. That said, there is nearly always a waiter who can translate. It's handy to learn a few words of Mallorquin, though, so you can decipher some menu items for yourself. Bottled mineral water *(aigua mineral)* is the norm; order it either with *(amb)* or without *(sense)* gas.

If you're extended the honour of being invited to dine in someone's home, bring a small gift of wine or chocolates and prepare yourself for a feast. A Mallorquin host will go all out to entertain guests. Family lunches are often big, boisterous affairs – you'll barely get a word in edgeways but have fun trying! Say '*bon profit*' (enjoy your meal) before eating and '*salut!*' (cheers) when drinking a toast.

The one who invites usually foots the bill. Service charge is included, but you might want to reward good service with an additional tip of around 5%.

Top: Seafood paella

Bottom: Cookies in a Mallorcan bakery

Plan Your Trip

Outdoor Activities

Whether you're hiking along the north coast's ragged cliff tops, negotiating the Tramuntana's limestone wilderness by mountain bike or kayaking to secluded coves too tiny to appear on maps, Mallorca's outdoors exhilarates and enthrals. Mountains, canyons and 550km of gorgeous coast are all squeezed into this island. Go forth and explore!

Planning Your Trip

When to Go

Mallorca's outdoor activities are, in theory, possible year-round thanks to the island's relatively mild winters and oft-touted 300 days of sunshine. That said, many organised activities will only be doable from roughly Easter to October, particularly water-based sports.

The ideal conditions for most activities, particularly hiking and cycling, is in spring and autumn. Daytime temperatures in summer can be uncomfortably hot and the traffic on the roads can make cycling a stop-start affair. These drawbacks are partly compensated for by the long daylight hours.

What to Take

Most activities operators in Mallorca can provide you with all of the necessary equipment, while high-quality bicycles can be rented all over the island. Although professional-standard equipment is available for purchase on Mallorca, anyone planning on hiking should bring their own boots – the trails of the Serra de Tramuntana are not the place to be breaking in new footwear.

Best Outdoor Activities

Hiking

The twin peninsulas of Cap de Formentor and Cap des Pinar offer coastal hiking at its finest, with pine-cloaked cliffs dropping suddenly to a sea of bluest blue.

Cycling

Mountain bikers and road cyclists are in their element in the high peaks of the Serra de Tramuntana, with thigh-burning climbs, epic descents and hairpin bend after beautiful hairpin bend.

Scuba Diving

South Mallorca is a diver's dream. Go to Illa de Sa Dragonera and Illa de Cabrera for wrecks, cave drops and pristine water swirling with rays, octopuses and barracuda.

Canyoning

The Serra de Tramuntana is rippled through with gorges and canyons. For drama, delve into Gorg Blau Sa Fosca or Torrent d'es Pareis.

Windsurfing & Kitesurfing

These thermal winds that whip off the sea rolling into Sa Marina in the Badia de Pollença create the idea conditions for windsurfing and kitesurfing.

On the Land

Hiking

From the bald and dramatic limestone mountains in the west to the rocky coastal trails of the north and east where the lure of the sea is a constant, Mallorca offers some of the finest hiking anywhere in Europe. The Consell de Mallorca (www.conselldemallorca.net) has become serious about signposting and maintaining the island's trekking routes, many of which have been used for centuries by pack animals and wayfaring pilgrims.

The Tramuntana cannot rival the Alps in height but its serrated peaks, crags and ravines are every bit as wild and not to be underestimated, and the hiking season here is longer. A network of *refugis* (mountain refuges; p167) gives weary hikers a place to bed down for the night, as do the hilltop monasteries and hermitages that have been converted into simple accommodation.

While short distances between trails mean you can cover more ground, it's worth bearing in mind that you may need your own wheels to reach many of the trailheads. But once you get there, you'll have them more or less to yourself.

Best Day Hikes

Just about every tourist office in Mallorca can advise on local day hikes in the area and help you find a route to match your fitness. Five favourites:

➡ **Cap de Ses Salines to Colònia de Sant Jordi** (p160) This half-day hike along the south coast takes in captivating seascapes. Plenty of opportunities for swimming.

➡ **Finca Can Roig to Cala Magraner** (p153) Slip away from east-coast crowds with this glorious, easygoing cove-to-cove walk.

➡ **Sóller to Mirador de Ses Barques** (p102) Stride through olive groves to a magical viewpoint, then return via pretty hill town Fornalutx.

➡ **Ermita de la Victòria to Penya Rotja** (p125) Walk through forests of pine and gaze out across the north coast from this cliff-hugger of a hike.

➡ **Cala en Gossalba to Fumat** (p120) Formentor's most dramatic coastal hike – begins gently and ends spectacularly with 360-degree views from the 334m crag of Fumat.

Multiday Hikes

There are two main long-distance hiking trails in Mallorca. As in the rest of Spain, the two GR (long-distance) trails are signposted in red and white.

➡ Keen hikers can tackle the **Ruta de Pedra en Sec** (Route of Dry Stone, GR221; www.gr221.info), a four- to seven-day walk going from Port d'Andratx to Pollença, crossing the Serra de Tramuntana. At a few points along the GR221 there are *refugis de muntanya* (rustic mountain huts) where trekkers can stay the night.

➡ Signposting is currently under way on the **Ruta Artà-Lluc** (GR222), which will eventually link the two towns, although development of this route is slow.

Hiking Maps & Guides

The best hiking maps are the 1:25,000 *Tramuntana Central, Tramuntana Norte* and *Tramuntana Sur* maps by Editorial Alpina. While these can be picked up at many bookshops around the island, your best bet is to head to the source at La Casa del Mapa (p75) in Palma. Cicerone's *Walking in Mallorca* details and maps 80 routes.

If you need more than a map, there are some reputable guides on the island:

➡ **Tramuntana Tours** (p101) Respected activities operator based in Sóller and Port de Sóller; its focus is on the Serra de Tramuntana.

➡ **Mon d'Aventura** (p111) This Pollença adventure specialist offers myriad hikes, graded from easy to advanced, including the Ruta de Pedra en Sec.

➡ **Rich Strutt** (☑609 700826; www.mallorcanwalkingtours.puertopollensa.com) An English-speaking guide based in Port de Pollença with (at last count) 63 day hikes or longer treks to choose from for groups of four or more.

PEAK BAGGER

Fancy something tougher? Mallorca's highest peak, Puig Major (1445m), may be an off-limits military zone, but you can trek up to the second highest, **Puig de Massanella** (1365m). Make sure you take plenty of provisions and a decent map for this 11km, five-hour hike. From the summit, you'll be rewarded with 360-degree views over the buckled Tramuntana to the Badia d'Alcúdia. On clear days you can even spy the island of Menorca on the horizon. For more details, see www.lluc.net.

Cycling

Mallorca's popularity as a destination for road cycling and mountain biking continues to soar, not least thanks to the likes of British cyclist Bradley Wiggins, who trains for the Tour de France in the Tramuntana.

Nearly half of Mallorca's 1250km of roads have been harnessed for cycling, with everything from signposts to separate bike lanes. The lycra peak season in mountainous regions is from March to May and late September to November, when the weather is refreshingly cool.

Mountain bikers will find abundant trails too, ranging from flat dirt tracks to rough-and-tumble single tracks. Be sure to get a good highway or trekking map before you set out on any cycling expedition.

Bike-rental agencies are ubiquitous across the island, and local tourist offices can usually point you in the right direction. Prices can vary between €8 per day for a basic touring bike and €30 for a high-end mountain or racing bike. Kids bikes and kiddie seats are also widely available.

Best Cycling Routes

There are many great areas for biking; trails cover the island like a web and, depending on your skills and interests, anywhere can be the start of a fabulous ride. That said, here are some of our favourites:

➧ **Palma to Capocorb Vell** Palma and Southern Mallorca.

➧ **Andratx to Monestir de Lluc** Western Mallorca.

➧ **Parc Natural de la Península de Llevant** Eastern Mallorca.

➧ **Cap de Formentor** Northern Mallorca.

➧ **Port d'Alcúdia & Cap des Pinar** Northern Mallorca.

Cycling Guides

If you don't fancy going it alone, you can hook onto some terrific excursions with guides that know Mallorca like the back of their hands:

➧ **Bike & Kite** (p117) Based in Port de Pollença, Kite & Bike offers guided mountain-bike tours in the north, bike hire and an MTB downhill shuttle service.

➧ **Tramuntana Tours** (p101) As the name suggests, these guys take you into the heart of the Tramuntana.

HIKING RESOURCES

The Consell de Mallorca publishes two excellent brochures, both of which should be available from the **Consell de Mallorca tourist office** (Map p56; ☎971 71 22 16; www.infomallorca.net; Plaça de la Reina 2; ☻8am-8pm Mon-Fri, 9am-2pm Sat) in Palma. The brochures' maps are orientative in scope and you'll need to supplement them with detailed hiking maps:

➧ **Rutes per Mallorca (Mallorca Itineraries)** Six treks ranging from 33.2km to 113.5km.

➧ **Caminar per Mallorca (Walking in Mallorca)** Twelve day hikes from 4.5km to 14km.

➧ **Rock and Ride** (p106) Runs skill courses and publishes an excellent mountain-biking booklet (£10) with maps and GPX files.

Cycling Resources

The **Federació de Ciclisme de les Illes Balears** (Balearic Islands Cycling Federation; ☎971 75 76 28; www.webfcib.es) can provide contact information for local cycling clubs. A growing number of hotels cater specifically to cyclists, with garages and energy-packed menus.

Canyoning

The ultimate Mallorcan adrenalin rush, canyoning is an exhausting but exhilarating mix of jumping into ravines and trudging down gorges and gullies. An average excursion might include boulder hopping, abseiling down waterfalls, shimmying up cliffs and swimming in ice-cold rock pools of crystal blue.

Going with a professional guide is essential. Among the best are **Món d'Aventura** (☎606 879514; www.mondaventura.com), Rock and Ride (p106), Tramuntana Tours (p101) and Experience Mallorca (p127), all of which cater to all levels with tours graded from easy to difficult.

Canyoning Routes

The best places for canyoning are concentrated in the central Serra de Tramuntana between Valldemossa and Sa Calobra. It's here that you'll find two of our favourite sites:

MALLORCA FROM ABOVE

Mallorca looks tiny as you rise gently above it or glide on thermals. **Illes Balears Ballooning** (☏607 647647; www.ibballooning.net) offers hot-air balloons for charter, with a bird's-eye view of the entire island. As you approach Port d'Alcúdia you'll often see paragliders drifting high on the thermals. If you're keen to join them, try Tandem Mallorca (p123). In addition to tandem flights for beginners, there are also beginners' and intermediate courses year-round.

➡ **Gorg Blau-Sa Fosca** Tough, 2.5km route with 300m-high walls, 40cm-wide gaps and a 400m stretch in total darkness to negotiate.

➡ **Torrent de Pareis** A moderate 8km trek, with boulder scrambling and sensational limestone scenery – rock formations, caves and the like.

Rock Climbing

The mere thought of Mallorca's majestic limestone walls has climbers rubbing their hands in glee. The island counts among Europe's foremost destinations for sport climbers, with abundant overhangs, slabs and crags. Climbing here concentrates on three main areas: the southwest for multi-pitch climbing, the northwest for magnificent crags and the east for superb Deep Water Soloing (DWS).

A holy grail to climbers, Sa Gubia is a huge fist of rock combed through with multipitch routes. Other climbing hot spots include the ragged limestone crags of the Formentor peninsula and the coves of Porto Cristo and Cala Barques in the island's east.

Experienced climbers can go it alone. Rock and Ride (p106) offers guided multi-pitch climbs and intro courses. **Rockfax** (www.rockfax.com) publishes guides and PDF mini guides on climbing in Mallorca.

Caving

Mallorca's pocked limestone terrain means caving conditions are fantastic. Kitted out with headlamps, spelunkers can head into the cool twilight of the numerous cave complexes that burrow into the cliffs of the southern, northern and eastern coasts. A guide is highly recommended.

Experience Mallorca (p127) leads half-day caving excursions year-round. You'll pass through subterranean chambers dripping with stalactites. One minute you're crawling through narrow passageways, the next you are in a cathedral-like vault big enough for 30 people to stand at ease. It's not one for claustrophobes.

Coasteering

A summer alternative to canyoning (being that bit closer to the sea), coasteering is a heart-pumping mix of swimming, climbing, scrambling, abseiling, cliff jumping and traversing the rock horizontally using the sea to catch your falls. Locations reach from Bonaire near Alcúdia in the north to Peguera in the southwest. Adventure specialists offering coasteering provide all the gear you need, such as helmets and life jackets. Mon d'Aventura (p35) arranges two different levels – the easier one is suitable for kids. Half-day trips run by **Experience Mallorca** (p127) are suitable for over-12s.

Golf

Palma is a popular golfing destination, which is not surprising given the mix of warm Mediterranean climate and fine natural setting. At last count there were around 22 golf courses scattered around the island; some of the best cluster around Capdepera and Artà in the east. Green fees for 18 holes start from €30 and can go as high as €130, although the average is €40 to €75. Cart rental costs €30 to €45. Prices dip in summer when it's often simply too hot to have fun, and can soar in spring and autumn.

Golfing Resources

Useful resources on golfing in Mallorca:

➡ The **Consell de Mallorca** (www.infomallorca. net) tourist authority publishes a brochure entitled *Mallorca Golf* with brief coverage of all 22 courses. Its website also has links to each course's website; click on 'Tourist Information', then 'Themes', then 'Sports', then 'Golf'.

➡ **Federació Balear de Golf** (Balearic Golf Federation; ☏971 72 27 53; www.fbgolf.com) General golfing info.

➡ **Simply Mallorca Golf** (☏971 58 82 96; www. simplymallorcagolf.com) A handy website with details on all courses.

Horse Riding

With its extensive network of rugged trails making their way over the hilly countryside and alongside the Mediterranean, Mallorca is a fine place to saddle up. Many towns and resorts have stables where you can sign up for a class (€10 to €20) or join a group excursion (about €15 for the first hour, with two five-hour rides generally costing around €25–€60 per person. Longer trips are also possible. Some stables also offer pony rides for small children.

Horse-Riding Routes

Cala Ratjada, Colònia de Sant Jordi and Pollença are all popular riding areas; ask at local tourist offices for the nearest stables. Cala Ratjada in particular allows you to ride along a largely undeveloped coast towards Cala Mesquida. Rancho Bonanza (p149), Cala Ratjada's main stables, are German run. Besides countryside and coastal excursions, staff arrange pony rides for kids.

Horse-Riding Resources

Get more information from the **Federació Hipica de les Illes Baleares** (Equestrian Federation of the Balearic Islands; ☑971 75 67 54; www.fhbalear.com; Avinguda Uruguay). Its website lists 15 stables in Mallorca under 'Clubes Illes Balears'.

Water Sports

Scuba Diving & Snorkelling

Mallorca is one of southern Europe's premier diving and snorkelling destinations. The combination of superclear waters and professional dive centres make this an excellent place for a leisure dive or even the open-water PADI diving-accreditation course.

Mallorca Diving (www.mallorcadiving.com) lists 10 reputable dive centres. Diving is best from May to October. A one-tank dive will set you back around €45, a two-hour intro course around €80. The per-dive rate falls markedly the more dives you take. Diving equipment and insurance are sometimes, but not usually, included in the quoted prices, so always ask. Snorkelling starts from €15 per hour.

Dive Sites

The options around the Mallorcan coast are close to endless, from Port d'Andratx in the southwest to Formentor at the island's northernmost tip. Three favourites:

➡ **Badia de Pollença** Experienced divers rank this the island's best diving, with caves and decent marine life along the southern wall of the Cap de Formentor peninsula or the southern end of the Cap des Pinar.

➡ **Parc Nacional Marítim-Terrestre de l'Arxipèlag de Cabrera** (p163) A national park, so special permission required for scuba diving, but also great snorkelling.

➡ **Illa de Sa Dragonera** The best underwater views off the island's southwest.

Windsurfing & Kitesurfing

While the relatively calm wind and waves of Mallorca don't make the island a natural hot spot for fans of windsurfing or kitesurfing, exceptions to the rule are the Badia de Pollença and Port d'Alcúdia, where stiff breezes ensure plenty of action. Three-day beginners' windsurfing courses cost around €145, with hourly rental starting from €16. Kitesurfing is a more expensive affair – rental will set you back around €120 per day, and a three-day course €390.

➡ **WSM** Kitesurfing lessons in Playa de Muro and Sa Marina.

➡ **Bike & Kite** (p117) Kitesurfing lessons and rental in Port de Pollença.

➡ **Sail & Surf Pollença** (p118) Sailing and windsurfing courses and rental in Port de Pollença.

JUMPING OFF A CLIFF

Yes, cliff jumping sounds more death wish than delightful beach holiday, but with guides who know the rocks inside and out, this suicidal-sounding pursuit is perfectly safe. On the same level as bungee jumping on the Richter scale of nerve-shredding pursuits, you jump off cliffs between 3m and 12m high – not colossal by any means, but it feels that way in the freeze-frame moment when you leap and plunge. Listen for the euphoric whoops and yells in north coast Cala Sant Vicenç, where locals doing dives and somersaults show how it's done properly.

BOAT EXCURSIONS

From Easter to October, glass-bottomed boats drift up and down the eastern coast and can be a fun way to enjoy the water without having the responsibility of sailing your own boat. Most are half-day trips only and rarely last more than four hours. All sell return tickets, but on some east-coast routes you can travel one way. If we had to choose just three routes, they would be these:

➡ **Transportes Marítimos Brisa** (p123) Port d'Alcúdia to Cala Sant Vicenç and back, via Cap de Formentor.

➡ **Barcos Azules** (p104) Port de Sóller to Sa Calobra.

➡ **Excursions a Cabrera** (p163) Round-trip tours by speedboat or slower boats from Colònia de Sant Jordi to the Parc Nacional Marítim-Terrestre de l'Arxipèlag de Cabrera.

Sailing

Among the 35 marinas that ring Mallorca's coast, many offer yacht charters, sailboat rentals and sailing courses. There are large sailing schools in Palma, Port de Pollença and other resorts; expect a two-day course to cost around €400; the Palma Sea School (p63) is the most professional outfit.

One place that rents yachts is Llaüts (p88) in Port d'Andratx; prices start at €150 per day.

Sailing Routes

If you charter or bring your own yacht, your options for sailing are unlimited. Popular routes:

➡ **Palma to Illa de Cabrera** To enter the national park, you'll need prior permission.

➡ **Port d'Andratx to Port de Sóller** The best of the Serra de Tramuntana coast.

➡ **Cala Sant Vicenç to Port d'Alcúdia** Round the inspiring Cap de Formentor.

Sailing Resources

Sailing is a serious busines in Mallorca and there are plenty of organisations to promote the sport and provide information or to ensure that sailors leave the environment as they found it.

➡ **Harbours & Marinas Guide** Free guide to moorings and marinas published annually by Tallers de Molí; available from tourist offices or marinas.

➡ **Conselleria de Medi Ambient** (☑971 17 68 00; www.caib.es; Avinguda de Gabriel Alomar i Villalonga 33) Contact this organisation for guidelines for anchoring your yacht in open water to protect the sea floor.

➡ **Federación Balear de Vela** (Balearic Sailing Federation; ☑971 40 24 12; www.federacionbalearvela.org; Avinguda de Joan Miró 327) Another good source of information.

Sea Kayaking

Mallorca's craggy coastline is indented with lovely bays and coves – many of which can only be reached by boat. A sea kayak allows you to tune into the soothing rhythm of the sea and explore rock formations, caves and quiet beaches at your own pace. Marine falcons, cormorants and wild goats are frequently sighted, and you might even spot the odd dolphin or flying fish. The coast around Sóller in the west, Porto Cristo in the east and Port de Pollença in the north is perfect for paddling.

Sea-Kayaking Routes

Guide and rental companies are clustered around Alcúdia and Port de Pollença.

➡ **Escola d'Esports Nàutics Port de Sóller** (p104) Port de Sóller.

➡ **Kayak Mallorca** (p118) Port de Pollença.

➡ **Piraguas Mix** (p158) Colònia de Sant Jordi.

➡ **Nemar Kayaks** (p165) Cala d'Or.

➡ **Skualo Adventure Sports Centre** (p154) Portocolom.

➡ **Skualo Adventure Sports & Dive Centre** (p152) Porto Cristo.

Sea-Kayaking Resources

For details on courses for kids and adults, as well as a list of nautical clubs with a kayak presence, check out the **Federación Balear de Piragüismo** (Balearic Federation of Canoeing & Kayaking; ☑971 79 20 19; www.fibp.org; Carrer Joan Miró 327).

Plan Your Trip

Travel with Children

If you're off to Mallorca with the family, you're going to have a blast. Travelling here with kids in tow is child's play. There are castles (sand and real), shallow sea and water parks to splash in, caves to explore, brilliant beaches for energy-burning activities, and warm welcomes all round.

Mallorca for Kids

Resorts up and down the island cater for families with their well-tended seafront promenades, playgrounds, pools, round-the-clock activities and child-friendly hotels and restaurants. And the Mallorquins simply adore tots, so wherever you go, you can be sure they'll be made a fuss of – having their hair ruffled, cheeks pinched and being given sweets and masses of attention.

It's the little things that are likely to spark imaginations: eating snail-shaped *ensaïmada* pastries for breakfast, building castles in the sand, taking a (whoa!) helter-skelter ride along the coast to Sa Calobra, or a rickety train ride to Sóller.

There's plenty to appease older children too: mountain biking, scuba diving, spelunking in sea caves or even cliff jumping – sure to gain them kudos in the classroom back home.

Sights & Attractions

Mallorca is full of kid-friendly attractions. Swap the beach for a ramble around hilltop forts in Capdepera (p146) Alaró (p107) and Artà (Santuari de Sant Salvador; p143) – perfect for playing king (or queen) of the castle. Children are enchanted by the petrified forests of stalactites and stalagmites in the labyrinthine caves that

Best Regions for Kids

Northern Mallorca

Alcúdia and Port de Pollença are natural family-pleasers, with giant sandy bays ideal for go-easy days. Hit Hidropark (p123) for whizzy slides and Parc Natural de S'Albufera (p126) for gentle bike rides and birdwatching expeditions. There are tons of activities for teens – from kayaking to spooky caving.

Eastern Mallorca

Tell tales of troglodytes as you duck through the glittering chambers of vast caves – none more impressive than the Coves del Drac (p151). There are castles for fantasy play, pony rides, boat trips, safari encounters and a cluster of lovely, gently shelving bays in the island's east too.

Palma & Badia de Palma

The island's capital is like a history lesson come to life, whether playing spot-the-gargoyle at the cathedral (La Seu; Carrer del Palau Reial 9; adult/child €4/3; ☺10am-5.15pm Mon-Fri, to 2.15pm Sat) or clambering up to Castell de Bellver (p62). Nearby, find giant water parks and an aquarium with brilliantly scary shark sleepovers.

honeycomb the east and interior, such as the Coves del Drac (p151), Coves d'Artà (p150) and Coves de Campanet (p135).

Water parks take the heat out of summer – Aqualand ($\square$ 971 13 08 11; www.aqualand.es; Carretera de Cala Figuera; adult/child €21/13; ⊙10am-6pm mid-May–Jun & Sep) in Palma is arguably the best, but Western Water Park (p83) in Magaluf and Hidropark (p123) in Alcúdia also offer cooling fun, with wave pools, slides and pulse-raising flumes. Palma Aquarium (p79) is a big hit with marine life from sharks to glow-in-the-dark jellyfish, as is Artestruz (p159) near Ses Salines, where kids have a whale of a time petting and feeding ostriches.

Tourist offices should be able to point you in the direction of child-geared activities and playgrounds.

Outdoor Activities

Mallorca is an outdoorsy wonderland. Kids can release energy playing on the beaches and swimming in the sea. Depending on how old they are, there's all manner of water-based activities to engage their interest in the main resorts: from bouncy banana boat rides to PADI Bubblemaker scuba diving courses, snorkelling and coastal kayaking. Glass-bottomed-boat rides allow a peek at marine life with minimal effort.

On dry land, rent bikes and make the most of the island's bike paths, like the flat stretch that heads through the Parc Natural de S'Albufera (p126) wetlands. Horse riding is a thrill for older kids, and even toddlers will enjoy the pony rides available at many of the stables.

Just off the highways of the Serra de Tramuntana are two dozen or so public recreational areas, parks and rural estates that now have barbecues and play areas.

Eating Out

Eating out with children is a breeze in Mallorca, where large family lunches are a way of life and the mood is laid-back in all but the most formal of places. You'll get lots of smiles if you have kids with you and letting a tot wander around a restaurant – as long as they're not breaking wine bottles or bothering anyone – is usually OK.

Many resort restaurants offer inexpensive children's menus – simple grilled meats, French fries, spaghetti and tortillas and the like, followed by ice cream. If not, most chefs are generally happy to improvise to suit children's appetites and whip up smaller portions. Kids with more adventurous tastes might like to try *pa amb oli* (bread rubbed with oil and tomatoes with a variety of toppings) and paella, while Sóller orange ice cream always goes down a treat.

You cannot rely on restaurants having high chairs, although many have a couple – getting there early increases your chances of snaffling one. It's worth bringing your own harness, though, as these are often lacking. Few places have nappy-changing facilities. Nappies (diapers), baby food and formula milk are widely available in town and resort supermarkets and chemists.

Children's Discounts

Discounts are available for children (usually aged under 12) on public transport, while under-fives ride for free. You can also expect substantial reductions on sights, though ages vary widely, with free entry ranging from 0 to 16 years. As a rule, under-fours are free and under-12s pay half price, and there are concessions for youths. Most tours (for instance boat tours) offer a 50% reduction for children.

TOP TIPS FOR TRAVELLING WITH CHILDREN

➡ Ask for extra tapas in bars to suit younger tastebuds, such as olives or raw carrot sticks.

➡ Adjust your children to Spanish time (ie late nights) as quickly as you can – otherwise they'll miss half the fun.

➡ Unlike in the USA, crayons and paper are rarely given out in restaurants – bring your own.

➡ Kids who share your bed won't incur a supplement – extra beds usually cost €20 to €30.

➡ Ask the local tourist office for the nearest children's playgrounds.

Children's Highlights

Energy Burners

➡ **Water babies** Swimming, snorkelling, scuba diving, windsurfing and kayaking all around the island.

➡ **Hiking** Go for strolls along the coast and through the nature parks (keep an eye out for wild goats and wading birds).

➡ **Cycling** Gentle pedals along the coast and in the bird-rich wetlands of Parc Natural de S'Albufera. Mountain biking in the Tramuntana for active teens.

➡ **Adventure thrills** The north is a giant playground for active pursuits from caving to coasteering, cliff jumping to canyoning (suitable for over-12s).

Water & Amusement Parks

➡ **Aqualand** (p79) Kids love hurtling down the slides and flumes at this mammoth water park near Palma.

➡ **Artestruz** (p159) Ostriches to stroke, feed and admire in full sprint at this one-of-a-kind park near Ses Salines.

➡ **Palma Aquarium** (p79) Some 8000 marine creatures splash around in the tanks here. There are shark sleepovers for little nippers.

➡ **Western Water Park** (p83) Fearless kids will love the twisting, near-vertical slides at this Wild West–themed water park.

➡ **Safari-Zoo** (p151) In the island's east, this is a rare chance to spot giraffe, emus and lions on a safari train.

➡ **Marineland** (p83) Somersaulting dolphins, playful penguins, sea lions and more.

➡ **Hidropark** (p123) A kid-friendly water park handy for the northern resorts.

Natural Wonders

➡ **Coves del Drac** (p151) Go underground to boat through caverns encrusted with stalactites millennia in the making.

➡ **Serra de Tramuntana** (p90) Marvel at faces and weird formations in the bizarrely weathered peaks of this mountain range.

➡ **Sa Calobra** (p108) Feel your stomach drop on the roller-coaster road down to Sa Calobra, with snapshot views of sheer cliffs and canyons.

➡ **Coves d'Artà** (p150) A magical cave with a forest of formations, including the 'Queen of Columns' and 'Chamber of Hell'.

➡ **Blue Cave** (p163) Look in wonder at its surreal blue waters on a boat trip to the Illa de Cabrera, part of Mallorca's only national park.

➡ **Parc Natural de S'Albufera** (p126) Bring binoculars to spot wading birds, turtles and even water buffalo in this reed-fringed nature park.

Family Beaches

➡ **Platja de Muro** (p126) Fabulous sweep of silky sand and shallow turquoise sea in the north's Badia d'Alcúdia. It backs onto the Parc Natural de S'Albufera.

➡ **Cala Mondragó** This southern Blue Flag bay in the Parc Natural de Mondragó (p164) is gorgeous, with brilliantly clear water and powder-soft sand. Great for snorkelling.

➡ **Cala Agulla** (p147) Fringed by pines and dunes, this beautiful arc of a Blue Flag bay sits just north of Capdepera. The water is shallow enough for paddling.

➡ **Platja de Formentor** (p119) Getting to this north-coast beach by boat or the hair-raising coastal road is part of the fun. Tiptoe away from the crowds on this pine-flanked slither of sand.

➡ **Cala Mesquida** (p151) Another east-coast favourite, this gently shelving bay has dazzling clear water. It's better for older kids because of stiff winds and waves.

Back in Time

➡ **Castell de Bellver** (p62) The Badia de Palma shrinks to postcard format from this mighty circular castle.

➡ **Train from Palma to Sóller** (p77) This rattling vintage train is a real blast from the past – a hit with kids and parents.

➡ **Santuari de Sant Salvador** (p143) Ramble along the ramparts of this hilltop castle above Artà.

➡ **Medieval Walls** (p121) Travel back in time with a walk atop the old city walls in Alcúdia.

➡ **Torre des Verger** (p92) Play pirates at this watchtower precariously perched above the sea near Estellencs.

Planning

When to Go

It's worth bearing in mind that many kid-geared sights and activities are open only from May to October. The best season to go depends on what you want to see and do. Spring and autumn are dry, warm and fantastic for hiking, cycling and other active pursuits. Families (including locals) descend en masse on the coast during the summer holidays, so if you are going then, you might want to choose a quieter resort or base yourself slightly inland at a *finca* (farm).

Accommodation

Whether you're looking for a self-catering apartment, a coastal resort for families or a rural farm-stay complete with resident goats and donkeys to pet, we list dozens of family-friendly accommodation options in this guide, which are flagged with a 👪 icon.

Many hotels in coastal resorts offer apartments big enough for families or one-bedroom suites with a small sitting area and sofa bed. The vast majority of places will squeeze in a baby's cot for free or a child's bed for a small extra charge – mention it when booking.

The all-inclusive resorts that dominate the southern, eastern and (to a lesser extent) northern coastline do one thing very well: most places employ kids' entertainers to organise children's activities, from games and discos to craft workshops and outdoor excursions. See p166 for more information.

Baby Equipment

Most airlines – including Ryanair and easyJet – will take your pushchair from you as you embark for no extra charge (this needs to be tagged at the check-in or bag-drop desk). For additional items such as booster seats and travel cots, they often levy a fee of around £30–€36.50 per flight. You can take baby food, milk and sterilised water in your hand baggage.

If you would rather not schlep it all with you, companies such as **Multi-Hire** (www.multi-hire.com) and **Baby Equipment Hire Mallorca** (www.babyequipmenthiremajorca.co.uk) rent out the essentials, and it's often a more cost-effective way of doing it than paying through the nose with airlines.

Baby Food

You can buy baby formula in powder or liquid form, as well as sterilising solutions such as Milton, at *farmacias* (pharmacies). Disposable nappies (diapers) are widely available at supermarkets and *farmacias*. Fresh cow's milk is sold in cartons and plastic bottles in supermarkets in big cities, but can be hard to find in small towns, where UHT is often the only option.

If you've brought baby food with you, just ask for it to be warmed up in the kitchen; most restaurants will have no problem with this.

Child Care

Some of the better hotels can generally arrange babysitters for an hourly fee. You could also check out the website **Canguroencasa** (www.canguroencasa.com), where you can search for English-speaking *canguros* (babysitters); click on 'Canguros Baleares'. The going rate is between €5 and €10 per hour.

If you want to explore safe in the knowledge that your kids are in good hands, check out **Jelly and Ice Cream** (www.jellyandice-cream.com), which arranges English-speaking child care with qualified nannies and babysitting. **Little Ducklings** (www.littleducklings.es), **Little Puffs** (www.littlepuffschildcaremallorca.com) and **Angels** (www.angelsnursingagency.com) also come recommended. Expect to pay around €15/70 per hour/half-day. A deposit is required to confirm your booking.

Car Hire

You can hire car seats for infants and children (usually for a per-day fee) from most car-rental firms, but book them well in advance.

It's worth bearing in mind that most compact cars are short on space, so you may struggle to squeeze in your luggage and pushchair in the boot. Check the car's dimensions before booking or consider upgrading to a bigger model.

Regions at a Glance

Western Mallorca

Villages
Landscapes
Hiking

Northern Mallorca

Landscapes
Old Towns
Beaches

Palma & the Badia de Palma

Architecture
Galleries
Food

Medieval Architecture

Palma is like a 3D textbook on Mediterranean architectural history. The Gothic cathedral is the show-stealer, but the old town's tightly packed lanes hide Modernista masterpieces, medieval mansions and baroque *patis* (patios).

Miró, Barceló, Picasso & Dalí

Many of Spain's premier 20th-century artists had a soft spot for Palma. Miró has left his playful mark all over the city, Miquel Barceló came from nearby Felanitx, and Picasso and Dalí originals cram the city's stellar galleries.

The Mallorcan Kitchen

Mallorca's culinary star shines brightest in Palma, from the island's best seafood restaurants to the coterie of restaurants overseen by celebrity chef Marc Fosh, to intimate tapas bars around Plaça Major and irresistible pastry shops.

p46

Hilltop Villages

What poet or artist wouldn't want to capture the goldstone beauty of western Mallorca's hilltop villages? Slow tour the Tramuntana's foothills to commit the loveliness of Valldemossa, Deià, Fornalutx, Binaraix and Orient to memory.

Mallorca's Spine

In Mallorca's repertoire of lovely landscapes, the Serra de Tramuntana deserves a standing ovation, with its wild limestone peaks, plunging cliffs and sea backdrop.

Mountain Hikes

The multiday Ruta de Pedra en Sec traversing the Tramuntana is the biggie, but you can also scramble up Puig de Massanella, mooch through Sóller's citrus groves or make the pilgrimage to Monestir de Lluc.

p84

Cap de Formentor

The northern crescendo of the Serra de Tramuntana is a peninsula of Tolkienesque mountain summits, razor-edge cliffs and sheltered coves. Drive, cycle or hike it.

Cultured Towns

In the northern coastal hinterland reside two of Mallorca's most engaging midsized towns: Pollença with its cobblestone streets and 365 steps to Calvari, and Alcúdia with Roman ruins and defensive walls.

Glorious Beaches

The masses gravitate to the broad sands and crystal-clear water of the north's twin bays: Badia de Pollença and Badia d'Alcúdia. Quieter coves punctuate Cala Sant Vicenç, Cap de Formentor and Cap des Pinar.

p110

The Interior

Eastern Mallorca

Southern Mallorca

Wines
Food
Architecture

Beaches
Caves
Landscapes

Beaches
Scenery
Archaeology

Wines & Wineries

Mallorca's wine-producing areas range across the island's vine-cloaked interior; some of the wineries offer tours, others just cellar-door sales.

Hearty Inland Fare

From the *celler* restaurants of Inca and Sineu, lodged in old wine cellars, to the rural *fincas* (farms) transformed into hotels and restaurants, eating in the interior is all about authenticity.

Monasteries & Medieval Towns

Almost every hilltop in inland Mallorca was long ago colonised by a monastery from where the views ripple for kilometres, while towns like Sineu and Petra are places of quiet, underrated charm.

p128

Beyond the Resorts

Go off-piste to the wild beaches northeast of Cala Ratjada, some of Mallorca's most desirable stretches of coastal real estate. The serene *cales* (coves) south of Porto Cristo are similarly lovely.

Underground Cathedrals

The epic formations and stalactite forests of eastern Mallorca's caves rank among the island's most eye-catching phenomena – try Coves del Drac, Coves d'Artà and Coves dels Hams.

Protected Peninsula

North of Artà, the Parc Natural de la Península de Llevant allures birdwatchers and hikers. Cap Ferrutx bookends the peninsula, while Ermita de Betlem affords quiet contemplation.

p141

Unspoiled Sands

The south has a prize collection of beaches and limpid waters for diving. Loll on the seemingly never-ending sands of Platja des Trenc, or cove-hop to coastal lovelies like Cala Pi, Cala Llombards and the Parc Natural de Mondragó.

Coastal Ramparts

The high cliffs of the coast have spared much of the south from developers' bulldozers, especially from Cap Blanc to Cap de Ses Salines. Illa de Cabrera is a treasure.

Mallorca's Mysterious Past

The island's prehistory is shrouded in uncertainty; Talayotic sites such as Capocorb Vell and those close to Ses Salines offer insights into pre-Roman Mallorca.

p155

On the Road

Western Mallorca
p84

Northern Mallorca
p110

Palma & the Badia de Palma
p46

The Interior
p128

Eastern Mallorca
p141

Southern Mallorca
p155

Palma & the Badia de Palma

Best Places to Eat

➡ Simply Fosh (p66)

➡ Can Cera Gastro Bar (p66)

➡ Wine Garage (p67)

➡ Toque (p70)

➡ Misa Braseria (p66)

Best Places to Stay

➡ Can Cera (p168)

➡ Hotel Tres (p169)

➡ Palma Suites (p168)

➡ Boutique Hotel Calatrava (p168)

➡ Puro Oasis Urbano (p169)

Why Go?

Petite, sea-splashed, party-loving Palma is one of Europe's most underrated capitals. For a city of its size, its sights play in the premier league with major metropolises. Take its immense Gothic cathedral, moored like the prow of a great ship on the Mediterranean's edge. Or its astounding galleries: fortified Es Baluard with its Mirós and Picassos, and Museu Fundació Juan March with its Dalís and Barcelós are just tip-of-the-iceberg stuff. In the labyrinthine backstreets of Old Palma, medieval palaces jostle for space with patrician mansions that hide some of Spain's most beautiful inner courtyards.

If the sights don't grab you, the soulful sea views, fabulous food and happening bar scene surely will. Need a breather? Within minutes you can be at a hilltop castle, on a vintage train rattling through the mountains or stretched out on a beach, which means Palma is permanently switched on relaxed mode.

When to Go

Unlike the rest of the island, Palma's energy levels remain fairly constant throughout the year; most sights, hotels and restaurants are open year-round. That said, the city does have an irresistible feel-good atmosphere when the weather's warm, the yacht harbour is filled with masts and one of the numerous sailing regattas brings the beautiful people to town – this applies from April to October. Scarcely a month passes in Palma without a festival of some kind: pre-Lenten carnival parades in February, the crazy pyrotechnics of Nit de Foc in June and December's Christmas market are top diary dates. The beach resorts of the Badia de Palma effectively shut down in winter.

Palma's Patios

Few experiences in Palma beat simply milling around the backstreets of the city's old quarter, which spreads east of the cathedral. Iron gates conceal the city's *patis* (patios), the grand courtyards where nobles once received guests and horse-drawn coaches clattered to a halt. Patios were the intersection of public and private life, and as such they were showpieces – polished until they gleamed and filled with flowers and plants.

There are around 150 patrician houses with patios in Palma today, though most can only be observed from a distance. They vary in style from Gothic to Renaissance, baroque to Modernista, but most have the same defining features: graceful arches and Ionic columns, sweeping staircases with wrought-iron balustrades, and a well or cistern. Our walking tour (p61) passes some of our favourites. For a closer look, join one of the guided tours run by Mallorca Rutes (p64).

To Market

Palma's produce markets are a great way to get under the skin of the city as you mosey around the fresh-produce stands. There's all you need to assemble your own picnic, from cheeses and cold meats to fruit and veg. The most engrossing is the central Mercat de l'Olivar (p69), where you'll find everything from plump olives to never-heard-of legumes, melons as big as footballs, strings of *sobrassada* (paprika-flavoured cured pork sausage), hunks of Serrano ham and enough fish to fill a small ocean. Make a morning of it and linger for lunch at the deli stalls for tapas or oyster shucking. Equally busy but with few tourists are the **Mercat de Santa Catalina** (Map p66; Plaça de la Navegació; ⊘ 8am-2pm & 5-8pm Mon-Fri, 8am-2pm Sat) and **Mercat de Pere Garau** (Map p52; Plaça de Pere Garau; ⊘ 8am-2pm & 5-8pm Mon-Fri, 8am-2pm Sat).

Top Five Galleries

➡ **Museu Fundació Juan March** (p55) Contemporary art stars, including Mallorca's own Miquel Barceló.

➡ **Es Baluard** (p60) Picasso, Miró and fine city views at this gallery atop the Renaissance sea wall.

➡ **Fundació Pilar i Joan Miró** (p81) Total Miró immersion, with 2500 works on show.

➡ **Museo Can Morey de Santmarti** (p52) A feast of Dalí in a lavish town mansion.

➡ **Palau March** (p51) Paintings by Dalí and sculpture by Moore, Rodin and Chillida in an exquisite palace.

Cathedral Photo Ops

For that must-have cathedral snapshot of Palma's Catedral, head to Parc de la Mar during the blue hour (twilight) to frame it perfectly and see it spectacularly illuminated.

Need to Know

➡ Many of Palma's headline attractions close on Mondays, including the Fundació Pilar i Joan Miró and Es Baluard.

➡ Sunday closures include the Catedral, Palau March and Palau de l'Almudaina.

Advance Planning

➡ Book accommodation up to several months ahead if you're coming in high season.

➡ Reserve tables at Palma's fine-dining restaurants up to two weeks ahead.

➡ Plan your itinerary (taking into account sight closing days) one week in advance.

➡ Arrange guided walking and city tours several days ahead.

Resources

➡ **Ajuntament de Palma** www.palmademallorca.es

➡ **Consell de Mallorca tourist office** www. infomallorca.net

➡ **Visit Calvia** www. visitcalvia.com

➡ **EMT Palma public transport** www. emtpalma.es

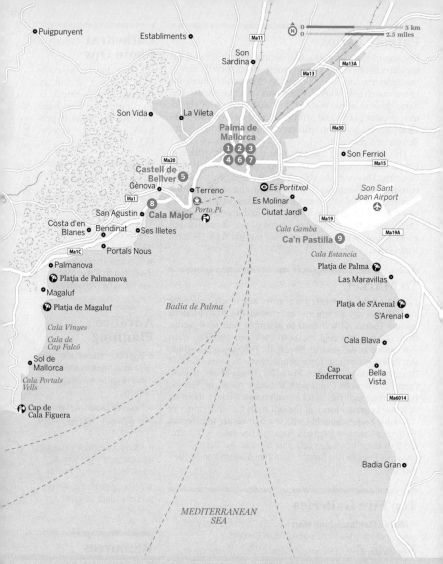

Palma & the Badia de Palma Highlights

1 Admire Barceló, Gaudí and a rainbow of stained glass in the Gothic **Catedral** (p49).

2 Tap into Palma's contemporary art scene in top-of-the-ramparts **Es Baluard** (p60).

3 Discover baroque patios and the Moorish **Banys Àrabs** (p53) in labyrinthine Old Palma.

4 Glimpse Picasso, Miró and Dalí at the **Museu Fundació Juan March** (p55).

5 Survey the Badia de Palma from hilltop **Castell de Bellver** (p62).

6 Swing with Palma's boho groove in the bars and boutiques of **Santa Catalina** (p73).

7 Marvel at the cathedral at dusk from the seafront **Parc de la Mar** (p52).

8 See the light from Miró's perspective at the **Fundació Pilar i Joan Miró** (p81) in Cala Major.

9 Hang out with cool, cocktail-sipping kids at **Puro Beach** (p81) in Ca'n Pastilla.

PALMA DE MALLORCA

POP 407,650

Nestled in the crook of the Badia de Palma, Mallorca's capital is the most agreeable of all Mediterranean towns. Shaped and defined by the sea and backed by not-so-distant mountains, it is a city of open horizons and oft-blue skies, with good looks and a festive nature. Surveying it all from a gentle rise is the old quarter, crowned by its colossal Gothic cathedral. Slip away from the crowds that swarm around the trophy sights for just a minute and you will find yourself deep in a labyrinth of cobbled lanes, which call for serendipitous strolls. Take your lead from the locals and wander here at ease, pausing for market banter, boutique shopping, snapshots of baroque churches, palaces and patrician courtyards, and lunches that linger long into the afternoon.

History

Palma has been occupied since Roman times, when the city was known as Palmeria or Palma. By the 12th century, Medina Mayurka (City of Mallorca) was one of the most flourishing Muslim capitals in Europe. After the Christian conquest in 1229, it again entered a period of prosperity as a trade centre in the 14th century – the Christians renamed the city Ciutat de Mallorca or Ciudad Capital (City Capital).

By the 16th century, along with the rest of the island, the city was sinking into a protracted period of torpor. The great seaward walls that you see today were largely built in the 16th and 17th centuries, when the city's seasonal torrent, the Riera, was diverted from its natural course along Passeig d'es Born to its present location west of the city walls. The old city centre then went into decline. The bulk of the sea walls were demolished at the beginning of the 20th century to allow rapid expansion of the city. But the heart of the city has been spruced up beyond recognition since tourist cash began to flow into the island in the 1960s. A report in 2007 claimed that property around the Dalt Murada was among the most expensive in Spain.

The planting of bombs by the Basque separatist group ETA in July and August 2009, which was reportedly linked to the impending arrival of the King and Queen of Spain on their annual summer holiday visit to Mallorca, thrust the city briefly into the international spotlight.

◉ Sights

◎ Old Palma

★ **Catedral** CATHEDRAL
(La Seu; Map p56; www.catedraldemallorca.org; Carrer del Palau Reial 9; adult/child €6/free; ☉10am-6.15pm Mon-Fri, to 2.15pm Sat) Palma's vast cathedral is the city's major architectural landmark. Aside from its sheer scale and undoubted beauty, its stunning interior features, designed by Antoni Gaudí and renowned contemporary artist Miquel Barceló, make this unlike any cathedral elsewhere in the world. The awesome structure is predominantly Gothic, apart from the main facade, which is startling, quite beautiful and completely mongrel.

The Catedral occupies the site of what was the central mosque of Medina Mayurka,

---

PALMA IN TWO DAYS

Palma makes a fabulous city break and with a will to cram you can do a lot in a weekend. Start touring with the obvious: the colossal Gothic **Catedral** (p49) and **Palau de l'Almudaina** (p51). You could spend hours meandering the old town's mazy lanes and, to add a little structure, throw in visits to Dalí-filled **Museo Can Morey de Santmarti** (p52) and the **Banys Àrabs** (p53). Lunch at **Can Cera Gastro Bar** (p66). Continue touring with the **Basílica de Sant Francesc** (p53) and **Es Baluard** (p60), where you can stop to snack alongside the battlements. For a night out, make for nearby Santa Catalina, with dinner at **Koh** (p68), drinks at **Idem Café** (p73) and clubbing along Passeig Marítim. The following day, head east out of town up to **Castell de Bellver** (p62) and the **Fundació Pilar i Joan Miró** (p81), book lunch at **Ca'n Eduardo** (p70) and spend the afternoon exploring the **Museu Fundació Juan March** (p55), then end with a drink at **Guiness House** (p73). Later, have an *ensaïmada* (a delicate, croissant-like pastry dusted with icing sugar, and sometimes filled with cream) at **Ca'n Joan de S'Aigo** (p67), dinner at **Simply Fosh** (p66) or **Misa Braseria** (p66), then hit the bars of Sa Gerreria, beginning at **L'Ambigú** (p71).

DON'T MISS

TOP TREASURES OF PALMA CATHEDRAL

Enter the cathedral from the north flank. You get tickets in the first room and then pass into the sacristy, which hosts the main part of the small **Museu Capitular** (Chapter Museum). At the centre of this is a huge gold-plated monstrance, dating to 1585, which comes out for the annual Corpus Christi procession. Interesting items include a portable altar, thought to have belonged to Jaume I. Its little compartments contain saints' relics. Other reliquaries include one purporting to hold three thorns from Christ's crown of thorns.

Next come two chapter houses. In the **Gothic chapter house** by Guillem Sagrera, note the tomb of Bishop Gil Sánchez Muñoz (Antipope Clement VIII), the *Tabla de l'Almoina* (Alms Panel) and two paintings by the master Monti-Sion – *El Calvario* (The Calvary) and *Nuestra Señora de la Misericordia* (Our Lady of Mercy) – which allude to a terrible flood in Palma in 1403 that left 5000 dead. The **baroque chapter house** is exquisite, with its delicately carved stonework and 16th-century *relicario de la vera cruz* (reliquary of the true cross) encrusted with gemstones. Your attention will also be drawn to a matching pair of silver candelabras, each weighing 243kg.

On passing through one of the side chapels into the cathedral itself, your gaze soars high to the cross vaults, supported by slender, octagonal pillars. The broad **nave** and aisles are flanked by chapels. The walls are illuminated by kaleidoscopic curtains of stained glass, including 87 windows and eight magnificent rose windows. The grandest (the **oculus maior** or 'great eye'), featuring a Star of David, comprises 1115 panes of glass and shimmers ruby, gold and sapphire. It is the largest Gothic rose window in the world. Visit in the morning to see the stunning effect of its coloured light and shapes reflected on the west wall. This spectacle is at its best at 8.30am on 2 February and 11 November when the image of the main rose window appears superimposed below that of the other.

The cathedral's three strikingly different **apses** show the Eucharist in three stages left to right: institution, celebration and adoration. The left apse displays the golden wonder of the Corpus Christi altarpiece, an elaborate baroque confection by Jaume Blanquer (1626–41), devoted to the institution of the Eucharist at the Last Supper.

Antoni Gaudí carried out renovations from 1904 to 1914. His most important contribution was the strange **baldachin** that hovers over the main altar. Topped by a fanciful sculpture of Christ crucified and flanked by the Virgin Mary and St John, it looks like the gaping jaw of some oversized prehistoric shark dangling from the ceiling of an old science museum. Some 35 lamps hang from it and what looks like a flying carpet is spread above it. The genius of Barcelona Modernisme seems to have left behind an indecipherable pastiche, but then this was supposed to be a temporary version. The definitive one was never made.

Not content with this strangeness, the parish commissioned contemporary Mallorquin artist Miquel Barceló (an agnostic) with the remake of the **Capella del Santíssim i Sant Pere**, in the right apse. Done in 15 tonnes of ceramics, this dreamscape representing the miracle of the loaves and fishes was unveiled in 2007. On the left, fish and other marine creatures burst from the wall. The opposite side has a jungle look, with representations of bread and fruit. In between the fish and palm fronds, and standing above stacks of skulls, appears a luminous body that is supposed to be Christ but is modelled on the short and stocky artist.

Other notable elements of the interior include the **giant organ**, built in 1798 (free recitals are held at noon on the first Tuesday of each month), and the two pulpits, the smaller of which was partly redone by Gaudí.

capital of Muslim Mallorca for three centuries. Although Jaume I and his marauding men forced their way into the city in 1229, work on the Catedral (La Seu in Catalan), one of Europe's largest, did not begin until 1300. Rather, the mosque was used in the interim as a church and dedicated to the Virgin Mary. Work wasn't completed until 1601.

The original was a Renaissance cherry on the Gothic cake, but an earthquake in 1851 (which caused considerable panic but no loss of life) severely damaged it. Rather than mend the original, it was decided to add some neo-Gothic flavour. With its interlaced flying buttresses on each flank and soaring pinnacles it forms a masterful example of the style. The result is a hybrid of the Renaissance original (in particular the main doorway) and an inevitably artificial-feeling, 19th-century pseudo-Gothic monumentalism.

Mass times vary, but one always takes place at 9am.

★ **Palau de l'Almudaina**   PALACE
(Map p56; Carrer del Palau Reial; adult/child €9/4, audioguides €4, guided tours €6; ⊙ 10am-8pm Apr-Sep, to 6pm Oct-Mar) Originally an Islamic fort, this mighty construction opposite the Catedral was converted into a residence for the Mallorquin monarchs at the end of the 13th century. The King of Spain resides here still, at least symbolically. The royal family are rarely in residence, except for the occasional ceremony, as they prefer to spend summer in the Palau Marivent (in Cala Major). At other times you can wander through a series of cavernous stone-walled rooms that have been lavishly decorated.

The Romans are said to have built a *castrum* (fort) here, possibly on the site of a prehistoric settlement. The Wālis (governors) of Muslim Mallorca altered and expanded the Roman fort, while Jaume I and his successors modified it to such an extent that little of the Muslim version remains.

The first narrow room you enter has a black-and-white ceiling, symbolising the extremes of night and day, darkness and light. You then enter a series of three grand rooms. Notice the bricked-in Gothic arches cut off in the middle. Originally these three rooms were double their present height and formed one single great hall added to the original Arab fort and known as the **Saló del Tinell** (from an Italian word, *tinello*, meaning 'place where one eats'): a giant banqueting and ceremonial hall. The rooms are graced by period furniture, tapestries and other curios. The following six bare rooms and terrace belonged to the original Arab citadel.

In the main courtyard, the **Patio de Armas**, troops would line up for an inspection and parade before heading out into the city. The lion fountain in its centre is one of the palace's rare Arab remnants. Up the grand Royal Staircase are the **royal apartments**, a succession of lavishly appointed rooms (look up to the beautiful coffered timber *artesonado* ceilings), whose centrepiece is the Saló Gòtic, the upper half of the former Saló del Tinell, where you can see where those Gothic arches wind up. Next door to the apart-

ments is the royal **Capella de Sant'Anna**, a Gothic chapel whose entrance is a very rare Mallorcan example of late Romanesque in rose and white marble.

After the death of Jaume III in 1349, no king lived here permanently again.

In the shadow of the Almudaina's walls, along Avinguda d'Antoni Maura, is S'Hort del Rei (King's Garden).

★ **Palau March**   MUSEUM
(Map p56; Carrer del Palau Reial 18; adult/child €4.50/free; ⊙ 10am-6.30pm Mon-Fri, to 2pm Sat) This house, palatial by any definition, was one of several residences of the phenomenally wealthy March family. Sculptures by 20th-century greats, such as Henry Moore, Auguste Rodin, Barbara Hepworth and Eduardo Chillida, grace the outdoor terrace. Within lie many more artistic treasures from some of Spain's big names in art, such as Salvador Dalí, and Barcelona's Josep Maria Sert and Xavier Corberó, as well as an extraordinary 18th-century Neapolitan baroque *belén* (nativity scene).

Entry is through an outdoor terrace display of modern sculptural works. Centre stage is taken by Corberó's enormous *Orgue del Mar* (1973).

Inside, more than 20 paintings by Dalí around the themes 'Alchemy and Eternity' catch the eye, as does the *belén* with hundreds of incredibly detailed figures, from angels and kings to shepherds and farm animals and market scenes, making up a unique representation of Christ's birth.

Upstairs, the artist Josep Maria Sert (1874–1945) painted the main vault and music room ceiling. The vault is divided into four parts, the first three representing three virtues (audacity, reason and inspiration) and the last the embodiment of those qualities in the form of Sert's client Juan March. One of the rooms hosts an intriguing display of medieval maps of the Mediterranean by Mallorquin cartographers.

Museu Diocesà   MUSEUM
(Map p56; Carrer del Mirador 5; adult/child €3/free; ⊙ 10am-2pm Mon-Sat) Opened in 2007 in its magnificent new home of the Palau Episcopal (bishop's residence), the Museu Diocesà, behind the cathedral to the east, is a fascinating excursion for those interested in Mallorca's Christian artistic history. It contains works by Antoni Gaudí, Francesc Comes and Pere Niçard, and a mind-boggling *retaule* (*retablo* in Spanish; an altarpiece) depicting

Palma

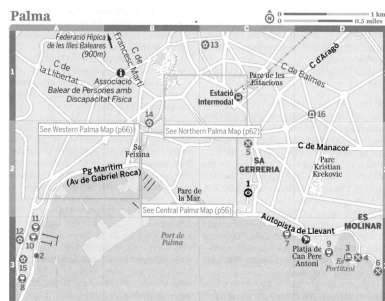

the Passion of Christ (c 1290–1305) and taken from the Convent de Santa Clara.

The episodes of the Passion are shown with effusive detail: Palm Sunday, the Last Supper, St Peter's kiss of betrayal. Christ flailed looks utterly unperturbed, while the image of his being nailed to the cross is unsettling. Off to the right, a key work is Comes' *St Jaume de Compostela* (St James, known to the Spaniards as the Moor-slayer). Niçard's *Sant Jordi* (St George), from around 1468–70, is remarkable for its busy detail. The City of Mallorca (Palma) is shown in the background as St George dispatches the dragon. Below this painting is a scene by Niçard and his boss Rafel Mòger depicting the 1229 taking of Palma. The final room in this wing is the Gothic Oratori de Sant Pau, a small chapel. The stained-glass window was a trial run done by Gaudí in preparation for the windows he did in the Catedral.

Otherwise, a succession of rooms showcases Mallorquin artists such as Pere Terrencs and Mateu López (father and son), while upstairs is a thin collection of baroque art, ceramics and some lovely views of the bay.

Dalt Murada & Parc de la Mar WALLS, PARK
(Map p56) Most of Palma's defensive walls were destroyed in the early 20th century to allow easier expansion of the city. Only a section of the Renaissance sea wall, the Dalt Murada (begun in 1562, finished in 1801), remains impressively intact. In 1984, Parc de la Mar (with its artificial lake, fountain and green spaces) was opened. Head slightly east and you'll reach a children's playground.

The park is an appealing place for a breezy drink at a terrace cafe in summer. It is also the best vantage point for photographing the cathedral in all its colossal glory, especially when it is lit up after dark.

Museo Can Morey de Santmartí GALLERY
(Map p56; www.museo-santmarti.es; Carrer de la Portella 9; adult/child €9/5; ⊙9.30am-8.30pm Apr-Oct, shorter hours rest of year) A grand town mansion set around an inner courtyard was revamped and reopened as this museum in 2012. A dream come true for German art dealer Wolfgang Hörnke, the museum is an ode to the wonderfully weird world of Catalan surrealist artist Salvador Dalí (1904–89). Some 226 original works from the 1930s to the 1970s are displayed on three levels.

Sorcery, bullfighting (with the matador often given a monstrous touch) and mythology are recurring themes in the works that grace the opulent wood-floored rooms. Among the standouts are series of lively engravings, including *Faust* (1968) and *Les Hippies* (1969–70).

Palma

Jardí del Bisbe
GARDENS
(Map p56; Carrer de Sant Pere Nolasc 6; ⊙9am-3pm Mon-Fri) **FREE** Adjoining the Palau Episcopal is the Jardí del Bisbe; this modest botanic garden is an oasis of peace. Have a quiet stroll among the palms, pomegranates, water lilies, thyme, artichokes, kumquats, orange and lemon trees, and more. Or just sit on a bench and contemplate.

Can Bordils
HISTORIC SITE
(Map p56; Carrer de l'Almudaina 9) This 16th-century mansion with a 17th-century courtyard is home to the Arxiu Municipal, which sometimes holds temporary exhibitions.

Porta de l'Almudaina
GATE
(Map p56; Carrer de l'Almudaina) Part of a rare stretch of defensive wall and tower, this arch down the street (east) of Can Bordils is intriguing for history buffs. It is said to have been in use from antiquity until about the 13th century. Although largely medieval in appearance, it is almost certain that this was part of the Roman wall.

Museu de Mallorca
MUSEUM
(Map p56; www.museudemallorca.es; Carrer de la Portella 5; ⊙11am-8pm Mon-Fri, to 2pm Sat) **FREE** This excellent city museum remains closed for extensive renovations until at least late 2014, when it will reopen in this rambling ensemble of 17th-century mansions on Carrer de la Portella. Until then, it occupies a temporary home at Fundació Sa Nostra (p59), and showcases a collection of archaeological artefacts, religious art, antiques and ceramics – from Talayotic bronzes to intricate Almohad gold jewellery.

Banys Àrabs
BATHHOUSE
(Map p56; Carrer de Serra 7; adult/child €2/free; ⊙9am-7.30pm) These modest Arab baths are the single most important remaining monument to the Muslim domination of the island, although all that survives are two small underground chambers, one with a domed ceiling supported by a dozen columns, some of whose capitals were recycled from demolished Roman buildings. The site may be small, but the two rooms – the caldarium (hot bath) and the tepidarium (warm bath) – evoke a poignant sense of abandonment.

Normally there would also have been a third, cold bath, the frigidarium. As the Roman terms suggest, the Arabs basically took over a Roman idea, here in Mallorca and throughout the Arab world. These ones probably were not public but attached to a private mansion. The baths are set in one of Old Palma's prettiest gardens, where you can sit and relax.

Església de Santa Eulàlia
CHURCH
(Map p56; Plaça de Santa Eulàlia 2; ⊙9.30am-noon & 6.30-8.30pm Mon-Fri, 10.30am-1pm & 6.30-8.30pm Sat, 9.30am-1.30pm, 6.30-7.30pm & 9-10pm Sun) **FREE** One of the first major churches raised after the 1229 conquest, the Església de Santa Eulàlia is a soaring Gothic structure with a neo-Gothic facade (a complete remake was done between 1894 and 1924). It is the only such church in Mallorca, aside from the Catedral, with three naves. The baroque *retablo* (altarpiece) is rather worn and you can't get to the chapels in the apse.

Basílica de Sant Francesc
CHURCH
(Map p56; Plaça de Sant Francesc 7; admission €1.50; ⊙9.30am-12.30pm Mon-Sun, 3.30-6pm Mon-Sat) One of Palma's oldest churches, the Franciscan Basílica de Sant Francesc was begun in 1281 in Gothic style and its baroque facade was completed in 1700. In the splendid Gothic cloister – a two-tiered, trapezoid affair – the elegant columns indicate it was

PALMA & THE BADIA DE PALMA PALMA DE MALLORCA

PALMA FOR CHILDREN

With its beaches, parks and water activities, touring Palma with children in tow should be a breeze. Tell tales of knights and damsels exploring Castell de Bellver (p62) and **Castell de Sant Carles** (Carretera del Dic de l'Oest; ⊙ 9am-1pm Mon-Sat) **FREE**; you can also combine art with fun on the ramparts at Es Baluard (p60). Palma Aquarium (p79), east of Palma, is also outstanding and you could easily spend half a day there; kids can spend a (possibly sleepless) night at one of the shark sleepovers. Aqualand (p79) water park near S'Arenal is another surefire hit, with its slide, pools and speedball flumes.

Playgrounds are scattered about town, for instance in **Parc de les Estacions**, behind the train and bus station, and **Sa Feixina** park near Es Baluard. There's a brilliant adventure playground further along near the walls just east of **Parc de la Mar**.

some time in the making. Inside the lugubrious church, the fusion of styles is clear. The high vaulted roof is classic Gothic, while the glittering high altar is a baroque lollipop, albeit in need of a polish.

In the first chapel (dedicated to Nostra Senyora de la Consolació) on the left in the apse is the church's pride and joy, the tomb of and monument to the 13th-century scholar and evangelist Ramon Llull. He is Mallorca's favourite son (apart perhaps from the tennis genius Rafael Nadal). Llull's alabaster tomb is high up on the right. Drop a few coins in the slot for the campaign to have him canonised (he has only made it to beatification). Check out the Capilla de los Santos Mártires Gorkomienses, on the right side of the apse. In 1572, 19 Catholics, 11 of them Franciscans, were martyred in Holland. In this much faded portrayal of the event, you can see them being hanged, disembowelled, having their noses cut off and more.

Arab City Wall   HISTORIC SITE
(Map p52; Carrer de Mateu Enric Lladó) One block east of the Església de Sant Jeroni, you strike a portion of the 12th-century Arab city wall (with some heavy blocks from the Roman wall at the base), beyond which is a park named after the city gate that once stood here: Porta d'es Camp (Gate of the Countryside). The Muslims knew it as Bab al-Jadid (the New Gate).

Església del Monti-Sion   CHURCH
(Map p56; Carrer del Monti-Sion; ⊙ 5.15-7pm) The gaudy baroque facade of the Església del Monti-Sion was converted from a Gothic synagogue. It got a serious baroque makeover, inside and out, in the 16th to 17th centuries. Gothic giveaways include the ogive arches in front of the chapels, the key vaulting in the ceiling and the long, low Catalan Gothic arch just inside the entrance.

As you wander in, a priest sitting in a booth by the entry may flip a switch and light up the curves-and-swirls baroque *retablo* at the back of the church.

Ajuntament   HISTORIC BUILDING
(Town Hall; Map p56; Plaça de la Cort 1) Dominating the square that has long been the heart of municipal power in Palma is the *ajuntament*. The baroque facade hides a longer history: the town hall building grew out of a Gothic hospital raised here shortly after the island's conquest. On the top floor of the main facade sits En Figuera, as the town clock is affectionately known. The present mechanism dates to 1863 and was purchased in France, but a clock has tolled the hours here for centuries.

You can generally enter the foyer only, in which you will see a Gothic entrance, a fine sweeping staircase and, probably, half a dozen *gegants* (huge figures of kings, queens and other characters that are paraded around town on people's shoulders during fiesta) in storage.

Centre Cultural Contemporani Pelaires   CULTURAL CENTRE, GALLERY
(Map p56; www.pelaires.com; Carrer de Can Verí 3; ⊙ 10am-1.30pm & 4.45-8pm Tue-Fri, 10am-1.30pm Sat) This private cultural centre is as interesting for its architecture as for its content (changing art exhibitions). The building, Can Verí, is a beautiful 17th-century town house that was also used for a while as a convent. This narrow pedestrian lane is rather chichi, home to galleries, antique shops and fashion boutiques.

Convent de Santa Clara   CONVENT
(Map p56; Carrer de Can Fonollar 2; ⊙ 9am-12.30pm & 4.15-6.15pm) This church is a gloomy baroque affair. It was closed for

renovation when we were here, but, in any event, locals prefer to pop into the adjacent building, because the handful of cloistered nuns maintain a centuries-old tradition of baking sweets for sale.

You will see a *torno,* a kind of timber turnstile set in a window. Ring for a nun, order what you want and put money into the turnstile. This swivels around and out come your *bocaditos de almendra* (almond nibbles) or *rollitos de anís* (aniseed rolls), at €3 for 200g.

Arc de sa Drassana   HISTORIC BUILDING
(Map p56; off S'Hort del Rei) A grand arch, the Arc de sa Drassana is one of the city's few reminders of its Arab past. When the Riera, the city's river, coursed along what is now Passeig d'es Born and the sea lapped the city walls, this was the seaward entrance into the Arab palace and early shipyards.

◉ Plaça Major & Around

★Museu Fundació Juan March   GALLERY
(Map p56; www.march.es/arte/palma; Carrer de Sant Miquel 11; ⊙10am-6.30pm Mon-Fri, 10.30am-2pm Sat) **FREE** This 17th-century mansion gives an insightful overview of Spanish contemporary art. On permanent display are some 70 pieces held by the Fundación Juan March. Together they constitute a veritable who's who of mostly 20th-century artists, including Miró, Juan Gris (of cubism fame), Dalí and the sculptors Eduardo Chillida and Julio González.

After starting with the big names, the collection skips through various movements in Spanish art, such as that inspired in Barcelona by the Dau al Set review (1948–53) and led by Antoni Tàpies. Meanwhile, in Valencia, Eusebio Sempere and Andreu Alfaro

---

GET YOUR BEARINGS

Use the cathedral as your compass. The heart of the old city (the districts of **Sa Portella** and **Sa Calatrava**) has always been centred on its main place of worship and the one-time seat of secular power opposite it. The bulk of Palma's sights are jammed into this warren of tight, twisting lanes and sunny squares, where massive churches sidle up to noble houses. The bright Mediterranean light and glittering sea are never far away.

To the north lies **Plaça Major**, a typically Spanish central square, lined with arcades, shops and cafes. Lively by day, it falls eerily silent at night. To the east, Carrer del Sindicat spokes out towards the avenues that mark the limits of historic Palma. It crosses a district known as **Sa Gerreria**. For decades run-down and slightly dodgy, Sa Gerreria is enjoying a revival and it's becoming a trendy hub of the city's nightlife. Off Plaça Major, the shopping boulevard, Carrer de Sant Miquel, leads north towards the vast **Plaça d'Espanya**, the city's major transport hub. Plaça Major and Carrer de Sant Miquel are on high ground that falls away to the west down to tree-lined **Passeig de la Rambla** boulevard.

West of the cathedral is **Passeig d'es Born**, a classic strolling boulevard and one of Palma's major arteries. It frames the historic quarter of **Es Puig de Sant Pere**, which is buttressed by the fortress walls of Es Baluard to the west and the shop-lined Avinguda de Jaume II to the north. Crossing the Sa Riera river brings you to **Santa Catalina**, with its long, grid-pattern streets and traditional low-slung one- and two-storey houses, which was once a down-at-heel sailors' district. As early as the 17th century, windmills were raised in the area (still known as Es Jonquet) south of Carrer de Sant Magí, the oldest street in the *barri* (district). In recent years gentrification has transformed Santa Catalina into an artsy, bohemian quarter, filled with one-of-a-kind boutiques, galleries, bars and restaurants. Follow the seafront **Passeig Marítim** further west still and you reach the ferry port and western Palma's major drawcard: Castell de Bellver.

A 1km walk from the city-centre end of the Platja de Can Pere Antoni brings you to **Es Portitxol**. The 'little port' has a quiet abundance of pleasure craft and is closed off inland by the motorway (at a discreet distance). You can walk, cycle or rollerblade here along the Passeig Marítim from central Palma. From Es Portitxol, walking around the next point brings you to **Es Molinar**. This simple, waterfront 'suburban' district of low fishing folks' houses has become a dining haunt, with a handful of places at the Es Portitxol end. Over the bridge is **Ciutat Jardí**, a low-key residential area with a broad, sandy beach.

Central Palma

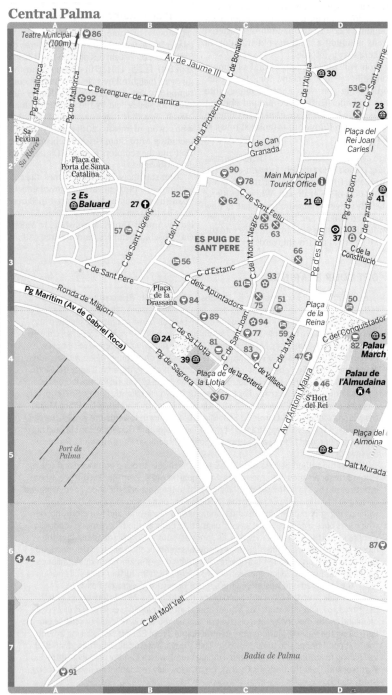

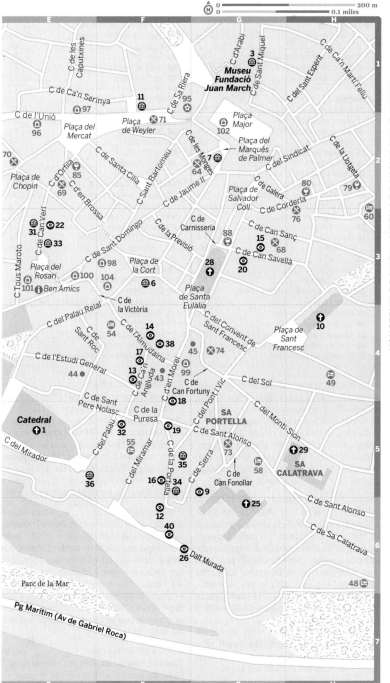

Central Palma

◉ Top Sights

1 Catedral	E5
2 Es Baluard	A2
3 Museu Fundació Juan March	G1
4 Palau de l'Almudaina	D4
5 Palau March	D4

◉ Sights

6 Ajuntament	F3
7 Almacenes El Águila	G2
8 Arc de sa Drassana	D5
9 Banys Àrabs	G5
10 Basílica de Sant Francesc	H4
11 CaixaForum	F1
12 Cal Marquès de la Torre	F6
13 Cal Poeta Colom	F4
14 Can Bordils	F4
15 Can Catlar del Llorer	G3
16 Can Espanya-Serra	F5
17 Can Marquès	F4
18 Can Oleza	F4
Can Oms	(see 14)
19 Can Salas	F5
20 Can Vivot	G3
21 Casal Solleric	D2
22 Centre Cultural Contemporani Pelaires	E3
23 Círculo de Bellas Artes	D1
24 Consolat de Mar	B4
25 Convent de Santa Clara	G6
26 Dalt Murada & Parc de la Mar	F6
27 Església de Santa Creu	B2
28 Església de Santa Eulàlia	G3
29 Església del Monti-Sion	H5
30 Fundació Sa Nostra	D1
31 Galeria K	E3
32 Jardí del Bisbe	F5
33 La Caja Blanca	E3
34 Museo Can Morey de Santmartí	F5
35 Museu de Mallorca	F5
36 Museu Diocesà	E5
37 Passeig d'es Born	D3
38 Porta de l'Almudaina	F4
39 Sa Llotja	B4
40 Sa Portella	F6
41 Sala Pelaires	D2

◉ Activities, Courses & Tours

42 Cruceros Marco Polo	A6
43 Die Akademie	F4
44 Estudi Lul·lià de Mallorca	E4
45 Mallorca Rutes	G4
46 Palma City Sightseeing	D4
47 Palma on Bike	D4

◉ Sleeping

48 Boutique Hotel Calatrava	H6
49 Can Cera	H4
50 Consell de Mallorca Tourist Office	D3
51 Hostal Apuntadores	C3
52 Hostal Pons	B2
53 Hotel Born	D1
54 Hotel Dalt Murada	F4
55 Hotel Palacio Ca Sa Galesa	F5

were leading the way down abstract paths. Sempere's *Las Cuatro Estaciones* (1980) reflects the four seasons in subtle changes of colour in a series of four panels with interlocking shapes made of fine lines. Other names to watch for are Manuel Millares, Fernando Zóbel and Miquel Barceló, who is represented by works including his large-format *La Flaque* (The Pond; 1989).

Església de Sant Miquel   CHURCH

(Map p62; Carrer de Sant Miquel 21; ☺9.30am-1.30pm & 5-7.30pm) Raised after the conquest of Mallorca, this church is a striking mix. It was one of the first four churches built on the site of a mosque where the island's first Mass was celebrated on 31 December 1229. The facade and entrance, with its long, low arch, is a perfect example of 14th-century Catalan Gothic. The squat seven-storey bell tower is also a Gothic creation.

Otherwise, the church, with its barrel-vaulted ceiling, is largely the result of a baroque makeover. Note the statue of Pope John Paul II on the right as you enter.

Claustre de Sant Antoniet   GALLERY

(Map p62; Carrer de Sant Miquel 30; ☺10am-2pm & 3.30-8pm Mon-Fri, 10am-1.30pm Sat) FREE The Claustre de Sant Antoniet is a baroque gem that belongs to the BBVA bank. The two-tiered, oval-shaped enclosure was built in 1768 and is now used for temporary art exhibitions. It was originally attached to the Església de Sant Antoni de Viana, which was closed for restoration when we visited, next door.

Almacenes El Águila   HISTORIC BUILDING

(Map p56; Plaça del Marquès de Palmer 1) Gaspar Bennàssar (1869–1933) – one of the most influential architects in modern Palma, his native city – played with various styles during his long career, including Modernisme. An outstanding example of this is the Almacenes El Águila, built in 1908. Each of the three floors is different and the generous use of wrought iron in the main facade is a herald of the style.

Círculo de Bellas Artes   GALLERY

(Map p56; www.circulopalma.es; Carrer de l'Unió 3) Casal Balaguer – with the grand if unevenly cobbled courtyard, graced by four thin, leaning palms – is home to a faded but weighty art institution, the Círculo de Bellas Artes. The site was closed for much-needed major renovations at the time of our visit, and is set to reopen and host exhibitions in 2015.

CaixaForum GALLERY
(Map p56; www.lacaixa.es/ObraSocial; Plaça de Weyler 3; ⏰10am-9pm Mon-Sat, to 2pm Sun) **FREE** This exhibition centre is run by one of Spain's biggest building societies, the Barcelona-based La Caixa. CaixaForum is housed in the wonderful Modernista building (the island's first) that was once home to the Grand Hotel. Pick up a free program at reception and flick through it at the ground-level cafe. There's also an excellent bookshop.

The Grand Hotel was a city landmark built in 1900–03 by the Catalan master architect Lluís Domènech i Montaner and the first building in Palma with electricity and a lift. The hotel was shut down during the Civil War and never recovered. As well as the art exhibitions, other frequent activities here include lectures, workshops, film cycles and concerts.

Fundació Sa Nostra GALLERY, CULTURAL CENTRE
(Map p56; www.obrasocialsanostra.com; Carrer de la Concepció 12; ⏰8am-8pm Mon-Fri, 11am-2pm Sat) **FREE** The big Balearics building society, Sa Nostra, has a cultural foundation in Can Castelló, where it stages exhibitions. It is worth popping by just to check out the fine 18th-century courtyard, which now hosts a hip cafe. The temporary exhibitions at the centre are always worth a look.

The original house dates to the 17th century, and it even has a few Modernista touches from renovation work in 1909. Just in front of it is **Font del Sepulcre**, a Gothic baptismal font left over from a long-disappeared church. Inside it is a 12th-century Muslim-era well. Carrer de la Concepció used to be known as Carrer de la Monederia, as the Kingdom of Mallorca's mint was on this street.

Església de Sant Jaume CHURCH
(Map p62; Carrer de Sant Jaume 10; ⏰11.30am-1.30pm & 5.30-8.30pm) **FREE** Despite its baroque facade, this is one of Palma's older surviving Gothic churches. This grey soaring

eminence is one of the first four parish churches to be built 'under the protection of the Royal House of Mallorca' from 1327. It is said that the Bonapart family (later Bonaparte) lived around here until they moved to Corsica in 1406. Napoleon could have been a Mallorquin!

Església de Santa Magdalena   CHURCH
(Map p62; Plaça de Santa Magdalena; ☺9am-12.30pm & 5.30-7.30pm Mon-Sat) **FREE** The main claim to fame of the baroque Església de Santa Magdalena is as being the resting place of Santa Catalina Thomàs of Valldemossa. Her clothed remains are visible through a glass coffin held in a chapel to the left of the altar and are an object of pilgrimage.

It is said that the future saint sat weeping by a great clump of stone one day as none of the convents would accept her because she was too poor. Then someone told her that the convent once attached to the Església de Santa Magdalena would take her in. She was overjoyed. The stone in question is now embedded in the rear wall of the 14th-century Església de Sant Nicolau on Plaça del Mercat.

Església de Sant Crist de la Sang   CHURCH
(Map p62; Plaça de l'Hospital; ☺7.30am-1pm & 4-8pm) **FREE** Within the Hospital General (founded in the 16th century), you can behold the Gothic facade of this church. It is the object of pilgrimage and devotion, since the *paso* (a sculpted image used in processions) of 'Holy Christ of the Blood' is considered to be miraculous.

If you happen on a Mass, it's moving to see the devotion of the faithful who climb up behind the altar to venerate the image of Christ crucified, with long, flowing *real* hair and embroidered loincloth. Just on your left as you enter the church is a 15th-century nativity scene, probably imported from Naples.

◉ Es Puig de Sant Pere

★ Es Baluard   GALLERY
(Museu d'Art Modern i Contemporani; Map p56; www.esbaluard.org; Plaça de Porta de Santa Catalina 10; adult/child €6/free, temporary exhibitions €4; ☺10am-8pm Tue-Sat, to 3pm Sun) Built with flair and innovation into the shell of the Renaissance-era seaward walls, this contemporary art gallery is one of the finest on the island. Its temporary exhibitions are worth viewing, but the permanent collection – works by Miró, Barceló and Picasso – give the gallery its cachet.

The 21st-century concrete complex is cleverly built among the fortifications, including the partly restored remains of an 11th-century Muslim-era tower (on your right as you arrive from Carrer de Sant Pere).

Inside, the ground floor houses the core of the permanent exhibition, starting with a section on Mallorcan landscapes by local artists and others from abroad; the big names here include Valencia's Joaquín Sorolla, Mallorca's own Miquel Barceló and the Catalan Modernista artist Santiago Rusiñol; the latter did a lot of work in and around the town of Bunyola. A broad swath of local and mostly Catalan landscape artists is also on show here. Also on the ground floor and part of the permanent collection is a room devoted to the works of Joan Miró, while on the top floor is an intriguing collection of ceramics by Pablo Picasso; after viewing the latter, step out onto the ramparts for fine views. In sum, it's an impressive rather than extraordinary collection that's well worth a couple of hours of your time.

Sa Llotja   HISTORIC BUILDING
(Map p56; Plaça de la Llotja; ☺11am-1.45pm & 5-8.45pm Tue-Sat, 11am-1.45pm Sun) **FREE** Gorgeous 15th-century sandstone Gothic Sa Llotja, opposite the waterfront, was built as a merchants' stock exchange and is used for temporary exhibitions, such as the eye-catching sculpture of British artist Tony Cragg. Designed by Guillem Sagrera, it is the apogee of civilian Gothic building on the island and was completed in 1450.

Inside, six slender, twisting columns lead to the lofty vaulted ceiling. In each corner of the building rises a fanciful octagonal tower. The flanks are marked with huge arches, fine tracery and monstrous-looking gargoyles leaning out overhead.

Passeig d'es Born   STREET
(Map p56) One of Palma's most appealing boulevards, Passeig d'es Born is capped by Plaça del Rei Joan Carles I (named after the present king and formerly after Pope Pius XII), a traffic roundabout locally known as Plaça de les Tortugues, because of the obelisk placed on four bronze turtles. On the east side of the avenue, on the corner of Carrer de Jovellanos, the distorted black face of a Moor, complete with white stone turban, is affixed high on a building.

Known as the Cap del Moro (Moor's Head), it represents a Muslim slave who is said to have killed his master, a chaplain, in

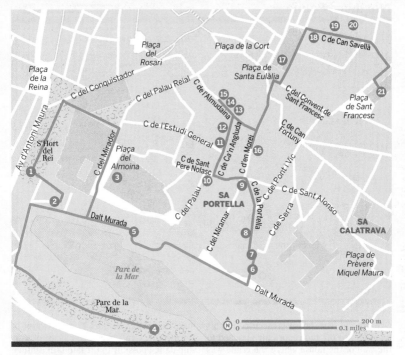

Walking Tour
Historic Palma & Hidden Patios

START S'HORT DEL REI
END BASÍLICA DE SANT FRANCESC
LENGTH 2.5KM; TWO TO THREE HOURS

Begin in ① **S'Hort del Rei** (King's Garden), where ② **Arc de sa Drassana** (p55) arches above a pond. Amble north to Miró's bronze sculpture ('the egg'). Climb the steps past Palau March to the immense Gothic ③ **Catedral** (p49). Head down to ④ **Parc de la Mar** (p52), with its fountain-draped lake.

Soak up views along the Renaissance sea wall ⑤ **Dalt Murada** (p52). Turn left at medieval gateway ⑥ **Sa Portella**, with a keystone and coat of arms. Carrer de la Portella hides historic courtyards: 17th-century ⑦ **Cal Marquès de la Torre** and 19th-century ⑧ **Can Espanya-Serra**, with a neo-Gothic staircase. Swing left onto Carrer de la Puresa, pausing at ⑨ **Can Salas**, one of Palma's oldest patios, with carved pillars, a beautiful loggia and a 13th-century coat of arms.

Pause in tiny ⑩ **Jardí del Bisbe** (p53) or continue to ⑪ **Cal Poeta Colom**, named for its one-time resident poet. Its baroque patio reveals tapered columns. Further along is grand medieval manor ⑫ **Can Marquès**.

On Carrer de l'Almudaina, the medieval gateway ⑬ **Porta de l'Almudaina** (p53) was originally part of the Roman walls. Close by is ⑭ **Can Bordils** (p53), a 17th-century courtyard, and neighbouring ⑮ **Can Oms**, with its Gothic portal. Nearby, on Carrer d'en Morei, ⑯ **Can Oleza** is a baroque patio with a loggia, Ionic columns, low arches and wrought-iron balustrade. Pass spired ⑰ **Església de Santa Eulàlia** (p53) to Carrer de Can Savellà, home to Corinthian-column-lined ⑱ **Can Vivot** and ⑲ **Can Catlar del Llorer**, one of Palma's oldest Gothic patios. Stop for hot chocolate at old-school ⑳ **Ca'n Joan de S'Aigo** (p67) before finishing at ㉑ **Basílica de Sant Francesc** (p53).

Northern Palma

October 1731. The slave was executed and his hand lopped off and reportedly attached to the wall of the house where the crime was committed. Chronicles claim the withered remains of the hand were still in place, behind a grille, in 1840.

Casal Solleric
HISTORIC BUILDING

(Map p56; www.solleric.org; Passeig d'es Born 27; ⊙ 11am-2pm & 3.30-8.30pm Tue-Sat, 11am-2.30pm Sun) This grand 18th-century baroque mansion with the typical Palma courtyard of graceful broad arches and uneven stone paving is at once a cultural centre with temporary exhibitions, bookshop and tourist information office. Displays are usually free and found over a couple of floors.

Consolat de Mar
HISTORIC BUILDING

(Map p56; Passeig de Sagrera) The Consolat de Mar was founded in 1326 as a maritime tribunal. The present building, one of Mallorca's few examples of (albeit impure) Renaissance design, was completed in 1669. It was tacked onto, and faces, a late Gothic chapel completed around 1600 for the members of Sa Llotja.

Església de Santa Creu
CHURCH

(Map p56; Carrer de Sant Llorenç 4; ⊙ Mass) Work on this Gothic church began in 1335. The main entrance (Carrer de Santa Creu 7) is a baroque addition. What makes it interest-

ing is the Cripta de Sant Llorenç (Crypt of St Lawrence), an early-Gothic place of worship dating possibly to the late 13th century. Some paintings by Rafel Mòger and Francesc Comes are scattered about the interior.

◎ Passeig Marítim & Western Palma

Castell de Bellver
CASTLE

(www.cultura.palma.es; Carrer de Camilo José Cela 17; adult/child €4/2, Sun free; ⊙ 8.30am-1pm Mon, to 8pm Tue-Sat, 10am-6pm Sun) Straddling a wooded hillside, the Castell de Bellver is a 14th-century circular castle (with a unique round tower), the only one of its kind in Spain. Jaume II ordered the castle built atop a hill known as Puig de Sa Mesquida in 1300 and it was largely complete 10 years later. The best part of a visit is to mosey around the castle and enjoy the spectacular views over the woods to Palma, the Badia de Palma and out to sea.

The castle was conceived above all as a royal residence but seems to have been a white elephant, as only King Sanç (in 1314) and Aragón's Joan I (in 1395) moved in for any amount of time. In 1717 it became a prison. Climb to the roof and check out the prisoners' graffiti etched into the stonework.

Northern Palma

The ground-floor **Museu d'Història de la Ciutat** (City History Museum) consists of some explanatory panels and a modest collection of pottery. Upstairs you can visit a series of largely empty chambers, including the one-time kitchen. These are kept closed on Sundays, when admission is free.

About the nearest you can get to the castle by bus (3, 46 or 50) is Plaça de Gomila, from where you'll have to hoof it about 15 minutes (1km) up a steep hill. Instead, combine it with the Palma City Sightseeing open-top bus, which climbs to the castle as part of its circuit of the city.

🏃 Activities

Marenostrum BOAT TRIPS
(Map p66; ☑ 971 45 61 82; www.marenostrum-catamarans.com; Passeig Marítim 8; with/without hotel pick-up €57/49; ⊙ 10am-3pm & 3.30-8.30pm Apr-Oct) Marenostrum puts on twice-daily five-hour catamaran tours to either Cala Portals

Vells or Cala Vella (depending on wind direction), just east of the Badia de Palma. The price includes food on board and snorkelling gear.

Cruceros Marco Polo BOAT TRIPS
(Map p56; ☑ 647 843667; www.crucerosmarcopolo.com; off Passeig Marítim; 1hr cruise €12; ⊙ hourly 11am-4pm Mon-Sat, 2-4pm Sun Mar-Oct) This operator offers a one-hour whiz around the bay up to six times daily.

Palma on Bike BICYCLE RENTAL
(Map p56; ☑ 971 71 80 62; www.palmaonbike.com; Avinguda d'Antoni Maura 10; city/mountain/e-bike rental per day €14/22/24, per week €67/95/130; ⊙ 10am-2pm & 4-8pm) Palma on Bike has city bikes to get around Palma, as well as mountain bikes, rollerblades and kayaks. Bike rates include insurance and a helmet.

Mallorca Vintage SCOOTER HIRE
(Map p62; ☑ 620 476285; www.mallorcavintage.com; Plaça Espanya 6; ⊙ 9.30am-7.30pm) Take a breather from the city by hopping on one of Mallorca Vintage's Vespas to zip across the island to villages and secluded beaches. Prices start from around €42 per day. It's located on the underground level of the train station.

🎓 Courses

Dialog LANGUAGE
(Map p62; ☑ 971 71 99 94; www.dialog-palma.com; Carrer del Carme 14; 2-week course €395; ⊙ 9.30am-2pm & 4.30-8.30pm Mon-Fri, 10am-2pm Sat) This bookshop offers well-regarded two-week intensive Spanish courses.

Estudi Lul·lià de Mallorca LANGUAGE
(Map p56; ☑ 971 71 19 88; www.estudigeneral.com; Carrer de Sant Roc 4; from €400) Offers intensive summer courses in Spanish language and culture.

Die Akademie LANGUAGE
(Map p56; ☑ 971 71 82 90; www.dieakademie.com; Carrer d'en Morei 8; per week €140-285; ⊙ 9am-1.30pm & 5-7.30pm Mon-Fri) Housed in a late-Gothic mansion, Die Akademie runs a variety of Spanish-language courses.

Palma Sea School SAILING
(Map p52; ☑ 971 10 05 18; www.palmaseaschool.com; Passeig Marítim 38; 2-day yachting courses from €400) Whether you're cutting your teeth or honing your skills, this Royal Yachting Association–affiliated school offers a wide range of courses in yachting, sailing, power-boating and jet-skiing.

PALMA & THE BADIA DE PALMA PALMA DE MALLORCA

☞ Tours

★ Mallorca Rutes
WALKING

(Map p56; ☑ 971 72 89 83; www.mallorcarutes.com; Carrer d'en Morei 1; per person €15-35) Mallorca Rutes runs a wide range of guided walking tours, which afford insight into different aspects of Palma. These range from basic city walking tours covering the main sights to walks with a themed angle, such as the excellent one revealing Palma's hidden courtyards and palaces. It also arranges tastings of wine and typical Mallorcan products. The tours can be booked through Típika, next to Plaça de Santa Eulalia.

Palma City Sightseeing
BUS

(Map p56; ☑ 902 101081; www.mallorcatour.com; Avinguda d'Antoni Maura; adult/child €15/7.50; ⊘ 9.30am-10pm) This hop-on hop-off bus has commentary in various languages. Tickets are valid for 24 hours (a slightly more expensive 48-hour version is also available). The bus departs from Avinguda d'Antoni Maura and runs every 15 minutes. Apart from doing a circuit of the city centre, it runs along the waterfront and even climbs up to the Castell de Bellver.

★ Festivals & Events

Festa de Sant Sebastiá
MUSIC

(⊘ 19-20 Jan) On the eve of the feast day of Palma's patron saint, concerts (from funk to folk) are staged in the city squares, along with flaming pyres and the *aiguafoc*, a fireworks display over the bay. It's a big (if chilly) night.

Sa Rueta & Sa Rua
CARNIVAL

(⊘ Feb-Mar) Palma's version of Carnaval (celebrated in the last days before Lent starts) involves a procession for kids (Sa Rueta) followed later by a bigger one (Sa Rua) with floats and the like.

Semana Santa
RELIGIOUS

(Holy Week; ⊘ Mar-Apr) Processions dot the Easter week calendar, but the most impressive are those on Holy Thursday evening. In the Processó del Sant Crist de la Sang (Christ of the Blood), robed and hooded members of *confraries* (lay brotherhoods) parade with a *paso* (heavy sculpted image of Christ, borne by a team of men). It starts at 7pm in the Església de Sant Crist de la Sang, where the *paso* is kept, and returns hours later.

Boat Show Palma
BOAT FAIR

(www.boatshowpalma.com; ⊘ May) Usually held around the first week of May, this is a major boat fair held at the Moll Vell docks.

Corpus Christi
RELIGIOUS

(⊘ May-Jun) The feast of the Body of Christ (the Eucharist) falls on the Thursday of the ninth week after Easter, although the main procession from the cathedral takes place on the following Sunday at 7pm. On that day, carpets of flowers are laid out in front of the Catedral and in Plaça de la Cort. Concert cycles (many held in the city's *patis,* which can also be visited at this time) add a celebratory note for about a month around the feast day.

Nit de Foc
LOCAL FIESTA

(⊘ 23 Jun) The night before the feast of St John (24 June) is celebrated with fiery feasting. As night falls, the *correfoc* (fire-running) begins in Parc de la Mar. People dressed up as demons, and armed with pyrotechnical gear that would probably be illegal in hell, leap and dance in an infernal procession. Locals then head for the beaches, where wandering musical groups

---

GALLERY ALLEY

Contemporary-art enthusiasts will get a buzz out of the plethora of galleries that populate the narrow streets just east of the Passeig d'es Born.

La Caja Blanca (Map p56; www.lacajablanca.com; Carrer de Can Verí 9; ⊘ 11am-2pm & 5-8pm Mon-Fri, 11.30am-2pm Sat) Edgy Mallorquin and international artists are showcased in this stark, minimalist space. It stages three to four exhibitions annually.

Galeria K (Map p56; www.galeria-k.com; Carrer de Can Verí 10; ⊘ 10.30am-2.30pm & 4-8pm Mon-Fri, 10.30am-6pm Sat) This innovative little gallery presents Spanish and international painters and sculptors.

Sala Pelaires (Map p56; www.pelaires.com; Carrer de Pareires 5; ⊘ 10am-1.30pm & 4.45-8pm Mon-Fri, 10am-1.30pm Sat) An arm of the Centre Cultural Contemporani Pelaires and Palma's first contemporary gallery, this is a wonderful place to see works by top Spanish artists.

LOCAL KNOWLEDGE

PATIOS & PALACES

Mallorca Rutes tour guide Mateu Masegosa gives the inside scoop on his favourite Mallorcan *patis* (patios) and oft-missed details in Palma's labyrinth of cobbled backstreets.

Noblemen and merchants There is something of a class distinction among Palma's patios. The elite (nobles and landowners) lived in luxury in the historic quarter, Palma Alta, around Sa Portella. Merchants and sailors resided in Palma Baixa, around Es Puig de Sant Pere, where patios often feature details such as boat engravings or motifs of Mercury, god of commerce.

A man with vision Juan March was an affluent businessman and a flamboyant fellow who went all out to impress. Palau March (p51) has Palma's most unusual patio: a loggia open on all sides to maximise views of the cathedral and Palau de l'Almudaina.

Courtly flirtations Above the Porta de l'Almudaina (p53) medieval gate, a tiny window pays testament to theatrical courtship rituals. Here beautiful señoras would peer out and flirt with moustachioed caballeros below by unfolding their fans or fluttering their handkerchiefs.

Legends of dragons On the corner of Carrer de la Portella, look up to notice a crocodile-like stone figure – El Drac de Na Coca. Legend has it that back in the 17th century a bloodthirsty dragon roamed the sewers of Palma's old quarter, instilling terror in all who beheld it. A brave knight came here to visit his love. When the dragon appeared from the shadows to attack her, the knight slayed the beast with his sword.

and pyres add flaming cheer to a partying crowd until dawn.

Cinema a la Fresca   SUMMER FESTIVAL
(www.imtur.es; ☉ Jul & Aug) Catch the open-air cinema, folk music and theatre at a stage set up in Parc de la Mar.

Nit de l'Art   CULTURAL
(www.nitdelartartpalma.com; ☉ Sep) An established art event; galleries and institutions all over town throw open their doors to expose the latest trends in art.

TaPalma   FOOD FESTIVAL
(www.tapalma.es; ☉ late Oct–early Nov) Nibble your way around Palma at this event celebrating the city's best tapas. Some 40 restaurants take part and there are dedicated tapas trails to follow – see the website for a map.

Christmas Market   MARKET
(Plaça Major; ☉ 10am-9pm) The Christmas market takes over the Plaça Major from 1 December to 6 January.

 Eating

✕ Old Palma

Confitería Frasquet   PASTELERÍA €
(Map p56; www.confiteriafrasquet.com; Carrer d'Orfila 4; pastries & cakes €1.50-4; ☉ 10am-8pm Mon-Sat) This distinguished sweets shop with its 19th-century decor has an astonishing range of sweets and specialises in pralines, almond sponges and *embatumats* (a cake and chocolate confection); everything's tempting. There's been a sweets shop here since the 17th century.

Forn del Santo Cristo   PASTELERÍA €
(Map p56; www.hornosantocristo.com; Carrer de Paraires 2; ensaïmades from €1.30; ☉ 8am-8.30pm Mon-Sat, 8.30am-1pm Sun) Has been baking up *ensaïmades* (delicate, croissant-like pastries dusted with icing sugar, and sometimes filled with cream) since 1910; also has good traditional goodies including *cocas de patata* (sweet potato buns).

La Taberna del Caracol   SPANISH €€
(Map p56; ☎ 971 71 49 08; www.tabernacaracol. com; Carrer de Sant Alonso 2; tapas €1.50-17, tapas tasting plate €14; ☉ 7.30-11pm Mon, noon-3pm & 7.30-11pm Tue-Sat) Descend three steps into this high-ceilinged Gothic basement. Through a broad vault at the back you can see what's cooking – tasty tapas that include grilled artichokes, snails and a host of other Spanish delicacies. Amid soothing background music, a broad assortment of tapas (four choices for €14, minimum of two people) is a meal in itself.

Las Olas   MEDITERRANEAN, VIETNAMESE €€
(Map p56; ☎ 971 21 49 05; www.lasolasbistro.com; Carrer de Can Fortuny 5; meals €25-30, tapas €2-9;

Western Palma

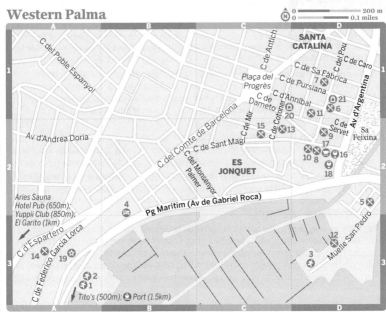

⊙12.30-4pm & 8.30-11.30pm Wed-Sat, 12.30-4pm Mon & Tue; 🌐) Now here's something special. Run by an Irish-Cambodian couple, Las Olas divides the day into two: lunch is all about fresh Mediterranean flavours with international twists, while dinner is a Vietnamese-Cambodian affair.

🍴 Plaça Major & Around

★**Simply Fosh**   MODERN EUROPEAN €€€
(Map p62; ☑971 72 01 14; www.simplyfosh.com; Carrer de la Missió 7A; mains €23-29, menus €21.50-76; ⊙1-3.30pm & 7-10.30pm Mon-Sat) Lovingly prepared Mediterranean cooking with a novel flourish is the order of the day at this 17th-century convent refectory, one of the home kitchens of chef Marc Fosh, whose CV twinkles with Michelin stars. A slick, monochrome interior and courtyard provide the backdrop for high-quality, reasonably priced menus. The three-course lunch menu for €21.50 is a terrific deal. Flavours are clean, bright and seasonal. Reservations are essential.

Can Cera Gastro Bar   MEDITERRANEAN €€
(Map p56; ☑971 71 50 12; www.cancerahotel.com; Carrer del Convent de Sant Francesc 8; mains €14-22, menus €18-31; ⊙1-3.30pm & 7.30-10.30pm) How enchanting: this restaurant spills out into one of Palma's loveliest inner patios

at the hotel of the same name, housed in a 13th-century *palacio*. Dine by lantern light on tapas or season-focused dishes such as watermelon and tomato gazpacho, and creamy rice with aioli, saffron and calamari. Note the vertical garden that attracts plenty of attention from passers-by.

Misa Braseria   MEDITERRANEAN €€
(Map p62; ☑971 59 53 01; www.misabraseria.com; Carrer de Can Maçanet 1; mains €17-23; ⊙1-3.30pm & 7.30-10.30pm Mon-Sat) Marc Fosh's second baby is this nouveau-rustic brasserie, which combines a basement restaurant with an attractive upstairs patio. The food is slickly presented and tastes are typically fresh. Dishes that change with the seasons star alongside classics such as butter-soft roast chicken and grilled beef with truffle-potato purée. The three-course daytime menu (€15.50) is outstanding value.

Restaurant Celler Sa Premsa   SPANISH €
(Map p62; ☑971 72 35 29; www.cellersapremsa. com; Plaça del Bisbe Berenguer de Palou 8; mains €9-14; ⊙12.30-4pm & 7.30-11.30pm Mon-Sat) A visit to this local institution is almost obligatory. It is a cavernous tavern filled with huge old wine barrels and has walls plastered with faded bullfighting posters – you find plenty such places in the Mallorcan interior

Western Palma

but they're a dying breed here in Palma. Mallorcan specialities dominate the menu.

Come here for the roast lamb, *tumbet* (Mallorcan-style vegetable ratatouille), *frit Mallorquí* (sautéed lamb offal with fried potatoes, onions and herbs), pork with cabbage, and rabbit with onion.

Quina Creu   TAPAS €€
(Map p56; ☑971 71 17 72; www.quinacreu.com; Carrer de Corderìa 24; mains €9-35, lunch menus €9.90; ⊙noon-1am Mon-Sat) With its mishmash of vintage furniture, flickering haunted-house chandeliers and poster-plastered walls, Quina Creu works the shabby chic look. The bar has a designer feel, as do the tapas lined up along the bar and chalked on the blackboard. Each is a mini taste sensation, from *sobrassada* (paprika-flavoured cured pork sausage) with quail egg to cod with *gambas* (prawns) and salsa verde.

Ca'n Joan de S'Aigo   PASTELERÍA, CAFE €
(Map p56; Carrer de Can Sanç 10; pastries €1.30-3; ⊙8am-9pm) Tempting with its sweet cre-

ations since 1700, this is *the* place for thick hot chocolate (€2) and pastries in what can only be described as an antique-filled milk bar. The house speciality is *quart*, a feather-soft sponge cake that children love, with almond-flavoured ice cream.

La Bodeguilla   SPANISH €€
(Map p56; ☑971 71 82 74; www.la-bodeguilla.com; Carrer de Sant Jaume 3; mains €17-28; ⊙noon-11.30pm) This gourmet restaurant does creative interpretations of dishes from across Spain; try the *cochinillo* (suckling pig) from Segovia or the *lechazo* (young lamb, baked Córdoba-style in rosemary). Also on offer is an enticing range of tapas – the marinated cubes of salmon with dill chutney caught our eye.

Bar España   SPANISH €€
(Map p56; ☑971 72 42 34; Carrer de Ca'n Escurrac 12; tapas menus €12-22; ⊙6.30pm-12.30am Mon-Sat) Happening upon this place in the evening when everything else in the vicinity is closed is like discovering some hidden secret. Hugely popular and deservedly so, this place has stone walls and an agreeable hum of conversation accompanies the fine *pintxos* (Basque tapas), which are lined up along the bar or chalked up on a board.

Horno San Antonio   PASTELERÍA €
(Map p52; Plaça Sant Antoni 6; ensaïmades from €1.30; ⊙8am-8pm Tue-Fri, to 2pm Sat & Sun) Considered by most Mallorquins to be the best of the best when it comes to *ensaïmades*, this wonderfully traditional old pastry shop does a roaring trade in all sizes and types, from plain to chocolate, with cream or apricot filling. You can get them nicely packed if you plan on taking one home.

Forn des Teatre   PASTELERÍA €
(Map p56; www.forndesteatre.com; Plaça de Weyler 9; ensaïmades from €1.30; ⊙8am-8pm) This pastry shop does feather-light *ensaïmades* (a light, spiral pastry emblematic of the island) and is a historic landmark. Larger ones are prepared to order, but smaller, takeaway ones start from €1.30. Also on offer is a mean almond cake.

✕ Es Puig de Sant Pere

★ Wine Garage   INTERNATIONAL €€
(Map p56; ☑971 72 44 83; Carrer de Montenegro 10; 3-course menus incl wine & water €40; ⊙1-4pm & 7.30-11pm Mon-Fri, 7pm-midnight Sat & Sun) The Wine Garage cuts a cool, urban picture

with its exposed stone, high ceilings, claret-red walls and perennial buzz. Everything is executed with a razor-sharp eye for detail, be it a simple steak and chips or a dreamily smooth chocolate panna cotta with mint salsa. Bone-white crockery shows off dishes to great effect, and the wine list is predictably excellent.

Opio
ASIAN €€

(Map p56; ✍971 42 54 50; www.purohotel.com; Carrer de Montenegro 12; mains €14-23; ◌restaurant 7.30-11.30pm, bar to 2am) It may be the haunt of the glam and the gorgeous, with its DJ beats, champagne hues and candlelit courtyard, but Opio at the Puro Hotel has substance as well as style. Go for cocktails, people-watching and artfully assembled Asian fusion cuisine, along the lines of salmon in a miso crust and beef sirloin with shitake mushrooms.

13%
TAPAS €

(Map p56; ✍971 42 51 87; www.13porciento.com; Carrer de Sant Feliu 13a; tapas €3-11, lunch/tasting menus €11/20; ◌6-11pm Mon-Wed, 12.30-4pm & 7pm-midnight Thu-Sat; ✍) At the quieter end of the old town, this L-shaped barn of a place is at once a wine and tapas bar, bistro and delicatessen. Most items are organic and there's plenty of choice for vegetarians. You'll find everything from canapés, salads and carpaccio of monkfish with parmesan and truffle oil to fresh sardine fillets in *cava* (sparkling wine). The lunch menu is a selection of three tapas.

Aramís
SPANISH €€

(Map p56; ✍971 72 52 32; Carrer de Sant Feliu 7; mains €8-17; ◌1-3.30pm & 7.30-10.30pm Mon-Fri, 7.30-10.30pm Sat) This carefully orchestrated gourmet hideaway, with dark-timber floors and art on the walls, is surprisingly well priced. The creative cooking includes dishes such as sautéed calamari with *sobrassada* and pine nuts.

Bruselas
INTERNATIONAL €€

(Map p56; ✍971 71 09 54; www.restaurantebrusel-las.com; Carrer d'Estanc 4; mains €9-25; ◌1-4pm & 8pm-midnight Mon-Sat) Once a Belgian-owned piano bar, Bruselas is all about red meat for aesthetes, with pleasantly contemporary decor in the stone-vaulted basement and Argentine steaks – such as *solomillo con foie* (sirloin with foie gras) – dominating the menu. There are also gourmet hamburgers and it all goes down particularly well with a throaty Mallorcan red, such as Son Bordils Negre.

Bon Lloc
VEGETARIAN €

(Map p56; ✍971 71 86 17; www.bonllocrestaurant. com; Carrer de Sant Feliu 7; menus €14.50; ◌1-4pm Mon-Wed, 1-4pm & 7.30-11pm Thu-Sat; ✍) ✔ This 100% vegetarian place is light, open and airy with a casual but classy atmosphere. All produce is organic and you're in assured hands here – this was Palma's first veggie restaurant and there are no agonising decisions, just a satisfying, take-it-or-leave-it four-course menu. Bookings recommended.

Santa Catalina & Around

Koh
ASIAN €€

(Map p66; ✍971 28 70 39; www.kohmallorca.com; Carrer de Servet 15; mains €10-15; ◌7-11pm Mon-Sat) Craving a little spice? Slide across to

---

SAILING EVENTS IN PALMA

Sailing is a big deal in Palma and numerous regattas are held in the course of the year. In addition to those listed, the **Real Club Náutico** (Map p66; www.realclubnauticopalma. com), the most prestigious of Palma's yacht clubs, organises more than 20 events (some in collaboration with other clubs) throughout the year.

Copa del Rey (King's Cup; ◌Jul-Aug) Held over eight days in summer, and a high point on the sailing calendar. The king, Juan Carlos I, and his son Felipe frequently race on competing boats.

PalmaVela (www.palmavela.com; ◌late Apr) Has hundreds of yachts of all classes from around the world.

Trofeo SAR Princesa Sofía (www.trofeoprincesasofia.org; ◌Apr) One of six regattas composing the World Cup Series, attracting Olympic crews from all over the world.

The Superyacht Cup (www.thesuperyachtcup.com; ◌Jun) Held over three days, this is one of the major races for superyachts of anything from 25m to 90m in size.

Trofeo Ciutat de Palma (www.trofeociutatdepalma.com; ◌Dec) A huge four-day event for smaller boats.

LOCAL KNOWLEDGE

PALMA'S FOOD SCENE

Renowned British chef and proprietor of Misa Braseria (p66) and Simply Fosh (p66), Marc Fosh has revolutionised Palma's dining scene in recent years with what he describes as 'modern yet simple cuisine, with clean tastes and big flavours.'

Why Mallorca? Mallorca is slowly but surely becoming a great gastronomic destination. There are several young chefs who have opened great little restaurants bursting with enthusiasm over the last few years, and thefood scene is really buzzing with so many new wineries along with top olive oils, cheeses and salts being produced on the island.

Favourite dish Mallorcan food has its roots firmly planted in rustic, country-style cooking and one of my favourite dishes is *arròs brut*. It's a flavour-packed dish of rice, meat and vegetables in a hearty stock. I enjoy going to Sa Cuina de n'Aina in Sencelles, where the cook makes the best *arròs brut* on the island.

Palma's markets The Mercat de l'Olivar (Map p62; Plaça de l'Olivar; ⊙ 8am-2pm & 5-8pm Mon-Fri, 8am-2pm Sat) in Palma is a must for any discerning foodie. The fish stalls are spectacular and they have an amazing array of wonderful seafood on offer. There is also an oyster bar in the middle of the market and you could walk to both Misa and Simply Fosh from there for a spot of lunch.

In season Everyone knows Palma as a great summer destination, but the winter also has so much to offer. The local wild mushrooms, *esclata-sangs*, come into season. They are large, big-flavoured mushrooms that are just perfect for grilling or roasting. Simply sprinkle them with a little sea salt, olive oil, crushed garlic cloves and chopped parsley.

---

this upbeat, modern Thai in Santa Catalina, where chefs Abel Denhard and Mika Drouin put a fresh, herby take on Asian flavours. The flavours are punchy, whether you go for delicate Vietnamese summer rolls, sticky ribs glazed in hoisin sauce or Malaysian curry.

Ummo   SPANISH, BASQUE €€
(Map p66; ☑ 871 953873; Carrer de Sant Magí 66; mains €13-18; ⊙ 8am-11.30pm Tue-Sun) This stylish wood-floored bistro keeps it sweet, simple and season-focused. The chef, from San Sebastián, puts his own novel twist on tapas in creations such as stuffed baby squid on polenta, and Mallorcan white-pepper jelly and Burgos blood sausage with red pepper and quail egg. It's this approach that won him gold at the Tapalma tapas awards in 2013.

Room   SPANISH €€
(Map p66; ☑ 971 28 15 36; www.theroompalma.es; Carrer de Cotoner 47; snacks €3-7, 2-course lunch menus €13; ⊙ 8am-5pm Mon-Fri, 9.30am-5pm Sat; ⊕) This slick, contemporary cafe is a much-loved breakfast and lunch spot, with its easygoing air and colouring books to amuse tots. The menu is strong on wholesome, homemade pastries, torte, salads, pastas and tapas.

El Perrito   SWEDISH €
(Map p66; ☑ 971 45 59 16; Carrer d'Anníbal 20; mains €8-11; ⊙ 8am-5pm Mon-Sat) The 'little dog' takes its canine moniker from the black-

and-white photos of customers' pooches that hang on its walls. Run by Swedes, this cute-as-a-button cafe is a pleasantly relaxed, boho-flavoured haunt for bagels, homemade cakes, fresh juices and hearty day specials such as goulash and meatballs with lingonberries. Bear in mind that portions are on the small side.

Hórreo Veinti3   MEDITERRANEAN €€
(Map p66; ☑ 649 033806; Carrer de Sa Fàbrica 23; mains €15-45; ⊙ 1pm-12.30am Thu-Mon, 7pm-12.30am Tue & Wed) Transparent chairs and monochrome hues set the scene at this modern, upbeat pick, with tables spilling out onto a pavement terrace. Dishes range from risotto to grilled tuna and chateaubriand.

La Baranda   ITALIAN €€
(Map p66; ☑ 971 45 45 25; www.labaranda.co.uk; Carrer de Sant Magí 29; pizzas €8-16, mains €16-40; ⊙ 1-3.30pm & 6.30pm-midnight) An easygoing Italian – with exposed stone, warm-yellow-hued walls, and simple timber furniture and art scattered about – this is a good choice for wood-fired pizzas, pasta dishes and homemade cakes for dessert. You can also get tapas downstairs.

Japo Express   SUSHI €
(Map p66; ☑ 971 73 83 21; www.ilovejapo.com; Carrer de Sant Magí 25; sushi per piece €1-4; ⊙ 1.30-4pm & 7-11.30pm) You can't miss the hot-pink

facade of this funky Santa Catalina sushi bar, which is frankly deserving of a more inspired name. Paper lanterns hang in the white-washed interior, where you can dig into winningly fresh sushi, maki, sashimi and nigiri. The two-course lunch is a snip at €9.

Passeig Marítim & Western Palma

★ Toque INTERNATIONAL €€
(Map p66; ✆971 28 70 68; www.restaurante-toque. webs.com; Carrer Federico García Lorca 6; mains €14-20, 3-course lunch menus €13; ☺1-3.30pm & 7-11pm Tue-Sat, 1-3.30pm Sun; ⚓) Yes, it looks like just another neighbourhood restaurant on a nondescript backstreet, but don't be fooled – there's good reason Toque consistently receives rave reviews. Honest home cooking (Belgian with a Med twist), wallet-friendly prices (wine starts at a modest €13 per bottle) and a heartfelt welcome make it stand head and shoulders above the competition. Go for starters such as mussels in cream and mains such as butter-soft suckling pig confit served with its own juices and sweet potato purée, and you won't be disappointed.

Nautic SEAFOOD €€
(Map p66; ✆971 72 63 83; www.nautic-restaurant. com; Muelle San Pedro 1; mains €16-29, 3-course lunch menus €25; ☺1-3.30pm & 8-11.30pm Tue-Sun) One of Palma's standout seafood options in the Royal Sailing Club, Nautic does all the usual grilled fishes and shellfish, as well as rice dishes, but you'll also find surprises such as zucchini stuffed with lobster in a *sobrassada* sauce. It's a classy, skylit, white-walled space, with wraparound windows overlooking the marina and a decked terrace.

Caballito de Mar SEAFOOD €€
(Map p56; ✆971 72 10 74; www.caballitodemar. info; Passeig de Sagrera 5; mains €17-34; ☺noon-11.30pm Sun-Thu, to midnight Fri & Sat) One of Palma's seafood beacons, the 'Little Seahorse' presents its food in a contemporary key. There are monkfish medallions, *sobrassada* and *butifarrón* (blood sausage) wrapped in cabbage leaves in a nut sauce, for example. Or you could go for something more traditional, such as the fresh fish of the day, rice dishes or red shrimp from Sóller. Grab a seat on the sunny terrace.

Ca'n Eduardo SEAFOOD €€€
(Map p66; ✆971 72 11 82; www.caneduardo.com; 3rd fl, Travesía Contramuelle, Es Mollet; mains €20-38; ☺1-11.30pm; ⚓) What better place to sample fish than here, right above the fish market? With its bright, contemporary decor and picture windows overlooking the fishing port, Ca'n Eduardo has been in business since the 1940s. Black-vested waiters serve up grilled fish and seafood and some fantastic rice dishes (minimum of two) – the *arroz bogavante* (lobster rice) is a favourite.

Casa Jacinto SPANISH, MALLORCAN €€
(✆971 40 18 58; www.casajacintomallorca.com; Camí de la Tramvía 37; mains €9-23, 3-course lunch menus €15-22; ☺1-5pm & 7pm-12.30am) A classic since the 1980s, this huge and no-nonsense eatery attracts Mallorquins from far and wide for copious servings of mainland Spanish and local food, especially grilled meats, including game cuts such as venison and wild boar. It's situated in Gènova, 4km west of the centre of town.

Es Portitxol, Es Molinar & Ciutat Jardí

Portixol MEDITERRANEAN €€€
(Map p52; ✆971 27 18 00; www.portixol.com; Carrer de la Sirena 27; mains €17-40, 3-course lunch menus €19; ☺7.30am-10.30pm) This harbourside restaurant at Hotel Portixol is a bright and breezy affair, with sea views and a blue-and-white colour scheme. The menu is ingredient-driven, playing up Med flavours with the occasional international twist in dishes as simple as grilled scallops, spot-on sirloin steak and red tuna with wasabi mayonnaise.

MOMO Seabar INTERNATIONAL €
(Map p52; ✆871 711798; www.momoportixol.com; Carrer Vicari Joaquim Fuster 93; mains €8-16; ☺9am-7pm Sun-Thu, to 11pm Fri & Sat) We love the sea views, easy-going vibe and global menu at this cafe. It does a fine line in salads and *bruschetti,* as well as mains such as wok dishes, Thai curries and steaks. The €12.50 lunch menu represents good value, too.

Mares Marisquería SEAFOOD €€€
(✆971 49 19 78; www.maresmarisqueria.com; Carrer de l'Illa de Xipre 12; menus €40-55; ☺1-3.30pm & 8-11pm Mon-Fri, 1-3.30pm Sat) One of the classic seafood restaurants in Palma, Mares Marisquería attracts local businessfolk and seafood-lovers of every ilk. On your way into the overlit but otherwise tasteful dining area you'll see fresh fish (sold by weight). There are no views (it's a block inland), but the seafood more than makes up for it. It's located 3km east of Portixol.

Es Mollet SEAFOOD €€€
(Map p52; ☑971 24 71 09; www.restaurantees
mollet.com; Carrer de la Sirena 1; mains €18-40;
☉1-3.30pm & 7.30-10.30pm Mon-Sat) With its
covered veranda just over the road from a
little bay (Cala Portixolet), this is a classic
seafood joint, where your main course, the
freshest catch of the day, is sold by weight
(€45 to €60 per kg). There's a price to pay,
but the produce here is selected direct from
local fishers and grilled to utter perfection.

♟ Drinking & Nightlife

Palma will never be voted Spain's party capital, but there's always plenty going on and
dozens of appealing little bars. For the truly
raucous summer tourist scene, head for
Platja de Palma or Magaluf. The epicentre of
Palma's clubbing scene remains around the
Passeig Marítim (Avinguda de Gabriel Roca)
and the Club de Mar, where you'll find the
city's largest and most popular *discotecas*.

Although most clubs open around midnight or earlier, don't expect to find much
action until at least 2am. Things will continue going strong until 5am, when glassy-
eyed clubbers stumble outside. Some may
head home, while others head to the 'afters',
early-morning clubs (some around Plaça de
Gomila) that keep the music going past the
breakfast hour.

Admission prices range from €10 to €20,
usually including your first drink, although
if you're not dressed to impress you may
be turned away no matter how much cash
you're willing to spend.

Old Palma

Gibson BAR
(Map p56; Plaça del Mercat 18; ☉8am-3am) This
chirpy cocktail bar with outside seating is
still busy with (mostly local) punters on a
weekday night when everything else around
has pulled the shutters down.

Cappuccino CAFE
(Map p56; www.grupocappuccino.com; Carrer del
Conquistador 13; ☉8.30am-10pm Mon-Wed, to
11pm Thu & Sun, to midnight Fri & Sat) The location is a winner, a terrace at the 'prow' end
of Palau March. It serves light meals and
snacks with international staples, but we
like it best for its (slightly overpriced) name-
sake, and the people-watching. It's the sort
of place that sells its own lounge-music CDs.

Plaça Major & Around

L'Ambigú TAPAS BAR
(Map p56; Carrer de Carnisseria 1; ☉noon-4pm &
7pm-1am Mon-Sat) Tucked in behind the Església de Santa Eulàlia, this irresistible little
bar rocks on Tuesday and Wednesday nights
when you can scarcely see the tapas perched
atop the bar, but we like it any night for its
sense of a tiny hub of modern, casual so-
phistication beneath the high stone walls of
medieval Palma.

Bar Flexas BAR
(Map p56; www.barflexas.com; Carrer de la Llot-
geta 12; ☉1-5pm & 8pm-1am Mon-Fri) Retro-cool
Bar Flexas took up residence long before
the streets southeast of the Plaça Major became trendy and that whiff of authenticity
remains. It's a lively locals' bar with a hint
of grunge and a great spot for a noisy chat
far from the tourist haunts. You'll find art
exhibitions, occasional live acts and bar staff
with just the right sort of attitude.

Café L'Antiquari BAR
(Map p62; www.facebook.com/cafeantiquari; Carrer
d'Arabi 5; ☉11am-1am Mon-Sat) This old antique
shop has been transformed into one of the
most original places in Palma to nurse a
drink and nibble on tapas. Antiques adorn
every corner and inch of wall space, and
even the tables and chairs belong to another
age. It also has occasional live music and the
coffee is unbeatable.

LA RUTA MARTIANA

The Sa Gerreria neighbourhood of Palma, southeast of the Plaça Major, has undergone
an extraordinary makeover, from the no-go area of central Palma to one of its hottest
nightlife districts. Part of the momentum is attributable to the inexplicably named **La
Ruta Martiana** (the Martians' Route), whereby 25 bars clustered tightly around these
streets offer a small morsel to eat (known as a tapa, or a *pintxo*) and a drink for €2 from
7.30pm to midnight on Tuesday and from 7.30pm to 2am on Wednesday. Apart from
being great value and allowing you to go on a tapas and bar crawl without breaking the
bank, it has breathed life into this long-neglected corner of town. Among the bars taking
part are Barafina, L'Ambigú and Ca La Seu.

BEACH CLUB COOL

When the city turns up the heat in summer, many gravitate towards Palma's chill-out lounges to linger by the poolside, slurp cocktails and hang with a cool, bronzed crowd. Here's our pick of the beachfront bunch:

Nikki Beach (www.nikkibeach.com; Avenida Notario Alemany 1; ☺11am-8pm) Sushi, champagne, plush white loungers, bronzed bods, DJ beats and summertime barbecues are what Magaluf-based Nikki Beach has to offer.

Anima Beach (Map p52; www.anima beachpalma.com; Platja de Can Pere Antoni; ☺10.30am-1.30am) Beachfront chill-out lounge and much-loved spot for a sundowner and tapas.

Nassau Beach (Map p52; www.nassaubeach-palma.com; Passeig Portixol; ☺9am-1am) Slick beach club in Es Portixol, with views out to sea and back along the bay to the cathedral.

Ca La Seu
TAPAS BAR

(Map p56; Carrer de Cordería 17; ☺8pm-2am Mon-Sat) Set in an artfully converted 500-year-old barn of a place, this is one of our favourite bars in Palma with marble-top tables, creative tapas to accompany your drinks and an agreeable buzz most nights. If other places come and go in the neighbourhood, we reckon this place is destined to last the distance.

Es Puig de Sant Pere

Ginbo
BAR

(Map p56; Passeig de Mallorca 14; ☺9.30pm-3am Mon-Sat, 6pm-3am Sun) Ginbo does the best G&T in Palma for our money. Besides around 100 different kinds of gin, the bar-tenders mix some superb cocktails, including the Porn Star Martini (the mind boggles), which you can sip in the buzzy, stylishly urban, backlit bar or on the terrace.

Abaco
BAR

(Map p56; www.bar-abaco.es; Carrer de Sant Joan 1; ☺8pm-midnight Sun-Thu, to 3am Fri & Sat) Behind a set of ancient timber doors is this extraordinary bar. Inhabiting the restored patio of an old Mallorcan house, Abaco is filled with ornate candelabras, elaborate floral arrangements, cascading towers of fresh fruit, and bizarre artworks. It hovers between extravagant and kitsch. Paying this much for a cocktail is an outrage, but one might just be worth it here.

Rocco's
BAR

(Map p56; Carrer de Sant Feliu 16) All warm colours, vintage furnishings and cosy nooks, this lantern-lit, boho-style newcomer is a terrific spot for an intimate chat, mellow music and a glass of vino. It often does a *caña* (small glass of beer) and tapa for €2.

Atlantico Café
BAR

(Map p56; Carrer de Sant Feliu 12; ☺10pm-3am Mon-Sat) This is one of the most enticing bars in town. Think spot-on mojitos, 'Hotel California' for the music and US car number plates on the walls (along with generous and ever-expanding swaths of graffiti).

Café La Lonja
CAFE

(Map p56; Carrer de Sa Llotja 2; ☺10am-1am Mon-Thu, 10am-3am Fri, 11am-3am Sat Easter-Nov) With its curved marble bar, tiled-chessboard floor and smattering of tables and benches, this place is as appealing for breakfast as it is for tapas and a *pomada* (Menorcan gin and lemon soft drink). Many choose to sit outside in the shadow of Sa Llotja.

Mojo
BAR

(Map p56; Carrer Jaume Ferrer 14 ; ☺5pm-1am Tue-Thu, 5pm-3am Fri, 6pm-3am Sat, 6pm-1am Sun) Chilled music plays at this chandelier-lit bar, with a nicely relaxed vibe and three happy hours (from 5pm to 8pm) when cocktails go for €6 a pop. It also hosts the occasional crazy party and pub quiz.

Escape Bar
BAR

(Map p56; Plaça de la Drassana 13; ☺5pm-1am Mon-Thu, 5pm-3am Fri, 10am-3am Sat, 10am-1am Sun) A largely international crowd (with Brits generally well represented) fills up the two rooms of this small bar in the early stages of the evening. Grab one of a couple of tables out the front for an afternoon refreshment or come along in the morning for a full English breakfast. It also whips up some inexpensive lunch specials.

Es Jaç
COCKTAIL BAR

(Map p56; Carrer de Vallseca 13; ☺8pm-1am Thu & Sun, to 3am Fri & Sat) This designer cocktail bar is slick in all the right places, with stunning decor and bar staff who know their cocktails and are adept at helping those who aren't really sure what they want.

Santa Catalina & Around

Soho BAR
(Map p66; Avinguda d'Argentina 5; ⏰7pm-2.30am; 🛜) This self-proclaimed 'urban vintage bar' has a green-lit beer fridge, 1960s decor (including totally groovy wallpaper), velour sofas and a wonderfully retro look. The music's mostly indie and the laid-back crowd seems oblivious to the traffic pounding past the footpath tables. The day's cocktail special goes for €5.

Idem Café CAFE
(Map p66; Carrer de Sant Magí 15A; ⏰9pm-3am) Slink into this bordello-chic cocoon of deep, dark-red velvet, chandeliers and baroque mirrors, where some of the wall art is risqué. With a fabulously burlesque look and pre-clubbing vibe, Idem is a unique spot to sip a mojito or gin.

Hostal Cuba Colonial BAR
(Map p66; Carrer de Sant Magí 1; ⏰8am-2am Sun-Thu, to 4am Fri & Sat) Inhabiting an early 20th-century Santa Catalina landmark for sailors passing through Palma, this place has been reborn as a watering hole of a more sophisticated kind. You'll find everything from coffee to full meals, and a chill-out zone on the 1st floor.

Novo Café Lisboa LIVE MUSIC
(Map p66; Carrer de Sant Magí 33; ⏰9pm-3am Thu, 10pm-4am Fri & Sat) The curved timber bar gives this place a homey appeal. When some Latin and bossa nova, indie rock and electropop sounds get thrown on, it gets even better. It fills up quickly on evenings when live music is staged.

Passeig Marítim & Western Palma

Pacha CLUB
(Map p52; www.pachamallorca.es; Passeig Marítim 42; ⏰11.30pm-6am daily Jul-Aug, Thu-Sat Sep-Jun) This new glamour puss of a club brings a splash of Ibiza to the dance floor. Opened in 2013, it's a three-floor temple to hedonism, with regular fiestas, DJs pumping out house and chill-out terraces. Entry costs around €15.

El Garito LIVE MUSIC
(Map p52; www.garitocafe.com; Dàrsena de Can Barberà; ⏰8pm-4.30am) DJs and live performers, doing anything from nu jazz to disco classics and electro beats, heat up the scene from around 10pm. Admission is generally free, but you're expected to buy a drink.

Varadero BAR
(Map p56; www.varaderomallorca.com; Carrer del Moll Vell; ⏰9am-2am Sun-Thu, to 4am Fri & Sat) This minimalist, glass-fronted bar's splendid fore position makes it feel as though you've weighed anchor. The squawking of seagulls mixes with lounge sounds as you sip your favourite tipple and gaze east across the bay or back to a splendid cathedral from the sprawling terrace.

Guiness House BAR
(Map p56; Parc de la Mar; ⏰8am-midnight Sun-Thu, to 2am Fri & Sat) It's all about location here between the Catedral and the sea. The views of the former are unrivalled, especially when floodlit at night. It's at its best for an early-morning coffee before the crowds arrive, or after dark.

Tito's CLUB
(Map p52; www.titosmallorca.com; Passeig Marítim 33; admission €15-20; ⏰11.30pm-6am daily Jun-Sep, Thu-Sun Oct-May) Ray Charles, Marlene Dietrich and Frank Sinatra once used to let their hair down at this clubbing classic, which has been going strong since the 1950s. Today DJs spin a mix of music to a crowd who come for the upbeat vibe, sweeping city views and the occasional sexy floor show.

☆ Entertainment

From live concerts to opera, from a good movie to a summer bullfight, from sailing regattas to a football match, there's plenty to do in Palma. You can book tickets to many events online through www.ticketmaster.es. You can also get tickets to many events at El Corte Inglés department store.

Go to http://ocio.diariodemallorca.es for up-to-date event listings.

Cinemas

Palma has at least seven cinema complexes, each with several screens, but only one showing films that aren't dubbed into Spanish.

Cine Ciutat CINEMA
(📞971 20 54 53; www.cineciutat.org; Carrer Emperadriu Eugènia 6) This cinema has a roster of art-house films, some of which are shown in their original language with Spanish subtitles. It's situated around 2km north of the centre.

GAY & LESBIAN PALMA

The bulk of gay life on the island happens in and around Palma. The biggest concentration of gay bars is on Avinguda de Joan Miró, south of Plaça de Gomila. To get your night going, you could start with the following:

Dark (Map p52; www.darkpalma.com; Carrer de Ticià 22; ☉ 6.30pm-2.30am Sun-Thu, to 10.30am Fri & Sat)

Aries Sauna Hotel Pub (Map p52; www.ariesmallorca.com; Carrer de Porras 3; ☉ sauna 4pm-midnight, bar 10pm-6am)

Yuppii Club (Map p52; Carrer de Joan Miró 98; ☉ midnight-late Thu-Mon)

Useful websites for plugging into Palma's gay networks:

➡ www.mallorcagaymap.com (a paper version is available from some tourist offices)

➡ www.gay-mallorca.blogspot.com (in Spanish)

Theatre

Auditòrium CLASSICAL MUSIC
(Map p66; ☑ 971 73 47 35; www.auditoriumpalma.es; Passeig Marítim 18; ☉ box office 10am-2pm & 4-9pm) This spacious, modern theatre is Palma's main stage for major performances (as well as congresses), ranging from opera and light rock to ballet and musicals. The Sala Mozart hosts part of the city's opera program (with the Teatre Principal), while the Orquestra Simfónica de Balears (Balearic Symphony Orchestra) are regulars from October to May.

Teatre Principal THEATRE
(Map p56; ☑ 971 21 96 96; www.teatreprincipal.com; Carrer de Sa Riera 2; ☉ box office 11am-2pm & 5-9pm Tue-Sat) Built in 1854 and restored in 2007, this is the city's prestige theatre for drama, classical music, opera and ballet. The renovation works recreated the theatre's neoclassical heyday majesty of 1860 and combined it with the latest technology, resulting in great acoustics.

Teatre Municipal DANCE
(Map p52; ☑ 971 71 09 86; Passeig de Mallorca 9; ☉ box office 1hr before show) You might see anything from contemporary dance to drama.

Live Music

Most of Palma's live acts perform on the stages of intimate bars around Sa Llotja. Concerts begin between 10pm and midnight and wrap up no later than 2am.

Jazz Voyeur Club LIVE MUSIC
(Map p56; ☑ 971 90 52 92; www.jazzvoyeurfestival.com; Carrer dels Apuntadors 5; admission free-€25; ☉ 8.30pm-1am Mon-Thu & Sun, to 3am Fri & Sat) A tiny club no bigger than most people's living rooms, Voyeur hosts live bands nightly for much of the year – jazz is the focus, but you'll also hear flamenco, blues, funk and the occasional jam session. Red candles burn on the tables and a few plush chairs are scattered about – get here early if you want to grab one. In autumn it hosts a fine jazz festival.

Blue Jazz Club BLUES, JAZZ
(Map p56; ☑ 971 72 72 40; www.bluejazz.es; 7th fl, Passeig de Mallorca 6; ☉ 10pm-late Thu-Sat, 8.30pm-late Mon) Located on the 7th floor of the Hotel Saratoga, this sophisticated club with high-altitude views over Palma offers after-dinner jazz, soul and blues concerts from Thursday to Saturday, and a Monday evening jam session. Admission may be free but you're expected to buy a drink.

Bluesville BLUES
(Map p56; Carrer de Ma d'es Moro 3; ☉ 10.30pm-4am Tue-Sat) As dark and moody as a blues bar should be, this intimate spot a stone's throw from the busy Carrer dels Apuntadors hosts free blues concerts usually around midnight, mostly attracting a young hippie crowd.

Football

Palma's top division **RCD Mallorca** (☑ 971 22 12 21; www.rcdmallorca.es) is one of the better football sides battling it out in the Primera Liga. They have never finished as champions but usually wind up with a respectable spot about halfway down the ladder. The side has played at the **Iberostar Estadi** (Camí dels Reis, Polígon Industrial), about 3km north of central Palma, since 1999. You can get tickets at the stadium or call the ticket booking number.

🔒 Shopping

Start your browsing in the chic boutiques around Passeig d'es Born. The Passeig itself is equal parts high street and highbrow, with chain stores such as Massimo Dutti and Zara alongside elitist boutiques. In the maze of pedestrian streets west of the Passeig, you'll find some of Palma's most tempting (and expensive) stores. Another good shopping street is the pedestrianised Carrer de Sant Miquel.

🔒 Old Palma

Colmado Santo Domingo FOOD
(Map p56; www.colmadosantodomingo.com; Carrer de Sant Domingo 1; ⊙10am-8pm Mon-Sat) It's almost impossible to manoeuvre in this narrow little shop, so crowded are its shelves with local Mallorcan food products – cheeses, honey, olives, olive oil, pâté, fig bread, balsamic vinegar, Sóller marmalade to name just a few – while *sobrassada* hangs from the ceiling.

Chocolate Factory CHOCOLATE
(Map p56; www.chocolatfactory.com; Plaça des Mercat 9; ⊙10.30am-9pm Mon-Sat) The Chocolate Factory does precisely what it says on the tin. Besides irresistible pralines, macaroons and slabs of amazingly intense 100% cocoa chocolate, it also does a fine line in chocolate-filled *ensaïmades*, chocolate fondues, cakes and ice cream.

Típika FOOD, HANDICRAFTS
(Map p56; www.tipika.es; Carrer d'en Morei 1; ⊙10am-7.30pm Mon-Fri, to 4pm Sat) This small shop is dedicated to promoting the craftsmanship and gastronomy of Mallorca. Here you'll find wines, olive oils and a small but carefully chosen selection of other food products, as well as ceramics and other handicrafts from small family artisan businesses across the island.

Carmina SHOES, ACCESSORIES
(Map p56; www.carminashoemaker.com; Carrer de l'Unió 4; ⊙10am-2pm & 5-8pm Mon-Fri, 10am-2pm Sat) A classic of traditional Mallorcan shoemaking, Carmina makes a virtue of dark tones, brogues and loafers that will set you back between €300 and €500.

Món CLOTHING
(Map p56; Plaça del Rosari 2; ⊙10am-1.30pm & 4-8pm Mon-Fri, 10am-1.30pm Sat) You can find great deals at this outlet, where flirty, feminine fashions from labels such as Essentiel and Hoss hang on the racks. They're the still-desirable leftovers from the mother store, Addaia (Map p62; Carrer de Sant Miquel 57).

La Casa del Mapa BOOKS, MAPS
(Map p56; Carrer de Sant Domingo 11; ⊙9.30am-2pm Mon, to 7pm Tue-Fri) You could come to this government-run shop for topographical maps and other hiking resources, but we like it just as much for facsimiles of some examples from Mallorca's ancient cartographical heritage – the 1375 map of the known world by Abraham Cresques is a real find.

Fine Books BOOKS
(Map p56; Carrer d'en Morei 7; ⊙9.30am-8pm Mon-Sat, to 2pm Sun) This extraordinary collection of secondhand books, including some really valuable treasures, rambles over three floors. If you can't find what you're looking for, Rodney will try to track it down for you.

Quesada ARTS & CRAFTS
(Map p56; Passeig d'es Born 12; ⊙10am-8pm Mon-Fri, to 2pm Sat) The typical Mallorcan two-toned patterned textiles called *roba de llengües* (striped cloths) have been sold here since 1890, as well as other exquisite pieces.

Vidrierias Gordiola ARTS & CRAFTS
(Map p56; www.gordiola.com; Carrer de la Victòria 2; ⊙10.15am-1.45pm & 4.30-8pm Mon-Sat) Looking back over a 150-year tradition, Mallorca's best-known glassmakers offer everything from traditional goblets to dinky heart pendants and contemporary works of art.

🔒 Plaça Major & Around

Dialog BOOKS
(Map p62; www.dialog-palma.com; Carrer del Carme 14; ⊙9.30am-2pm & 4.30-8.30pm Mon-Fri, 10am-2pm Sat) The selection of German- and English-language books here is small but very carefully chosen, with especially good sections on languages and books about Mallorca.

Bordados Valldemossa HANDICRAFTS
(Map p62; Carrer de Sant Miquel 26; ⊙10am-8pm Mon-Sat) Embroidered linens, many made on the island, fill this old-timey shop.

Rosario P ARTS & CRAFTS
(Map p62; Carrer de Sant Jaume 20; ⊙10.30am-1.30pm & 5-8pm Mon-Fri, 10.30am-1.30pm Sat) Artisan boutiques such as this one dot central Palma. Here you'll find delicate hand-painted tops, dresses and shawls, all made with light-as-breath silk.

🏠 Es Puig de Sant Pere

Millésimée WINE
(Map p62; www.millesimee.com; Carrer de Sant Joan 4; ⊙10.30am-1.30pm & 5-8.30pm Mon-Fri, 10.30am-1.30pm Sat) If you're looking for a special bottle of vino, stop by this new wine specialist, where you'll find a carefully selected array of boutique and dessert wines, *cavas* and champagnes. It's run by Marina Mut, a trained sommelier, who oversees the regular tastings and wine-related events.

Camper SHOES
(Map p62; www.camper.com; Avinguda de Jaume III 16; ⊙10am-8.30pm Mon-Sat) Best known of Mallorca's famed shoe brands, funky, eco-chic Campers are now incredibly popular worldwide.

🏠 Santa Catalina & Around

★Cronopios FASHION, CRAFT
(Map p66; www.cronopiospalma.com; Carrer del Pou 33; ⊙11am-3pm & 6-9.30pm) A theatrical fantasy of a boutique crammed with the hand-crafted art and fashion of Argentinian brother and sister duo, Marcelo and Mara, this is quite possibly the most original shop in Palma. Enter and your gaze is drawn up to the high-wire theatrics of circus acrobats in papier mâché and upside-down chicken bags.

Marcelo and Mara studied fashion in Buenos Aires and their range of clothing and accessories is colourful and versatile, often with bold prints, flashes of imagination and eye-catching details. We also love their zipper necklaces and funky shoes and wellies.

B Connected Concept Store FASHION, HOMEWARES
(Map p66; www.bconnected-conceptstore.com; Carrer de Dameto 6; ⊙10am-2.30pm & 5-9pm Mon-Fri, 10am-3pm Sat) This designer 'concept' store is very much at home in Santa Catalina. Apart from furnishings and a few fashion items (it has another shop devoted to vintage fashions a few blocks away), you'll find all sorts of knick-knacks that you never knew you needed but just have to have. The look is oh-so-contemporary with the occasional retro touch.

Trading Place BOOKS
(Map p66; www.mallorca-books.com; Carrer de Pou 35; ⊙10am-1.30pm & 5-7.30pm Mon-Fri, 10am-1.30pm Sat) One of the largest dealers in secondhand books (mostly English, but some Spanish and German), it also sells furniture and serves as something of a meeting and information point for Palma's expat community.

ℹ Information

EMERGENCY
Ambulance (🕿061) Emergency phone number, valid in Palma and across the island.
General EU Emergency Number (🕿112) Catch-all emergency number.
Policía Local (🕿092, 971 22 55 00; Carrer de Son Dameto 1) Municipal Police station, northwest of the centre.
Policía Nacional (🕿091, 971 22 52 45; www.policia.es; Carrer Simó Ballester 8) National Police.

INTERNET RESOURCES
Asociación Hotelera de Palma de Mallorca (www.visit-palma.com) Has hotel and general information for Palma de Mallorca.
City of Palma Tourist Site (www.imtur.es) The city's main tourist portal

MEDIA
For local news in English have a look at the *Daily Bulletin* (www.majorcadailybulletin.es). More substantial are the weekly German-language newspapers, *Mallorca Magazin* (www.mallorca-magazin.net) and *Mallorca Zeitung* (www.mallorcazeitung.es).

For an idea of what's on, try the fortnightly *Youthing* (www.youthing.es). *Dígame* (www.digamemallorca.com) is a free monthly with islandwide events, activities and up-to-date

---

MARKET WATCH

Flea markets, speciality markets and artisan markets abound in Palma. For handicrafts, head to the **Plaça Major Artisan Market** (Map p56; Plaça Major; ⊙10am-2pm Mon & Sat Mar-Jul & Oct-Dec, daily Aug & Sep) or **Plaça des Meravelles Artisan Market** (Plaça des Meravelles; ⊙8pm-midnight May-Oct). A sprawling **flea market** (Avinguda de Gabriel Alomar & Avinguda de Villalonga; ⊙10am-2pm Sat) takes over the *avingudes* west of the city centre (Avinguda de Gabriel Alomar and Avinguda de Villalonga) each Saturday. The **Christmas market** takes over the Plaça Major from 16 December to 5 January.

THE SLOW TRAIN TO SÓLLER

Welcome to one of the most rewarding excursions in Mallorca. Since 1912 a narrow-gauge train has trundled along the winding 27.3km route from Palma to Sóller (one way/return €12.50/19.50). The fragile-looking timber-panelled train, which replaced a stage-coach service, departs from Plaça de l'Estació seven times a day (five times from November to February) and takes about 1¼ hours; there are between four and five return trains every day. The route passes through ever-changing countryside that becomes dramatic in the north as it crosses the Serra de Alfàbia, a stretch comprising 13 tunnels and a series of bridges and viaducts.

The trip starts out heading through the streets of Palma but within 20 minutes you're in the countryside. At this stage the view is better to the left towards the Serra de Tramuntana. The terrain starts to rise gently and to the left the eye sweeps over olive gardens, the occasional sandy-coloured house and the mountains in the background. Half an hour out of Palma you call in at Bunyola. You could board here to do just half the trip (one way/return €6.25/12.50) to Sóller.

Shortly after Bunyola, as the mountains close in (at one point you can see Palma and the sea behind you), you reach the first of a series of tunnels. Some trains stop briefly at a marvellous lookout point, the Mirador Pujol de'n Banya, shortly after the Túnel Major (main tunnel, which is almost 3km long and took three years to carve out of the rock in 1907–10). The view stretches out over the entire Sóller valley. From there, the train rattles across a viaduct before entering another tunnel that makes a slow 180-degree turn on its descent into Sóller, whose station building is housed in an early 17th-century noble mansion. Return tickets are valid for two weeks.

At the train station in Palma, you can buy packages that include a tram from Sóller, and then a boat from there to Sa Calobra, and then back to Palma again. It costs around €49. For more information, call ☑ 902 364711, or visit www.trendesoller.com.

listings. You'll find them in the tourist offices and distributed in bars. Another useful resource for events and listings is the website www.seemallorca.com.

There is a growing stable of glossy monthlies in English and German. The free *abcmallorca* (www.abc-mallorca.com) has articles on the city and island. *Contemporary Balears* (www.contemporarybalears.com) is published three times a year and has interesting articles and listings. Look out for it in hotels and some restaurants, bars and galleries. *Anglo Info* (www.angloinfo.com) has a forum, events listings and a directory of English-speaking businesses.

The annual *Mallorca Geht Aus!* (€9.80; also available in Germany, Austria and Switzerland) has more than 200 glossy pages packed with stories and reviews of anything from *fincas* (farmhouses) to clubs. It can be ordered online at www.mallorca-geht-aus.de.

MEDICAL SERVICES

In the main newspapers (such as the *Diario de Mallorca*) you will find a list of pharmacies open from 9am to 10pm and others (a handful) from 10pm to 9am.

Hospital Universitari Son Espases (☑ 871 205000; www.hospitalsonespases.es; Carretera de Valldemossa 79) Situated 4km north of town, Palma's new hospital is best reached with bus lines 20, 29, 33 and 34.

Farmácia Castañer-Buades (☑ 971 71 15 34; Plaça de Joan Carles I 3; ⊙ 8.30am-10.30pm)

Farmácia Salvà Saz (☑ 971 45 87 88; Carrer de Balanguera 15; ⊙ 24hr)

SAFE TRAVEL

Palma is fairly safe. The main concern is petty theft – pickpockets and bag-snatchers. Some streets are best avoided at night, when the occasional dodgy character comes out to play; one such area is around Plaça de Sant Antoni and the nearby avenues, such as Avinguda de Villalonga and Avinguda d'Alexandre Rosselló.

TOURIST INFORMATION

You can get lots of local city info by dialling ☑ 010, with luck even in English.

Airport Tourist Office (☑ 971 78 95 56; Aeroport de Palma; ⊙ 8am-8pm Mon-Sat, to 4pm Sun)

Consell de Mallorca Tourist Office (Map p56; ☑ 971 17 39 90; www.infomallorca.net; Plaça de la Reina 2; ⊙ 8am-6pm Mon-Fri, 8.30am-3pm Sat; 🖝) Covers the whole island.

Main Municipal Tourist Office (Map p56; ☑ 971 72 96 34; www.imtur.es; Casal Solleric, Passeig d'es Born 27; ⊙ 9am-8pm)

Municipal Tourist Office (Map p62; ☑902 102365; ⊘9am-8pm Mon-Sat) In one of the railway buildings off Plaça d'Espanya.

ℹ Getting There & Away

AIR

Palma de Mallorca Airport (PMI) lies 8km east of the city and receives an impressive level of traffic. A number of airlines service Mallorca (p214).

BOAT

Palma is the island's main port. There are numerous boat services to/from Mallorca from mainland Spain and the other islands of the Balearics.

BUS

All island buses to/from Palma depart from (or near) the **Estació Intermodal de Palma** (Map p62; ☑971 17 77 77; www.tib.org; Plaça d'Espanya). Services head in all directions, including Valldemossa (€2, 30 minutes, four to nine daily), Sóller (€3.50, 30 minutes, up to five daily), Pollença (€5, 45 minutes, up to 12 daily) and Alcúdia (€5, 45 minutes, up to 16 daily). Other coastal and inland centres are served by less-frequent bus lines. A handful of areas are more easily reached by train.

TRAIN

Two train lines run from Plaça d'Espanya. The Palma–Sóller railway is a popular panoramic run. From the main Estació Intermodal de Palma, the other line is more prosaic, running northeast to Inca (€3) and then splitting into a branch to Sa Pobla (€4, 58 minutes) and another to Manacor (€4, 66 minutes). Services start at 5.45am and finish at 10.10pm on weekdays. Departure times on weekends (when both lines are all-stops trains) vary but the frequency remains about the same.

ℹ Getting Around

TO & FROM THE AIRPORT

Bus 1 runs every 15 minutes from the airport to Plaça d'Espanya (on the train-station side) in central Palma (€3, 15 minutes) and on to the entrance of the ferry terminal. It makes several stops along the way, entering the heart of the city along Avinguda de Gabriel Alomar i Villalonga, skirting around the city centre and then running back to the coast along Passeig de Mallorca and Avinguda d'Argentina. It heads along Avinguda de Gabriel Roca (aka Passeig Marítim) to reach the Estació Marítima (ferry port) before turning around. Buy tickets from the driver.

Taxis are generally abundant (when not striking) and the ride from the airport to central Palma will cost between €18 and €22.

TO & FROM THE FERRY PORT

Bus 1 (the airport bus) runs every 15 minutes from the ferry port (Estació Marítima) across town (via Plaça d'Espanya) and on to the airport. A taxi from/to the centre will cost between €10 and €12.

BICYCLE

Bicycle is a great way to explore the Badia de Palma. There are plenty of operators who rent out city and mountain bikes. These include Palma on Bike (p63) and **Palma Lock & Go** (Map p62; ☑971 71 64 17; www.palmalockandgo.com; Estació Intermodal de Palma, Plaça d'Espanya; bikes per day €6-10; ⊘9am-8pm Apr-Sep, 9.30am-7.30pm Oct-Mar).

BUS

There are 30 local bus services around Palma and its bay suburbs run by **EMT** (☑971 21 44 44; www.emtpalma.es). These include line 1 between the airport and port, and line 23 Palma–S'Arenal–Cala Blava via Aqualand. Single-trip tickets cost €1.50, or you can buy a 10-trip card for €10.

CAR & MOTORCYCLE

Parking in the centre of town can be complicated. Some streets for pedestrians only and most of the remaining streets, including the ring roads (the *avingudes,* or *avenidas*) around the centre, are either no-parking zones or metered parking. Metered areas are marked in blue and generally you can park for up to two hours (€2.50), although time limits and prices can vary. The meters generally operate from 9am to 2pm and 4.30pm to 8pm Monday to Friday, and 9am to 2pm on Saturday.

METRO

Of limited use to most travellers, a metro line operates from Plaça d'Espanya to the city's university. A single trip costs €0.75; return costs €1.40.

TAXI

For a taxi call ☑971 72 80 81, ☑971 75 54 40, ☑971 40 11 14, ☑971 74 37 37 or ☑971 20 09 00. For special taxis for the disabled, call ☑971 703 529. Taxis are metered but for trips beyond the city fix the price in advance. A green light indicates a taxi is free to hail or you can head for one of the taxi stands in the centre of town, such as those on Passeig d'es Born. Flagfall is €3/4 by day/night; thereafter you pay €0.80/1 per kilometre per day/night (more on weekends and holidays). There's a €0.60 supplement for every piece of luggage. Other extras include €2.70 for the airport or the port, and €0.60 for Castell de Bellver.

BADIA DE PALMA

The broad Badia de Palma stretches east and west away from the city centre. Some of the island's densest holiday development is to be found on both sides, but the beaches, especially to the west, are quite striking in spite of the dense cement backdrop.

East of Palma

Beyond the quiet beach of Ciutat Jardí and the Cala Gamba marina, you arrive in the mass beach-holiday area focused on Platja de Palma and S'Arenal. A couple of nearby escape hatches allow respite from the madding crowds.

Ca'n Pastilla to S'Arenal

POP CA'N PASTILLA 5390; S'ARENAL 9560

In the shadow of the airport, heavily built-up Ca'n Pastilla is where Palma's eastern package-holiday coast begins. The **Platja de Ca'n Pastilla** marks the western and windier end of the 4.5km stretch of beach known as **Platja de Palma**; the windsurfing here can be good. Just west of Ca'n Pastilla is the pleasant **Cala Estancia**, a placid inlet whose beach is perfect for families. The waterfront, with a pedestrian walkway, is backed by low-rise developments with hotels, eateries, cafes and bars. Just a two-minute walk further west from Cala Estancia along the waterfront is the überlaid-back, sunset-chill lounge, Puro Beach (p81), where the hip crowd hangs out when the weather warms.

S'Arenal hosts produce and flea markets on Tuesdays and Thursdays.

☉ Sights & Activities

★ Palma Aquarium
AQUARIUM
(☑ 902 70 29 02; www.palmaaquarium.com; Carrer de Manuela de los Herreros i Sorà 21; adult/child €24/17, shark sleepover/scuba dive €50/200; ☉ 9.30am-6.30pm daily May-Sep, 10am-3.30pm Mon-Fri, to 6.30pm Sat & Sun Oct-Apr; ⊞) This aquarium is one of the best in the Med and one of few good reasons for visiting Platja de Palma. Five million litres of salt water fill the 55 tanks, home to sea critters from the Mediterranean (rays, seahorses, coral and more) and far-away oceans. The central tank, which you walk through via a transparent tunnel, is patrolled by 20 sleek sharks. You could easily spend half a day here.

In total, some 8000 specimens are found here ranging across a number of marine environments, with some stirring exhibits covering the threat to world tuna stocks. Yes, you'll see Nemo and there are good information panels in English, French, German and Spanish. If the kids fancy spending the night, the monthly Friday shark sleepover will certainly crank up the fear factor for little nippers. Adults after a *Jaws* fix can slip into a wetsuit to scuba dive with sharks in the 8.5m-deep tank. Pre-booking is essential.

Aqualand
AMUSEMENT PARK
(www.aqualand.es; Ma6014; adult/child €26/19; ☉ 10am-6pm Jul & Aug, to 5pm mid-May–Jun & Sep; ⊞) A surefire hit with the kids, this giant water park has plenty of splashy fun, including dedicated pools for tots, rapids, flumes and thrill-a-minute slides with names like Anaconda, Harakiri and Kamikaze that leave little to the imagination.

Attraction
BOAT TRIPS
(Map p66; ☑ 971 74 61 01; www.attractioncatamarans.com; Carrer de Nanses; adult/child incl meal & drink €54/31; ☉ mid-Apr–Sep) Attraction arranges 4½-hour catamaran trips around the Badia de Palma, taking in caves and bathing spots and including a paella lunch. There are departures from Palma, Ca'n Pastilla and Magaluf.

Ciclos Quintana
BICYCLE RENTAL
(☑ 971 44 29 25; www.ciclosquintana.com; Carrer de San Cristóbal 32; bikes per day €12-30, per week €70-195) You'll find plenty of rental outlets along S'Arenal's beachfront but if you're after a road bike try Ciclos Quintana, just up from the main drag. Opening hours vary; see the website for details.

☞ Tours

Segway Tours
SEGWAY
(☑ 605 666365; www.segwaypalma.com; Carretera del Arenal 9; 1/2/2½hr tours €35/65/79) See the city by Segway (zippy battery-powered two-wheel scooters), with one-hour beach tours, two-hour tours to Es Portitxol and 2½-hour excursions that go to the Catedral and back to Platja de Palma.

✕ Eating

There's no shortage of places to eat in Platja de Palma and S'Arenal, offering anything from German sausages to mediocre paella; most people come here for the partying, not fine food. A predominantly German crowd

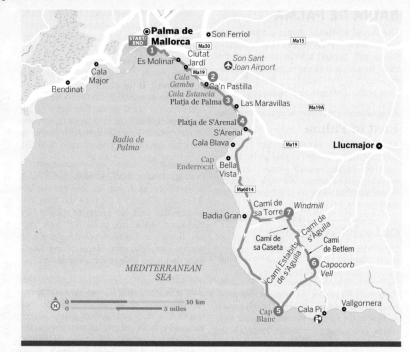

Cycling Tour
Palma to Capocorb Vell

START/FINISH PALMA
DISTANCE 67KM
DIFFICULTY EASY TO MODERATE
BIKE ROAD OR TOURING BIKE

Covering a huge swath of the Badia de Palma, this circular ride follows an easygoing seafront cycle path, then heads slightly inland towards Cap Blanc on the island's south coast. The return journey winds through peaceful country lanes, before a deserved downhill reverses the route back to town.

Pick up the waterfront bike path in ❶ **Central Palma** and head southeast. Hugging the coast for most of the way, the path is a breezy sweep to ❷ **Ca'n Pastilla**. From here follow the seafront road to the end of the long sandy strip of ❸ **Platja de Palma** and its extension ❹ **S'Arenal**. Then follow the wooden signs for ❺ **Cap Blanc**. Although along a major road, the 23km ride cuts through pleasant countryside, and motorists are used to lycra-clad cyclists plying the

route. The road rises to 150m but the ascent is not too gruelling.

You're unable to reach the lighthouse at the cape, so scoot left round the bend, rather than taking the signed road to the right. When you come to a junction (with signs right to Cala Pi), take a left for ❻ **Capocorb Vell**, whose entrance is on the left. There's a rustic bar at the ruins.

Exit the bar to the right and take the Camí de Betlem, a quiet country lane (also signed Carreró de Betlem). Follow this to the junction, and continue onto the Camí Estabits de s'Àguila, surrounded by farmland. Turning sharp right, it becomes the Camí de s'Àguila. After 200m, a left turn will bring you onto the Camí de sa Caseta, shaded by overhanging trees and lined by dry-stone walls. The end of the lane is marked by a ❼ **windmill** and, to the left, a church. Turn left here, where a wooden sign points along tranquil Camí de sa Torre and onwards to S'Arenal. Take a right when you hit the Ma6014 and follow the wooden signs to Platja de Palma. From here, retrace your tracks back to the capital.

CALA BLAVA

Nothing could be further removed from the beer gardens of Platja de Palma than residential Cala Blava (population 340), 2.5km southwest of S'Arenal. There are several rocky locations for a dip and one sandy beach. After the fork in the Ma6014 road (to Cala Blava and Cala Pi), take the first right – it's a few hundred metres down to the beach (bus stop Carrer D'Ondategui 36). Look for the Pas a Sa Platja sign and stairs opposite Carrer de Mèxic.

The continuation south of Cala Blava is Bella Vista. Part of the coast is off-limits as a protected area, but you could slip down to the **Calò des Cap d'Alt** for a swim in crystal-clear waters.

On the west side of the Badia de Palma, you could head south of Magaluf to a couple of pretty inlets. **Cala Vinyes** has placid water, and the sand stretches inland among residential buildings. The next cove, **Cala de Cap Falcó**, is an emerald lick of an inlet surrounded by tree-covered rocky coast. Unfortunately, the developers are getting closer and closer. Follow signs south for Sol de Mallorca and then the signs for each of these locations. Bus 107 from Palma reaches Cala Vinyes via Magaluf.

pours in for endless drinking and deafening music, a phenomenon known as *Ballermann* (after the name of a famous beachside drink-and-dance local – Balneari 6).

🍷 Drinking & Nightlife

The core of the nightlife takes place in enormous beer gardens on or near Carrer del Pare Bartomeu Salvà, known to German revellers as Schinkenstrasse (Ham St) and about three-quarters of the way along the beach east towards S'Arenal (orientation points are Balneario 5 and 6 on the beach). There's very little to distinguish one from the other.

Puro Beach   LOUNGE, BAR
(www.purobeach.com; ⏱11am-1am May-Sep, to 7pm Apr & Oct; 🛜) This laid-back lounge carries more than a hint of Ibiza with a tapering outdoor promontory over the water and an all-white bar that's perfect for sunset cocktails, DJ sessions and open-air spa treatments. Most of the toned, bronzed bods here wear white to blend in with the slinky decor.

Our tip: go for a drink or two and skip the sky-high-priced fusion food. It is a two-minute walk east of Cala Estancia (itself just east of Ca'n Pastilla).

🛈 Getting There & Away

Bus 23 runs from Plaça d'Espanya to Ca'n Pastilla and parallel to Platja de Palma through S'Arenal and on past La Porciúncula to Aqualand (€1.25, one hour). Buses run every half-hour or so and once every two hours they continue on to Cala Blava (€1.35; one hour 50 minutes). Bus 15 runs from Plaça de la Reina and passes through Plaça d'Espanya on its way to S'Arenal every eight minutes. For the aquarium, get off at Balneari 14.

West of Palma

The Badia de Palma stretches to the southwest of central Palma in a series of little bays and beaches that are the nucleus of a series of heavily built-up resort areas. The beaches themselves are mostly very pretty and clean; the tourism is at its English-breakfast-and-binge-drinking worst in Magaluf. Beyond, the coast quietens considerably until rounding Cap de Cala Figuera.

Cala Major

POP 5630

Cala Major, once a jet-set beach scene about 4km southwest of the city centre, is a pretty beach and the first you encounter on your way west of the city. Sandwiched in between the multistorey hotels and apartments right on the beach is a motley crew of bars, snack joints and dance spots.

Aside from the beach, the main attraction here is a major art stop, the **Fundació Pilar i Joan Miró** (http://miro.palma.cat; Carrer de Saridakis 29; adult/child €6/free; ⏱10am-7pm Tue-Sat, to 3pm Sun), inland from the waterfront. Take bus 3 or 46 from the Palma city centre (Plaça d'Espanya) to reach it.

Top Spanish architect Rafael Moneo designed the main building in 1992, next to the studio in which Miró had thrived for decades. With more than 2500 works by the artist (including 118 paintings), along with memorabilia, it's a major collection. No doubt influenced by his Mallorquin wife and mother, Miró moved to Palma in 1956 and remained there until his death in 1983. His friend, the

MALLORCA ROCKS

For clubbers and concert-goers, one of the most exciting additions to the party scene in Magaluf (or Palma for that matter) is **Mallorca Rocks** (☑++44 (0)207 9522 919; www.mallorcarocks.com; Carrer Blanc 8, Magaluf), the younger sister of the legendary venue in Ibiza. Opened in 2010, the complex comprises a monster-sized hotel (656 rooms) gathered around pools with pulsating music. The vibe? Fun but not lairy. Sleep? Way overrated.

The two big weekly sessions are Tuesday's gigs and Thursday's W.A.R!, where the crème of Europe's DJs spin techno, electro and house. Dizzee Rascal played in 2013, and the 2014 opening line-up is set to star Californian dudettes Haim and British rock/indie band The 1975. Guests get entry to all events, while nonguests can book tickets online (around €40 for gigs).

architect Josep Lluís Sert, designed the studio space for him above Cala Major.

A selection of his works hangs in the Sala Estrella, an angular, jagged part of Moneo's creation that is the architect's take on the artist's work. The rest of the building's exhibition space is used for temporary shows. Miró sculptures are scattered about outside. Beyond the studio is Son Boter, an 18th-century farmhouse Miró bought to increase his privacy. Inside, giant scribblings on the whitewashed walls served as plans for some of his bronze sculptures.

Gènova & Around

POP 4100

Most travellers come up here, around 1km roughly north of the Fundació Pilar i Joan Miró in the satellite settlement of Gènova, to visit the closest caves to the capital, **Coves de Gènova** (Carrer d'es Barranc 45; adult/child under 10yr €9/5; ☉11am-1.30pm & 4-6pm Tue-Sun). Discovered in 1906, the caves are not as interesting as the Coves del Drac in the east of the island, but are a pleasant enough distraction with stalactites and stalagmites to poke around.

You reach a maximum depth of 36m and will be shown all sorts of fanciful, backlit shapes. The temperature is always around 20°C in the caves and water has been dripping away for many millennia to create these natural 'sculptures'.

From Palma or Cala Major, take bus 46 to Coves de Gènova. Alight at Camí dels Reis 19; from here it's about a 300m walk. If you have wheels, follow the signs to Na Burguesa off the main road from the centre of Gènova (a short way north of the Coves turn-off). About 1.5km of winding, poor road takes you past the walled-in pleasure domes of the rich to reach a rather ugly monument to the Virgin Mary, from where you have sweeping views over the city (this is about the only way to look *down* on the Castell de Bellver) and bay.

Palma folk love escaping up here for a hearty feed in one of the crowded restaurants. One of the best is **Mesón Ca'n Pedro** (☑971 70 21 62; Carrer del Rector Vives 4; mains €12-25, 4-course lunch €26; ☉12.30pm-12.30am), famous for its *pa amb oli* (rye bread rubbed with olive oil and topped with chopped tomatoes), snails and sizzling steaks that you cook on a hot slate at your table.

Ses Illetes & Portals Nous

POP 2650

Ses Illetes and Portals Nous lie just off pine-backed beaches. This is a classy holiday-residential zone and the most appealing stretch of the Badia de Palma. The coast is high and drops quite abruptly to the turquoise coves, principally Platja de Ses Illetes and, a little less crowded, Platja de Sa Comtesa. Parking is a minor hassle.

Virtually a part of Ses Illetes is **Bendinat**, named after the private castle of the same name (a neo-Gothic reworking of the 13th-century original that can only be seen from the Ma1 motorway). The area is jammed with high-class hotels and villas that are not for the financially faint-hearted. Next up is **Portals Nous**, with its supermarina for the superyachts of the superrich at restaurant-lined **Puerto Portals**. The beach that stretches north of the marina is longer and broader than those in Ses Illetes.

On a scenic perch overlooking Ses Illetes and Portals Nous, clifftop **Restaurante Port'Alt** (☑971 67 61 79; www.restauranteportalt.com; Carrer Oratori 1; mains €16-25, 3-/4-course menus €26/33) has dreamy sea views and a pretty garden where the palms are lit by fairy lights after dusk. The mood is relaxed and the food a model of Mediterranean simplicity – from crispy calamari to just-right rack of lamb rubbed with lemon, garlic and mint.

Afterwards, head to **Virtual Club** (www. virtualclub.es; Passeig d'Illetes 60; ☺10am-1am Apr-Oct). This hipper-than-thou waterside chill-out space has a long list of cocktails, wicker sofas, hammocks, cabana chairs and wicked DJ sounds. Poncy or perfect? You decide. There's also a cave-like bar that fills with strange strobe lighting at night. We suggest skipping the overpriced food and going for a drink.

Local Palma bus 3 reaches Ses Illetes from central Palma (€1.50); you can pick it up on Passeig de la Rambla or Avinguda de Jaume III. Buses 103, 104, 106 and 111 from Palma's bus station call in at Portals Nous (€1.45; 30 to 50 minutes).

Palmanova & Magaluf

POP PALMANOVA 7020; MAGALUF 4410

About 2km southwest from Portals Nous' elite yacht harbour and much-flaunted €500 notes is a whole other world. Palmanova and Magaluf have merged to form what is the epitome of the sea, sand, sangria and shagging (not necessarily in that order) holiday that has lent all of Mallorca an undeserved notoriety. The good news? Change is afoot, with a planned multimillion-euro investment and an impending public drinking ban that is set to change the face of this bad-boy resort.

◎ Sights & Activities

There is a reason for Palmanova and Magaluf's popularity: the four main beaches between Palmanova and Magaluf are beautiful and immaculately maintained. The broad sweeps of fine white sand, in parts shaded by strategically planted pines and palms, are undeniably tempting and the development behind them could be considerably worse.

Marineland   AMUSEMENT PARK

(🖉971 67 51 25; www.marineland.es; Carrer Garcilaso de la Vega, Costa d'En Blanes; adult/child €24/16.50; ☺9.30am-5.30pm late Mar-Oct) Flipper and Co perform playfully for cheering crowds at 11.45am and 3.45pm daily at this marine-themed amusement park. Other big-hitters include the sharks in the aquarium, the monkeys in the tropical house, the penguin pools and the sea lion show (11.30am and 3.30pm daily). It's at the Puerto Portals roundabout near Portals Nous.

Western Water Park   AMUSEMENT PARK

(🖉971 13 12 03; www.westernpark.com; Carretera de Cala Figuera a Sa Porrasa; adult/child €26/18.50;

☺10am-6pm Jul & Aug, to 5pm May, Jun & Sep) The Wild West in Mallorca...well, why not? This is the bucking bronco of Magaluf water parks, with wave pools and slides such as the Tijuana Twists and the Beast, with a near-vertical 30m drop. Let kids loose in Kidzworld.

Cruceros Costa de Calvià   BOAT TRIPS

(🖉971 13 12 11; www.cruceroscostadecalvia.com; Avinguda Magaluf 10; adult/child €17/9; ☺11am, 1pm & 3pm Mon-Fri, 11am & 3pm Sat & Sun May-Sep) This operator offers two-hour boat trips in a glass-bottomed boat with the chance of seeing dolphins. There are departures from the main beach in Magaluf, calling at Palmanova 15 minutes later.

Big Blue Diving   DIVING, SNORKELLING

(🖉971 68 16 86; www.bigbluediving-mallorca.net; Carrer de Martí Ros García 6; snorkelling per person €35,1-/2-dive package €60/89; ☺Apr-Oct) A well-run dive centre right on Palmanova beach offering the whole array of PADI courses. The prices quoted include equipment.

🍸 Drinking & Nightlife

While restless young Germans party at the Platja de Palma beer gardens east of the city, their British equivalents are letting themselves loose on the nightspots of Magaluf. This is big stag- and hen-night territory, and few holds are barred. The drinking antics of the Brits in Magaluf have long been legendary (for all the wrong reasons). The bulk of the action is concentrated around the north end of Carrer de Punta Ballena. Pubs and bars are piled on top of one another.

ℹ Information

Hotel Information (www.palmanova-magaluf. com) Run by the local hoteliers' association.

Magaluf Tourist Office (🖉971 13 11 26; Carrer de Pere Vacquer Ramis 1; ☺9am-6pm)

Palmanova Tourist Office (🖉971 68 23 65; Passeig de la Mar 13; ☺9am-6pm daily Apr-Oct, to 3pm Mon-Fri Nov-Mar)

ℹ Getting There & Away

The most direct bus from Palma to Palmanova and Magaluf is the 105 (€3; 45 minutes), which runs 11 times a day. Bus 107 (seven times a day) takes five minutes longer as it stops at Marineland en route. The 106 (one hour) is the most frequent service.

Western Mallorca

Best Places to Eat

➡ Trespaís (p88)

➡ Es Verger (p107)

➡ QuitaPenas (p96)

➡ Es Passeig (p104)

➡ Béns d'Avall (p103)

Best Places to Stay

➡ Ca N'Aí (p173)

➡ Es Petit Hotel de Valldemossa (p171)

➡ Alqueria Blanca (p174)

➡ Hostal Miramar (p172)

➡ Gran Hotel Son Net (p171)

Why Go?

'A sky like turquoise, a sea like lapis lazuli, mountains like emerald, air like heaven,' enthused Romantic composer Chopin of his new home Valldemossa in 1838. His words ring true almost 200 years later in western Mallorca.

The Serra de Tramuntana range ripples all along the west coast, surveying the Mediterranean from above. Skirted by olive groves and pine forest, its razorback limestone mountains plunge 1000m down to the sea like the ramparts of some epic island fortress. Whether you hike its highland trails, bike its obstacle course of serpentine roads, or breeze along the cliff-flanked coastline by boat, these mountains will sweep you off your feet with their cinematic beauty.

Some of the island's loveliest towns and villages perch high on hilltops and deep in verdant valleys, with grandstand mountains and sea views. Wander their higgledy-piggledy lanes and be smitten, like so many artists, poets and celebrities before you.

When to Go

Spring and autumn are peak season for cyclists in the Tramuntana, but otherwise you'll have its gorgeous coves, trails and flower-flecked heights pretty much to yourself. Most hotels and restaurants open Easter to October. In summer, coastal resorts and villages are full to bursting point, but vast expanses of wilderness means you can always find a quiet retreat, be it a *finca* (farm), castle or monastery. The festival season gets into full swing as the heat rises: both Deià and Valldemossa host classical-music concerts in summer. True pilgrims walk through the night from Palma to Lluc in August.

THE SOUTHWEST

Look beyond the occasional blip of tasteless development and you'll find a sprinkling of little-known treasures in Mallorca's southwest crook. Use Andratx, Port d'Andratx or Sant Elm as your springboard for day trips to the exquisite coves of Portals Vells or a boat trip over to Illa de Sa Dragonera. Activities on this stretch abound, with crystal-clear sea for all manner of water sports. The epic, multiday Ruta de Pedra en Sec, Mallorca's greatest walk, begins here, too.

Andratx

POP 12,150 / ELEV 132M

Andratx is the largest town in the southwest. Typically for Mallorca, it lies well inland as a defensive measure against pirate attack, while its harbour, Port d'Andratx, lies 4km southwest. Andratx has a low-key, untouristy vibe and makes a relaxed base for exploring the coast to the west and the mountains that spread to the northeast. Its most important buildings stand tall on two rises. The 16th-century **Castell de Son Mas**, on the hill at the northern end of town, is an elegant defensive palace that now houses the *ajuntament* (town hall). From it you can see the hulk of the **Església de Santa María d'Andratx**, built in the 18th century on the site of the original 1248 church.

✗ Eating

Bar Restaurante Sa Societat   MALLORCAN €€
(☑ 971 23 65 66; Avinguda Juan Carlos I 2; mains €11-19, 2-course menus €8.50-15.50; ☺1-4pm & 7.30-11pm Wed-Sun, 1-4pm Mon) For island fare in a time-warp atmosphere, head to Bar Restaurante Sa Societat. There's a courtyard out the back or you sit inside beneath exposed beams for some *trampó* (tomato, pepper and onion salad), followed by paella, suckling pig with crackling or cod in an aioli crust. The two-course lunch is a snip at €8.50.

❶ Information

Tourist office (☑ 971 62 80 19; Avinguda de la Curia; ☺10am-2pm Mon-Fri) Housed in the town hall at the top end of town.

❶ Getting There & Away

Bus 102 operates a roughly hourly service daily between Palma and Andratx (€4.55, 65 minutes).

Port d'Andratx

POP 3150

Port d'Andratx surrounds a fine, long natural bay that attracts yachting fans from far and wide, and moves to an international beat rather than a Mallorquin one. It has an affluent air and a pleasant promenade for a walk and a waterfront meal. This is a relaxed west-coast base for water sports (sailing, diving and the like) and kicking back on the coves that spread picturesquely to the south.

◉ Sights

The port is short on sights.

Museo Liedtke   GALLERY
(☑ 971 67 36 35; www.liedtke-museum.com; Carrer de l'Olivera 35; ☺hours vary) FREE The eccentric Museo Liedtke, 2km south of the port centre, was built between 1987 and 1993 into the cliffs near Cap de Sa Mola by German artist Dieter Walter Liedtke. Home to his art and temporary exhibitions, it's also a selling point for Liedtke's theories on life. The coastal views alone warrant the detour. Opening hours vary – it's worth calling ahead to check.

Cala Llamp   BEACH
What a difference a bay makes. Located 2km south of Port d'Andratx, Cala Llamp is where locals gravitate for silence and sparkling, bottle green water. There's no sand but the scenery is quite special, with rugged, pine-cloaked cliffs rearing like an amphitheatre around the crescent-shaped cove. Go for a dip or relax over a drink at the Gran Folies Beach Club. It's around a 30-minute walk, or drive by taking the Ma1020 from Port d'Andratx and following the signs over the ridge.

☗ Activities

Like any Mallorcan coastal resort, Port d'Andratx has a small number of operators offering diving, snorkelling and boat rental.

Diving Dragonera   DIVING
(☑ 971 67 43 76; www.aqua-mallorca-diving.com; Avinguda de l'Amirante Riera Alemany 23; 6-/10-dive package €204/320, 2hr snorkel adult/child €19.50/15; ☺8am-7pm mid-Mar–Oct) If you fancy exploring the underwater caves and wrecks around Port d'Andratx and Sa Dragonera, you can take the plunge with this friendly German-run dive shop. It offers the whole shebang of PADI and SSI courses.

Western Mallorca Highlights

1 Relish the poetic loveliness of **Deià** (p97), the winner in Mallorca's hill-town beauty pageant.

2 Drive the length of the coast from seaside **Port d'Andratx** (p85) to the monastic peace of **Monestir de Lluc** (p109).

3 Listen to Chopin on your iPod as you wander through narrow lanes in **Valldemossa** (p94).

4 Tread through citrus, almond and olive groves to cute-as-a-button **Biniaraix** (p105) and **Fornalutx** (p105).

5 Find vintage trains, Miró and Modernista flair in the island's zesty orange capital, **Sóller** (p99).

6 Feel your heart do somersaults as you drive the snaking road down to **Sa Calobra** (p108).

7 Climb to the impregnable fortress ruins of **Castell d'Alaró** (p107).

8 Dive the transparent depths off the **Illa de Sa Dragonera** (p89).

9 Wander to **Sa Foradada** (p97) as the setting sun paints the Mediterranean in aquarelles.

10 Disappear into timeless **Orient** (p106) in Mallorca's quiet hinterland.

Llaüts
BOATING

(☑971 67 20 94; www.llauts.com; Carrer de San Carlos 6A; per hour/half-day/day €40/110/150; ☺Apr-Oct) A good place for boat rentals, Llaüts offers 4m crafts for those with no boat licence, with prices on request for more experienced boat users. Rates leap by about 10% in August. You'll find it southwest of the main waterfront restaurant strip; opening hours are prone to change so call ahead.

✖ Eating

The waterfront is lined with restaurants, all with terraces right on the water. Quality varies as always in such ports, but there are a few places that stand out.

★ Trespaís
MEDITERRANEAN €€

(☑971 67 28 14; www.trespais-mallorca.com; Carrer Antonio Callafat 24; mains €10.50-29.50, 3-course menu €29.90; ☺6pm-midnight Tue-Sun) With its sleek monochrome interior and tree-rimmed patio all aglow with candles, Trespaís is a flicker of new-wave romance, and chef Domenico Curcio with his Michelin-starred background has made it the top table in town. Together with his wife Jenny Terler, he assembles memorable dishes that play up integral flavours. Advance booking advisable.

Restaurante El Coche
SEAFOOD €€

(☑971 67 19 76; Avinguda de Mateu Bosch 13; mains €13.50-21; ☺1-3.30pm & 7-10.30pm Wed-Mon) A slightly classier option than most along the waterfront, El Coche has been going strong since 1977. The dishes are Mallorcan seafood classics with the occasional unusual twist, such as the sea bream with garlic, vinegar and chilli.

Rústico da Giuliano
ITALIAN €€

(☑971 23 85 64; www.rusticodagiuliano.com; Carrer Isaac Peral 43; tapas €3-15, mains €15-25; ☺noon-3pm & 6-11pm) This sweet and simple Italian place pulls in the punters with its chipper service and prime people-watching terrace. The food is good too, whether you go for tapas, wood-oven pizza or a just-right steak.

♟ Drinking

Most of the harbourside restaurants morph into bars as the night wears on. There are some reasonable choices at the southwestern end of the strip.

Gran Folies Beach Club
BAR

(www.granfolies.net; Carrer de Congre 2, Cala Llamp; ☺10am-11.45pm May-Oct) This bar-restaurant sits right above the rocky cove in Cala Llamp and offers use of a saltwater pool to cavort in between frozen margaritas. It also does breakfast, tapas and full meals and runs events from Mexican nights to G&T tastings.

Tim's
BAR

(Avinguda de l'Almirante Riera Alemany 7; ☺10am-late) Overlooking the marina, this bar has a great buzz and can stay open as late as 4am at the height of summer. It's a fine spot to sink a beer or mojito as the sun sets. Live football is shown on the big screen, and there is live music on Friday and Saturday nights.

❶ Information

Tourist office (☑971 67 13 00; Avinguda de Mateu Bosch; ☺9am-4pm Tue-Sat, 9.30am-2.30pm Sun) Next to the bus stop.

❶ Getting There & Away

Most of the 102 buses from Palma continue from Andratx to the port (€1.50, 10 minutes). Bus 100 runs seven or eight times a day between Andratx and Sant Elm (€2.10, 40 minutes), calling in at Port d'Andratx en route.

Sant Elm

POP 410

The narrow country Ma1030 road twists deep into pine forest from S'Arracó to emerge in Sant Elm. While it's by no means a secret, the relative remoteness of this beach resort has kept mass tourism at bay, and there's something magical about watching the sun plop behind the silhouetted Illa de Sa Dragonera.

◉ Sights & Activities

A couple of nice walks head north from Plaça del Monsenyor Sebastià Grau, at the northeast end of town. One follows the GR221 long-distance route for about 1¼ hours or 4km to **La Trapa**, a ruined former monastery. A few hundred metres from the building is a wonderful lookout point. You can start on the same trail but branch off west about halfway (total walk of 2.5km; about 45 minutes) to reach **Cala d'En Basset**, a lovely bay with transparent water but not much of a beach.

Platja Sant Elm
BEACH

Sant Elm's main town beach is a pleasant sandy strand (no shade) that faces the gently lapping Mediterranean to the south. Within swimming distance for the moderately fit is

PORTALS VELLS & CAP DE CALA FIGUERA

A short detour 20km south of Andratx, the Cap de Cala Figuera peninsula's eastern flank is one of the last remaining stretches of unspoilt coastline in this much-developed corner of the southwest. It feels light years away from the crowds and bustle in nearby Magaluf.

Three dreamlike inlets collectively known as Portals Vells reside in blissful seclusion, backed by pine-clad sandstone cliffs and dazzlingly clear water. **Cala Mago** is two narrow inlets. The one on the right has a restaurant and is frequented by nudists, while the longer inlet with the narrow, shady beach to the right is prettier.

Fairest of all is **Cala Portals Vells**. Turquoise waters lap the beach, the sands of which stretch back quite a distance beneath rows of straw umbrellas. To the south of here a walking trail leads to caves that honeycomb the rock walls, one of them containing the rudiments of a **chapel**, where the altar has been hewn from the rock. According to local lore, Genoese sailors built it in the 15th century to give thanks for their lives being spared in a shipwreck.

Factor around three hours for a 10km circuit walk from Cala Portals Vells to the lighthouse-dotted Cap de Cala Figuera cape, which commands sweeping views across the Badia de Palma. The gentle and mostly flat coastal hike takes you along cliff tops and to small bays.

You'll need your own wheels to reach Portals Vells as there is no public transport. Take exit 14 off the Ma1 towards Portals Vells, passing the Western Park water park and golf club. About 2km through pine woods you reach a junction: turn left following signs to Cala Mago and park above the bay, or head 1.8km south to reach Cala Portals Vells.

WESTERN MALLORCA SANT ELM

Illa Es Pantaleu, a rocky islet that marks one of the boundaries of a marine reserve. To the south of Sant Elm's main beach is **Cala es Conills**, a sandless but pretty inlet (follow Carrer de Cala es Conills).

Illa de Sa Dragonera   ISLAND
Part of the marine reserve is dominated by the 4km-long **Illa de Sa Dragonera**, a ripple of an island that stretches out like a slumbering dragon to the west. Constituted as a natural park, it can be reached by ferry. The ferry lands at a protected natural harbour on the east side of the island, from where you can follow trails to the capes at either end or ascend the **Na Pòpia peak** (Puig des Far Vell, 349m). The ferry operators also do **glass-bottomed-boat tours** around the island. If you want to dive off the island, try Scuba Activa.

Keida   ADVENTURE SPORTS
(☑971 23 91 24; www.keida.es; Plaçs de na Caragola 3; ☉hours vary) Keida offers a huge array of activities, from guided hikes (€38 to €60) to half-day boat excursions to Illa de Sa Dragonera (€42), three-hour horse-riding excursions (€60) and 1½-hour paddle-surfing courses (€45). You can also hire a bike (half-/full day €10/15) or a kayak (half-/full day €11/15) here.

Scuba Activa   DIVING, SNORKELLING
(☑971 23 91 02; www.scuba-activa.com; Plaça del Monsenyor Sebastià Grau 7; dive incl equipment

€38, equipment per day €15-17; ☉9am-6pm Apr-Oct) This well-run dive centre takes you into the depths of the brilliantly clear waters around Illa de Sa Dragonera, among Mallorca's best for scuba diving, with equipment rental and a full range of courses. It also runs one-hour snorkelling trips (€29).

Eating

★ **Es Molí**   MEDITERRANEAN €€
(☑971 23 92 02; http://esmoli.cat; Plaça de Mossèn Sebastià Grau 2; mains €14.50-21; ☉1-4pm & 7-11pm Tue-Sun Apr-Oct; ⊞) Tucked away on a plaza close to the sea, this is without shadow of a doubt our favourite restaurant in town – and we'd love to take a ride in the baby blue Seat 600 car parked outside. The decor is stripped-back minimalism, the team young and upbeat, and the food Mediterranean with distinct Italian overtones. Everything from salmon carpaccio with mango to homemade ravioli with wild mushrooms, truffle oil and Iberian ham hits the mark.

El Pescador   SEAFOOD €€
(☑971 23 91 98; Avinguda de Jaume I 48; mains €15-25; ☉1-3.30pm & 7.30-10.30pm; ⊞) El Pescador is perched off Plaça de Na Caragola, halfway into town (past the tourist office). Paella is a good midday option, but the best bet is the fish of the day (sold by weight). Service can be hit-and-miss.

DON'T MISS

HIKING THE RUTA DE PEDRA EN SEC

A breathtaking week of walking in Mallorca will see you traverse the entire mountainous northwest, from Cap de Formentor to Sant Elm. Old mule trails constitute the bulk of the (still incomplete) 167km GR221 walking route, aka the Ruta de Pedra en Sec (**Dry Stone Route**). The name refers to the time-honoured dry stone building technique here and throughout the island. In the mountains you'll see paved ways, farming terraces, houses, walls and more built of stone without the aid of mortar.

The GR221 begins in **Pollença** near Can Diable and the Torrent d'en Marc stream, but you could start with a day's march from Cap de Formentor. A reasonably fit walker can accomplish the eight-stage stretch from Pollença to Port d'Andratx in four days, but it's worth adding on an extra few days to include stops in some of the beautiful villages en route.

The first stretch is an easy walk of about four to five hours gradually curving southwest to the Monestir de Lluc (p109), where you can stay overnight. You will ascend about 600m in the course of the day, before dropping back down a little to the monastery. The following day sees another fair climb to over 1000m, taking you past the Puig de Massanella (1365m), southwest to the Embassament de Cúber dam, past Puig de l'Ofre (1093m), which many like to tick off the list, and down the Biniaraix ravine to Sóller to sleep. You might want to spend a couple of days here to explore the surrounding area.

To **Deià** (www.deia.info) you're looking at two to three hours' walking (from Sóller you could follow several trails, not just the GR221) and another two hours for **Valldemossa** (www.valldemossa.com). Those in a hurry could make it as far as **Estellencs** but, again, you might want to spread the walking over a couple of days. The last day would see you hiking from Estellencs to Sant Elm via **La Trapa**.

The walking requires a reasonable level of fitness but no special skills or equipment, other than good boots, sun protection, water bottle and so on. Good map-reading and compass skills are essential, as paths are not always well marked (one of the delays in completing the GR221 trail has been that 92% of the Serra de Tramuntana is private property and many rights of way are disputed). With various alternative routes, it is easy to become disoriented.

There are five refuges along the way, in Pollença, Monestir de Lluc, Escorca, Port de Sóller and Deià (to book a sleeping berth, call ahead on ☏ 971 13 77 00 from 9am to 2pm Monday to Friday, or visit www.conselldemallorca.net/refugis). There are plenty of other overnight options in the villages. For more information on the route, check out the Consell de Mallorca's web page, **Pedra en Sec i Senderisme** (www.conselldemallorca.net/?id_section=3198).

ℹ️ Information

Tourist office (☏ 971 23 92 05; Avinguda de Jaume 1 28B; ⏱ 9am-4pm Mon-Sat & 9.30am-2pm Sat) A short walk from the beach.

ℹ️ Getting There & Away

Seven or eight buses run from Andratx to Sant Elm (€2.10, 40 minutes) via Port d'Andratx and S'Arracó. You can also take the boat between Sant Elm and Port d'Andratx (€8, 20 minutes, daily February to October). If you are driving, dodge the €3.50 beachfront parking fee by heading a little uphill.

Ferries to Illa de Sa Dragonera (return €12, 15 minutes, three to four daily February to November) operate from the small harbour north of Sant Elm's main beach. One of the main operators is **Cruceros Margarita** (☏ 639 617545; www.crucerosmargarita.com); in peak season it is advisable to book tickets ahead.

SERRA DE TRAMUNTANA

Dominated by the Serra de Tramuntana range, Mallorca's northwest coast and its hinterland form a spectacular contrast to the built-up resorts you leave behind around Palma. The landscape is remarkably wild, ensnared by limestone peaks scarred by wind and water and cliffs that drop abruptly to the brilliant blue sea like natural ramparts. Gold-stone villages and hamlets sit atop hillsides, providing a tantalising taste of Mallorca before mass tourism kicked in. The terraces that march up from the coast date back centuries, and the high, rugged interior is beloved of walkers for its pine forests, olive groves and spring wildflowers. The region's unique cultural and geographical features have been inscribed by Unesco on to its World Heritage List.

The range covers 1100 sq km and is 90km long, extending all the way north to the Cap de Formentor. The highest peaks are concentrated in the central mountain range. The highest, Puig Major de Son Torrella (1445m), is off limits and home to a military base. It is followed by Puig de Massanella (1365m). The area is virtually bereft of surface watercourses, but rich in subterranean flows that feed the farming terraces of the coastal villages.

Andratx to Valldemossa Coast Road

Welcome to the one of the Mediterranean's most exhilarating stretches of coastline, embraced by the Ma10 road that climbs away from Andratx into the pine-clad hills marking the beginning of the majestic Serra de Tramuntana range. Pasted to cliff tops and hillsides, the hamlets and lookouts that dot this mostly lonely stretch of road have arresting views of raw coastal beauty.

Estellencs

POP 380 / ELEV 151M

Estellencs is an enticingly laid-back village of warm-stone buildings scattered around the rolling hills below the Puig Galatzò (1025m); the views of the village are stunning, especially from the main road as you approach from the north. The village is best observed as you climb down the hill away from the main road.

◉ Sights & Activities

Cala d'Estellencs   BEACH

From Estellencs, a 1.5km road winds down through terraces of palm trees, citrus orchards, olives, almonds, cacti, pines and flowers to Cala d'Estellencs, a rocky cove with bottle green water.

Puig Galatzò   MOUNTAIN

To ascend Puig Galatzò (1052m), a walking trail starts near the Km 97 milestone on the Ma10 road, about 2.5 km west of Estellencs. It's not easy going, so you'll need good maps and plenty of water and food. Prepare for a five- to six-hour round trip. An alternative but easily confused trail leads back down into Estellencs.

✖ Eating

Cafeteria Vall-Hermós   CAFE €

(☑ 971 61 86 10; www.vallhermos.com; Carrer de Eusebio Pascual 6; mains €8-17.50; ⊗ 10am-11pm

Thu-Tue) It's all about the sea view at this simple cafe on the main drag through town, particularly at sunset. Go for a coffee and a *bocadillo* (filled roll) by day or linger over a glass of red and some tapas by night.

★ Arandora   INTERNATIONAL €€

(☑ 638 417595; Plaça de la Constitució 6; mains €13-18; ⊗ 2pm-midnight Wed-Mon) Our favourite in Estellencs is sweet, Swedish-run Arandora right opposite the church. On summer evenings the terrace is great for watching the world go lazily by over a glass of *cava* (sparkling wine) with dishes like beetroot, goat's cheese and rocket salad and lamb burger on focaccia with feta and spicy sauce. You'll want to finish every last morsel, but save an inch for the stellar desserts.

Montimar   MALLORCAN €€

(☑ 971 61 85 76; Plaça de la Constitució 7; mains €20-30; ⊗ 1-3.30pm & 7-10.30pm Tue-Sun) This bastion of traditional Mallorcan cooking sits next to Arandora. Dishes range from grilled sardines to rice, suckling pig or *sobrassada* (Mallorcan cured sausage) with honey, while local cheeses are the pick of the desserts.

🛍 Shopping

Estel@rt   FOOD, CRAFT

(Carrer de Sa Siquia; ⊗ 10am-2pm & 5-8pm Mon & Wed-Sat, 10am-2pm Sun) At the northern end of town, this engaging little place sells primarily Mallorcan and Menorcan clothes, jewellery, ceramics, speciality foods and wine; the selection is small but well chosen. There's a two-room art gallery downstairs.

Banyalbufar

POP 560 / ELEV 112M

Eight kilometres northeast of Estellencs, Banyalbufar is positioned in a cleft in the Serra de Tramuntana's seaward wall, high above the coast. It's a tight, steep rabbit-warren of a town, with quiet pot-plant-lined lanes winding down towards the sea that beckon strollers.

The village was founded by the Arabs in the 10th century; the name Banyalbufar means 'built next to the sea' in Arabic. All around the village are carved-out, centuries-old, stone-walled farming terraces, known as *ses marjades* and forming a series of steps down to the sea; they are kept moist by mountain well water that gurgles down open channels and is stored in cisterns.

WESTERN MALLORCA ANDRATX TO VALLDEMOSSA COAST ROAD

⊙ Sights

Torre des Verger TOWER

(Torre de Ses Animes; Carretera de Banyalbufar-Andratx) **FREE** One kilometre out of town on the road to Estellencs, the Torre des Verger is a 1579 *talayot* (watchtower), an image you'll see on postcards all over the island. It's one of the most crazily sited structures on the island – one step further and it would plunge into the Mediterranean far below.

Cala Banyalbufar BEACH

A steep 1km walk downhill past terraced slopes from Banyalbufar brings you to this rugged shingle cove, where you can swim or sip a cold one at the beach shack on the rocks; there's also a lovely waterfall nearby.

Bodega Son Vives WINERY

(☑609 601904; www.sonvives.com; Carretera de Banyalbufar-Andratx, Font de la Vila 2; ☺11am-7pm Thu-Sun May-Oct) High on the hill at the southern entrance to the village, this small winery has cellar-door tastings and sales in summer. It offers a number of fusion wines, but its best drop comes from the locally grown malvasia grape.

✕ Eating

Pegasón y el Pajarito Enmascarado MEDITERRANEAN €

(☑971 14 87 13; www.pegasonyelpajaritoenmascarado.com; Carrer del Pont 2; mains €7-16; ☺12.30-4pm & 7.30-11pm Sat-Wed, 7.30-11pm Fri) Stone walls, checked tablecloths and cobbled-together vintage furnishings give this button-cute bistro a distinctly boho feel. It's tucked in the corner of a narrow backstreet, with a plant-dotted patio for people-watching over everything from *tumbet* (Mallorcan ratatouille) with roast pork to lamb meatballs. The bargainous three-course €15.50 lunch includes water, wine and olives.

Ca'n Paco MALLORCAN €€

(☑971 61 81 48; www.canpaco.es; Carrer de la Constitució 18; mains €11.50-17.50; ☺1-5pm & 7.30-11pm Tue-Sun) On the road leading down to Cala de Banyalbufar, this traditional haunt stays true to its Mallorcan roots with generous portions of *arroz negro* (black rice cooked in squid ink) and grilled fish. Its *gato con helado de almendra,* a moist sponge with almond ice cream, takes some beating, as do the terrace views as the sun sinks into the sea.

Son Tomás MALLORCAN €€

(☑971 61 81 49; Carrer de Baronia 17; mains €14-21; ☺12.30-4pm & 8-10.30pm Wed-Mon; ♿) A clas-sic spot, this place almost seems to lean over the main road at the southwest end of town. Although it draws cyclists seeking snacks to its streetside tables, the upstairs restaurant is first class. Crackling *lechona* (suckling pig) and one of the best renditions of rice with lobster we tasted on the island await.

🔒 Shopping

Malvasia de Banyalbufar WINE

(☑971 14 85 05; www.malvasiadebanyalbufar.com; Carrer de Comte Sallent 5; ☺11am-2pm & 5-8pm Tue-Sat, 11am-2pm Sun Jun-Aug, shorter hours rest of year) This shop run by a cooperative of local wineries was set up to promote the locally grown malvasia grape. As such, it's the perfect place to pick up a bottle of wine for a picnic or to take back home.

Esporles & the Inland Circuit

A few hundred metres beyond the Port des Canonge turn-off, the Ma1100 breaks off southward towards Esporles. After 1km you reach a road junction and La Granja.

From La Granja, those with wheels could make a circuit inland. Follow the Ma1101 south, which plunges through thick woods and slithers down a series of hairpin bends to reach **Puigpunyent**. This typical inland town offers few sights but the luxury, rose-hued hilltop Gran Hotel Son Net (p171) is reason enough to detour here if money is no object.

From Puigpunyent, make a dash for **Galilea**, a high mountain hamlet about four serpentine kilometres south. Climb to the town's church square for views across the valleys and a drink in the bar next door, or head even higher up this straggling place for a greater sense of altitude.

Back in Puigpunyent, take the Ma1101 to Esporles. Cradled between the mountain folds in the foothills of the Tramuntana, this pretty village of ochre-stone town houses is set beside a generally dry stream and has a Saturday market. The pace is laid-back in the cafe-lined alleys presided over by a neo-Gothic church. Esporles can be animated by night, as many folk from Palma have opted to live here and commute to the capital.

⊙ Sights

La Granja HISTORIC BUILDING

(www.lagranja.net; Carretera de Esporles-Banyalbufar; adult/child €12.50/6; ☺10am-7pm) This magnificent *possessió* (rural estate) has been turned into something of a kitsch Mallorca-land exhibit, with folks

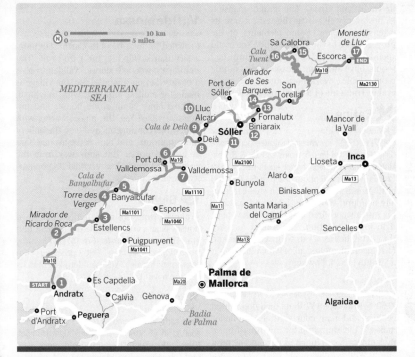

🏃 Driving Tour
Andratx to Monestir de Lluc

START ANDRATX
END MONESTIR DE LLUC
LENGTH 140KM; SIX HOURS

To appreciate the sheer drama of this coast-line, we recommend driving this 140km route from Andratx in the south to Monestir de Lluc in the north. From ① **Andratx**, the road climbs through pine forests to your first glimpse of the Mediterranean below. Fourteen kilometres from Andratx, pull into the parking lot opposite Restaurant El Grau and climb up to the ② **Mirador de Ricardo Roca** for some of the most extraordinary views anywhere along this coast. A further 4km on you pass through ③ **Estellencs**, before continuing on 5km to the ④ **Torre des Verger**, one of the Mediterranean's most dramatically sited watchtowers. The tower lies on the outskirts of ⑤ **Banyalbufar**, another charming coastal village, whereafter the road winds inland. At the road junction after 7km, take the narrow road north, which climbs through pine

trees and boulders before crossing a high plateau. Take the turn-off west to ⑥ **Port de Valldemossa**, an exhilarating descent down to the water's edge, and then return to the main road. By now, you're almost in ⑦ **Valldemossa**, which is always worth a pause, as is ⑧ **Deià**, which is nine spectacular kilometres beyond the Valldemossa turn-off along the Ma10. Don't miss the brief detour down off the main road to ⑨ **Cala de Deià**, one of Mallorca's prettiest coves, while the views of ⑩ **Lluc Alari** from the main road are exceptional. ⑪ **Sóller** has a fabulous location and is the gateway to ⑫ **Biniaraix** and ⑬ **Fornalutx**, two of the loveliest villages on the island. From the latter, the Ma10 climbs up to the ⑭ **Mirador de Ses Barques**, before passing high-altitude lakes in the shadow of Mallorca's highest mountains. By the time you reach the turn-off to ⑮ **Sa Calobra**, the mountains are bare and otherworldly. Follow the hairpin bends down to Sa Calobra and detour to ⑯ **Cala Tuent**, before returning to the main road bound for ⑰ **Monestir de Lluc**.

in traditional dress. The grand mansion is, however, well worth the visit, as are its extensive gardens. Some elements of the property date to the 10th century. You could spend hours exploring the period-furnished rooms, olive and wine presses, grand dining room, stables, workshops and some medieval instruments of torture in the cellars.

✕ Eating

El Mesón La Villa   MALLORCAN €€

(☑971 61 09 01; www.mesonlavilladesporles.com; Calle Nou de Sant Pere 5; mains €15-25; ⊘8-11pm Mon-Sat Jun–mid-Sep, shorter hours rest of year) Locals wax lyrical about the *asados* (roasts) at El Mesón La Villa, where a chef can usually be found shovelling lamb and suckling pig into a wood-fired clay oven to slow-bake it to juicy perfection. The setting matches the rustic, hearty food, with its beams and farming implements; all of which has won it a faithful local following.

Es Brollador   SPANISH €€

(☑971 61 05 39; Passeig del Rei 10; mains €11.50-21.50; ⊘10am-10pm) With its tiled floors, high ceilings and rear courtyard, Es Brollador makes a pleasant stop for anything from a morning coffee to lunch or dinner. The pork sirloin with a sauce made with *sobrassada* is memorable; it also serves lighter meals. The outdoor tables are perfect for people-watching.

❶ Getting There & Away

The 200 Palma–Estellencs bus (€3.85, one hour 20 minutes, four to 11 times daily) passes through Esporles and Banyalbufar.

Valldemossa

POP 2027 / ELEV 425M

Crowned by the spire of its Carthusian monastery that slowly lifts the gaze to the Tramuntana's wooded slopes, Valldemossa is a beauty. Set on a gentle rise, the village is made for aimless ambling, with tree-lined, cobbled lanes, stout stone houses and impressive villas. Yes, the place swarms with tourist-bus contingents and, yes, the bulk of the restaurants and bars serve average fare at inflated prices. But slip away from the crowds and you'll discover that its popularity is well founded.

◎ Sights

Around town you may notice that most houses bear a colourful tile depicting a nun and the words '*Santa Catalina Thomàs, pregau per nosaltres*' ('St Catherine Thomas, pray for us'). Yes, Valldemossa has its very own saint.

★Real Cartuja de Valldemossa   MONASTERY

(www.cartujadevalldemossa.com; Plaça Cartoixa; adult/child €8.50/4; ⊘9.30am-6.30pm Mon-Sat, 10am-1.30pm Sun) This grand old monastery and former royal residence has a chequered history, once home to kings, monks and a pair of 19th-century celebrities: composer Frédéric Chopin and George Sand. A series of cells now shows how the monks lived, bound by an oath of silence they could only break for half an hour per week in the library. Various items related to Sand's and Chopin's time here, including Chopin's pianos, are also displayed.

SAILING FROM ANDRATX TO PORT DE SÓLLER

Driving, walking, cycling...whichever way you choose to explore the dramatic coast of the Serra de Tramuntana you're in for some spectacular views. But there's also a different approach worth considering. Take a sailing route from Port d'Andratx in the southwest, around past Sant Elm and Illa de Sa Dragonera and northeast to Port de Sóller, a good, quiet port to overnight in. Places to stop during the day for a dip (they are no good for dropping anchor overnight) are Port des Canonge, Cala de Deià and Lluc Alcari. The inlets of Estellencs and Valldemossa are too shallow for most yachts. The next stage, tracking to Cap de Formentor and rounding it to find shelter in the Badia de Pollença, takes longer under equal conditions. Good daytime stops are Cala Tuent, Sa Calobra, Cala Sant Vicenç and Cala Figuera. The total trip is around 60 nautical miles.

One of the main factors to consider is weather. Wind is more of a rule than an exception, which means you can get your sails out. However, depending on conditions, it can also be uncomfortable. In winter it is often dangerous to sail along this coastline. It is possible to charter yachts in Port d'Andratx at Llaüts, or ask at the tourist office.

Valldemossa

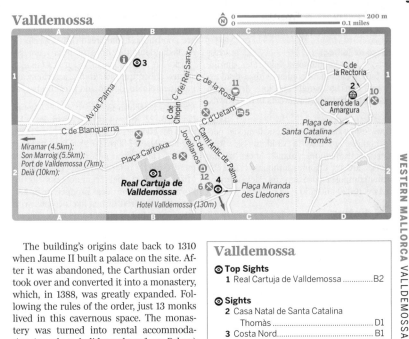

The building's origins date back to 1310 when Jaume II built a palace on the site. After it was abandoned, the Carthusian order took over and converted it into a monastery, which, in 1388, was greatly expanded. Following the rules of the order, just 13 monks lived in this cavernous space. The monastery was turned into rental accommodation (mostly to holidaymakers from Palma) after its monks were expelled in 1835. Entry includes piano recitals (eight times daily in summer) and Jaume II's 14th-century **Palau de Rei Sanxo**, a muddle of medieval rooms jammed with furniture and hundreds of years of mementoes, gathered around a modest cloister.

Casa Natal de Santa
Catalina Thomàs　　　HISTORIC BUILDING
(Carrer de la Rectoria) The Casa Natal de Santa Catalina Thomàs, birthplace of St Catherine Thomas, is tucked off to the side of the parish church, the **Església de Sant Bartomeu**, at the east end of the town. It houses a simple chapel and a facsimile of Pope Pius VI's declaration beatifying the saint in 1792; she was canonised in 1930. There are no fixed opening hours, but you'll rarely find the doors closed.

Miranda des Lledoners　　　VIEWPOINT
For an exquisite view taking in the terraces, orchards, gardens, cypresses, palms, the occasional ochre house through the mountains and the distant plains leading to Palma, walk down Carrer de Jovellanos to Miranda des Lledoners.

Valldemossa

◉ **Top Sights**
　1 Real Cartuja de Valldemossa B2

◉ **Sights**
　2 Casa Natal de Santa Catalina
　　　Thomàs D1
　3 Costa Nord... B1
　4 Miranda des Lledoners C2

▢ **Sleeping**
　5 Es Petit Hotel de Valldemossa C1

✕ **Eating**
　6 Casa de Sa Miranda........................... C2
　7 Forn Ca'n Molinas B2
　8 Gelatimossa... B2
　9 Hostal Ca'n Marió C1
　10 QuitaPenas D1

◉ **Drinking & Nightlife**
　11 Aromas.. C1

◉ **Shopping**
　12 Es Carreró C2

Costa Nord　　　CULTURAL CENTRE
(☑ 971 61 24 25; www.costanord.es; Avinguda de Palma 6; adult/child €6/free; ◷ 9am-5pm) The brainchild of part-time Valldemossa resident and Hollywood actor Michael Douglas, Costa Nord describes itself as a 'cultural centre' and begins well with a 15-minute portrayal of the history of Valldemossa, narrated by Douglas himself. The subsequent virtual trip aboard *Nixe*, the 19th-century yacht of Austrian Archduke Luis Salvador, who owned much of western Mallorca, will be of less interest to most.

✦ Festivals & Events

Sunday is market day in Valldemossa.

Festa de la Beata   RELIGIOUS
On 28 July, Valldemossa celebrates the life of Santa Catalina Thomàs, with a donkey-drawn carriage parade and kids dressed in peasant garb throwing sweets to the crowds.

Festival Chopin   MUSIC
(www.festivalchopin.com) Classical-music performances are held in Valldemossa's Real Cartuja throughout August; most of the works are by Chopin, although music by other composers also appears. Tickets go for between €20 and €30.

✗ Eating

★ QuitaPenas   TAPAS €
(☑ 675 993082; www.quitapenasvalldemossa.com; Carreró de la Amargura 1; tapas €3-15; ☺ noon-4pm & 6-8pm) Descend cobbled steps to this sweet deli for tapas prepared with care and first-class seasonal ingredients. Grab one of the half-dozen spots outside for interesting takes on *pa amb oli* (bread with olive oil and vine-ripened tomatoes) or tangy *sobrassada* with caramelised fig. Couple with chilled Mallorcan wine and magical mountain views and this is a little slice of heaven.

Forn Ca'n Molinas   BAKERY €
(Carrer de Blanquerna 15; coca de patata/ensaïmada €1.15/1.20; ☺ 7.30am-8pm; 🖐) This place along the main pedestrian drag has been baking up the local speciality of *coca de patata* (a bready, sugar-dusted pastry) and the island-favourite *ensaïmades* (light pastry spirals dusted with icing sugar) since 1920. It stays open later in the height of summer.

Gelatimossa   ICE CREAM €
(www.gelatimossa.com; Plaça de Cartoixa 18; ice cream per scoop €1.60; ☺ 11am-10pm Jun-Sep, shorter hours rest of year) Pistachio, Mallorcan almond, peach, coffee and yoghurt....how ever will you choose? It's all homemade and delicious at this *gelateria*. Grab a cone and head to the garden behind the Real Cartuja (50m away).

Hostal Ca'n Marió   MALLORCAN €
(☑ 971 61 21 22; http://hostalcanmario.net; Carrer d'Uetam 8; mains €8.50-14; ☺ 1.30-3.30pm & 8-10.30pm Wed-Mon, shorter hours in winter) If you can grab a window table at this homely restaurant half the job is done, as you'll have views almost clear to Palma. On the menu are good honest Mallorcan dishes perfectly cooked, along the lines of *lomo com col* (pork loin with cabbage), *caracoles* (snails), stuffed aubergine and *tumbet*, a garlicky aubergine, tomato, potato and zucchini bake.

Casa de Sa Miranda   FUSION €€
(☑ 971 61 22 96; www.samiranda.com; Plaça Miranda des Lladoners 3; tapas €8-10, mains €14-24; ☺ 7-10pm Mon, 1-3.30pm & 7-10pm Tue-Sat) What a view! The entire town and valley spreads picturesquely before you at Casa de Sa Miranda. Here chef Fecundo puts his innovative stamp on local produce in bright, expertly prepared dishes like octopus in miso sauce and pear ravioli with gorgonzola and strawberries – all big on flavour and delivered with flair. The tapas are great too.

🍷 Drinking

Aromas   CAFE
(Carrer de la Rosa 25; ☺ 11am-9pm; 🐦) With its chequerboard floor, warm terracotta walls and jazzy music, this arty cafe is a wonderfully relaxed spot to sip speciality teas (there are 60 to choose from) or thick hot chocolate. Out the back there's a fragrant garden. In summary – very cool!

🔒 Shopping

Es Carreró   CRAFT
(Carrer de Jovellanos 6B; ☺ 11am-9pm Jun-Sep, shorter hours rest of year) Vicky Vidal's artistic eye rarely misses a beat. The homewares, jewellery and accessories at this petite boutique are mostly either handmade or recycled by her – from button rings to wooden sunglasses, dishes crafted from newspaper cuttings to origami fish and birds. It's a cut above your average Valldemossa souvenir shop.

ℹ Information

Tourist office (☑ 971 61 20 19; www.ajvalldemossa.net; Avinguda de Palma 7; ☺ 10am-6.30pm Mon-Fri, to 2pm Sat & Sun) On the main road running through town, about two minutes' walk from the main bus stop.

ℹ Getting There & Away

The 210 bus from Palma to Valldemossa (€1.85, 30 minutes) runs four to nine times a day. Three to four of these continue to Port de Sóller (€2.25, one hour) via Deià.

WORTH A TRIP

AN ARCHDUKE'S ROMANTIC ABODES

Head northeast of Valldemosa on the spectacular coastal road that twists to Deià and you will come across two of the most remarkable residences on the island, both of which belonged to Habsburg Archduke Luis Salvador (1847–1915), a hopeless romantic who found his idea of heaven right here.

The first is **Miramar** (www.sonmarroig.com; Carretera de Valldemossa-Deià; adult/child €4/free; ⊙10am-6pm May-Oct, shorter hours rest of year), a splendid sea-facing mansion, built on the site of a 13th-century monastery, with a *tàfona* (olive-oil press), cloister and landscaped gardens to explore. The evangelist and patron saint of Catalan literature, Ramon Llull, founded the monastery, where he wrote many of his works and trained brethren for the task of proselytising among the Muslims. Walk out the back and enjoy the clifftop views.

Seven kilometres from Valldemosa is another of Salvàdor's residences, **Son Marroig** (www.sonmarroig.com; Carretera de Valldemossa-Deià; adult/child €4/free; ⊙10am-6pm May-Oct, shorter hours rest of year). It's a delightful, rambling mansion jammed with furniture and period items, including many of the archduke's books. But above all, the views are the stuff of dreams.

Ask permission to wander down to **Sa Foradada**, the strange hole-in-the-wall rock formation by the water, which resembles an elephant from afar. It's a stunning 3km walk (one way) down through olive groves tinkling with sheep bells and along paths flanked by pine trees and caves. A soothing swim in the lee of this odd formation is the reward. Avoid the midday heat as there is little shade. The fiery sunsets here are riveting stuff.

Port de Valldemossa

About 1.5km west from Valldemossa on the road to Banyalbufar, a spectacular mountain road (the Ma1113) clings to cliffs all the 5.5km down to Port de Valldemossa. The giddying sea and cliff views are breathtaking and the descent is akin to traversing a precipice with a village glimpsed through the trees a very long way down below; drivers shouldn't take their eye off the road and there's only one place to pull over for photos. At journey's end, there is a shingle and algae 'beach' backed by low red cliffs and a cluster of a dozen or so houses, one of which is home to the justifiably popular Restaurant Es Port.

✕ Eating

Restaurant Es Port SEAFOOD €€
(☏971 61 61 94; Carrer Ponent 5; mains €12.50-23.50; ⊙10am-10pm Jun-Aug, shorter hours rest of year) Seafood is the mainstay here, as you'd expect, and it all somehow tastes better out on the 1st-floor terrace on a midsummer's evening. Rice dishes steal the show, as does the mixed seafood platter, while the *calamares al ajillo con patatas* (cuttlefish cooked with potato cubes and lightly spiced) is perfectly prepared.

Deià & Around

POP 750 / ELEV 222M

When the late afternoon sun warms Deià's honey-coloured houses, which clamber breathlessly up a conical hillside, and the sea deepens to darkest blue on the horizon, it's enough to send even the most prosaic of souls into romantic raptures. This eyrie of a village in the Tramuntana is flanked by steep hillsides terraced with vegetable gardens, citrus orchards, almond and olive trees and even the occasional vineyard – all set against the mountain backdrop of the **Puig des Teix** (1062m).

Deià was once a second home to writers, actors and musicians, the best known of whom (to Anglo-Saxons at any rate) was the English poet Robert Graves.

◎ Sights & Activities

Climbing up from the main road, the steep cobbled lanes, with their well-kept stone houses, overflowing bougainvillea and extraordinary views over the sea, farm terraces and mountains, make it easy to understand why artists and other bohemians have loved this place since Catalan artists 'discovered' it in the early 20th century.

★ **Casa Robert Graves** HISTORIC BUILDING
(Ca N'Alluny; www.lacasaderobertgraves.com; Carretera Deià-Sóller; adult/child €7/3.50; ⊘10am-5pm Mon-Fri, to 3pm Sat) Casa Robert Graves is a fascinating tribute to the writer who moved to Deià in 1929 and had his house built here three years later. It's a well-presented insight into his life; on show you'll find period furnishings, audiovisual displays and various items and books that belonged to Graves himself.

The three-storey stone house, **Ca N'Alluny** (House in the Distance), is a testament to his life and work. Graves left hurriedly in 1936 at the outbreak of civil war, entrusting the house to the care of a local. The Spanish authorities allowed him to return 10 years later and he found everything as he had left it. 'If I had felt so inclined, I could have sat down and...started work straight away', he later commented. And even now, the whole place is set up as if Graves had just stepped out for a stroll. His voice rings out through the rooms as his reading of his poem *The Face in the Mirror* is played in a loop of seemingly eternal playback; the effect is curiously powerful.

Famous for such works as *I, Claudius,* the novelised version of the Roman emperor's life, Robert Graves also wrote reams of verse and a book on his adopted homeland, *Mallorca Observed* (1965); the prologue to his *The Golden Fleece* is set in Deià. A handful of his 146 works are available for sale at the ticket office, and ask there also for the 'Reading Suggestions' information sheet.

Es Puig VIEWPOINT, RELIGIOUS
From Es Puig, the hill at the heart of Deià, you peer across the rooftops of the higgledy-piggledy village and take in the full sweep of the valley to the glinting Mediterranean beyond. At the top is the modest parish church, the **Església de Sant Joan Baptista** (its Museu Parroquial, with a collection of local religious paraphernalia, rarely opens). Opposite is the town **cemetery**. Here lies 'Robert Graves, Poeta, 24-4-1895 – 7-12-1985 E.P.D' (*en paz descanse,* meaning 'may he rest in peace'). His second wife, Beryl Pritchard (Beryl Graves), who died in 2003, is buried at the other end of the graveyard.

Cala de Deià BEACH
A 3km drive from Deià (take the road towards Sóller), or a slightly shorter walk, is Cala de Deià, one of the most bewitching of the Serra de Tramuntana's coastal inlets. Accessible only on foot, the enclosed arc of the bay is backed by a handful of houses and the small shingle beach gives onto crystal-clear water. Competition for a parking spot a few hundred metres back up the road can be intense; get here early.

The beach is backed by a simple bar-eatery, Can Lluc, while on a rocky platform above the water, you can sit down for fresh fish at Ca's Patró March. Some fine walks criss-cross the area, such as the gentle Deià Coastal Path to the pleasant hamlet of Lluc Alcari. Three daily buses run from Deià (15-minute trip) from May to October.

Lluc Alcari VILLAGE
Three kilometres northeast of Deià, this is a magical hamlet nestled into the rocky mountainside. The village is largely consumed by its hotel, but the view from the main road of terracotta roofs and palm trees against the Mediterranean backdrop is one of the prettiest along this stretch of coast.

✦ Festivals & Events

Festival Internacional de Deià MUSIC
(⌖971 63 91 78; www.dimf.com; admission €20) Outside Deià on the Serra de Tramuntana coast, the Son Marroig mansion hosts the Festival Internacional de Deià, a series of light-classical concerts on Thursdays from April to September.

✕ Eating

The Ma10 passes though the town centre, where it becomes the main street and is lined with bars, restaurants and shops, particularly at the village's eastern end. Quality varies, but there are some high-quality mainstays sprinkled among the others that come and go with the years.

Village Cafe INTERNATIONAL €
(⌖971 63 91 99; www.villagecafedeia.com; Carrer Felipe Bauzà 1; mains €9-15; ⊘noon-11pm Wed-Mon Mar-Oct; ⊞) Swathed in flowers and vines, the terrace at this stone-walled cafe has broad views of the Tramuntana. The gourmet burgers are a fine pick, as are the salads and *bocadillos* (filled rolls). As the ceramic lanterns flick on and the cicadas chirp at dusk, it's a highly atmospheric spot for a G&T and tapas.

Sa Vinya MEDITERRANEAN €€
(⌖971 63 95 00; www.restaurant-savinya.com; Carrer de Sa Vinya Vella 4; mains €15-29; ⊘1-11pm Wed-Mon Feb-Nov; ⊞) Cobbled steps trail up

to Sa Vinya and its subtly lit terrace, overlooking citrus groves and the Tramuntana's wooded peaks. It's a magical spot for dinner, and freshness shines through in sunny Mediterranean flavours like melon gazpacho with tarragon, hake with saffron risotto and whole sea bass. BBQ nights are popular and the friendly service is unfaltering.

Ca's Patró March
SPANISH €€

(☑ 971 63 91 37; Cala Deià; mains €10-25; ⊙ 10am-11pm Jun-Aug, shorter hours rest of year) This is probably the pick of the two places overlooking the water for its slightly elevated views, but it's a close-run thing. It has a wide range of grilled meat and fish dishes – the star of which seems to be the Sóller *gambas*. It's run by the third generation of a local fishing family.

Can Lluc
SEAFOOD €€

(☑ 649 198618; Cala Deià; mains €10-20; ⊙ 10.30am-7pm May-Oct) If you can't bear to drag yourself too far from your towel, this simple bar-eatery couldn't be more convenient. Cold drinks, grilled sardines and calamari with just a squirt of lemon on a lazy summer's afternoon – bliss.

★ Es Racó d'es Teix
FUSION €€€

(☑ 971 63 95 01; www.esracodesteix.es; Carrer de San Vinya Vella 6; mains €36-38, 3-course lunch menu €35, 4-/6-course tasting menu €72/98; ⊙ 1-3pm & 7-10pm Feb-Oct) An island legend, Josef Sauerschell has one Michelin star and it is well deserved. He tends to concentrate on elaborate but hearty meat dishes – anything from braised veal shoulder in sherry-vinegar sauce with marrow to Mallorcan suckling pig and trotters with foie gras.

The cooking's not as outlandish as other places of this kind, but the results are every bit as rewarding, and the mountain backdrop just sublime. Each month a different Mallorcan vineyard is in the spotlight.

Sebastian
MEDITERRANEAN €€€

(☑ 971 63 94 17; Carrer de Felip Bauzà 2; mains €26-30; ⊙ 7.30-10.30pm) With bare stone walls and crisp white linen, Sebastian is a refined experience. The short, sweet menu offers three fish and three meat mains, each enhanced with a delicate sauce or purée. What's available depends on the season, but you might expect such dishes as goat's cheese millefeuille with hazelnut pesto or sea bass ceviche with avocado and cherry tomatoes.

ⓘ Getting There & Away

Deià is 15 minutes up the winding road from Valldemossa on the 210 bus route between Palma (€2.85, 45 to 60 minutes) and Port de Sóller (€1.60, 30 to 40 minutes).

Sóller

POP 14,150 / ELEV 40M

As though cupped in celestial hands, the ochre town of Sóller lies in a valley surrounded by the grey-green hills of the Serra de Tramuntana. The Arabs saw the potential of the valley, known as the Vall d'Or (Golden Valley), and accounts of orange and lemon groves, watered from sources in the hills, date to the 13th century.

Worth exploring in its own right, with its vintage train and tram rides, graceful Modernist architecture and galleries showcasing Picasso and Miró, Sóller is a wonderful base for exploring the west coast and the Tramuntanal. It is also the trailhead for some stirring mountain hikes.

◉ Sights

Simply wandering Sóller's peaceful, often cobbled, streets is a pleasure. In any direction, within a few minutes you exchange tight, winding lanes for country roads bordered by stone walls, behind which flourish orange and lemon groves.

★ Ca'n Prunera –
Museu Modernista
GALLERY, HISTORIC BUILDING

(http://canprunera.com; Carrer de Sa Lluna 86-90; adult/child €5/free; ⊙ 10.30am-6.30pm Mar-Oct, closed Mon Nov-Feb) One of Mallorca's standout galleries, Ca'n Prunera occupies a landmark Modernista mansion. The list of luminaries here is astonishing – works by Joan Miró, along with single drawings by Toulouse-Lautrec, Picasso, Gauguin, Klimt, Kandinsky, Klee, Man Ray and Cezanne. Also part of the permanent collection is a gallery devoted to Juli Ramis (1909–90), a Sóller native and world-renowned painter who had his studio in the neighbouring village of Biniaraix, plus works by Miquel Barceló, Antoni Tapiès and Eduardo Chillida.

There's also the strangely mesmerising *Movement* (2006) by Francesca Martí, a sculpture garden out the back, and a display of dolls from the early 20th century... In total, a rich and varied selection.

But this is so much more than a who's who of European masters and the building

WESTERN MALLORCA SÓLLER

Sóller

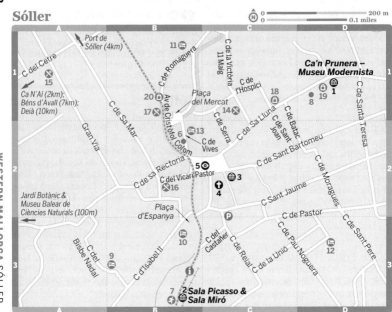

Sóller

◎ Top Sights

◎ Sights

⊕ Activities, Courses & Tours

⊜ Sleeping

⊗ Eating

⊜ Shopping

itself complements the eclectic collection. The mansion is a study in Modernista style, from the muted but intriguing stone and wrought-iron facade to the elaborate ceilings and early-20th-century furnishings.

★ **Sala Picasso & Sala Miró** GALLERY
(Plaça d'Espanya 6, Estación de Tren; ⊙10am-6.30pm) **FREE** Few train stations have such a rich artistic legacy. In two rooms at street level in Sóller's station, there are two intriguing art exhibitions, the Sala Picasso and Sala Miró. The former has more than 50 ceram-

ics by Picasso from 1948 to 1971, many bearing the artist's trademark subjects: dancers, women, bullfighting. The latter is home to a series of playful, colour-charged prints by the Catalan master; Miró's maternal grandfather was from Sóller.

Església de Sant Bartomeu CHURCH
(Plaça de la Constitució; ⊙11am-1.15pm & 3-5.15pm Mon-Thu, 11am-1.15pm Fri & Sat, noon-1pm Sun) A disciple of architect Antoni Gaudí, Joan Rubió got some big commissions in Sóller. The town didn't want to miss the wave of moder-

nity and so Rubió set to work in 1904 on the renovation of the 16th-century Església de Sant Bartomeu. The largely baroque church (built 1688–1723) preserved elements of its earlier Gothic interior, but Rubió gave it a beautiful if unusual Modernista facade.

The interior is gilded yet sombre with dimly lit chapels offset by the ornate altarpiece. Our favourite perspective is to walk towards the altar, and then turn for a view of the chandelier, organ and luminous rose window. The church's candelabra-like summit is visible from all over town, set against the backdrop of the Serra de Tramuntana.

Banco de Sóller   HISTORIC BUILDING
(Plaça de la Constitució) Joan Rubió is responsible for the strikingly Modernista frontage of the 1912 Banco de Sóller (nowadays Banco de Santander), right beside the Església de Sant Bartomeu. It's a daring effort, with two massive, circular galleries and windows draped in lacy wrought-iron grilles.

Plaça de la Constitució   SQUARE
(Town Centre) The main square, Plaça de la Constitució, is 100m downhill from the train station. Surrounded by bars and restaurants, filled with children playing in the evenings and home to the *ajuntament*, this is Sóller's heart and soul.

**Jardí Botànic & Museu Balear
de Ciències Naturals**   GARDENS, MUSEUM
(www.jardibotanicdesoller.org; Carretera Palma-Port de Sóller; adult/child €5/free; ⊙10am-6pm Mon-Sat) A pleasant stroll 600m west from Sóller's town centre brings you to the peaceful Jardí Botànic, with collections of flowers and other plants native to the Balearic Islands – from holm oaks to magnolias, myrtle to the endangered caraway pine – alongside other Mediterranean samples. The same ticket gives you free entry to the Museu Balear de Ciències Naturals (Natural Science Museum), which provides some basic insight on the flora and fauna of the Balearics – the fossil collection is of particular note.

🏃 Activities

For planning walks around and beyond the Sóller basin, pick up the Editorial Alpina *Tramuntana Central* map (1:25,000). Lonely Planet's *Hiking in Spain* describes two splendid day walks that set out from the village. For guided hikes, contact Tramuntana Tours.

Trams   VINTAGE TRAM
(Tranvías; 1 way €5; ⊙every 30 or 60 min 7am-11.30pm; ♿) A real blast from the past, Sóller's old-world, open-sided trams trundle 2km down to Port de Sóller on the coast. They depart from outside the train station; pick up a timetable from the tourist office.

Tramuntana Tours   ADVENTURE SPORTS
(☑971 63 24 23; www.tramuntanatours.com; Carrer de Sa Lluna 72; bike rental per day €12-30; ⊙9am-1.30pm & 3-7.30pm Mon-Fri, 9am-1.30pm Sat) This experienced operator organises a range of activities-based guided excursions, including canyoning (€45), sea kayaking (€50), hiking (€25 to €45) and mountain biking (from €40) in the Serra de Tramuntana, as well as renting out as-new bikes. It also has a gear shop. If it's not open, try the sister shop in Port de Sóller, which has longer opening hours.

🏅 Courses

Lengua Sóller   LANGUAGE COURSE
(☑674 216677; http://lenguas-soller.es; Carrer de Vives 5; ⊙11am-1pm & 5-8pm Mon-Fri) This central language school runs intensive Spanish-language courses.

🎭 Festivals & Events

Es Firó   LOCAL FIESTA
Around the second weekend of May, Sóller is invaded by a motley crew of Muslim pirates. Known as Es Firó, this conflict (involving about 1200 townsfolk) between *pagesos* (town and country folk) and Moros (Moors) is full of good-humoured drama and copious drinking. It re-enacts an assault on the town that was repulsed on 11 May 1561. The centrepiece of this event is remembered as **Ses Valentes Dones** (Valiant Women). Two sisters, instead of cowering as corsairs barged into their house, took a heavy bar and proceeded to kill several of the pirates, thus contributing to the town's final victory.

🍴 Eating

Cafe Scholl   CAFE €
(☑971 63 23 98; Carrer de la Victòria 11 Maig 9; light bites & mains €5-15; ⊙9am-8pm Mon-Fri, to 5pm Sat) With its chandeliers, brass mirrors and pretty patio, this boho-retro cafe is a fab place to linger. Pull up an art nouveau chair for breakfast with flaky croissants and fresh orange juice, a light lunch (we can recommend the goat's cheese salad and homemade ravioli) or coffee with a slice of moist orange-almond cake.

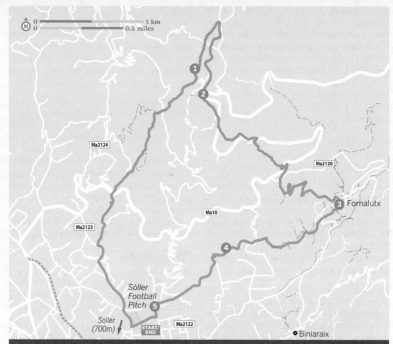

Walking Tour
Sóller to Mirador de Ses Barques Circuit

START/END SÓLLER
LENGTH 8KM; 3¾–4¼ HOURS

This stunning circuit is best attempted when it's cooler. Editorial Alpina's 1:25,000 *Tramuntana Central* map is recommended.

Begin at the football pitch on Sóller's northern fringes. Head briefly along Camí de Sa Figuera towards Port de Sóller, turning right into Camí de ses Argiles. Follow this track to reach the sign for **1 Camí Vell de Bàlitx**, then turn right onto Camí de son Blanco. At a fork in the track, turn left, then immediately right onto a path that climbs quickly to the Ma10. Veer left, then right onto a paved track. Take the cobbled trail to the left that weaves up through olive groves. At the sign to Cala Tuent, turn left onto the Camí Vell de Bàlitx. Bear right at the first gate and continue your ascent. The cobbled trail leads alongside a ditch and opens out before reaching a gravel road. Ignore the signs left to Cala Tuent, instead turning right for the

final ascent to **2 Mirador de ses Barques** (1¾ to two hours) lookout, with views of Port de Sóller.

Turn right on the Ma10, then right again, following signs to Fornalutx and Sóller. A narrow trail picks its way through pine and holm oak woods, zigzagging downhill and crossing the Ma10 several times. After 2¾ to three hours, you reach **3 Fornalutx**, one of the Tramuntana's prettiest hill towns. From here, follow the **4 Camí Binibassí** past almond terraces and the municipal cemetery. A cobbled trail leads through olive groves and narrows on the approach to the hamlet of Binibassí. A bend right brings you to a gravel road, which becomes a footpath. Turn left at the house, following a stream, then veer right onto a road. At a Y-junction, continue straight to reach **5 Camí de ses Marjades**, with lovely views over citrus groves to Sóller below. Head left downhill, traverse the Pont de Can Rave bridge and bear right onto the Camí des Maurterar to return to the football pitch.

Sa Fàbrica de Gelats ICE CREAM €

(Avinguda de Cristòfol Colom 13; ice cream per scoop €1.20; ⏱9am-10pm Jul & Aug, shorter hours rest of year) Legendary ice cream. Among the 40 or so trays of locally made flavours, those concocted from fresh orange or lemon juice are outstanding. There's a small patio with a handful of tables.

Ca'l Bisbe MALLORCAN €€

(⏱971 63 12 28; www.hotelcalbisbe.com/restaurante; Carrer del Bisbe Nadal 10; menus €29.50-38.50; ⏱8-10.30pm Mar-Oct) An old olive mill has been reincarnated into this restaurant, where you eat below heavy wood beams in the lantern-lit dining room or on the poolside terrace. The menu transcends the norm with refined dishes like slow-cooked cod with calamari noodles and black-olive-crusted lamb with basil risotto, all expertly matched with local wines.

Ca'n Boqueta MEDITERRANEAN €€

(⏱971 63 83 98; Gran Via 43; 3-/5-course menu €15/29.50; ⏱1-3.15pm & 7.45-10.15pm Tue-Sat, 1-3.15pm Sun) A tastefully converted townhouse bistro, with art on the walls, beamed ceilings and a garden patio, Ca'n Boqueta offers creative cooking with a seasonal touch. Starters like cherry gazpacho and scallops with white zucchini cream are a delicious lead to mains like Mallorcan black pork with tangy orange sauce.

Casa Alvaro TAPAS €€

(⏱871 709315; Carrer del Vicari Pastor 17; tapas €4.50-7, mains €16-24.50; ⏱1-4pm & 6-11pm) Scoot down a cobbled lane off the main plaza to reach Casa Alvaro, which pulls off its minimalist-traditional bodega look with ease. Under the beams you can dig into the superb tapas the jovial staff bring to the table: crispy calamari, tender rabbit, artichoke hearts and the like. Pair with a decent bottle of Mallorcan wine and enjoy!

★ Béns d'Avall SEAFOOD €€€

(⏱971 63 23 81; www.bensdavall.com; Urbanització Costa Deià, off Carretera Sóller-Deià; tasting menus €54-75; ⏱1-3.30pm & 7.30-10pm Wed-Sun, 7.30-10pm Tue) From its cliff-top perch overlooking the sea, this restaurant's romantic terrace is pop-the-question-at-sunset stuff. Not only that, it's the home turf of Benet Vicens, one of the island's foremost chefs. The nouvelle Balearic-style tasting menu goes with the seasons, but might include taste sensations like Sóller prawn carpaccio and fruit-filled suckling pig slow-cooked to crackling perfection. Find Béns d'Avall 7km west of Sóller on the road to Deià.

🛍 Shopping

Ben Calçat SHOES

(www.bencalcat.es; Carrer de Sa Lluna 74; ⏱9.30am-8.30pm Mon-Fri, to 1.30pm Sat) This is the place to come for authentic Mallorcan handcrafted *porqueras*, shoes made from recycled car tyres. The funky bowling-shoe designs in rainbow-bright colours won't appeal to everyone, but this is very Mallorca. Prices start at around €54.

Fet a Sóller FOOD

(www.fetasoller.com; Carrer de Romaguera 12; ⏱10am-8pm May-Oct, shorter hours rest of year) Fet a Sóller is an altogether different culinary experience. Mallorcan products, primarily from Sóller, line the shelves with olive oils, wines, almonds, jams, figs in cognac, charcuterie and balsamic vinegar made from Sóller oranges.

Arte Artesanía JEWELLERY

(www.arteartesania.com; Carrer de Sa Lluna 43; ⏱10.30am-8pm Mon-Fri, to 3pm Sat) A dynamic artistic space, Arte Artesania is at once classy and avant-garde, with its designer jewellery and small range of paintings, ceramics and sculpture. They're the work of Spanish and international artisan-designers and exhibitions are often hosted here.

ℹ Information

Tourist office (⏱971 63 80 08; www.visit-soller.com; Plaça d'Espanya 15; ⏱9.45am-4.15pm Mon-Fri, 9am-1pm Sat) In an old train carriage beside the station.

ℹ Getting There & Away

BUS

Bus 211 shoots up the Ma11 road from Palma to Sóller (€3.50, 30 minutes, up to five daily). Bus 210 takes the long way to/from Palma (€3.50) via Deià and Valldemossa (€2, 40 to 50 minutes). A local service connects Sóller with Fornalutx (€1.50, 15 minutes, two to four daily) via Biniaraix.

CAR & MOTORCYCLE

When coming from Palma, you have the option of taking the tunnel (€5.05 toll per car and €2 per motorbike) or adding 7km to the trip and taking the switchbacks up to the pass with some great views back down towards Palma on the way.

TRAIN

The Palma–Sóller train (p77) is a highlight.

Port de Sóller

Sóller's outlet to the sea is a quintessential Mallorcan fishing and yachting harbour, arrayed around an almost perfectly enclosed bay. In mid-2007 millions of euros were poured into sprucing up the port. Even so, as with all such places, the atmosphere wavers between classy and crass. The architecture reflects French and even Puerto Rican influences, as these were the two main destination countries of many Mallorcan emigrants, some of whom returned with cash and imported tastes.

◉ Sights

The bay is shaped something like a jellyfish and shadowed by a pleasant, pedestrianised and restaurant-lined esplanade. It makes for pleasant strolling, especially around the northern end where the heart of the original town is gathered together.

The beaches are OK, although hardly the island's best. The pick of the crop is **Platja d'en Repic** at the southern end of the bay, not least because it's nicely removed from the streams of passers-by. The same can't be said for **Platja d'es Port**, which is alongside the marina.

🏃 Activities

Tramuntana Tours   ADVENTURE SPORTS
(☑ 971 63 27 99; www.tramuntanatours.com; Passeig Es Travès 12; bicycle rental per day €12-30, 3hr sea-kayaking excursion €50; ☺ 9am-7.30pm Mar-Oct) This excellent gear shop and activity-tours operator right on the waterfront is the place to come for sea kayaking and bicycle hire. It can also arrange guided hikes into the Serra de Tramuntana, canyoning, mountain biking, boat charters and deep-sea fishing. There's another office in Sóller.

Barcos Azules   BOAT TOUR
(☑ 971 63 01 70; www.barcosazules.com; Passeig Es Travès 3; adult/child 1 way €15/8, return €25/13; ☺ hours vary) **FREE** Tour boats do trips to Sa Calobra (up to four times daily Monday to Saturday) and Cala Tuent (once a day Monday to Friday from Easter to June and in September). Get tickets at a booth on the dock.

Octopus Dive Centre   DIVING
(☑ 971 63 31 33; www.octopus-mallorca.com; Carrer del Canonge Oliver 13; 1 dive with/without own equipment €39/49, 2 dives €67/88; ☺ 8.30am-7pm mid-May–Oct) Dive with Octopus Dive Centre, a five-star English-run PADI centre with

first-rate equipment, courses (including the Bubblemaker for kids) and dives taking you from beginners to experts, shore to boat. It operates boat dives at about 30 sites along the Serra de Tramuntana coast.

Nàutics Sóller   SAILING
(☑ 609 354132; www.nauticsoller.com; Platja d'en Repic; 1-person sea kayak per hour/half-day/day €10/25/40, 2-person €15/35/60) This place rents out sea kayaks and can also arrange motorboat rental (half-day €120) and water-skiing (€110 per hour).

✖ Eating

The Port de Sóller waterfront is lined with eateries. Most serve fish and seafood but quality varies wildly. The following are safe bets.

★Es Passeig   MALLORCAN €€
(☑ 971 63 02 17; www.espasseig.com; Paseo de la Playa 8; mains €20-26, 4-course tasting menu €36.90; ☺ 12.30-10.30pm Mar-Oct) Grab one of the sea-facing terrace tables or try for one by the window at this artfully understated restaurant. The bright, imaginative dishes are richly inflected by the seasons and presented with a razor-sharp eye for detail – no coincidence given chef Marcel Battenberg's Michelin-star background.

Randemar   INTERNATIONAL €€
(☑ 971 63 45 78; www.randemar.com; Passeig Es Travès 16; mains €13.50-23; ☺ 12.30pm-midnight mid-Mar–early Nov) You could almost feel like you're turning up to a Great Gatsby–style party in this pseudo-waterfront mansion, but most rarely make it that far, preferring to linger over cocktails on the candlelit terrace to the backbeat of mellow music. The menu trots the globe from Thai curry to sushi, pizza to Peruvian ceviche.

Espléndido   MALLORCAN €€€
(☑ 971 63 18 50; www.esplendidohotel.com; Passeig Es Travès 5; mains €26-29; ☺ 8am-midnight daily) Cheerfully done out in nautical blues and whites, this slick, modern bistro resides on Port de Sóller's waterfront promenade. The menu has a fishy angle, with simple mains like grilled tuna and plump Sóller *gambas* taking centre stage. The three-course lunch is a steal at €15.

🍷 Drinking

Like any Mallorcan harbourside town where yacht masts crowd the skyline, summer evenings are long and happy – you could easily take up residence in a cafe-bar-restaurant terrace by the port or along Passeig de Sa Platja in the afternoon and find yourself still there in the wee small hours. There are plenty of lively bars, but few have anything to distinguish them from the rest.

ℹ Information

Tourist office (☑ 971 63 30 42; Carrer del Canonge Oliver 10; ⊘ 9am-3.15pm Mon-Fri Apr-Oct) The tourist office is right in the heart of the town, near the bus terminus.

ℹ Getting There & Away

Most buses to Sóller terminate in Port de Sóller. If driving, you must choose between going to the centre (take the tunnel) or the Platja d'en Repic side (follow the signs). The *tranvías* (trams) to Sóller run along the waterfront. Several car-rental offices line Passeig Es Través.

Biniaraix

From Sóller it's a pleasant 2km drive, pedal or stroll through narrow laneways to the sweet hamlet of Biniaraix, with the brooding Tramuntana peering over its shoulder. Sights are few – hence the reason most people continue on to neighbouring Fornalutx – but there's something special about pausing in a place where most visitors arrive on foot, or along narrow country lanes lined with drystone walls. The village started life as an Arab *alquería* (farmstead), and has a shady central square, Plaça de Sa Concepció. The walking trail to Biniaraix is well signposted from the centre of Sóller.

Fornalutx

There are two ways to reach Fornalutx, one of Mallorca's loveliest stone-built villages in the shadow of high mountains. The first is along a narrow, scenic route from Biniaraix, passing through terraced groves crowded with orange and lemon trees. The other is the road that drops down off the Ma10, with aerial views of the village's stone houses and terracotta roofs.

Either way, Fornalutx is postcard pretty, and the effect is heightened as you draw near, with green shuttered windows, flower boxes, well-kept gardens and flourishing citrus groves. Many of the houses are owned by expats, but it's a far cry from the (comparative) bustle of Sóller. Like Biniaraix, Fornalutx is believed to have its origins as an Arab *alquería*.

◎ Sights

Fornalutx rewards those who simply wander to get lost. Begin with the lanes around the central **Plaça d'Espanya** and pop into the **ajuntament** with its cool courtyard dominated by a palm tree. Outside, water gurgles cheerfully along one of several irrigation channels. You can follow the course of the town stream east past fine houses and thick greenery, or climb the stairs heading north out of the town from the **Església de la Nativitat de Nostra Senyora**.

✕ Eating

Fornalutx is liberally scattered with restaurants and cafes, most of which are located around central Sa Plaça or occupy shady roadside terraces about half a kilometre out of the centre on the Ma2121 road leading northeast out of town.

Es Turó   MALLORCAN €

(☑ 971 63 08 08; www.restaurante-esturo-fornalutx.com; Carrer Arbona-Colom 12; mains €9-19; ⊘ noon-10.30pm Fri-Wed) The front-row views over the village to the Tramuntana peaks steal the limelight at Es Turó, but the food is pretty good too. The menu is Mallorcan through and through, from *pa amb oli* to *arros brut* ('dirty rice') and nicely crisp *lechona* (suckling pig). Be sured to try the zingy juice, freshly squeezed from local oranges.

Ca'n Verdera   MALLORCAN €€

(☑ 971 63 82 03; www.canverdera.com; Carrer des Toros 1; mains €14-25; ⊘ 7.30-10.30pm mid-May–mid-Oct) Climb the stone steps to a candlelit terrace that plays up the romance as well as the extraordinary mountain views. Sunset is primetime viewing. The valley spreads scenically before you as you sample local flavours delivered with flair, along the lines of saffron ravioli and beautifully tender lamb confit with honey and rosemary.

🛍 Shopping

Tramuntana Gourmet   FOOD, WINE

(Carrer Arbona-Colom 4a; ⊘ 11am-8pm) Food products from the Serra de Tramuntana, with a few ring-ins from elsewhere on the island and the other Balearic Islands, are the staples at this fine little shop. There are free olive-oil tastings, besides a range of preserves, wines and unusual offerings, such as fig bread, available for purchase.

ℹ️ Getting There & Away

A local service connects Fornalutx with Sóller (€1.50, 15 minutes, two to four daily), via Biniaraix.

Road from Sóller to Alaró

A dramatic driving route winds its way south of Sóller. To begin with, climb the valley into the hills (the tunnel costs €5.05 and isn't as pretty) and enjoy the views to Palma as you follow the switchbacks on the other side. Before entering Bunyola and the towns that lie beyond, it's worth pausing to visit a grand reminder of Moorish Mallorca: the Jardins d'Alfàbia.

◎ Sights

★ Jardins d'Alfàbia   GARDENS
(www.jardinesdealfabia.com; Carretera de Sóller Km 17; adult/child €6.50/free; ⊙ 9.30am-6.30pm Mon-Sat Apr-Oct, 9.30am-5.30pm Mon-Fri, 9.30am-1pm Sat Nov, closed Dec-Feb) The Jardins d'Alfàbia reside in the shadow of the rugged Serra d'Alfàbia mountain range stretching east of Sóller. Here an endearingly faded *finca* with a baroque facade, which looks like it was stripped from a Florentine basilica, is surrounded by gardens, citrus groves, palm trees and a handful of farmyard animals. The murmur of water gurgling along irrigation canals hints at the place's past as the residence of an Arab *wāli* (viceroy), it's no coincidence that in the Quran, paradise is a garden.

Little remains of the original Arab house, except for the extraordinary polychromatic coffered ceiling, fashioned from pine and ilex, immediately inside the building's entrance. It is bordered by inscriptions in Arabic and is thought to have been made around 1170. To the right of the inner courtyard is the *tafona* (large oil press), a mix of Gothic, Renaissance and baroque styles. The rambling house is laden with period furniture and a 1200-volume library.

Bunyola

This drowsy town, known for olive oil and its *palo* (herbal liquor) distillery, resides at the foot of lush terraced hillsides and the wild grey peaks of the Tramuntana. The rickety wooden train that trundles between Palma and Soller stops here. It's a fabulous base for rock climbing and – back at ground level – observing Mallorcan village life in the central square, Sa Plaça, which hosts a small Saturday-morning market.

◎ Sights & Activities

Església de Sant Mateu   CHURCH
(Carrer de l'Església 2; ⊙ Mass) Next to the main square in the heart of town, the Església de Sant Mateu was built in 1230 but largely redone in 1756. You'll only be allowed to peek inside during Mass.

Sa Gubia   ROCK CLIMBING
Just west of Bunyola, where the foothills of the Tramuntana thin to the flatlands around Palma, rises this magnificent rock amphitheatre – a holy grail to climbers, who come to play on 125 multipitch routes graded 4 to 8, including some excellent, fully bolted long climbs. The Cara Oeste (West Face) ranks as one of Europe's most impressive limestone walls. **Rock and Ride** (☏ 0664 734512; www.rockandride-mallorca.com) offer guided climbs.

✖️ Eating

Ca'n Topa   MALLORCAN €
(☏ 971 14 84 67; www.cantopa.com; Careterra Palma a Soller Km 22.1; snacks €5-10; ⊙ hours vary) 'It's all downhill from here' is the strapline of Ca'n Topa – not a reference to the food, but to its high-on-a-hill location on the windy mountain road to Sóller. It's a much-loved pitstop of cyclists, who love its languid rhythm, poolside deck, snacks (pizzas, *bocadillos* and the like) and ice-cold drinks after tearing around the Tramuntana.

Orient

Orient is one of the loveliest little hamlets on the island with its huddle of ochre houses clustered on a slight rise. A few houses seem to slide off as if they're an afterthought on the north side of the road.

🏃 Activities

The 9km road (the Ma2100) that wends northeast from Bunyola to Orient attracts swarms of lithe, lycra-clad cyclists. The first 5km is a promenade along a valley brushed with olive and cypress trees that slowly crests a plain and the **Coll d'Honor** (550m) before tumbling over the other side of a forested ridge. The next 2km of serried switchbacks flatten out on the run into Orient. All the way, the **Serra d'Alfàbia** is in sight to the north.

✕ Eating

Mandala INTERNATIONAL €€
(☑971 61 52 85; Carrer Nou 1; mains €17-25; ☺8.30-10.30pm Tue-Sun Jun–mid-Sep, shorter hours rest of year & closed Dec-Feb; ☲) Spicy smells drift enticingly from this Swiss-run den of fusion cooking, run with love and a pinch of creativity. Snag a table on the patio for French classics like steak tartar and bouillabaisse (Provençal fish stew), or Asian takes like Thai prawn curry followed by a Yogi tea gourmand with a trio of mini desserts. Bookings are essential.

Alaró

Perkily topped by castle ruins, Alaró is pleasantly sleepy and rewards those who linger. Head for Plaça de la Vila, flanked by the Casa de la Vila (town hall), parish church and a couple of cafes. The square springs to life at its Saturday-morning market. Cafes also congregate around Carrer Petit and Carrer de Jaume Rosselló.

◉ Sights

★Castell d'Alaró CASTLE
(off Carretera Alaró-Bunyola) Perched at an improbable, almost comical angle on a gigantic fist of rock, Castell d'Alaró is one of the most rewarding castle climbs on the island. The ruins are all that remain of the last redoubt of Christian warriors who could only be starved out by Muslim conquerors around 911, eight years after the latter had invaded the island. The views, from Palma to Badia de Alcúdia, are something special.

If the two-hour walk doesn't appeal, you can cover most of the climb by car. The first 4.2km to nearby Es Verger restaurant are paved but have their fair share of potholes. The road deteriorates (but should be OK if it hasn't rained – ask at the restaurant for the current state of the road) for a further 1.2km beyond the restaurant to a parking area at the base of a path that leads (in 15 minutes) to the ruins. Once there, you'll see several stone arched doors and parts of the walls of what was once clearly a major fortress.

Another minute's walk uphill brings you to the **Ermita de la Mare de Déu del Refugi**, a decrepit 17th-century chapel that locals still visit to give thanks for miraculous events. If you can't bear to leave, bed down at the Refugi S'Hostatgeria (p174).

THE ROAD TO ALARÓ

One of the most scenic ways to approach Alaró is on the Ma210 from Orient, which takes you through bucolic scenery of cypresses and orchards of fig, olive and almond. The road meanders about 4km northeast before taking a leisurely turn around the outriders of the mighty rock plug **Puig d'Alaró** (822m) that thrusts up from the valley floor. Its identical twin to the east is **Puig de S'Alcadena** (815m). Ripped apart by a geological fault millions of years ago, these twin peaks are one of Mallorca's most distinctive images. To the south you can make out the flat interior of **Es Pla** (The Plain).

✕ Eating

★Es Verger SPANISH €€
(☑971 18 21 26; Camí des Castell; mains €8-16; ☺9am-9pm Tue-Sun; ☲) On the zigzagging road up to Castell d'Alaró, this gloriously rustic haunt is well worth the trek, bike ride or gear-crunching ascent. The sheep hanging out in the car park are a menu giveaway. In his *Mediterranean Escapes* series of books, UK-based chef Rick Stein praises the lamb as the moistest he has ever tasted – and right he is. Antonia fires up the wood oven every morning to slow cook the lamb for three-and-a-half hours in beer, herbs, carrots and onions until meltingly tender.

Traffic MALLORCAN €€
(☑971 87 91 17; www.canxim.com; Plaça de la Vila 8, Hotel Can Xim; mains €12-22; ☺12.15-5.15pm & 8-11.30pm Mon & Thu-Sun, 8-11pm Wed) The pick of the places on Plaça de la Vila, this countrified restaurant rolls out Mallorcan specialities with a few innovative twists. Meats such as rabbit and suckling pig are defintely the strong point, but the cod with *sobrassada* and honey is terrific too. Choose between the terrace and the beamed, tiled interior.

❶ Getting There & Away

Buses and trains running between Palma and Sóller stop at Bunyola (the bus stop is at Sa Plaça, and the train station a short walk west of the centre). From there local bus 221 runs twice a day east to Orient (€2, 30 minutes). This is a microbus service and you need to book a seat in advance by calling ☑617 365365.

The Palma–Inca train calls at the Consell-Alaró train station (20 to 30 minutes), where it connects with local bus 320 for Alaró (15 minutes).

Cala de Sa Calobra & Cala Tuent

Taking in the wide open sea, the island's highest mountains and plunging cliffs, the Ma10 road from Sóller to the Monestir de Lluc is one of Mallorca's great drives – or cycle rides, if you are that way inclined. The first stop is the **Mirador de Ses Barques**, about 6km out of Sóller, with phenomenal views all the way down to Port de Sóller; the cafe here serves great freshly squeezed orange juice, as well as snacks. The road unravels eastward to cross the Serra de Son Torrella range, and 16km out of Sóller a side road leads north up to the island's highest point, **Puig Major** (1445m). The peak is off limits, however, as this is Air Force territory and topped by a communications base. From here it wends its way around two dazzling patches of liquid blue, the Cúber and Gorg Blau dams.

All of which is just a tantalising prelude for the hairpin-riddled 12km helter-skelter of a road down to Sa Calobra. Whether you're swooning over the giddy ravine views, gulping as a coach squeezes through an impossibly narrow cleft in the rock, or aping Tour de France winner Bradley Wiggins with a thigh-burning pedal to the top (he does it in 26 minutes, for the record), this spectacularly serpentine road, which branches north off the Ma10, is pure drama. Carved through the rock and skirting narrow ridges as it unfurls to the coast, it is the feat of Italian engineer Antonio Paretti, who built it in 1932; its twists and turns were inspired by tying a tie, some say (whatever else?).

If you come in summer you won't be alone. Legions of buses and fleets of pleasure boats disgorge battalions of tourists. It's a different world to Sa Calobra on a quiet, bright midwinter morning. From the northern end of the road a short trail leads around the coast to a rocky river gorge, the **Torrent de Pareis**, and a small white-pebble cove with fabulous (but usually crowded) swimming spots.

If you want to skip the crowds, follow a turn-off west, some 2km before reaching Sa Calobra, to head to Cala Tuent, a tranquil emerald green inlet in the shadow of Puig Major. The broad pebble beach is backed by a couple of houses and a great green bowl of vegetation that climbs up the mountain flanks. About 200m back from the beach, a turn-off leads 1.5km to Es Vergeret.

✗ Eating

Es Vergeret   MALLORCAN **€€**
(☑ 971 51 71 05; www.esvergeret.com; Camí de Sa Figuera Vial 21; mains €10-19; ⊙ 10am-4.30pm Mar-Oct) A narrow country lane from Cala Tuent passes sheep farms and olive groves to reach this glorious old *finca*, where the view (ah, the view!) takes in the full sweep of the bay and mountains. The terrace is a cracking spot for a lazy lunch of paella, grilled fish or lamb chops. Ring ahead for a table, especially in summer.

❶ Getting There & Away

One bus a day (bus 355, Monday to Saturday, May to October) comes from Ca'n Picafort (9am) via Alcúdia, Cala Sant Vicenç, Pollença and the Monestir de Lluc. It returns at 3pm. The whole trip takes three hours and 50 minutes to Sa Calobra (with a one-hour stop at the Monestir de Lluc) and 2½ hours on the return leg. From Ca'n Picafort you pay €9.05 one way. Boats make excursions to Sa Calobra and Cala Tuent from Port de Sóller.

CANYONING THE SERRA DE TRAMUNTANA

The wild limestone peaks and boulder-strewn gorges of the central Serra de Tramuntana between Valldemossa and Sa Calobra create the ideal backdrop for canyoneers. By far the most challenging (rated 5–6, for experts only) is the 2.5km Gorg Blau-Sa Fosca, one of Europe's most dramatic canyons, descending north and then northeast from the dam of the same name. It's a tough route, with drops, scrambling, freezing water and a 400m stretch in total darkness to negotiate. An easier alternative (though by no means a walk in the park) is the 8km Torrent de Pareis, surrounded by majestic rock walls. Either way, a local guide is essential; try Experience Mallorca (p127), Tramuntana Tours (p104) or Món d'Aventura (p111).

Monestir de Lluc & Around

Back in the 13th century, a local shepherd claimed to have seen an image of the Vir-

THE PATHS OF PILGRIMS

Like so many before him, Antoni Gaudí made the pigrimage to the **Monestir de Lluc** in April 1908, leaving a donation of 25 pesetas. In October that same year he returned, this time with his protégé Joan Rubió in tow. He redesigned the church in the same baroque style as the chancel and oversaw the creation of the stone monuments that grace the **Pujol des Misteris** (Hill of the Mysteries), which rises behind the monastery complex.

An old stone trail, partly shaded by holm oaks, leads up this hill, which recounts the mysteries of the rosaries. Taking in monuments and three bronze reliefs, hidden in the twilight of a rock overhang, the trail is a place for peaceful contemplation. From the cross at the top, linger for grandstand views of the valley and the boulder-strewn peaks of the Tramuntana. The walk takes around half an hour to complete.

Numerous walking routes leave from the monastery. One is a challenging 11km, five-hour circuit of **Puig de Massanella** (1365m), Mallorca's second-highest peak, with sensational views from its summit. Another is a 9km, 3½ hour circuit of **Puig Tomir** (1103m), a stiff, rocky ascent into the lonely heights of the Tramuntana, where you may see vultures and falcons. Lluc is also a stop on the long-distance **GR221** between Sant Elm and Pollença.

For the true spirit of a blister-footed pilgrim, join thousands of Mallorcans on the **Marxa des Güell a Lluc a Peu** (http://desguellallucapeu.es), a 42km, all-night march on the first Saturday in August from the Plaça Güell in Palma to the Monestir de Lluc, taking in farmland, hill towns and the Serra de Tramuntana by torchlight.

gin Mary in the sky. Later, a similar image appeared on a rock. Another story says that a statuette of the Virgin was found here and taken to the nearest hamlet, Escorca. The next day it was back where it had been found. Three times it was taken to Escorca and three times it returned. A chapel was built near the site to commemorate the miracle, possibly around 1268. The religious sanctuary came later. Since then thousands of pilgrims have come every year to pay homage to the 14th-century (and thus not the original) **statue of the Virgin of Lluc**, known as La Moreneta (the Black Madonna) because of the statuette's dark complexion.

◎ Sights

★**Monestir de Lluc**   MONASTERY, GARDENS
(www.lluc.net; Plaça dels Peregrins; monastery & gardens free, museum adult/child €2/free, Lluc ticket €3; ◎10am-5pm) Entered via a cloistered garden, the monastery is a huge austere complex, dating mostly from the 17th to 18th centuries. Off the central courtyard is the late-Renaissance basilica, containing a fine altarpiece by Jaume Blanquer and the Virgin Mary statuette. The church was given an ornate, baroque-style revamp in the early 20th century, based on plans drawn up by Gaudí. If you're lucky, you might hear the Els Escolanets (also known as Els Blauets, the Little Blues, because of the soutane they wear), the monastery's boarding school boys choir. This institution dates to the early 16th century.

Centre d'Informació
Serra de Tramuntana   INTERPRETATION CENTRE
(☑971 51 70 83; www.serradetramuntana.net; Monestir de Lluc; adult/child €2/free; ◎9am-4.30pm) Opposite the monastery complex, this interpretation centre has audiovisual displays and a small museum providing background on the Serra de Tramuntana. Here you can brush up on regional flora, fauna and bird species such as the Eleonora's falcon and Balearic shearwater, and learn about farming in the mountains. The centre has a stock of multilingual leaflets detailing walks in the area, and the friendly staff can arrange camping in the grounds of Lluc for €5 per night.

✗ Eating

Sa Fonda   MALLORCAN €€
(☑971 51 70 22; Plaça del Lledoner; mains €9.50-18; ◎8.30am-9.15pm) Housed in the expanded pilgrims' refectory, this is a historic spot for lunch or a light bite below marble arches and wood beams. The all-Mallorcan menu stars dishes such as *frit Mallorquí* (a tasty lamb offal and vegetable fry-up), suckling pig and *pa amb oli*.

❶ Getting There & Away

Up to two buses a day (May to October) run from Ca'n Picafort to the Monestir de Lluc (€6.30, 1¼ hours) on their way to Sóller and Port de Sóller. From Palma, two all-stops buses (bus 330 and 354) to Inca continue to Lluc via Caimari from Monday to Saturday (one on Sunday).

Northern Mallorca

Best Places to Eat

➡ Mirador de La Victòria (p126)

➡ Restaurante Jardín (p123)

➡ Manzanas y Peras (p114)

➡ Ca'n Cuarassa (p118)

➡ S'Arc (p121)

Best Places to Stay

➡ Posada de Lluc (p175)

➡ Hotel Formentor (p176)

➡ Can Tem (p176)

➡ Hostal Los Pinos (p175)

➡ Pensión Bellavista (p175)

Why Go?

Northern Mallorca is the island's heart and soul, bundling coastal drama, cultured towns with spirited fiestas, a twin-set of white-sand bays and an exciting portfolio of adventure sports into one enticing package.

The Serra de Tramuntana is at its most fabulous where the range culminates on Cap de Formentor, flicking out into the Med like a dragon's tail. The road that wraps around its clifftops elicits gasps of wonder from drivers and cyclists. Across the water, the pine-forested peninsula of Cap des Pinar is hiking heaven. Elsewhere, kitesurfers, cliff-jumpers, scuba divers, cavers and paragliders harness its unique coastscapes and steady breezes.

Resorts here have a low-key, kid-friendly vibe. Inland, towns have retained an authentic Mallorcan air: from medieval-walled Alcúdia to Pollença, with its cafe-rimmed plazas, pilgrim trails and live-to-party summer festivals.

When to Go

Some of the beach resorts barely have a pulse until May or after October (Cala Sant Vicenç, for instance), and the best beach weather is from June to August. Pollença is one big fiesta in August. Yet, our favourite time to visit is spring and autumn – migrating birds flock to the Parc Natural de S'Albufera, the roads are quieter (especially out along Cap de Formentor), Pollença's Good Friday celebration is captivating, and Alcúdia hosts a terrific market in early October. Cooler weather is better for hitting the walking trails, too.

POLLENÇA & AROUND

Pollença

POP 16,190 / ELEV 41M

On a late summer afternoon, when its stone houses glow in the fading light, cicadas strike up their tentative drone and the burble of chatter floats from cafe terraces lining the Plaça Major, Pollença is like the Mallorca you always hoped you would discover. Pollença's postcard looks and vaguely bohemian air have drawn artists, writers and luminaries from Winston Churchill to Agatha Christie over the years. Saunter through its backstreets lined with galleries and boutiques or pull up a ringside chair on the square at sundown to watch the world go by and you too will be smitten.

◉ Sights & Activities

★ **Calvari**   PILGRIMAGE SITE
(Carrer del Calvari) They don't call it Calvari (Calvary) for nothing. Some pilgrims do it on their knees, but plain walking up the 365 cypress-lined steps from the town centre to the 18th-century hilltop chapel, the **Oratori del Calvari**, is penance enough. This may not be a stairway to heaven, but there are soul-stirring views to savour back over the town's mosaic of terracotta rooftops and church spires to the Tramuntana beyond.

**Església de la Mare de
Déu dels Àngels**   CHURCH
(Plaça Major; ⊙ 11am-1pm & 3-5pm Jun-Aug, shorter hours rest of year) A church was first raised on this site in Gothic style shortly after the conquest in 1229, but was given a complete makeover in the 18th century, so what you see today is mostly baroque. The unusually simple rough-sandstone facade is a lovely backdrop to the square. Lit by a rose window, the interior has an unusual barrel-vaulted ceiling and extravagant ceiling frescoes.

Museu de Pollença   MUSEUM
(Carrer de Guillem Cifre de Colonya; adult/child €1.50/free; ⊙ 10am-1pm & 5.30-8.30pm Tue-Sat Jun-Sep, shorter hours rest of year) This museum's star attraction is the 17th-century baroque cloister of the Convent de Sant Domingo, in which the museum is housed, and a bright Buddhist Kalachakra mandala donated by the Dalai Lama to the town in 1990. Other exhibits include archaeological finds from the surrounding area and some Gothic altarpieces.

Museu Martí Vicenç   MUSEUM
(www.martivicens.org; Carrer del Calvari 10; ⊙ 10.30am-2pm & 5-8pm Mon & Wed-Sat, 10.30am-2pm Sun) **FREE** A short way up the Calvari steps is the Museu Martí Vicenç. The weaver and artist Martí Vicenç Alemany (1926–95) bought this property, once part of a giant Franciscan monastery that also included the nearby former **Església de Monti-Sion**, in the 1950s. His works, mostly canvases and textiles, are strewn around several rooms.

Casa-Museu Dionís Bennàssar   MUSEUM
(www.museudionisbennassar.com; Carrer de Roca 14; adult/child €2/free; ⊙ 10am-2pm Tue-Sun mid-Mar–Oct) Casa-Museu Dionís Bennàssar, the home of local artist Dionís Bennàssar (1904–67), hosts a permanent collection of his works. Downstairs are early etchings, watercolours and oils, depicting mostly local scenes. Works on the other floors range from a series on fish that is strangely reminiscent of Miquel Barceló's efforts in Palma's cathedral, to a series of nudes and portraits of dancing girls.

Món d'Aventura   ADVENTURE SPORTS
(☑ 971 53 52 48; www.mondaventura.com; Plaça Vella 8; canyoning €40-50; ⊙ 10am-2pm & 5-9pm Mon-Fri, 10am-2pm Sat & Sun) Canyoning, caving, kayaking, climbing, coasteering, hiking – you name the pulse-racing sport, Món d'Aventura has it covered. This is one of the most repubtable adventure sports operators on the north coast.

✦ Festivals & Events

Davallament   RELIGIOUS
(⊙ Mar or Apr) At this haunting yet entrancing re-enactment of the Passion Play, on GOod Friday the body of Christ is solemnly paraded down the 365 steps of Calvari by torchlight. It is one of the island's most moving Easter celebrations.

Festival de Pollença   CULTURAL
(www.festivalpollenca.com; ⊙ late Jul-Aug) Orchestras, exhibitions and film screenings come to the atmospheric Sant Domingo cloister for this summer arts festival.

Festes de la Patrona   HISTORICAL
(⊙ late Jul-early Aug) Dress up as a swashbuckling pirate or all in white and throw yourself into the crowd to celebrate the big and boisterous Festes de la Patrona, with mock battles between the Moros i Cristians (Moors and Christians; see p116) to mark the siege and attack by Saracen pirates in 1550.

NORTHERN MALLORCA POLLENÇA

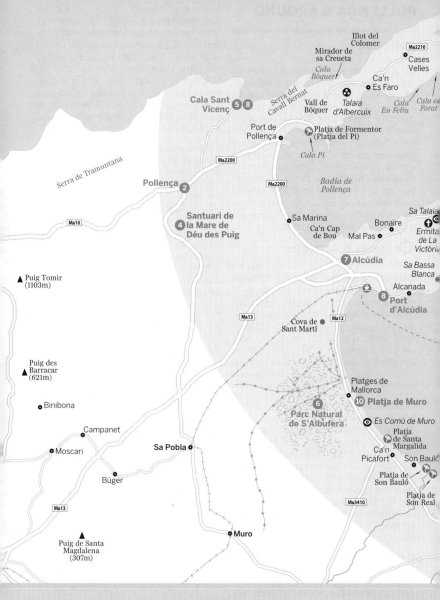

Northern Mallorca Highlights

1 Feel your jaw drop as low as the cliffs on coastal thriller **Cap de Formentor** (p119).

2 Count your blessings pilgrim-style on the 365-step Calvari in **Pollença** (p111).

3 Hike to **Penya Rotja** (p125) to see the north coast reduced to postcard format.

4 Lift your spi rits with sensational views at **Santuari**

de la Mare de Déu des Puig (p118).

5 Snorkel in translucent water and eat just-caught seafood in **Cala Sant Vicenç** (p116).

Cala Figuera

Cap de Formentor

① Moll del Patronet

▲ Fumat (334m)

Cala Murta   Cala Gossalba

MEDITERRANEAN SEA

N   0 _____ 5 km
    0 _____ 2.5 miles

Cap des Pinar

③ **Penya Rotja**

⑨ Platja des **Coll Baix**

Fundación Yannick y Ben Jakober

Badia d'Alcúdia

Cap Ferrutx

Cala Fosca

Punta des Caló   ▲ Talaia Moreia (432m)

Es Caló   S'Arenal et des Verger

Betlem ○   S'Alquera Vella d'Avall

Ma3331   ⊕ Parc Natural de la Península de Llevant

Necròpolis de Son Real   Illot dels Porros

inca Pública de Son Real   Son Serra de Marina   Platja de Sa Canova (S'Arenal)   Colònia de Sant Pere   ⊕ Ermita de Betlem

's Figueral de Son Real   ⊗ Talayot de Son Serra   ○ S'Estanyol   Son Morell Vell

Ma3333

⑥ Birdspot in the rushes of **Parc Natural de S'Albufera** (p126).

⑦ Wing back to Roman and medieval times exploring **Alcúdia** (p120).

⑧ Marvel at Mallorca's finest seascapes on a boat trip from **Port d'Alcúdia** (p123) to **Cala Sant Vicenç** (p116).

⑨ Descend on foot to the gorgeously remote **Platja des Coll Baix** (p124).

⑩ Stretch out on the powder-white sands of **Platja de Muro** (p126).

Pollença

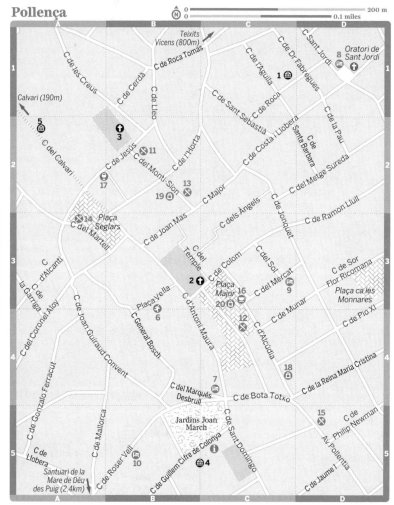

La Fira   MARKET
(⊙ 2nd Sun in Nov) A massive market held
in the Convent de Sant Domingo and elsewhere around town.

✗ Eating

★ **Manzanas y Peras**   TAPAS €
(☎ 971 53 22 92; www.manzanasyperas.es; Carrer
del Martell 6; tapas tasting menus €25; ⊙ 10am-
4pm & 7-11pm Mon-Sat, 10am-4pm Sun; 🛜 🖘)
Tiny but brilliant, Manzanas y Peras (Apples
and Pears) is a friendly oasis next to the Calvari steps, with tables set under trees lit by
fairy lights. The tapas menu is a real feast,

with taste sensations like crostini topped
with melted goat's cheese, blueberry jelly
and walnuts, and chicken cooked in Moroc-
can spices with dates. Kids have their own
dedicated menu (€11).

La Placeta   SPANISH €€
(☎ 971 53 12 18; Carrer Sant Jordi 29; mains €13.50-
16; ⊙ 12.30-3pm & 7.30-11pm Tue-Sun; 🖘) Everyone has been raving about La Placeta at
Hotel Sant Jordi recently, whether for its
pretty alfresco setting on the square, child-
friendly waiters or no-nonsense home cooking. Dishes as simple as prawns sautéed
with artichokes and lamb roasted in its own

Pollença

juices and Madeira wine reveal true depth of flavour.

Il Giardino   ITALIAN €€
(☑971 53 43 02; www.giardinopollensa.com; Plaça Major 11; mains €17-24; ☺9am-11pm Mar-Oct; 🖼) For our money, this is the pick of the restaurants on Plaça Major, with a fine terrace and upbeat service. The menu whispers longingly of *bella Italia*, with mains like wild mushroom ravioli and fresh tuna topped with avocado chilli and chives hitting the mark. Its adjacent patisserie and chocolate shop is a delectable post-dinner detour.

Cantonet   MEDITERRANEAN €€
(☑971 53 04 29; Carrer del Monti-Sion 20; mains €11-19; ☺12.30-3pm & 7-11pm) As day slides into dusk, this restaurant terrace in front of the Església de Monti-Sion is totally entrancing, with views reaching across the old town rooftops to the Puig de Maria beyond. The food has Italian undertones: mussels in oregano sauce, lamb slow-cooked in

thyme and honey, *malloreddus* (Sardinian gnocchi-shaped pasta) and the like. There's a mean tiramisu, too.

Restaurant Clivia   MALLORCAN €€
(☑971 53 36 35; Avinguda Pollentia 7; mains €12-23; ☺1-3pm & 7-10.30pm Thu-Tue) More contemporary than most, Clivia gathers around an inner courtyard, where a mosaic of pine panels and bell-shaped lights create an abstract artwork. The food (especially the fish) is prepared with panache. Prawn carpaccio with sweet red pepper is a delicious lead to the house speciality: wild sea bass steamed in malvasia wine.

La Font del Gall   MALLORCAN €€
(☑971 53 03 96; Carrer del Monti-Sion 4; mains €7.50-17, set menus €25-35; ☺6.30-11pm daily, plus noon-3pm Mon, Thu, Fri & Sun) You'll be lucky to bag a spot on the pavement terrace at La Font del Gall in summer. The chef keeps it simple, with spot-on Mallorcan dishes like crisp, slow-roasted suckling pig and seafood paella. Our only gripe is that portions can be small, though that means you have room for dessert!

🍷 Drinking & Nightlife

Club Pollença   CAFE, BAR
(Plaça Major 10; ☺7am-midnight) Observe life in all its guises over drinks and tapas on the terrace of this rambling colonial-flavoured cafe, which first opened its doors in 1910. Grab a front-row seat and enjoy.

U Gallet   BAR
(Carrer de Jesús 40; ☺7pm-2am Sun-Thu, to 4am Fri & Sat) Known also to locals as the 'Gallito' (cockerel) and full of enticingly cosy nooks, this drinking hole spills out onto a pavement terrace in summer. British owner and bartender Neil mixes great cocktails and G&Ts. The vibe is chilled, the music upbeat.

🛍 Shopping

Pollença is filled with engaging little boutiques and its shopping is – bar Palma – the best on the island.

★Hito   ARTS & CRAFTS
(www.hitohome.com; Carrer del Calvari 10; ☺10.30am-2pm & 5-8pm Mon & Wed-Sat, 10.30am-2pm Sun) A gallery, designer homeware store and artist-in-residence project rolled into one, Hito is run by New York expat jewellers Gillian Conroy and Danica Wilcox. On display are eye-catching, one-of-a-kind local crafts and accessories, from Teixits Vicens'

NORTHERN MALLORCA POLLENÇA

fine *robes de llengües* (Mallorcan striped fabrics) to sheepskin baby booties and faux hunting trophies made of felt.

There are rotating art exhibitions upstairs, many of which have a contemporary slant, and downstairs you'll find the Museu Martí Vicenç (p111).

La Merceria ARTS & CRAFTS
(Carrer del Monti-Sion 3; ⊙10am-2pm & 5-9.30pm Tue-Fri, 10am-2pm Sat & Sun) This gloriously retro emporium merges vintage style with contemporary design. Among the unique trinkets and gifts are nostalgic sepia postcards of old Pollença, Barcelona fashion, handmade straw boaters for a dash of Gatsby glamour, idiosyncratic ceramics (we dig the watering-can dog and sardine lights), glassware, art and jewellery. Out back there's a fab collection of kids' books and clothing.

Sunday Market MARKET
(Plaça Major; ⊙8.30am-1pm Sun) Held year-round, Pollença's Sunday market is one of the largest and liveliest in Mallorca. Fruit, veg, cheese, wine, herbs and spices are concentrated in the Plaça Major, with handicrafts and other stalls taking over an ever-widening arc of surrounding streets.

Enseñat FOOD, WINE
(www.ensenyat.com; Carrer d'Alcúdia 5; ⊙8.30am-3pm & 4.30-8.30pm Mon-Sat, 8.30am-2pm Sun) Pick up Mallorcan wines, salts, preserves, cheeses, meats, including homemade *sobrassada* (paprika-flavoured cured pork sausage), and Sóller marmalade at this gourmet deli, in business since the 1940s.

Teixits Vicens HANDICRAFTS
(www.teixitsvicens.com; Ronda Can Berenguer; ⊙9am-8pm Mon-Fri, 10am-2pm & 4-8pm Sat Apr-Sep, shorter hours rest of year) Artisans have been making the striped Mallorcan fabrics known as *robes de llengües* here at this family-run business since 1854, and the contemporary fabrics they turn out are faithful to traditional designs. Some of their works are on display at Hito (p115).

ⓘ Information

Tourist office (⊘971 53 50 77; www.pollensa. com; Carrer de Guillem Cifre de Colonya; ⊙8.30am-1.30pm & 2-4pm Mon-Fri, 10am-1pm Sun May-Oct, shorter hours rest of year) A mine of info on Pollença and its surrounds.

ⓘ Getting There & Away

From Palma, bus 340 heads nonstop for Pollença (€5.30, 45 minutes, up to 12 daily). It then continues on to Cala Sant Vicenç (€1.50, 20 minutes, six daily) and Port de Pollença (€1.50, 20 minutes, up to 30 daily).

Cala Sant Vicenç
POP 290

One of the loveliest little corners of the northern Mallorcan coast, Cala Sant Vicenç is arrayed around four jewel-like *cales* (coves) in a breach in the Serra de Tramuntana, with fine views across the turquoise waters northwest towards the sheer limestone cliffs of Cap de Formentor. The village is really only open for business from May to October.

🏖 Beaches

The first of the beaches, **Cala Barques**, is sandy until you hit the water, when you have to pick your way over rocks to reach submersion depth. Pretty (well, they're all pretty) **Cala Clara** is similar. **Cala Molins** is the biggest of the four, with a deep sandy strand and easy access into the shimmering waters of this tranquil inlet. **Cala Carbó**, around the headland, is the smallest and least visited. It doesn't take more than 20 minutes to walk the entire distance between the four.

MOORS & CHRISTIANS IN IMMORTAL COMBAT

August sees the staging in Pollença of one of the most colourful of Mallorca's festivals. This version of Moros i Cristians (Moors and Christians) celebrates a famous victory by townsfolk over a Moorish raiding party led by the infamous Turkish pirate Dragut (1500–65) in 1550. The 'battle' is the high point of the Festes de la Patrona (p111). Townsfolk dressed up as scimitar-waving Moorish pirates and pole-toting villagers engage in several mock encounters, to the thunder of drums and blunderbusses, around town on the afternoon of 2 August. The night before, the town centre is the scene of one almighty drinking spree, with folk thronging the bars and squares, and live concerts blaring through the night from 11pm. No wonder the following day's battles don't get started until 7pm! Spectacular fireworks conclude the festivities.

If you walk for 15 minutes along Carrer Temporal from behind Cala Clara and then down Carrer de Dionìs Bennàssar, you'll hit a rise with park benches and the **Coves de L'Alzineret**, seven funerary caves dug in pre-Talayotic times (c 1600 BC).

🏃 Activities

atemrausch ADVENTURE SPORTS
(📱622 122145; www.atemrausch.com; Carre Temporal 9; ☺10am-noon & 6-7pm Mon-Sat May-Oct) A German-run one-stop shop for adventure sports from kayaking and snorkelling to mountain biking and scuba diving. Also rents trekking/mountain/road bikes for €12/15/24.50 per day.

🍴 Eating

Cal Patró SEAFOOD €€
(📱971 53 38 99; Cala Barques; mains €14-22; ☺12.30-3.30pm & 7.30-10.30pm Jul & Aug, shorter hours rest of year) On the steps down to the beach, this breezy fisherman's shack has spirit-lifting views of the sea and serves the freshest catch of the day. You might want to plump for the cuttlefish Mallorcan-style (cooked in a rich casserole), followed by a rice dish or lobster stew.

Bar-Restaurant Cala Barques MALLORCAN €€
(📱971 53 06 91; Cala Barques; mains €14-25; ☺12.30-3.30pm & 7.30-10.30pm Tue-Sun May-Oct) The location, on a perch overlooking the beach, couldn't be better. Simply grilled fish and seafood is the big deal here, with a barbecue in the evenings.

ℹ️ Information

Tourist Office (📱971 53 32 64; Plaça de Cala Sant Vicenç; ☺8.30am-2pm & 2.30-4pm Mon-Fri, 10am-1pm Sat May-Oct) Fifty metres inland from Cala Clara.

ℹ️ Getting There & Away

Cala Sant Vicenç is 6.5km northeast of Pollença, off the road towards Port de Pollença. The 340 bus runs to Cala Sant Vicenç (€1.50, 20 minutes, up to six times a day) from Pollença and from Port de Pollença.

Port de Pollença

POP 6600

This low-key resort at the northern cusp of the Badia de Pollença has entrancing views over to the jagged formations of the Formentor peninsula. Yes, tourism has made its

---

DON'T MISS

CLIFF JUMPING IN CALA SANT VINCENÇ
....
Jumping off a cliff may sound suicidal, but it's a thrilling summer pursuit around the ragged cliffs of Cala Sant Vicenç, where locals diving from giddy heights make it look a piece of cake. If you plan to take the plunge, however, we highly recommend getting a guide.

Experience Mallorca (p127) guides know the rocks like the back of their hands. You'll jump off cliffs between 3m and 12m in height, which sounds easy-peasy but don't be fooled – the moment when you leap and plunge is every bit as nerve-shattering as it is exhilarating.

---

mark, but with its marina, cafe-lined promenade and long arc of sand, it still makes an appealing base for families and water-sports enthusiasts.

🏖️ Beaches

The beaches immediately south of the main port area are broad, sandy and gentle. Tufts of beach are sprinkled all the way along the shady promenade stretching north of town – these rank among Port de Pollença's prettiest corners. South along the bay towards Alcúdia, the beaches are a grey gravel mix, frequently awash with poseidon grass. At the tail end of this less than winsome stretch, the stiff breezes on **Ca'n Cap de Bou** and **Sa Marina** (just before entering Alcúdia) are among the best on the island for wind- and kitesurfing.

Some of the island's finest diving is in the Badia de Pollença. There's plenty of wall and cave action and reasonable marine life (rays, octopuses, barracuda and more) along the southern flank of the Formentor peninsula and the southern end of the bay leading to Cap des Pinar.

🏃 Activities

⭐ **Bike & Kite** ADVENTURE SPORTS
(📱971 09 53 13; www.bikeandkite.com; Carrer Temple H Fielding 3; guided hike/bike tour €45/55, 3hr kitesurfing lesson €150; ☺9am-1pm & 4-7pm Mon-Fri, 4-7pm Sun) Kai and Julia know the Serra de Tramuntana inside out and take you to its most exceptional places on their guided tours, which range from mountain-bike excursions to Lluc monastery and Cap de For-

mentor to hikes up to the Talaia d'Alcudia and through the Torrent de Pareis gorge.

This is also the go-to place for rock-climbing courses and kitesurfing lessons. Bike and equipment rental are available.

Boat Trips
BOAT TRIPS

(www.lanchaslagaviota.com; ⊙ May-Sep) At the small ticket booth alongside the car park entrance at Port de Pollença's marina, you'll find boat tickets to Platja de Formentor (adult/child €12/6, up to five daily departures in summer), Cap de Formentor (€23/11.50) and Cala Sant Vicenç (€28/14).

Scuba Mallorca
DIVE CENTRE

(☑ 971 86 80 87; www.scubamallorca.com; Carrer d'Elcano 23; 2-dive package €80, equipment extra €20; ⊙ 9.30am-7pm Mon-Thu, 9.30am-6.30pm Fri & Sat, 9am-6pm Sun Jun-Sep, shorter hours rest of year; ⊕) Scuba Mallorca is a PADI five-star outfit offering some 20 different diving courses, including the Bubblemaker for kids.

Sail & Surf Pollença
SAILING, WINDSURFING

(☑ 971 86 53 46; www.sailsurf.eu; Passeig de Saralegui 134; beginner windsurfing/sailing courses €122/133; ⊙ 9am-6pm Mon-Sat Apr-Oct, shorter hours rest of year) Come here for two- to three-day courses in sailing and windsurfing. Those with experience can rent equipment.

Kayak Mallorca
KAYAKING

(☑ 971 91 91 52; www.kayakmallorca.com; La Gola; 3hr trip incl transport per person €40-50, rental per hour/half-day €10/20; ⊙ 9.30am-1.30pm & 2.30-6pm) On the beach south of the marina, Kayak Mallorca organises trips for all levels, whether you fancy paddling around the coast to Cap des Pinar or via caves to Formentor. It also rents out kayaks and runs kayaking courses.

Rent March
BICYCLE RENTAL

(☑ 971 86 47 84; www.rentmarch.com; Carrer de Joan XXIII 89; bike rental per day €9-27; ⊙ 9am-1pm & 3.30-8pm) Rent March hires out all sorts of bikes, from basic jobs to mountain, electro, tandem and lightweight racer bikes. It also rents out scooters and motorbikes.

✗ Eating

A weekly market is staged on Wednesday, on Plaça Miguel Capllonch, two blocks inland, northwest of the marina.

Celler La Parra
MALLORCAN €

(☑ 971 86 50 41; www.cellerlaparra.com; Carrer de Joan XXIII 84; mains €10-16.50; ⊙ 1-3pm & 7.15-11pm; ⊕) In business since the 1960s, this atmospheric, old-style Mallorcan restaurant is something of a rarity in these parts. It serves up genuine island fare, from fresh fish to *frit Mallorquí* (a lamb offal fry-up), *lechona* (roast lamb) and *tumbet* (Mallorcan ratatouille). Throw in a wood-fired oven, wine-cellar decor and not a pizza in sight, and you'll soon see why we like it.

Ca'n Cuarassa
SPANISH, MALLORCAN €€

(☑ 971 86 42 66; www.cancuarassa.com; Carretera Port de Pollença-Alcúdia; mains €14.50-30, 3-course

---

SANTUARI DE LA MARE DE DÉU DES PUIG

South of Pollença, off the Ma2200, one of Mallorca's most tortuous roads bucks and weaves up 1.5km of gasp-out-loud hairpin bends to this 14th-century former **nunnery** (Puig de Maria; ⊙ 9am-6pm Oct-Mar, 8.30am-8.30pm Apr-Sep), which sits atop 333m **Puig de Maria**. If you come pilgrim style, the stiff hike through woods of holm oak, pine and olive will take you around an hour – Pollença shrinks to toytown scale as you near the summit. Be sure to avoid the midday heat.

No taxi driver is foolhardy enough to venture here, which speaks volumes about the road, but if you crank into first gear, take it steady and say your prayers, you might just make it to the final parking bay, around a 20-minute walk from the refuge.

At the top, take a contemplative stroll through the refectory, kitchen, heirloom-filled corridors and incense-perfumed Gothic chapel of the former nunnery. That's if you can tear yourself away from the view. Though modest in height, this fist of rock commands one of Mallorca's finest outlooks: to the west the hauntingly beautiful peaks of the Tramuntana range, to the east the gently curving bays of Alcúdia and Pollença and the jagged Formentor peninsula.

You can stay the night in a converted hermit's cell (p168) to rise at an ungodly hour for a spectacular sunrise, or simply enjoy the silence over a bite to eat. The paella is one of the best you'll get in these parts, but place your order well in advance. Life moves slooowly up here.

BIKING & HIKING IN MALLORCA

Kai Schwerte and Julia Rimpl, guides at Bike & Kite in Port de Pollença, filled us in on their favourite north coast and Serra de Tramuntana trails.

Favourite day hike La Victòria peninsula, especially the half-day hike to Talaia d'Alcudia (445m), has it all – sea, mountains, dramatic coastline, 360-degree views. On the descent there's a chance to swim in Platja des Coll Baix' turquoise water, and the track back through pine woods is fairly easygoing.

Top rides For experienced mountain bikers, the 55km day tour from Port de Pollença to Monestir de Lluc is a must. Mountain bikers love the moderate climbs, single trails through holm oak woods and downhill on stony pilgrim trails. There are incredible views of the Tramuntana and the Badia de Pollença. Less experienced cyclists could hook onto a guided sunrise tour to Formentor or a half-day spin of the Parc Natural de S'Albufera.

Best for peak baggers Puig de Massanella (1365m) is a dramatic ascent. Its Alpine character with several climbing passages along fixed ropes makes it a challenge, but the views reaching across the entire island make the effort worthwhile.

menus €30; ☉noon-3.30pm & 7-11pm; 🖭) With its sea views and tranquil garden terrace fringed by palm and tamarind trees, this genteel villa stands out. Homemade bread and tapas are a tantalising lead to dishes like fillet of turbot in a *cava* sauce and charcoal-grilled meats. There's a play area for kids. Ca'n Cuarassa sits 3km south of Port de Pollença.

Stay INTERNATIONAL €€€
(☑971 86 40 13; www.stayrestaurant.com; Moll Nou; mains €15-42, 3-course menus incl water, wine & coffee €34.90; ☉9am-11pm) This is a slick example of seaside chic, with an extensive outdoor dining area on the pier. Yachties and their ilk hang here. Seafood is the strong point, from simply grilled shrimp to local hake cooked in saffron sauce. It's classy but casual, pricey but almost always worth it.

Bellaverde INTERNATIONAL €
(☑971 86 46 00; www.pensionbellavista.com; Carrer Monges 14; lunch menus €6-12, mains €9.50-19.50; ☉8.30am-midnight Tue-Sun; 🍴🖭) Sit under the canopy of a fig tree on the patio of this arty enclave, which hosts the occasional sculpture workshop. The kitchen rustles up healthy, mostly vegetarian dishes, from creative salads to tofu curries to pumpkin and goat's cheese lasagne. Kids are catered for, too.

La Llonja MEDITERRANEAN €€€
(☑971 86 59 04; www.restaurantlallonja.com; Carrer del Moll Vell; mains €13.60-67; ☉12.30-4pm & 7.30-11pm Apr-Oct) Upstairs overlooking the water, La Llonja does seriously good seafood and meat dishes with splashes of creativity (such as the lemonfish carpaccio), although the lobster stew (€67) is seriously

overpriced. Downstairs **La Cantina** (☉10am-11pm Apr-Oct) is far easier on the pocket for breakfast, snacks and sandwiches.

🍷 Drinking & Nightlife

Port de Pollença doesn't exactly go off. You have to feel for those somewhat lost-looking adolescents wandering about late at night, dreaming of Ibiza clubs and wishing they hadn't been dragged here by their insensitive parents.

ℹ Information

Tourist Office (☑971 86 54 67; www.puerto-pollensa.com; Passeig Saralegui; ☉8am-8pm Mon-Fri, 9am-4pm Sat May-Sep, shorter hours rest of year) The tourist office is on the waterfront in front of the marina.

ℹ Getting There & Away

The 340 bus from Palma to Pollença continues to Port de Pollença (20 minutes direct or 30 minutes via Cala Sant Vicenç). Bus 352 makes the run between Port de Pollença and Ca'n Picafort (€2.55, one hour), stopping at Alcúdia (€1.50, 15 minutes) and Port d'Alcúdia (€1.55, 25 minutes) along the way. The 353 runs to Formentor (€1.50, 20 minutes).

CAP DE FORMENTOR

The most dramatic stretch of Mallorca's coast (no mean feat!), Cap de Formentor is an otherworldly domain of razor-edge cliffs and wind-buckled limestone peaks jutting far out to sea; from a distance, it looks like an epic line of waves about to break.

WALKING TRAILS ALONG CAP DE FORMENTOR

The peninsula has various trails that lead down to pebbly beaches and inlets. The walk from **Port de Pollença** to crescent-shaped **Cala Bóquer** is signposted off a roundabout on the main road to Cap de Formentor. This valley walk, with the rocky Serra del Cavall Bernat walling off the western flank, is an easy 3km hike.

About 11km along the peninsula from Port de Pollença, trails lead off left and right from the road (there is some rough parking here) to **Cala Figuera** on the north flank and **Cala Murta** on the south. The former walk is down a bare gully to a narrow shingle beach, where the water's colours are mesmerising. The latter is through mostly wooded land to a stony beach. Each takes about 40 minutes down.

Near Cala Murta is quiet **Cala Gossalba**, reached via a shady 30-minute walk (try to park at the bay just before Km 15 and descend the trail opposite). From here you can head right to traverse cliffs to the next cove. This is the trailhead for Formentor's most memorable hike. Ascend the boulder-speckled gully behind the cove and then follow the serpentine old military path up to the summit of 334m **Fumat** (around 1½ hours from the cove). The crag has knockout 360-degree views of the cape to the east and the Badia de Pollença to the south, with the peaks of the Tramuntana rising like shark fins to the west. From here, retrace your steps and veer left onto a trail that leads back to the road and the parking bay.

A couple of other small inlets to check out along the coast are **Cala des Caló** and **Cala En Feliu**. Walkers can also hike to or from the cape along the Camí Vell del Far, a poorly defined track that crisscrosses and at times follows the main road. At Port de Pollença you can link with the GR221 trail that runs the length of the Serra de Tramuntana.

The Pollença and Port de Pollença tourist offices can give you booklets that contain approximate trail maps, which for these walks should be sufficient.

The road quickly climbs away from Port de Pollença, with splendid views of the bay, and whips its way to the cape. The traffic moves at a snail's pace here in summer, owing to a succession of lookouts, such as the **Mirador de Sa Creueta** (232m), 3km northeast of Port de Pollença, with dizzying views along the ragged north coast. To the east floats the **Illot del Colomer**, a rocky islet. From the same spot you can climb a couple of kilometres up a side road to the **Talaia d'Albercuix** watchtower (380m). It was built to warn of pirates and you can see why; the views extend far out to sea. When the cliffs glow at sunset, it is the perfect photo op.

From here, the Ma2210 sinks down through the woods some 4km to **Platja de Formentor** (Platja del Pi), a fine ribbon of pale, pine-fringed sand, with crystal-clear water. Parking costs €10 for the day. The road slithers another 11km from Hotel Formentor out to the cape and its 19th-century **lighthouse**, where you'll find views to Cap Ferrutx to the south and a short walking track (the Camí del Moll del Patronet) south to another viewpoint.

ℹ Getting There & Away

The 18km stretch from Port de Pollença (via the Ma2210) is best done with your own vehicle, bicycle or two legs, although bus 353 runs from Port de Pollença to Platja de Formentor (€1.50, 20 minutes, four daily Monday to Saturday). Two extra services run between Port de Pollença and Cap de Formentor.

BADIA D'ALCÚDIA

Alcúdia

Just a few kilometres inland from the coast, Alcúdia is a place of quiet charm and character, ringed by mighty medieval walls that enclose a maze of narrow lanes, historic mansions, cafe-rimmed plazas and warmstone houses. On the fringes of town are the remains of what was once the island's prime Roman settlement.

◉ Sights

Tuesday and Sunday are market days in Alcúdia, held on and around Passeig de la Victòria.

★ **Pol·lentia**   ARCHAEOLOGICAL SITE
(www.pollentia.net; Avinguda dels Prínceps d'Espanya; adult/child incl Museu Monogràfic €3/2; ⊙ 9.30am-8.30pm Tue-Sat, 10am-2pm Sun May-

Sep, shorter hours rest of year) The ruins of the Roman town of Pol·lentia lie just outside Alcúdia's walls. Founded around 70 BC, it was Rome's principal city in Mallorca and is the most important archaeological site on the island. Pol·lentia reached its apogee in the 1st and 2nd centuries AD and covered up to 20 hectares – its sheer geographical spread (most of it unexcavated) suggests it was a city of some size and substance.

In the northwest corner of the site is the Portella residential area – the most interesting of the houses is the **Casa dels Dos Tresors** (House of the Two Treasures), a typical Roman house centred on an atrium, which stood from the 1st to the 5th centuries AD. A short stroll away are the remnants of the **Forum**, which boasted three temples and rows of *tabernae* (shops). Finally, you walk another few hundred metres to reach the small but evocative 1st-century-AD **Teatre Romà** (Roman Theatre), which seems to be returning into the rock from which it was hewn. The theatre alone is worth the entrance fee.

★ **Medieval Walls**   WALLS

Although mostly rebuilt, Alcúdia's city walls are impressive. Those on the north side are largely the medieval originals. Near the **Porta Roja** (Red Gate) are remnants of an 18th-century bridge. From the bridge you can walk around 250m atop the walls, as far as Carrer del Progres, with fine views over the rooftops and towards the distant hills en route. Beyond the bridge to the northeast, the Plaça de Toros (bullring) has been built into a Renaissance-era fortified bastion.

Museu Monogràfic de Pol·lentia   MUSEUM

(www.pollentia.net; Carrer de Sant Jaume 30; adult/child incl Pol·lentia €3/2; ☉ 9.30am-8.30pm Tue-Sat, 10am-2pm Sun May-Sep, shorter hours rest of year) This one-room museum has fragments of statues, coins, jewellery, household figurines of divinities, scale models of the Casa dels Dos Tresors and Teatre Romà and other odds and ends dug up at the ruins of the Roman town of Pol·lentia. It's well presented but labels are only in Catalan, so ask for the 'English guidebook' pamphlet.

Museu de Sant Jaume   MUSEUM

(Plaça de Jaume Ques; adult/child €1/free; ☉ 10am-1pm Mon-Sat) This museum, housed in the eponymous church, will hold your attention only if you're into priestly vestments and other religious paraphernalia.

★★★ **Festivals & Events**

Fira d'Alcúdia   MARKET

(☉ 1st weekend in Oct) The big annual market, which sees a produce market come together with traditional dances, music and parades.

✕ **Eating**

S'Arc   INTERNATIONAL €€

(☑ 971 53 91 78; www.restaurantsarc.com; Carrer d'en Serra 22; mains €18-24; ☉ noon-3.30pm & 6.30-11.30pm; 🖼) Part of the Petit Hotel Ca'n Simó, this old-town charmer with a pretty inner courtyard and exposed stone walls offers Mediterranean cuisine with some inventive twists, such as Iberian pork with lemon couscous. World flavours also shine here, from Peruvian ceviche to Thai red curry.

Ca'n Pere   MEDITERRANEAN €€

(☑ 971 54 52 43; www.hotelcanpere.com; Carrer d'en Serra 12; mains €8.50-22; ☉ noon-4pm & 6-10.30pm) An attractive stone-walled courtyard restaurant, Ca'n Pere, in the hotel of the same name, serves up fresh Mediterranean dishes such as black ravioli filled with prawns and salmon. Service can be slow when things are busy.

Ca'n Costa   MALLORCAN €€

(☑ 971 54 53 94; Carrer Sant Vicenç 14; mains €12-19; ☉ 1-3pm & 7-11pm Tue-Sun; 🖼) It feels little has changed at this grand old house since it was built in 1594, with its beams and oil paintings still intact. There's alfresco seating for balmy days and a menu packed with Catalan and Mallorcan classics like *suquet* (a rich fish casserole), cod with *sobrassada* and roast suckling pig.

Bistro 1909   TAPAS €€

(☑ 971 53 91 92; Carrer Major 6; mains €11-19; ☉ 11am-11pm Sun-Fri, 4.30-11pm Sat Apr-Oct) Chipper staff bring pepper steaks cooked to a T, paellas and tapas (a mixed platter for two costs €12.50) to the tables at this sweet bistro.

ALCÚDIA'S HISTORIC MANSIONS

Alcúdia's old town is dotted with handsome mansions. Among the finest examples:

➡ **Ca'n Canta** (Carrer Major 18)

➡ **Ca'n Domènech** (Carrer dels Albellons 7)

➡ **Ca'n Fondo** (Carrer d'en Serra 13)

➡ **Ca'n Torró** (Carrer d'En Serra 15)

NORTHERN MALLORCA ALCÚDIA

Alcúdia

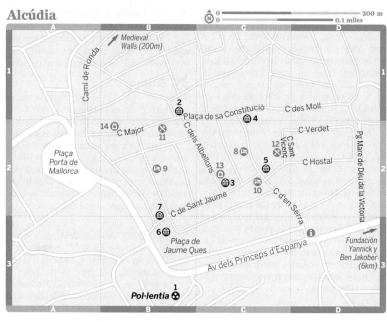

🛍 Shopping

Art i Costura ACCESSORIES, CLOTHING
(Carrer dels Albellons 5; ⊙10am-1pm & 5-8pm Tue-Fri) Designer Maren's funky little workshop

is a breath of fresh air from the souvenir tack. Find an array of beautifully fashioned bags with luxuriant details (a burst of floral material here, a dash of purple silk there), cotton tunics, beads and belts.

Flor de Sal d'es Trenc FOOD
(http://flordesaldestrenc.com; Carrer Major 30; ⊙10am-8pm) No time to go south? You can taste and buy Es Trenc's famous hand-harvested sea salt here in a variety of flavours, from rose to black olive. The shop also stocks extra virgin olive oils, tangy organic jams from Sóller and herbal liqueurs.

ℹ Information

Tourist Office (☎971 54 90 22; Avinguda dels Prínceps d'Espanya; ⊙9.30am-5pm Mon-Sat May-Oct, shorter hours rest of year) This helpful tourist office has maps, leaflets and stacks of info on Alcúdia and its surrounds.

ℹ Getting There & Away

The 351 bus from Palma to Platja de Muro calls at Alcúdia (€5.30, 45 minutes, up to 16 times daily). Bus 352 connects Ca'n Picafort (€1.70, 45 minutes) with Port de Pollença as often as every 15 minutes from May to October. Local service 356 connects Alcúdia with Port d'Alcúdia and the beach of Platja d'Alcúdia (€1.50, 15 minutes) every 15 minutes from May to October.

Port d'Alcúdia

POP 4850

Draped along the northeastern corner of the Badia d'Alcúdia, Port d'Alcúdia is a busy beach-holiday centre with a more appealing waterfront, marina and fishing harbour than many along this coast. Dotted with palms, its gently sloping, fine-sand beach has shallow water and plenty of activities geared towards families.

◎ Sights & Activities

Cova de Sant Martí CAVE, CHAPEL
Cova de Sant Martí is an otherworldly religious shrine and grotto in a 20m-deep hollow, which dates back to the 13th century. A pilgrimage leads to the cave on the Sunday after Easter. Find it at the foot of Puig de Sant Martí crag (behind the BelleVue Club hotel). Port d'Alcúdia's tourist office can point you in the right direction.

Transportes Marítimos Brisa BOAT TRIPS
(☑971 54 58 11; www.tmbrisa.com; Passeig Marítim; adult €18-55, child €9-27.50; ⊙May-Oct) Transportes Marítimos Brisa offers catamaran trips (adult/child €56/28, five hours), plus excursions to Platja de Formentor (€24/12, four hours) and Cala Figuera (€29/14.50, 3½ hours).

Alcudiamar Sports & Nature WATER SPORTS
(☑678 022866; www.sportsandnaturealcudiamar.com; Port Turistic i Esportiu; ⚑) This water sports specialist offers a full range of PADI courses, from day baptism courses to Advanced Open Water Diver certificates. It also arranges kayak rental and tours, sailing and windsurfing courses, and boat trips to sea caves.

Tandem Mallorca PARAGLIDING
(☑616 173402; www.mallorcaparapente.es; tandem flights €85; ⊙May-Oct) Tandem Mallorca takes you paragliding, with tandem flights for beginners. Most flights launch from 230m Puig de Sant Martí. There is a free pick-up service in the Alcúdia area.

Wind & Friends WATER SPORTS
(☑971 54 98 35, 661 745414; www.windfriends.com; Carrer de Neptú; ⊙Apr-Oct) At Wind & Friends, next to the Hotel Sunwing on the waterfront, you can get organised for sailing, windsurfing and kitesurfing. A five-day beginners' course in windsurfing will cost €210. Boat, kayak and stand-up paddle board rental is also available.

Hidropark AMUSEMENT PARK
(☑971 89 16 72; www.hidroparkalcudia.com; Avinguda del Tucá; adult/child 3-11yr/child under 3yr €20/14.50/free; ⊙10am-5pm May-Jun & Sep-Oct, 10am-6pm Jul & Aug) Amuse the kids at this water park with slides, wave pool and infants splash-pool area. It's about 600m inland from the beach.

✹ Festivals & Events

Festival de Sant Pere LOCAL FIESTA
(⊙29 Jun) This festival celebrates the port's patron saint. The week leading up to it is a time of concerts, kids' shows and activities. On the big day a statue of Sant Pere is paraded on land and sea.

✗ Eating

In general, the emphasis is on quantity rather than quality, but some places buck the trend and manage both.

Willy's Hamburger SNACKS €
(Carrer Joglars; snacks & light meals €4-8; ⊙8am-2.30am; ⚑) This *snackeria* in Platja de Muro is a hit with locals for its ultra-fresh, homemade fast food. Despite being as busy as a beehive in summer, Juan is always ready with a smile. Burgers are good, as is the *pepito de lomo* (pork loin in a bap with garlicky aioli).

Como en Casa SPANISH €€
(☑971 54 90 33; www.restaurantcomoencasa.com; Carrer dels Pins 4; mains €8-18; ⊙6pm-midnight Tue-Sun) Tucked down a side street near the marina, Como en Casa always has a good buzz and warm welcome. Snag a table on the terrace for dishes heavy on local ingredients and home-grown veg. We like the zingy, palate-awakening flavours in seared tuna on kiwi-mango salad and the prawn skewer with pineapple, lime and coriander salad.

Miramar SEAFOOD €€
(☑971 54 52 93; Passeig Marítim 2; mains €13-32.50; ⊙1-3.30pm & 7-11pm Mar-Dec; ⚑) Take up a spot on the ample terrace of this waterfront classic (since 1871) for one of a broad selection of paellas or *fideuá* (a paella-like noodle dish). Standard fish dishes (sole, bream etc) are well prepared, while the groaning seafood platter is epic in scale and price (€66.50 per person).

Restaurante Jardín MEDITERRANEAN FUSION €€€
(☑971 89 23 91; www.restaurantejardin.com; Carrer dels Tritons; tasting menus €85; ⊙1.30-3pm & 7.30-10pm Wed-Sun; ⚑) Chef Macarena de Castro

WORTH A TRIP

CULTURE BY THE COAST

Around 6km east of Alcúdia, in a Hispano-Moorish style house, is the **Fundación Yannick y Ben Jakober** (☑ tours 971 54 98 80; www.fundacionjakober.org; Camí de Coll Baix; admission Tue & Thu free, guided tours €9-15; ⊙ 9.30am-12.30pm & 2.30-5.30pm Tue, 10am-noon Thu, pre-booked guided tours 11am & 3pm Wed-Sat), an eclectic cultural institution that concentrates on children's portraits from the 16th to 19th centuries. It also has exhibition space devoted to contemporary artists, a sculpture garden featuring works by the British artist couple Ben Jakober and Yannick Vu, and the Espacio SoKraTES, showcasing art from the likes of Mallorquin painter Miquel Barceló and a 10,000-crystal curtain by Swarovski.

Spring, when the rose garden is in full bloom, is a fine time to visit. To reach the gallery, follow the signs to Fundación and Bonaire. At Bodega del Sol restaurant, turn right and follow the road, which turns into a potholed track. The foundation is on the right.

walks the culinary high wire at this Michelin-starred restaurant, its smart interior out of sync with its nondescript villa facade. Inspired by the seasons, the 11-course tasting menu brings nouvelle twists to essential Med products, from a simple red prawn carpaccio to sea popcorn – all exquisitely presented.

ⓘ Information

Tourist Office (☑ 971 54 72 57; www.alcudiamallorca.com; Passeig Marítim; ⊙ 9.30am-8.30pm Mon-Sat Mar-Oct) In a booth behind the marina.

ⓘ Getting There & Away

BUS
Regular buses run from here to Alcúdia (€1.50, 15 minutes) and Port de Pollença (€1.50, 25 minutes).

BOAT
Boats leave for Ciutadella on the island of Menorca from the ferry port.

Cap des Pinar

From Alcúdia and Port d'Alcúdia, the phenomenally beautiful Cap des Pinar thrusts eastward into the deep blue, and together with Cap de Formentor away to the north, encloses the Badia de Pollença within its embrace. The cape bristles with Aleppo pine woods at its eastern end as it rises to precipitous cliffs. Its walking trails are hands down some of the most spectacular on the island. The headland is military land and off-limits but the rest is well worth it.

From Alcúdia head northeast through residential Mal Pas and Bonaire to a scenic route that stretches to Cap des Pinar. After 1.5km of winding coastal road east of Bonaire you reach the beach and bar-restaurant of S'Illot. A little further on, there are turn-offs to Albergue La Victòria and Ermita de la Victòria (p168).

From Ermita de la Victòria, it's about a 40-minute uphill, signposted walk to **Sa Talaia**, a 16th-century lookout tower with views to the north, east and south. Back on the main road, walk about 1.5km east from the junction to where the road is blocked. It's worth the trip to continue savouring the changing views.

Another worthwhile ramble is to **Platja des Coll Baix** – oh, what a bay! Snug below sheer, wooded cliffs, this shimmering crescent of pale pebbles and translucent water is a soul-stirring sight. The catch (or not, depending on your point of view) is that it can only be reached on foot or by boat. Come in early morning or evening to see it at its peaceful best. From Alcúdia, it's about 8km to an open spot in the woods where you can park. Follow the directions for the Fundación Yannick y Ben Jakober and keep on for another 2km. From this spot, you could climb the south trail to Sa Talaia. Then follow the signs to Coll Baix, a fairly easy half-hour descent. The main trail will lead you to the rocks south of the beach, from where you have to scramble back around to reach it.

A curtain of pines rises behind **Platja S'Illot**, a pretty cove beloved of locals. Crystal-clear water and an islet makes it great for a spot of snorkelling. You'll need to bring a towel to lay on as there are no sunbeds, but there is a cafe for beachside snacking and the views reaching across to Cap de Formentor are something else. Just don't expect to have them all to yourself on a summer's day.

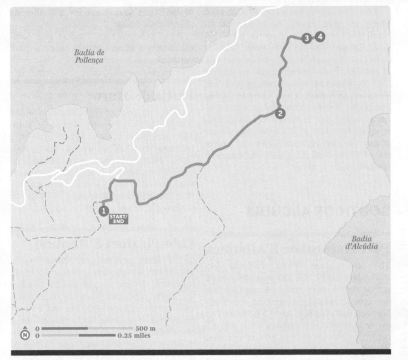

Badia de
Pollença

Badia
d'Alcúdia

0   500 m
0   0.25 miles

Walking Tour
Three Coastal Peaks

START/END ERMITA DE LA VICTÒRIA
LENGTH 6KM; 2½–3 HOURS

One of Mallorca's most dramatic coastal walks, this medium-level hike takes you along precipitous ridges and cliff tops to three crags, perched like eyries above the Cap des Pinar peninsula. Look out for the Mallorcan wild goat (*Capra ageagrus hircus*) that inhabits these rocky heights. It's wise to avoid the midday heat and take a map and plenty of water.

From the ❶ **Ermita de la Victòria** hermitage, a trail makes an easy ascent through shady pine forest, with tantalising views of the sea. Turn left after around 15 minutes, following signs to Penya Rotja and Penya des Migdia onto a narrow footpath, which wends uphill through woods, then gently downhill. Pause for sensational Badia de Pollença and Formentor views to the west. Sheer cliffs now rear above you and the sea glints far below. Pass overhanging cliffs and at a fork in the path, veer right and follow cairns uphill to

crest ❷ **Puig des Romaní** (387m) after 1½ hours, where a superb panorama awaits.

From the summit, return to the main trail, which descends gradually along a ridge as it skirts a bluff, with the cliffs to your left falling away sharply. Squeeze through a vertiginous tunnel that burrows through the rock. Entering old coastal fortifications with gun emplacements, follow the path that skirts the knife-edge cliff face, using the fixed rope to negotiate the steepest parts, to reach the top of ❸ **Penya Rotja** (354m) after 1½ hours. Topped by a cannon, the 360-degree lookout takes in the full sweep of Mallorca's north coast, reaching across Cap des Pinar to the Badia d'Alcúdia, Pollença and Formentor.

An optional boulder-strewn scramble takes you up to the cannon atop ❹ **Canó des Moró** (355m), where you'll most probably be alone with the goats, wild rosemary and striking views across the peninsula to the cobalt waters pummelling Platja des Coll Baix far below. Retrace your steps back to Ermita de la Victòria.

For eating, climb the steps through pine forest and past Ermita de la Victòria to reach **Mirador de La Victòria** (⟊971 54 71 73; Carretera Cap des Pinar; mains €7.50-25; ⊙1-3.45pm & 7-11pm May-Oct, shorter hours rest of year; ⓐ), a gorgeously rustic restaurant with no-nonsense home cooking and fine views out over the treetops towards Cap de Formentor. Besides local dishes like *caracoles* (snails) and *lomo con col* (pork loin wrapped in cabbage), it's deservedly proud of its grilled fish and rice dishes, and makes one of the best *ali olis* (garlic mayonnaise) on the island.

SOUTH OF ALCÚDIA

Parc Natural de S'Albufera

The 688-hectare **Parc Natural de S'Albufera** (⟊971 892 250; www.mallorcaweb. net/salbufera; ⊙visitor centre 9am-6pm Apr-Sep, 9am-5pm Oct-Mar) FREE, west of the Ma12 between Port d'Alcúdia and Ca'n Picafort, is prime birdwatching territory, with 303 recorded species (more than 80% of recorded Balearic species), 64 of which breed within the park's boundaries; more than 10,000 birds overwinter here, among them both residents and migrants. Entrance to the park is free, but permits must be obtained from the **visitor centre**, which is a 1km walk from the entrance gates.

The so-called **Gran Canal** at the heart of the park was designed to channel the water out to sea. The five-arched **Pont de Sa Roca bridge** was built over it in the late 19th century to ease travel between Santa Margalida and Alcúdia. The park is considered a Ramsar Wetland of National Importance, and in addition to the bird species, around 400 plant species have been catalogued here.

The visitor centre can provide information on the park and its birdlife, and is the trailhead for several walks through these protected wetlands. From here, 14km of signposted trails fan out across the park. There are four marked **itineraries**, from 725m (30 minutes) to 11.5km (3½ hours), two of which can be covered by bike. Of the six timber *aguaits* (birdwatching observatories) – come inside and watch in silence – some are better than others. You'll see lots of wading birds in action from the Bishop I and II *aguaits* on the north side

of the Gran Canal. There are a further six observation decks.

Buses between Ca'n Picafort and Alcúdia stop by a small car park near the park entrance.

Platja de Muro

Around 5km south of Port d'Alcúdia (on the bus line to Ca'n Picafort), Platja de Muro often makes the grade in lists of Mallorca's best beaches. While we are not entirely convinced about the better-than-the-Caribbean hype, it's certainly a beauty, with pale, soft sand backed by pines and the dunes of the Parc Natural de S'Albufera. The water is shallow and azure.

Ca'n Picafort & Around

Ca'n Picafort, and its southern extension, **Son Bauló**, is a package-tour frontier town, somewhat raw and raggedy. But the beaches are pretty good and there are some interesting archaeological sites. The main resort backs on to **Platja de Santa Margalida**, a crowded shallow beach with turquoise water.

For a wilder feel, swing southwest of town to **Platja de Son Real**. This almost 5km stretch of coast, with snippets of sandy strands in among the rock points, is backed only by low dunes, scrub and bushland dense with Aleppo pines.

⊙ Sights & Activities

★**Finca Pública de Son Real**   FARM
(adult/child under 12yr €3/free; ⊙10am-5pm) Much of the area between the coast and the Ma12 has been converted into the Finca Pública de Son Real. Its main entrance is just south of the Km 18 milestone on the Ma12, and the former farm buildings host an information office for those who wish to walk the property's several coastal trails. There's also a museum zooming in on traditional Mallorquin rural life.

Es Figueral de Son Real   ARCHAEOLOGICAL SITE
From the Finca Pública de Son Real, one trail leads through a largely abandoned fig plantation to the overgrown Talayotic ruins of Es Figueral de Son Real. This settlement dates at least to 1000 BC and consists of several buildings that you'll need considerable imagination to decipher.

BETLEM

Northeast along the coastal Ma3331, 3km from Colònia de Sant Pere, is somnolent Betlem. Not much goes on here – reason enough to visit. Along the coast, a 3km 4WD trail hugs the Aleppo-pine-fringed shoreline until it reaches a tiny protected bay called **Es Caló**, where a couple of sailboats occasionally find shelter and a handful of people stretch out on the stony strand and swim in the turquoise waters. Behind you, dramatic limestone hills rise sharply, some barely clothed in swaying grass. **Cap Ferrutx**, the windy cape north of Es Caló, is a tougher nut to crack as there are no trails. There are some hiking options in nearby Parc Natural de la Península de Llevant (p145).

Or strike out onto the old pilgrimage trail that leads to the serene hermitage **Ermita de Betlem** by taking the marked trail towards S' Alqueria Vella. This 6km round hike heads via the abandoned *finca* (farmhouse) Cases de Betlem and climbs through a wild and wonderfully remote valley to the hermitage. From here, it takes just a few minutes to clamber up to the 322m viewpoint **Sa Coassa**, where the entire Badia d'Alcúdia, bookended by Cap Ferrutx, spreads out before you.

Necròpolis de Son Real ARCHAEOLOGICAL SITE
On the sea about 10 minutes' walk southeast of Platja de Son Bauló, this impressive necropolis appears to have been a Talayotic cemetery with 110 tombs (in which the remains of more than 300 people were found). The tombs have the shape of mini-*talayots* (ancient watchtowers) and date as far back as the 7th century BC. Some suggest this was a commoners graveyard.

Illot dels Porros ARCHAEOLOGICAL SITE
Just north of the Necròpolis de Son Real, the island called Illot dels Porros also contains remains of an ancient necropolis. It's a fairly easy swim for the moderately fit.

Experience Mallorca ADVENTURE SPORTS
(☑687 358922; www.experience-mallorca.com; Avinguda Josep Trias 1, Vent-i-Mar Apts; activities €55-75; ☺Mar-Nov) If you want to crank up the thrill factor a notch or two, head for this adventure specialist, who will raise your pulse with activities such as canyoning, cliff-jumping, coasteering, caving, abseiling, trekking and rock climbing.

ⓘ Information

Tourist Office (☑971 85 07 58; Plaça Cervantes; ☺8.30am-1.30pm & 5-7.30pm Mon-Fri Easter-Oct) This helpful tourist office is located close to the beach.

ⓘ Getting There & Away

Bus 390 runs from Palma to Ca'n Picafort (€6.50, 1 hour 40 minutes, four to seven daily). Bus 352 is the main service between Ca'n Picafort and Port de Pollença (€4, 1¼ hours), via Port d'Alcúdia (€2, 45 minutes).

Son Serra de Marina

Spreading 5km east along the coast from Son Bauló, Son Serra de Marina keeps the mood low-key and relaxed. On its southeast edge starts the **Platja de Sa Canova**, a 2km stretch of virgin beach, backed by dunes and pine trees, which attracts the odd nudist. The stiff breezes and waves lure kite- and windsurfers. Some buses on the Palma–Ca'n Picafort route continue to Son Serra de Marina.

Colònia de Sant Pere

Named after the patron saint of fishers (St Peter), this peaceful former farming village is an antidote to the tourist resorts to the west. The huddle of houses has expanded beyond the central square and church to accommodate a small populace that seems to be on permanent vacation.

In the centre of town on the shady Passeig del Mar, some splash about in the water on the sandy, protected **Platja de la Colònia de Sant Pere**. Nearby is the small marina and fishing port. About 2.5km west, you'll find **Platja de Sa Canova**, a fine sweep of sand backed by dunes. From S'Estanyol the only way to Sa Canova is on foot.

Along the waterfront you'll find **Sa Xarxa** (☑971 58 92 51; www.sa-xarxa.com; Passeig del Mar; mains €12-20; ☺noon-11pm Tue-Sun Mar-Oct), with incredible sea and sunset views, and tables set under the tamarind trees. Seafood is the big deal, especially the catch of the day done simply in a salty crust. Everything, such as the carpaccio of angler fish with lime yoghurt, is done with a delicate touch.

The Interior

Includes ➡

Best Places to Eat

➡ Celler Es Grop (p136)

➡ Joan Marc Restaurant (p133)

➡ Es Celler (p138)

➡ Celler Ca'n Amer (p133)

➡ Celler Ca'n Carrossa (p134)

Best Places to Stay

➡ Read's Hotel (p176)

➡ Es Castell (p177)

➡ Sa Torre (p176)

➡ Agroturisme Monnàber Vell (p177)

➡ Possessió Binicomprat (p177)

Why Go?

Mallorca's serene interior is the alter ego to the island's coastal buzz. Although the beaches are rarely more than an hour's drive, the interior feels light years away, with its vineyards, hilltop monasteries and meadows stippled with olive, almond and carob trees. It's here that the island's rural heart beats strongly in church-topped villages where locals fiercely guard their traditions – and throw some of Mallorca's most spirited *festas* (festivals). Other towns preserve the time-honoured crafts of pot-throwing, shoemaking and glass-blowing.

Dip into the interior, if only for a day, for winery tastings, country walks and tucked-away *fincas* (farms), where you can spend idle moments lounging by poolsides and silent nights gazing up at the Big Dipper. The food here is earthy and authentic, especially in Inca's vaulted, barrel-lined cellar restaurants, where a jovial crowd gathers to guzzle local wines and eat spit-roasted suckling pig.

When to Go

Unlike the coast, inland Mallorca tends to remain open for business year-round: Palma folk like nothing better than escaping from city life in the depths of winter (such as it is) and finding a rural retreat for a heartwarming meal or a quiet night's sleep. The interior's festivals also rank among the most traditional on the island, from the Easter Sunday S'Encuentro of Montuïri to the 700-year-old livestock markets of Sineu in May or the yearly grape harvest in Binissalem in September.

THE CENTRAL CORRIDOR

Most travellers race quickly through the geographical heart of the island along the Ma13 motorway, although the older route (Ma13a) takes you through some interesting country. Sophisticated rural retreats and some of Mallorca's best vineyards are the main attractions, but charming villages such as Binibona in the Serra de Tramuntana foothills and Sineu further south are also compelling reasons to forsake the rush to the coast.

Santa Maria del Camí & Around

Santa Maria del Camí is a gateway to Mallorca's wine country and home to one of the island's biggest names in wine, **Bodegas Macià Batle** (☑971 14 00 14; www.maciabatle. com; Camí de Coanegra; ⊙9.30am-6.30pm Mon-Fri, 9am-1pm Sat), based just outside of central Santa Maria. In addition to winery visits and free tastings, you can admire their labels, all designed by renowned contemporary artists.

The village itself doesn't really catch the eye, but it does have a couple of pretty squares. If you're coming from Palma, the Ma13a widens to become the bar-lined **Plaça dels Hostals** as you roll into town. The original heart of Santa Maria del Camí is **Plaça de la Vila**, a quiet medieval square presided over by the 17th-century Casa de la Vila (Town Hall).

The centrepiece of Plaça dels Hostals is the 17th-century **Convent de Nostra Senyora de la Soledat** (Plaça dels Hostals 30), aka Can Conrado. If the main doors happen to be swung open, you can peer into the magnificent front courtyard, while a peek into the rear gardens can be had around the corner from Carrer Llarg.

The **Festes de Santa Margalida** (⊙Jul) is held here over almost three weeks, though the key day is 20 July. It involves concerts, traditional dances and communal meals.

Moli des Torrent (☑971 14 05 03; www. molidestorrent.de; Carretera de Bunyola 75; mains €20-26; ⊙1-3pm & 7.30-10.30pm Fri-Tue) is the area's most atmospheric restaurant – when you spot a stone windmill on the country road north of town that leads to Bunyola, you've found it. Sit in the vaulted interior or on the pretty patio for solid home cooking that makes the most of the seasons, from Mallorcan *gambas* (prawns) to perfectly cooked steaks. Book ahead.

❶ Getting There & Away

Santa Maria is around halfway along the Palma–Inca train line. Fares in either direction cost €2.10, and journey times range between 18 and 23 minutes.

Binissalem

POP 7800 / ELEV 131M

The Romans brought their wine-making nous to Binissalem some 2000 years ago and the placid little town at the foot of the Tramuntana hasn't looked back since. Its rich, velvety Manto Negro grapes produce the island's best DO (Denominación de Origen) wines. Besides vineyards, the gently rolling countryside here is cloaked in almond trees that scatter their pale blossom in February.

Like many towns in inland Mallorca, Binissalem has retained its Arabic name.

❍ Sights

José Luis Ferrer   WINERY
(☑971 51 10 50; www.vinosferrer.com; Carrer del Conquistador 103; guided tours €6; ⊙tours 11am & 4.30pm Mon-Fri & 11am Sat, shop 9am-7pm Mon-Fri, 10am-6pm Sat, 10am-2pm Sun) One of Mallorca's largest and most celebrated wineries, José Luis Ferrer, at the west end of the town, was launched in 1931. To get a better insight into the wine-making process, hook onto one of the 45-minute guided tours, which include a three-wine tasting. Call ahead to book.

Celler Tianna Negre   WINERY
(☑971 88 68 26; www.tiannanegre.com; Camí des Mitjans; guided tours €10; ⊙guided tours 10am-2pm Mon-Fri, shop 9am-6.30pm Mon-Fri, 10am-1pm Sat) ⏹ This 20-hectare winery has architect-designed buildings (we love the cork fence) and an aim for sustainability in its wine-production processes. It produces a range of whites, reds and rosés. Guided tours include a tasting of three wines and bread with Mallorcan olive oil.

Casa-Museu Llorenç Villalonga   MUSEUM
(www.fundaciocasamuseu.cat; Carrer de Bonaire 25; ⊙10am-2pm Mon-Fri plus 4-8pm Tue, 5-8pm Sat) **FREE** From the mid-18th to the early 19th century, Binissalem's prosperity as a wine-making town was reflected in the construction of several notable mansions. One

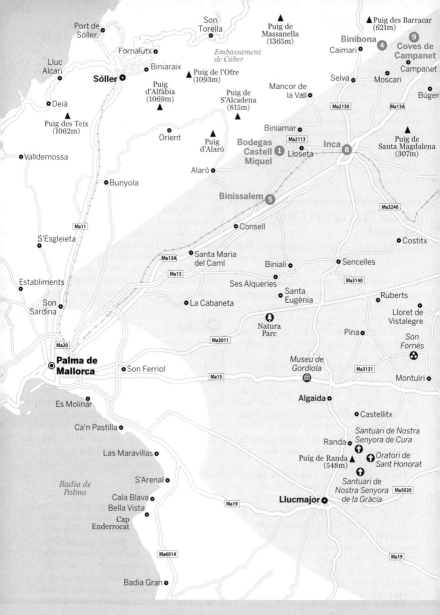

The Interior Highlights

1 Raise a toast in interior wineries like **Bodegas Castell Miquel** (p134).

2 Succumb to the low-key charm of stone-built **Petra** (p138).

3 Immerse yourself in the markets of the comely hill town of **Sineu** (p135).

4 Sleep in pin-drop peace in a rural hotel in **Binibona** (p134).

5 Join a giant grape fight and glimpse fire-breathing devils at the **Festes de la Verema** (p132) in Binissalem.

6 Take divine inspiration from the views at the **Santuari de Sant Salvador** (p140).

7 See how the rural señors lorded over the land at the mansion-museum of **Els Calderers** (p138).

8 Go on a leather-buying spree and feast traditionally in a *celler* in **Inca** (p132).

9 Venture underground into the glistening caverns of **Coves de Campanet** (p135).

10 Ascend **Castell de Santueri** (p140) for views that reach over patchwork fields to the sea.

THE FINAL CRUSH

Binissalem celebrates the fruits of its wine harvest in late September with lots of grape-stomping fun and a big, ridiculously messy grape fight. Every year at the **Festes de la Verema**, trucks rock up on a muddy field to disgorge tons of grapes, much to the delight of more than 1000 locals and visitors, who proceed to throw, jump and roll around in the grapey goodness. Anyone mad enough is welcome to join them, but take care to shield your eyes from the acidic juice.

The town divides into grape crushers and those getting down and dirty in the *batalles* (grape battles). The *festa* is actually a weeklong bash of wine tastings, concerts, readings and exhibitions. Besides grape fights, the highlight is a night-time *correfoc* (fire run), with fire-breathing devils dashing through the streets and firework displays. The full program is published nearer the time at www.ajbinissalem.net.

that has been well preserved is Can Sabater, a country residence for the writer Llorenç Villalonga and now the Casa-Museu Llorenç Villalonga. Inside, note the 18th-century wine vats and room set aside for the crushing of grapes underfoot. Summer concerts are held in the garden.

Ca'n Novell WINERY
(☑971 51 13 10; www.vinscannovell.es; Carrer de Bonaire 17; ☉8am-1pm & 3-8pm Mon-Fri, 8.30am-2pm Sat) Locals fill their own bottles from huge, 18th-century vats at this delightfully old-school winery. Made of olive wood and held together by sturdy rings of oak, these grand old barrels were a standard feature of cellars and mansions across much of this part of the island.

✘ Eating

Singló SPANISH, INTERNATIONAL **€€**
(☑971 87 05 99; Plaça de l'Església 5; mains €8-15; ☉1-4pm & 8-11pm Thu-Tue) You can eat well at Singló. Despite the cafeteria feel, it offers some enticing dishes, such as *porcella rostida* (roast suckling pig) or *bacallà a la mallorquina* (cod prepared with tomato and potato). It also has an extensive wine list.

❶ Getting There & Away

Binissalem is on the train line between Inca and Palma (€2.10, 20 to 30 minutes).

Santa Eugènia

Amid the quiet back roads south of Binissalem is the town of Santa Eugènia, home to a few picturesque windmills and lovely views from the hilltop on which it's perched.

Kids will love the **Natura Parc** (☑971 14 40 78; www.naturaparc.net; Carretera de Sineu

Km 15.4; adult/child 3-12yr/child under 3yr €11/7/free; ☉10am-6pm), a nature theme park with everything from kangaroos to flamingos prancing around. It's a couple of kilometres southwest of Santa Eugènia on the Ma3011 to Palma.

Worth the detour is the fabulous **Sa Torre** (☑971 14 40 11; www.sa-torre.com; 4-course tasting menus €40; ☉8-10.30pm Tue-Sat). The 15th-century cellar restaurant is a characterful backdrop, with its stone columns, high ceilings and giant wine casks. The four-course feast of a tasting menu changes weekly, but expect such simple, well-prepared dishes as cod gratin with aioli and chicken filled with plums and spinach. The restaurant is 2.5km north of Santa Eugènia along the Ma3020.

Inca

POP 30,070 / ELEV 130M

There are two main reasons for coming to Inca – it has some of the finest traditional *celler* restaurants on the island and it's at the heart of the island's leather industry: Spanish shoemakers Camper and Farrutx took their first baby steps here. Otherwise, it's not the most attractive of places.

◉ Sights

The first impression upon arriving in town is one of heat and traffic, and the new town sprawls without much charm. That said, a stroll down Carrer Major to Plaça de Santa Maria Major, dominated by the church of the same name and lively cafes, is pleasant.

★Ermita de Santa Magdalena HERMITAGE, VIEWPOINT
(☉church 11.30am-7pm May-Oct, shorter hours rest of year) FREE For extraordinary views,

make the pilgrimage to this hermitage with 13th-century origins, which sits astride the **Puig de Santa Magdalena** (307m). From the little chapel, your gaze will take in the full sweep of the plains to the Serra de Tramuntana and the Alcúdia and Pollença bays. It's a terrific starting point for hikes, providing you've brought sturdy footwear.

To reach the hermitage, head east of Inca for 2km, taking the turn-off to the Ermita de Santa Magdalena. Then head south another 2.5km and continue up Puig de Santa Magdalena.

Claustre de Sant Domingo   CLOISTER
(Plaça de Sant Domingo; ⊙ 10am-1.30pm & 5-8pm Mon-Fri, 10am-1.30pm Sat) FREE The last Dominican convent to be founded in Mallorca, Claustre de Sant Domingo is notable for its baroque cloister. It is now a cultural centre.

Església de Santa Maria Major   CHURCH
(Plaça de Santa Maria Major) FREE Inca's baroque church stands proud on Plaça de Santa Maria Major. Its greatest treasure is a Gothic retable of Santa Maria d'Inca, dating to 1373.

★☆ Festivals & Events

Dijous Bo   TOWN FESTIVAL
(Holy Thu; ⊙ 3rd Thu of Nov) This is the town's biggest shindig, with processions, livestock competitions, sporting events and concerts.

✖ Eating

A peculiarity of Inca is its *cellers,* basement restaurants in some of central Inca's oldest buildings, which dish out Mallorcan home cooking and robust local wines. The latter were once stored in the enormous 18th-century barrels that still line the *cellers'* walls.

★ Celler Ca'n Amer   SPANISH, MALLORCAN €
(☑ 971 50 12 61; www.celler-canamer.com; Carrer de la Pau 139; mains €9-18; ⊙ 1-4pm & 7.30-11pm Mon-Sat, 1-4pm Sun) Good old-fashioned Mallorcan cooking is the hallmark of this lively *celler,* big on rustic charm, where you'll eat below wood beams and beside huge wine barrels. The house speciality is lamb shoulder stuffed with aubergine and *sobrassada* (paprika-spiced cured pork sausage), but the suckling pig with spot-on crackling is equally delicious.

Joan Marc Restaurant   MEDITERRANEAN €€
(☑ 971 50 08 04; www.joanmarcrestaurant.com; Plaça del Blanquer 10; mains €15-20; ⊙ 1-3.30pm & 8-10.30pm Tue-Sat, 1-3.30pm Sun) A total contrast to Inca's dark and traditional *cellers* is this light, imaginative restaurant. The minimalist decor is softened by nature-themed design touches like tree-trunk coathangers and driftwood. Sunny, herby flavours ring true in chef Joan Marc's regional produce-focused menu, playing up Mediterranean dishes like snails in tomato salsa with garlic bread, and octopus with roast aubergine and peppers.

Celler Ca'n Ripoll   MALLORCAN €€
(☑ 971 50 76 39; www.cellercanripoll.com; Carrer de Jaume Armengol 4; mains €9.50-20, 3-course menus €17.50; ⊙ noon-4pm & 7.30-11.30pm Mon-Sat, noon-4pm Sun) Delve down to this enormous, cathedral-like 18th-century cellar, with a high-beamed ceiling resting on a series of stone arches. On the menu are hearty specialities like roast suckling pig and cod with *sobrassada*. It's not quite valet parking but they can arrange a place to park your bike.

Celler Sa Travessa   MALLORCAN €€
(☑ 971 50 00 49; Carrer de Murta 16; mains €9.50-19.50; ⊙ 1-4.30pm & 7-11.30pm Sat-Thu) Big on atmosphere and old-school charm, this *celler* dishes up house specialities from rabbit with onion to *llengua amb tàperes* (tongue with capers).

🛍 Shopping

Mercat d'Inca   MARKET
(⊙ 8am-1.30pm Thu) Sprawling over most of the town centre, Inca's Thursday market is one of the biggest on the island, with hundreds of stalls doing a brisk trade in everything from honey and herbs to ceramics, flowers, fabrics and fruit and veg. Local leather is wheeled out in massive fashion in the shape of jackets, bags and shoes.

ReCamper   SHOES
(www.camper.com; Polígon Industrial; ⊙ 10am-8pm Mon-Sat) Snag a bargain at Camper's factory outlet, which does a brisk trade in seconds and end of lines.

Lottusse Outlet   SHOES
(www.lottusse.com; Avinguda de Jaume II; ⊙ 10am-8pm Mon-Fri, 10am-2pm Sat) Upmarket shoes and accessories.

Munper   FASHION
(www.munper.com; Avinguda de Jaume II; ⊙ 9am-6.30pm Mon-Fri, 9am-2pm Sat) Leather goods in a variety of forms from a variety of brands.

THE INTERIOR INCA

Ballco SHOES
(www.ballco.com; Carrer de Vicente Enseñat 87; ⊙10am-1.30pm & 3.30-7.30pm Mon-Fri, 10am-1.30pm Sat) Another long-standing shoe manufacturer.

Barrats SHOES
(☑971 50 08 03; www.barrats1890.com; Avinguda del General Luque 480; ⊙10am-8pm Mon-Fri, 10am-2pm Sat) A classic look for men, with brighter colours for women.

❶ Getting There & Away

If you're not driving down the Ma13 motorway from Palma, get the train along the same route, which runs frequently (€2.10, 40 minutes).

Around Inca

A scattering of towns and hamlets riding up into the foothills of the Serra de Tramuntana invites gentle touring.

Lloseta & Around

Perfectly poised between the foothills of the Tramuntana and the open country of the interior, Lloseta is a sweet, ochre-hued town, with one of the top wineries on the island. It's at its photogenic best from late January to early March, when the almond trees burst into puffballs of pinkish white blossom. In early June it stages a fair in Plaça d'Espanya with local shoe manufacturers.

At **Celler Ca'n Carrossa** (☑971 51 40 23; Carrer Nou 28; 5-course tasting menus €25; ⊙1-3.30pm & 7-11pm Tue-Sun), sit inside by the exposed stone walls or opt for the garden at this converted 18th-century house. What's on the five-course tasting menu depends on the whim of the chef, Joan Abrines, but the food is superb. Despite residing inland, its fish dishes are especially regarded.

About 1.5km west of Lloseta on the road to Alaró is the German-owned and prize-winning **Bodegas Castell Miquel** (☑971 51 06 98; www.castellmiquel.com; Carretera Alaró-Lloseta Km 8.7; wine tastings €5, 2hr winery tours & tastings €15; ⊙noon-7pm Mon-Fri Apr-Oct, shorter hours rest of year). You can't miss the place – it looks like a little white castle. Besides wines like the 'Stairway to Heaven' rosé and 'Pearls of an Angel' *cava* (sparkling wine), the German pharmaceutical professor who runs it, Dr Michael Popp, has also developed a red-wine pill, Resveroxan, that supposedly contributes to a longer and healthier life. Tours and tastings should be booked ahead.

Caimari (☑971 873 577; www.aceites-olic-aimari.com; Carretera Inca-Lluc Km 6; ⊙9am-8pm Mon-Sat, 10am-2pm Sun), north of Lloseta, is known for olive oil. Visit the factory and shop of Oli Caimari. The best time to visit is in November and December, when the oil is made.

Binibona

A narrow lane northeast out of Caimari leads to the intriguing hamlet of Binibona. With its back to the Serra de Tramuntana, accessible only by quiet country byways and

---

WINES OF THE INTERIOR

Mallorca has been popping a cork on its own wines since Roman times. The island's vine-cloaked interior has two recognised wine-growing regions that have met the exacting standards of quality control known as DO (Denominación de Origen).

The smaller of the two, Binissalem doesn't extend much beyond the village of the same name. The much larger Pla i Llevant DO region covers almost the entire eastern half of the island. Around half of the reds produced in these DO regions come from the local Manto Negro grape, while around two-thirds of the whites come from the Moll grape variety.

If you're in the mood for a tasting, stop by one of the following wineries:

➡ Bodegas Castell Miquel (p134)

➡ Bodegas Crestatx (p136)

➡ Bodegas Miquel Oliver (p138)

➡ Celler Tianna Negre (p129)

➡ Mesquida Mora (p137)

➡ José Luis Ferrer (p129)

➡ Toni Gelabert (p139)

serenaded by sheep and cowbells, it has become a much-sought-out spot for those in search of tranquil but stylish rural getaways.

Campanet

Set in a beautiful stretch of little-visited countryside, among orchards and sheep-grazed meadows, Campanet is an appealing village for tiptoeing off the map for a spell. Encrusted onto a sharp ridge, the town's central square, Plaça Major, is dominated by a gaunt Gothic church, but the surrounding cafes are busier than the ill-attended Mass.

An eerie forest of wax-like stalactites and stalagmites, the **Coves de Campanet** (www.covesdecampanet.com; Camí de ses Coves; adult/child 5-10yr/child under 5yr €13.50/7/free; ⊙ 10am-7pm Apr-Sep, shorter hours rest of year) aren't as flashy as some of Mallorca's other cave systems, and are perhaps more authentic for it. There are guided tours every 45 minutes and visits last just under an hour. Scientists find these caves especially interesting as they're home to a local species of blind, flesh-eating beetle (nice...). Find them 3km north of town.

Sitting 3km southwest of town along the PMV2131 is **Ca'n Calco** (☑971 51 52 60; www.cancalco.com; Carrer Campanet 1, Hotel Ca'n Calco; menus €28-32; ⊙ 7-10.30pm Feb-early Nov), where dinner is an intimate affair on a poolside terrace lit by tealights. The emphasis is on seafood and, with its own boat in Badia d'Alcúdia, the catch couldn't be fresher. The five-course tasting menu is a snip at €28.

Sineu

POP 3760 / ELEV 151M

The ochre mass of Sineu rises on the horizon, draped across a ridgeback, 7km southeast of Inca along the Ma3240. This is without a doubt one of the most engaging of Mallorca's inland rural towns. It's also one of the oldest – a local legend traces the town's origins back to Roman Sinium, while the link to the Islamic settlement of Sixneu is less tenuous.

⊙ Sights

Sineu is famous throughout Mallorca for its markets. Downhill on the southeast flank of the town, Plaça des Fossar is where the town's big market days are held; the weekly Wednesday market takes over Sa Plaça up in the old town.

WORTH A TRIP

CARNIVAL TIME IN LLUBÍ

Overlooked most of the year, Llubí is especially worth the effort for the **Festa del Siurell** (⊙ Feb or Mar) on the Saturday before the Tuesday of Carnaval. This singular bit of fun involves townsfolk dressing up as *siurells*, the traditional Mallorcan whistles. That night, a big *siurell* is burned in effigy in Plaça de l'Església, which is dominated by the outsized parish church, the Església de Sant Feliu.

Llubí is on the Ma3440, midway between Inca and Sineu.

Convent dels Mínims   CONVENT
(Ajuntament; Carrer de Sant Francesc) **FREE** The town hall is housed in this 17th-century baroque convent. You can generally wander in any time to admire the somewhat neglected cloister. One block west is a beautiful example of a waymarking cross, the 1585 Renaissance **Creu dels Morts** (Cross of the Dead).

Convent de la Concepció   CONVENT
(Carrer del Palau 17) This 17th-century convent, an adaptation of the prior Muslim *al-qasr* (castle) and a two-minute stroll southwest of Sa Plaça, has a *torno,* a small revolving door through which you can receive pastries made by the nuns in return for a few euros. It was in the convent that King Jaume II had his inland residence built, making Sineu the de facto capital of rural Mallorca.

Sa Plaça   SQUARE
At Sineu's heart is Sa Plaça, a busy square fronted by several bars and the crumbling sandstone, late-Gothic facade of the 16th-century Església de Santa Maria.

Plaça des Fossar   SQUARE
On Plaça des Fossar, a **statue** honours Francisco Alomar, a Sineu-born professional cyclist who died in 1955; it has something of cult status among visiting cyclists.

★☆ Festivals & Events

Sineu's Easter processions are some of the largest on Mallorca.

Sa Fira   LIVESTOCK MARKET
(Plaça des Fossar; ⊙ 1st Sun May) Sineu's annual Sa Fira is a major produce market held on the first Sunday of May and dating to 1318.

Fira de Sant Tomás TOWN FESTIVAL
(☉2nd Sun Dec) In the depths of winter, the Fira de Sant Tomás features the annual *matanza* (pig slaughter). It's not for the faint-hearted.

🍴 Eating

Sa Fàbrica MALLORCAN €
(☎971 52 06 21; Carrer Estació 1; mains €8-15; ☉noon-4pm Wed & Fri, 7-11.30pm daily Jun-Oct, shorter hours rest of year) Most come for the seafood and beef steaks served sizzling hot from the grill at this convivial restaurant, housed in a former carpet factory, but the rice dishes are also top notch. Pep, the owner, keeps everything ticking over nicely and there's a pleasant terrace for summer dining.

Celler Es Grop MALLORCAN €
(☎971 52 01 87; Carrer Major 18; mains €8-19; ☉9.30am-4pm & 7-11pm Tue-Sun) Watch your step as you descend into this cheerful old whitewashed cellar with huge, aged wine vats. The roast spring lamb vies with the rice dishes for our favourite order. It's around 100m northeast of Sa Plaça.

ⓘ Getting There & Away

Trains on the Palma–Manacor line run here (from Palma €2.90, 50 minutes). The station is about 100m from Plaça des Fossar.

Sa Pobla & Muro

Sa Pobla, a grid-street rural centre and the end of the (railway) line from Palma, is in Mallorca's agricultural heartland. Five kilometres south across the potato flats from Sa Pobla, Muro boasts the sandstone **Església de Sant Joan Baptista**, a brooding Gothic creation reminiscent of Sineu's main church.

Sa Pobla hosts a lively Sunday market and one of the longest-standing winemakers on the island, **Bodegas Crestatx** (☎971 54 07 41; Carrer de Joan Sindic; ☉9am-1pm), which is well worth a visit.

Can Planes (www.ajsapobla.net; Carrer d'Antoni Maura 6; adult/child €2/free; ☉10am-2pm & 4-8pm Tue-Fri, 10am-2pm Sat & Sun) **FREE** houses the **Museu d'Art Contemporani**, a changing display of works by Mallorquin and foreign artists residing on the island. Upstairs, the **Museu de Sa Jugueta Antiga** is a touching collection of old toys, some with a bullfighting theme.

Jazz comes to Sa Pobla for the annual **Mallorca Jazz Festival** (http://jazz.sapobla.

cat; ☉Aug), while the **Festes de Sant Antoni Abat** (☉16-17 Jan) has a little bit of everything with processions, fireworks, folk music, dancing and blessings for work animals; the night of the 16th is the most lively time.

ⓘ Getting There & Away

Sa Pobla is an hour by train from Palma (€3.95, one hour) via Inca. The station, where buses also terminate, is about 1km southeast of central Plaça de la Constitució. Muro is on the same line.

THE SOUTHEAST

Small hamlets lie scattered across this region of Mallorca. While few warrant more than a passing glance, they sit alongside numerous wineries and sometimes in the shadow of former monasteries high on the hilltops. Apart from wine, local products to track down here include pearls, woodwork and glasswork. The two main towns of the region, Manacor and Felanitx, are useful for orienting yourself but otherwise have little to offer.

Algaida

POP 5370 / ELEV 201M

Centred on a Gothic church, the **Església de Sant Pere i Sant Pau**, this quiet farming community kicks up its heels for the Festes de Sant Honorat (16 January) and the Festa de Sant Jaume (25 July). On both occasions, *cossiers* dance for an appreciative local audience. The origins of the *cossiers* and their dances are disputed. A group of dancers (six men and one woman), accompanied by a devil, perform various pieces that end in defeat for the demon.

Algaida's main attraction lies 2.5km west on the Ma15. The **Museu de Gordiola** (www.gordiola.com; Carretera Palma-Manacor Km 19; ☉9am-7pm Mon-Sat, 9.30am-1.30pm Sun) **FREE** glassworks and museum, set in a mock-Gothic palace, has a factory area on the ground floor where you can observe the glassmakers working from 9am to 1.30pm. Upstairs, the museum has a curious collection of glass items from around the world. The on-site shop contains some lovely pieces amid the tack.

On Algaida's northern fringes, **Ca'l Dimoni** (☎971 66 50 35; www.restaurantecaldimoni.com; Carretera Vella de Manacor Km 21; mains €9-15; ☉8am-11pm Thu-Tue) is rustic Mallorca through and through, with wood beams, chunky tables, cured sausages hung from the rafters and an open fire where chefs sizzle up meaty mains. There's always a good local buzz here, as well as heart-warming dishes like *frit Mallorquí* (a lamb offal fry-up), *caracoles* (snails) and *arròs brut* (dirty rice).

ⓘ Getting There & Away

Various buses heading from Palma to the east coast stop here (€2.35, 20 to 25 minutes). The most regular service is the 490 Palma–Felanitx run (five to nine services daily).

Montuïri & Around

Montuïri, on a sharp ridge 8km northeast of Randa on the Ma5017, is known for its apricots. That very colour infuses the place with a soft glow in the early morning. The sandstone **Església de Sant Bartomeu** dominates Plaça Major, through which runs Carrer Major, graced by the occasional mansion and bar.

A few kilometres south is **Porreres**, a typical inland Mallorcan town that has always been a reasonably prosperous agricultural centre, sustained by wheat, fig, carob and wine crops. The local winery is the main reason to pass through.

◉ Sights

**Museu Arqueològic
de Son Fornés**   ARCHAEOLOGICAL MUSEUM
(☑971 64 41 69; www.sonfornes.mallorca.museum; Carrer d'Emili Pou; adult/child €3.50/free; ⊗10am-2pm & 4-7pm Mon-Fri Mar-Oct, shorter hours rest of year) On the eastern exit of town heading for Lloret de Vistalegre (the Ma3220), this museum is housed in a cactus-fronted former mill and explains the history of the Son Fornés *talayot* (watchtower), inhabited from around 900 BC to the 4th century AD. The *talayot* is one of the most important on the island and easy enough to visit. Head 2.5km northwest out of Montuïri on the Ma3200 towards Pina and you'll see it to the right (east) of the road.

Three-hour guided tours of the museum, *talayot* and mill can be booked by calling ahead; prices depend on group numbers.

Mesquida Mora   WINERY
(☑687 971457; www.en.mesquidamora.com; Pas des Frare, Porreres; ⊗9am-5pm Mon-Fri) 🖋 With a range of whites, reds and rosés, and a com-

OFF THE BEATEN TRACK

SANTUARI DE NOSTRA SENYORA DE CURA

This gracious **monastery** (Puig de Randa; ⊗daily) stands atop the 548m hill of Puig de Randa. Like most monasteries, it was built partly for defence purposes, though supposedly the monks enjoyed the heavenly views, too. Ramon Llull lived here as a hermit, praying in a cave (now closed to visitors). In the 16th century, the Estudi General (university) in Palma created the Collegi de Gramàtica here, and for centuries thereafter live-in students grappled with the complexities of Latin grammar, rhetoric and other classical disciplines.

There's a decent bar-restaurant within the monastery grounds. The Santuari, which is variously signposted as 'Santuari de Cura' or simply 'Cura', is 5km beyond the small village of Randa, southwest of Algaida.

mitment to sustainable production, this relative newcomer on Mallorca's winemaking scene is worth visiting – it arranges tastings, bike rides and even meals with wines as the centrepiece.

Sa Font   ARCHAEOLOGICAL SITE
FREE Sa Font is one of the few reminders of the Arab presence on the island. This complex qanawat (well and water distribution structure) is difficult to date but was taken over by the Muslims' Christian successors after 1229. It lies in Pina, 5.5km northwest of Montuïri, just 50m south of the Església de Sants Cosme i Damià, on the road to Lloret de Vistalegre.

✴ Festivals & Events

Festa de Sant Bartomeu   TOWN FESTIVAL
(⊗24 Aug) The main event of this celebration in honour of Montuïri's patron saint is traditional dancing by the *cossiers* (both on the eve and the 24th).

S'Encuentro   RELIGIOUS
(⊗Mar or Apr) On Easter Sunday, a figure of Christ resurrected is met in a parade by a figure of the Virgin Mary, who does some excited hops to show her joy at the resurrection of her son.

ELS CALDERERS

On a pretty country back road between Montuïri and Manacor, this stout rural mansion has been converted into a period museum. **Els Calderers** (www.elscalderers.com; adult/child €8/4; ☺10am-6pm Apr-Sep, shorter hours rest of year) was built around 1750, although the estate has been occupied since 1285. The mansion may lack the grandeur and elegant decay of other such Mallorcan estates, but is nonetheless well worth the detour.

On the ground floor of the main building, around a leafy courtyard, are the main salons and guest rooms, along with the family chapel and wine cellar – every decent *finca* (country estate) had one of each. You can sample a little house red. As a letter from 1895 (on display) notes, the Els Calderers wine was *muy flojito* (very average). This doesn't seem to have changed.

Els Calderers is 11km east of Montuïri. Take the Ma15 towards Manacor and turn left 300m after the turn-off to the village of Sant Joan and follow the signs.

Petra

POP 2910 / ELEV 120M

Petra's charms aren't immediately apparent, but stay a while and its long, straight and narrow streets and stone houses will quickly grow on you. With an in-town winery, a couple of terrific places to eat and an intriguing museum, it's a low-key place where you'll be pleased you lingered longer than planned.

◉ Sights

Petra's principal claim to historical fame is its favourite son, Juníper Serra, born here in 1713. A Franciscan missionary and one of the founders of what is now the US state of California, he could have had no inkling of his destiny as he grew up in this rural centre. The street on which the museum dedicated to his life is located is one of the prettiest in Mallorca.

Ermita de la Mare de Déu de Bonany   MONASTERY

Four kilometres southwest of Petra on a wooded hill stands this hermitage where Juníper Serra gave his last sermon in Mallorca before heading for the New World. Elements of the present church date to the 18th century but the place was overhauled in 1925. The views over the plains are magnificent.

Museu Fra Juníper Serra   MUSEUM

(Carrer des Barracar Alt 6; ☺by appointment) FREE The Museu Fra Juníper Serra contains mementos of Juníper Serra's missionary life. Next door at No 4 is the house in which he was born. Walk to Carrer des Barracar Baix 2 and ring the bell. If you get lucky, you'll get admission to the house and museum. All over the streets in this part of town are ceramic depictions of his eventful life.

Bodegas Miquel Oliver   WINERY

(☎971 56 11 17; www.miqueloliver.com; Carrer de Sa Font 26; ☺10am-2pm & 3.30-6.30pm Mon-Fri) Going strong since 1912, Bodegas Miquel Oliver is one of the island's most respected winemakers. You can pick up a decent bottle of red here for as little as €5.

✗ Eating

Es Celler   MALLORCAN €

(☎971 56 10 56; www.esceller.es; Carrer de l'Hospital 46; mains €8-14.50; ☺noon-11pm) Step down off the street and into this wonderfully cavernous cellar restaurant with soaring ceilings and old wine barrels. Its specialities are barbecued meats, roast lamb and roast suckling pig, but it also rustles up Mallorcan classics like *arròs brut* (dirty rice).

Ca n'Oms   SPANISH, MALLORCAN €

(☎971 56 19 20; www.canoms.com; Carrer de Caparrot de Ca N'Oms 7; mains €7-14; ☺9am-4pm & 7-11pm, shorter hours in winter; ⓕ) This is a lovely place to eat fine variations on *pa amb oli* (bread rubbed with olive oil and usually topped with tomato), including with cuttlefish, but it's also a wonderful chill-out space with a designer touch and occasional live music in the evenings. The shady garden is perfect on a warm summer's evening.

❶ Getting There & Away

Petra is one stop short of Manacor (nine minutes) on the Palma–Manacor train line and gets at least one service a day in both directions. From Palma the trip takes just under an hour and costs €3.95.

Manacor

POP 40,830 / ELEV 128M

Manacor, the island's second-largest city, is perhaps best known as the birthplace of tennis great Rafael Nadal and as a centre of furniture manufacturing. That we mention such things should speak volumes for its tourist appeal. That said, it does have a striking church at its centre, and there's some fine shopping to be had in the vicinity – from wineries to Mallorca's world-famous pearls, all on the city's outskirts.

⊙ Sights

Església de Nostra Senyora
Verge dels Dolors
CHURCH

(Plaça del General Weyler; ⊘ 8.30am-12.45pm & 5.30-8pm) **FREE** The massive Església de Nostra Senyora Verge dels Dolors lords it impressively over the Manacor skyline. It was raised on the site of the town's former mosque and has a hybrid Gothic/neo-Gothic style, which reflects the fact that construction began in the 14th century and wasn't completed until the 19th century.

Torre del Palau
HISTORIC BUILDING

(off Plaça del General Weyler) A short distance north of the main church, in the courtyard of an apartment block, is the dishevelled Torre del Palau, all that remains of a royal residence that Jaume II began in the late 13th century.

Església de Sant
Vicenç Ferrer
CHURCH, CLOISTER

(Carrer de Muntaner; ⊘ 8am-2pm & 5-8pm Mon-Fri) **FREE** On the corner of Carrer de Muntaner is the baroque Església de Sant Vicenç Ferrer, which first opened for worship in 1617. It's attached to a fetching 18th-century cloister, now home to government offices.

Torre de Ses Puntes
GALLERY, HISTORIC BUILDING

(Plaça de Gabriel Fuster Historiador) **FREE** Once part of the city's defences, this 14th-century tower is now used for the odd exhibition. It's around 500m west of the tourist office.

Toni Gelabert
WINERY

(🏠 971 55 24 09; www.vinstonigelabert.com; Camí dels Horts de Llodrà Km 1.3; ⊘ 9am-1.30pm & 3-7pm) The family-run winery of Toni Gelabert does superb whites. Visitors are welcome to pop by to see the bodega and sample the wine. Organised tastings, including three red/white wines and appetisers, cost €15 per person and must be booked in advance. Take the Ma14 south out of Manacor; after 2km is a small sign on the right to the vineyard.

🍴 Eating

Ca'n March SEAFOOD, MALLORCAN €€
(☎ 971 55 00 02; www.canmarch.com; Carrer de València 7; mains €9-14, menus €12-28; ⊙ 1-3.30pm & 8.30-11pm Tue-Sun) Fish prepared with a minimum of fuss using salt from Es Trenc and island olive oil is the house strong point at this warm, traditional haunt. Or opt for rice dishes like *arròs melós amb guàtleres i bolets* (creamy rice with quail and mushrooms). It's a block north of the Torre de Ses Puntes.

Reserva Rotana MEDITERRANEAN €€€
(☎ 971 84 56 85; www.reservarotana.com; Camí de Bendris Km 3; mains €28-32, 3-course lunch menus €25; ⊙ 1-4pm & 7-11pm late Feb–mid-Nov) A slice of rural luxury, this tucked-away *finca* escape has a genteel ambience in its beamed dining room and flower-draped garden. Farm-fresh ingredients and local sourcing are paramount in dishes like monkfish with Serrano ham and *fregola* (Sardinian durum-wheat pasta) and Asian-style lamb with mint yoghurt. Service is polished. The *finca* is 7km north of Manacor, off the Ma3321.

🛍 Shopping

Most visitors come to Manacor for the manufactured pearls, but you'll also find some fine woodwork on sale. There's a **craft market** on Plaça Sa Bassa on Saturday morning.

Majorica Showroom JEWELLERY
(www.majorica.com; Carretera Palma–Artà Km 47; ⊙ 9am-8pm Mon-Fri, 9am-7pm Sat & Sun) Majorica is the best-known Manacor pearl manufacturer. The company was founded by Eduard Heusch, a German, in 1902 and now has its two-storey showroom on the edge of town on the road to Palma. Upstairs you can see a handful of people working on the creation of pearls.

Orquidea JEWELLERY
(www.perlasorquidea.com; Carretera Palma–Artà Km 47; ⊙ 9am-7pm Mon-Fri, 9am-1pm Sat & Sun) Orquidea is one of Manacor's purveyors of Mallorcan pearls.

Oliv-Art CRAFT
(Carretera Palma–Artà Km 47; ⊙ 9am-7pm Mon-Fri, 9am-6pm Sat & Sun) Unless you're hankering for a Viking helmet or a gold-painted Pharaoh, the reason to come to this warehouse-style shop is olive wood. The pieces sold here aren't cheap but the craftsmanship is good.

ℹ Information

Tourist Office (☎ 662 350891; www.visit manacor.com; Plaça del Convent 3; ⊙ 9am-2pm Mon-Fri) In the town centre.

ℹ Getting There & Away

The train from Palma runs once an hour (€3.95, one hour). Various buses on cross-island routes also call in, terminating in front of the train station, a 10-minute walk from Plaça del General Weyler.

Felanitx

Felanitx is an important regional centre with a reputation for ceramics, white wine and capers (of the culinary variety). It makes an interesting stop in its own right, and as a gateway to two interesting hilltop monuments nearby.

Lording it over the heart of town, **Església de Sant Miquel** (Plaça de Sa Font de Santa Margalida; ⊙ Mass) has a baroque facade and acquired its current form in 1762. Above the Renaissance portal stands a relief of St Michael, sticking it to a discomfited-looking devil underfoot. Across the road and directly in front of the church, a flight of steps leads down to the Font, once the main town well.

One of inland Mallorca's most spectacular viewpoints, **Santuari de Sant Salvador** (www.santsalvadorhotel.com; ⊙ church 8am-11pm) is a hilltop hermitage 5km southeast of Felanitx. The hermitage was built in 1348, the year of one of the most disastrous waves of plague in Europe. It has undergone several refits since then, and is a strange mix with gaudy columns and an elaborate cave nativity scene offset by an unadorned barrel-vaulted ceiling and delicately carved stone altarpiece.

There's a prominent cross (built in 1957) on a neighbouring peak, and the car park is crowned by an enormous statue of Christ the King. At every turn, the views are heavenly. For the real experience, you can stay the night in one of the tastefully converted cells at the Petit Hotel Hostatgería Sant Salvador (p168).

For more spectacular views, which extend southeast far out to sea, scramble up to **Castell de Santueri**. The proud walls turn a craggy peak into a defensive bastion. The castle was built by the Muslims, and not taken until 1231, two years after the rest of the island had fallen. To get here from Felanitx, take the Ma14 for 2km, then follow the signs to the left (east). The road winds 5km to the base of the castle.

Eastern Mallorca

Best Places to Eat

➡ Forn Nou (p144)

➡ Cases de Son Barbassa (p146)

➡ Es Coll d'Os (p149)

➡ Restaurant Sa Llotja (p154)

➡ Sa Sal (p152)

Best Places to Stay

➡ Jardi d'Artà (p178)

➡ Cases de Son Barbassa (p178)

➡ Residence – The Sea Club (p178)

➡ Es Picot (p179)

➡ Hotel Sant Salvador (p178)

Why Go?

There's a reason that tourists arrive in eastern Mallorca in their hundreds of thousands on their annual sun pilgrimage: this is one of the prettiest coasts on an island of many. Yes, there are stretches of coastline that can seem like a poster child for all that's abhorrent about Mediterranean coastal tourism. But Mallorca's rocky eastern walls conceal perfectly formed caves, coves and inlets, some of which are accessible only on foot – among these are Mallorca's most beautiful, with turquoise waters and nary a hotel in sight. There are even resorts that are actually rather handsome, most notably Porto Cristo with its natural harbour and wild coastal beaches nearby. Also here is medieval Artà, one of the island's better-preserved inland towns.

When to Go

You could be forgiven for thinking that eastern Mallorca hibernates throughout the winter, rumbling into life only from April to October. There's an element of truth in this: many restaurants, hotels and other businesses only open in these months (sometimes waiting until May to dust off the cobwebs). That said, winters are relatively mild and the beauty of eastern Mallorca's coastal inlets have an alluring charm without the crowds, as long as you don't wish to swim. Plus most towns and villages celebrate Sant Antoni with great gusto in mid-January.

Eastern Mallorca Highlights

① Hike the wind-buckled hills of the **Parc Natural de la Península de Llevant** (p145) to reach pristine coves.

② Get a grasp on Moorish Mallorca by roaming the castle ramparts and backstreets of **Artà** (p143).

③ Delve into the bowels of the earth at the **Coves del Drac** (p151), Mallorca's most spectacular caves.

④ Puzzle over Mallorca's enigmatic Talayotic history at **Ses Païsses** (p143).

⑤ Hop from one gorgeous cove to the next ending at sublime **Cala Magraner** (p154).

⑥ Survey the land and sea from high-on-a-hillside **Castell de Capdepera** (p146).

⑦ Crank up the rural romance at *finca* **Cases de Son Barbassa** (p146), with the cicadas as your soundtrack.

⑧ Discover Cala Ratjada's cultured side wandering past Henry Moore and Rodin sculptures at **Sa Torre Cega** (p147).

⑨ Dive, snorkel or sea-kayak in the glassy waters around **Portocolom** (p152).

⑩ Bliss out on secluded east-coast bays like **Cala Torta** (p151) and **Cala Mitjana** (p151).

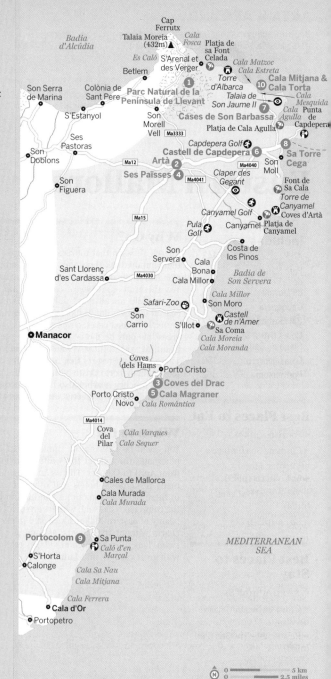

ARTÀ & AROUND

Boasting the poetic distinction of being the first place in Mallorca to receive the morning sunlight, the island's northeastern corner is a refreshingly low-key area where rounded hills stubbled with green radiate out in every direction, and calm, pine-lined beaches (a number of which are accessible only by foot, horseback or boat) dot the coastline. Fascinating historic monuments, good hiking territory and one of the best beach resorts on the east coast all provide convincing excuses for a visit.

Artà

POP 7630

The antithesis of the buzzing resort culture found just a few kilometres away, the quiet inland town of Artà beckons with its maze of narrow streets, appealing cafes and medieval architecture, which culminates in an impressive 14th-century hilltop fortress that dominates the town centre.

◎ Sights

The heart of Artà's historic centre is the shaded Plaça d'Espanya, home to the pretty *ajuntament* (town hall) building. On Tuesday morning, a market sets up on Plaça Conqueridor.

★ Santuari de
Sant Salvador   CASTLE, CHURCH

(Via Crucis; ⊘ 8am-8pm Apr-Oct, shorter hours rest of year) **FREE** Rising high and mighty above Artà, this walled fortress was built atop an earlier Moorish enclave and encloses a small church. A much-restored 4000-sq-metre complex, it reveals all the hallmarks of a medieval fortress, down to the stone turrets ringing the top and the metre-thick walls. The views from here sweep over the rooftops of the medina-like old town and beyond to the bald, bumpy peaks of the Serra de Llevant.

The walls were built in the 14th century to protect the town from pirates or invaders. Now you'll find walkways, a simple cafeteria and an unremarkable salmon-coloured neoclassical church, which was built in 1832 after the modest chapel that predated it was purposely burnt to the ground following a cholera epidemic.

From the Transfiguració del Senyor parish church, 180 steps lead up here along the grand, cypress-lined Via Crucis (Way of the Cross).

Museu Regional d'Artà   MUSEUM

(www.museuarta.com; Carrer de l'Estel 4; adult/child €2; ⊘10am-6pm Tue-Fri, to 2pm Sat & Sun) This little museum opens a window on Artà's fascinating past. There's an ornithology museum on the 1st floor, while the 2nd floor takes a chronological leap through time, with Bronze Age, Talayotic, Punic, Roman and Moorish artefacts. Among these are ceramics, jewellery, bronzes and votive double-edged axes. The ground floor hosts rotating exhibitions, such as the recent one showcasing works by Mallorcan abstract artist Miquel Barceló.

Transfiguració del Senyor   CHURCH, MUSEUM

(Carrer del Mal Lloc; adult/child €2/free; ⊘10am-2pm & 3-6pm Mon-Sat) This church, built atop the foundations of a Moorish mosque, was begun soon after the Christian reconquest, although the facade dates to the 16th century. Inside, note the large rose window, an ornately carved wooden pulpit, and an altar painting depicting Christ on Mt Tabor.

Ses Païsses   ARCHAEOLOGICAL SITE

(off Carretera Artà–Capdepera; adult/child €2/free; ⊘10am-5pm Mon-Fri, to 2pm Sat) Just beyond Artà proper lie the remains of a 3000-year-old Bronze Age settlement, the largest and most important Talayotic site on the island's eastern flank. The site's looming stone gateway is an impressive transition into the mystery-shrouded world of prehistoric Mallorca. You could easily spend an hour or two wandering the tree-shaded site.

We know little about the inhabitants' social or religious lives, but security was clearly an issue: they lived behind a double ring of stone walls, built between 650 BC and 540 BC. Within them, small stone houses were built in a circular pattern around a central *talayot* (watchtower). This was a centre of some size – the walls' perimeter

> ## ⓘ ARTÀ CARD
>
> If you're planning on doing a fair bit of sightseeing, buy the Artà Card (€3) at the tourist office. The card gets you entry into the major sights, including the Museu Regional d'Artà, the Transfiguració del Senyor and Ses Païsses, plus discounts elsewhere.

Artà

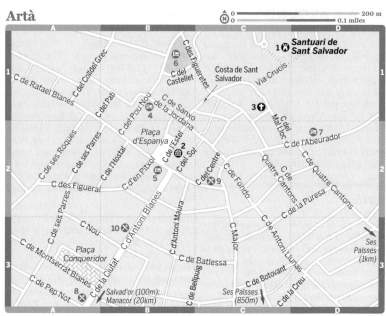

Artà

◎ Top Sights
1 Santuari de Sant Salvador..................C1

◎ Sights
2 Museu Regional d'Artà.........................B2
3 Transfiguració del Senyor C1

🛏 Sleeping
4 Can Moragues B1
5 Hotel Casal d'Artà................................B2
6 Hotel Sant Salvador B1
7 Jardí d'Artà D2

🍽 Eating
8 Bar Parisien A3
9 Forn Nou C2
10 Mar de Vins...B3
Salvador Gaudí.............................(see 6)

ℹ Information
Tourist Office................................(see 2)

extends 320m. The site was abandoned after the Romans arrived in 123 BC.

It's easy to get here from Artà. From the large roundabout east of the tourist office, follow the signs towards Ses Païsses; if you're walking or cycling, it's less than a kilometre from the main road.

🏃 Activities

The tourist office hands out an excellent brochure called *Bike Tours* that includes a dozen route maps and descriptions through the area that you can complete on foot or by bike. Particularly recommended is the demanding 7km route from Artà to the Ermita de Betlem hermitage.

🎊 Festivals & Events

Festes de Sant Antoni Abat   TOWN FESTIVAL
During this curious festival (16–17 January), everyone dresses in traditional costume and heads to the Santuari de Sant Salvador for dancing, music and a downright odd display of backward-facing equestrians swinging long sticks.

🍴 Eating

Artà has some brilliantly atmospheric restaurants and cafes, many with a boho vibe and sidewalk seating. Carrer de la Ciutat, the prettiest street in town, is lined with shops, restaurants and cafe-dotted squares.

★ Forn Nou   MEDITERRANEAN €€
(☎971 82 92 46; www.fornnou-arta.com; Carrer del Centre 7; lunch menu €12, dinner menus €28-38; ⏰noon-4pm & 7pm-midnight Thu-Tue) Forn Nou's bird's nest of a terrace perches high

above Artà's medieval maze and peers across the rooftops to the church and fortress. The season-driven menu changes twice monthly, but you can expect clean, bright Mediterranean flavours, along the lines of prawn-filled avocado with truffle mayonnaise and hake with garlic and crispy beetroot. In the slick downstairs restaurant, note the window in the flagstone floor that reveals the wine cellar below.

Mar de Vins INTERNATIONAL €

(📋 662 030460; Carrer d'Antoni Blanes 34; mains €6-11; ⊙10am-midnight Mon-Sat; 📶📶) Our favourite hang-out to linger over coffee and a good book, this cafe conceals one of Artà's loveliest garden patios. The interior is cosy, with its cobbled floor, paintings and marble-topped tables. The menu puts a worldly twist on organic, local ingredients in dishes like quinoa avocado salad with orange-soya dressing and oxtail stew with rosemary and chocolate. Upstairs is a boutique selling a hand-picked array of Mallorcan and Barcelonian clothing and accessories.

Bar Parisien MEDITERRANEAN €€

(📋 971 83 54 40; www.cafeparisien.es; Carrer de la Ciutat 18; 3 tapas €10, mains €11-22; ⊙10am-11pm Mon-Sat, 11am-11pm Sun) White wrought-iron chairs, modern art and 1930s swing music give this boho cafe a dash of Parisian class. Swathed in jasmine and vines, the courtyard is a beautiful spot on a balmy day. The food has a market-fresh, Mediterranean slant. Starters like seabass ceviche and strawberry gazpacho are a tantalising prelude to tapas or mains of grilled meat and shellfish.

Live music cranks up the atmosphere at 8.30pm on Friday and Saturday.

Salvador Gaudí MEDITERRANEAN €€

(📋 971 82 95 55; www.santsalvador.com; Carrer del Pou Nou 26; menus €16-33, mains €16-39; ⊙1-3pm & 7-10.30pm Wed-Mon) Gathered around an inner courtyard lit by tealights, this is a fabulously intimate setting for lunch or dinner. Rumour has it Gaudí himself designed the gracefully curving facade. Chefs prepare dishes like Atlantic lobster grilled in lemon oil served with nut butter, and acorn-fattened Iberian pork, with flair and imagination. Live music accompanies the tapas on Tuesday night.

ℹ Information

Tourist office (📋 971 82 97 78; Carrer de l'Estel 4; ⊙10am-5pm Tue-Fri, to 2pm Sat &

Sun) A helpful tourist office with plenty of info and maps of the area. Sells the Artà Card.

ℹ Getting There & Away

Bus services to/from Carrer de Costa i Llobera include bus 411 to Palma (€9.50, one hour 20 minutes, two to five daily) via Manacor (€2.80, 25 minutes) and bus 446 to Alcúdia (€5.65, 50 minutes, six daily Monday to Saturday) and Port de Pollença (€6.55, one hour).

The train station was being restored at the time of writing as part of the planned extension of the Palma–Manacor train line to Artà.

Parc Natural de la Península de Llevant

This beautiful nature park, 5km north of Artà, is one of the most rewarding corners of the island's east. It's dominated by the Serra de Llevant, a low mountain range of wind-sculpted limestone, cloaked in woods of holm oak, Aleppo pine and fan palms. The park culminates in the **Cap Ferrutx**, a dramatic finger of land that juts out into the Mediterranean and along the northern and eastern coasts. The **park office** (📋 606 096830; S'Alqueria Vella de Baix; ⊙information office 9am-3pm) can help with itinerary maps and organises guided walks, generally in Catalan and Spanish.

Although parts of the park are accessible by car, it's hugely popular with hikers, cyclists and binocular-wielding birdwatchers; the latter are drawn by the prevalence of cormorants, Audouin's gulls, peregrine and Eleonora's falcons. Wild goats, Balearic green toads and Hermann's tortoises can be spotted with a little luck too.

The remote nature of the park means that coves like **Cala Fosca** and **Platja de sa Font Celada** are quiet and pristine, with flour-soft sand and crystal-clear sea.

The 19th-century **Ermita de Betlem** is still home to hermits who live a life of

DON'T MISS

EASTERN MALLORCA'S BEST BEACHES

➡ **Cala Magraner** (p154)

➡ **Cala Mitjana** (p151)

➡ **Cala Marçal** (p152)

➡ **Platja de Cala Agulla** (p147)

➡ **Cala Matzoc** (p151)

HIKING IN THE PARC NATURAL DE LA PENÍNSULA DE LLEVANT

Hikers are in their element in the Parc Natural de la Península de Llevant. A classic walk leads from **S'Alqueria Vella d'Avall** – where you can park – to the coast and a little beach at **S'Arenal et des Verger**. Reckon on two hours' walking time. To reach the same point from the east along the coast, you could start at **Cala Estreta** (where it's also possible to park). This walk follows the coast to **Cala Matzoc**, on past the medieval watchtower **Torre d'Albarca** and west. It takes another hour to reach S'Arenal et des Verger. Beyond that, the coast becomes harder to negotiate.

At the main car park, close to S'Arenal et des Verger, a map highlights nine trails totalling 25km through the park. Take the Ma3333 north of Artà in the direction of the Ermita de Betlem and follow the signposted turn-off right at Km 4.7, from where it's a further 600m to the car park.

seclusion and self-sufficiency. The alluring views over country and wind-whipped coast make the pilgrimage to this hermitage worthwhile. There is a small church with irregular opening hours – its lovely stone-built exterior stands in contrast to the modern whitewashed interior and cave nativity scene, complete with stalactites and stalagmites. Strolling up the neighbouring hilltops brings some fine vistas into play.

To reach the hermitage, take the narrow paved road (the Ma3333) beginning in Artà, which meanders for around 5km through pine woodland and fields before climbing steeply to reach the top of the ridge at around 7km.

Capdepera

POP 11,420

More of a castle with a town than a town with a castle, Capdepera's stirring medieval fortress is visible from afar. The remainder of the village that tumbles down the hill has a workaday feel and little to detain you.

⊙ Sights

★ **Castell de Capdepera**　　　CASTLE
(www.castellcapdepera.com; Carrer Castell; adult/child under 12yr €3/free; ⊙9am-8pm May-Oct, shorter hours rest of year) Lording it over Capdepera is this early-14th-century fortress. A walled complex built on the ruins of a Moorish fortress, the castle is one of the best preserved on the island. It was constructed under the orders of Jaume II (son of the conquering Jaume I), who envisioned it as the boundary of a protected town at a time when pirate attacks were rife.

Within the walls, the church contains a valuable wooden crucifix dating to the 14th century but is otherwise a simple stone af-

fair. The watchtower, **Torre Miquel Nunis**, predates the rest of the castle and is probably of Moorish construction. In the 1800s a taller, round tower was built inside the original rectangular one. The views reach over the town rooftops to the wooded hills and glistening sea beyond.

✦ Festivals & Events

Festes de Sant Antoni　　　RELIGIOUS
(St Anthony's Feast Day) A traditional animal-blessing ceremony held on 17 January.

Mercat Medieval　　　MEDIEVAL
Medieval costumes and food stalls on the third weekend in May.

Festa de Sant Bartomeu　　　TOWN FESTIVAL
A week of exhibits, concerts, parades and fireworks in the third week of August.

✕ Eating

★ **Cases de Son Barbassa**　　　MEDITERRANEAN €€
(☑971 56 57 76; www.sonbarbassa.com; Camí de Son Barbassa; mains €15-25, menu €28; ⊙12.30-3pm & 7-10pm) Follow a narrow lane to this blissfully secluded *finca* (farm), which notches up the romance with its lantern-lit terrace and sweeping country views. Set among olive, almond and carob trees, it makes the most of garden and market produce in dishes likes turbot in champagne with clams, and suckling pig cooked to crackling perfection – all prepared with home-grown olive oil. The wine list features some excellent Mallorcan choices.

ℹ Information

Tourist office (☑971 55 64 79; Carrer de la Ciutat 22; ⊙8.30am-2.30pm Mon-Fri, plus 4-6.30pm Tue) In the town centre.

⊕ Getting There & Away

Bus 411 links Capdepera to Palma (€10.60, 1½ hours, up to five daily), via Artà (€1.50, 10 minutes) and Manacor (€3.90, 35 minutes). Bus 441 runs along the east coast, stopping at all the major resorts, including Porto Cristo (€3.20, 55 minutes, up to 10 daily) and Cala d'Or (€9.10, one hour 25 minutes).

Cala Ratjada

POP 6240

Cala Ratjada is the Jekyll and Hyde of Mallorca's eastern resorts. Wander along the promenade that skirts the contours of the coast and plump for one of the quieter bays and it can be pretty, peaceful even. It's also a terrific base for water-borne activities. But come high season the resort adopts a second persona as the Costa del Bavaria, with rollicking beer gardens attracting a tanked-up 18–30 crowd, doing a brisk trade in schnitzel and other German grub. You'll need to tiptoe beyond the centre to find Mallorca again.

⊙ Sights

★Sa Torre Cega   GALLERY, HISTORIC BUILDING
(☑ 971 81 94 67; www.fundacionbmarch.es; off Carrer Leonor Servera; adult/child under 12yr €4.50/ free; ⊙ tours 10.30am-noon Wed-Thu, 10.30am-6pm Fri, 11am-6pm Sat & Sun) On a hilltop west of the harbour, this estate was named for the 15th-century 'blind tower' (ie windowless tower) that sits at its centre. The beautiful Mediterranean garden is home to a collection of some 70 sculptures by greats such as Eduardo Chillida, Josep Maria Sert, Henry Moore and Auguste Rodin. All guided visits must be booked in advance through the tourist office.

Platja de Cala Agulla   BEACH
(Cala Agulla) At the northern edge of town this horseshoe-shaped beach wraps around a calm, pale-sand bay bathed by turquoise waters and hemmed in by hills blanketed in pine trees. There's precious little development to be seen from the sand, but the beach itself is packed with umbrellas for rent.

Just north of Cala Agulla is the quieter Platja de ses Covasses, where the lack of a wide beach keeps visitors at bay.

Far de Capdepera   LIGHTHOUSE
This lighthouse on Mallorca's easternmost tip is the endpoint of a lovely drive, walk or cycle through pine forests; it's around 1.5km east of Sa Torre Cega. The lighthouse, which sits 76m above the sea, began operating in 1861, and the views from here (all the way to Menorca on a clear day) are wonderful.

Font de Sa Cala   BEACH
South of Cala Ratjada is Font de Sa Cala, where the crystalline waters are perfect for snorkelling. The serene beach is surrounded by a harshly beautiful rocky coast.

Cala Gat   BEACH
East of Cala Ratjada harbour, beyond Sa Torre Cega, this fine little cove has a pretty beach backed by pine forests and receives far fewer visitors than others in town.

Platja de Son Moll   BEACH
Cala Ratjada's most accessible beach is the busy Platja de Son Moll, just in front of Passeig Marítim in the centre of town.

🏃 Activities

Skualo Adventure Sports   DIVING
(☑ 971 56 43 03; www.mallorcadiving.com; Carrer Lepanto 1; 3hr intro course €90, 2hr snorkelling

EASTERN MALLORCA CALA RATJADA

GOLF IN NORTHEASTERN MALLORCA

A handful of golf courses are within easy reach of Artà, Capdepera, Cala Ratjada and Cala Millor, including the following:

Pula Golf (☑ 971 81 70 34; www.pulagolf.com; Carretera Son Servera–Capdepera Km 3; 9 holes €37-47, 18 holes €60-75; ⊙ 8am-7pm) Designed by José María Olazabal, this PGA Tour, 18-hole course is Mallorca's longest.

Canyamel Golf (☑ 971 84 13 13; www.canyamelgolf.com; Avinguda d'es Cap Vermell; 9/18 holes €63/97; ⊙ 8am-8pm) On clear days spy the neighbouring island of Menorca from this scenic 18-hole course.

Capdepera Golf (☑ 971 81 85 00; www.golfcapdepera.com; Carretera Artà–Capdepera Km 3.5; 9 holes €49-59, 18 holes €64.50-89; ⊙ 8am-7pm) One of Mallorca's most scenic, this 18-hole course bears the hallmark of US golf architect Dan Maples.

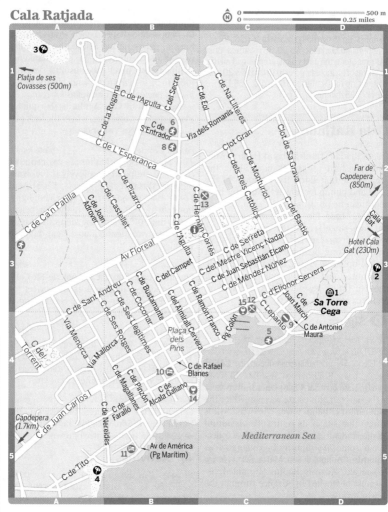

Cala Ratjada

€45) This reputable dive centre has an array of PADI courses and snorkelling excursions, many to the pristine waters around the Llevant natural park. It also arranges other activities from stand-up paddle boarding to kayaking.

Illa Balear   BOAT TOURS
(☑971 81 06 00; www.illabalear.com; adult 1 way/return from €15/20, child €8; ☺Apr-Oct) Round-trip excursions in glass-bottom boats to Porto Cristo, Sa Coma, Cala Millor and Cala Bona, with up to two daily departures.

Segpark   SEGWAY
(☑634 317266; www.segpark.es; Carrer de l'Agulla 85D; 90min Segway tour adult/child €44/29, e-bike 1hr/day €7/22; ☺10am-8pm) If you fancy a whiz around an obstacle course on a nifty two-wheeled, self-balancing scooter, this is the place to come. A taster session costs €5, a 15-minute circuit €10. It also runs 90-minute tours and rent out e-bikes that take the sweat out of pedalling.

M Bike   CYCLING
(☑639 417796; www.m-bike.com; Carrer de l'Agulla 95; bike rental per day €10-32, per week €60-180, 1-/3-/4-day cycle tours €53/150/200; ☺9am-

Cala Ratjada

12.30pm & 4-6pm Mon-Fri, 9-11am & 6pm for returns only Sat, 10-11am & 5-6pm Sun) M Bike rents out quality mountain, racing and trekking bikes. From March to October, it also runs daily cycle tours along coastal trails and to the Ermita de Betlem; all tours start at 10am.

Rancho Bonanza HORSE RIDING
(☑619 680688; www.ranchobonanza.com; Carrer de Ca'n Patilla; 1hr/2hr rides €18/30; full-day excursion per person €55) Runs excursions daily to quiet bays and along rural lanes. One-hour pony rides (€8) are available for kids six years and under, as well as riding lessons (€18).

 Festivals & Events

Festes del Carme RELIGIOUS
(⊙15-16 Jul) Cala Ratjada's main festival celebrates the Verge del Carme, the holy patroness of fishers. It includes an elaborate maritime procession, fireworks and a host of cultural events.

✖ **Eating**

★**Es Coll d'Os** MEDITERRANEAN €€
(☑971 56 48 55; www.escolldos.com; cnr Carrer Hernán Cortés & Carrer l'Esperança; mains €18-28, 3-course tasting menu €30; ⊙7.30-10.30pm

Mon-Tue, 1.30-3pm & 7.30-10.30pm Wed-Sat) This family-run *finca* restaurant feels light years away from some of the tacky tourist places in town. Sit on the vine-draped terrace for a meal that tastes profoundly of the seasons, creatively prepared with organic, home-grown herbs and veg. The fish is caught in local waters. The menu changes frequently, but might include dishes like meltingly tender leg of lamb with black olive butter, and duck with tangy *sobrassada* (spicy cured sausage).

Restaurante del Mar INTERNATIONAL €€
(☑680 133381; www.mallorca-delmar.com; Avinguda de América 31; lunch menus €9.90, mains €15-26; ⊙11.30am-3pm & 6.30-11pm Thu-Tue mid-Apr–early Nov, dinner only Jul & Aug) A Swiss couple run this restaurant, with breezy sea views from the terrace. The big deal is seafood, including a superb *parrillada*, with five kinds of fish, shellfish and grilled vegetables. Otherwise the food has an international slant, along the lines of black tiger prawns cooked in ginger served with lemon rice, and Zurich-style veal stew with crispy rösti potatoes.

Ca'n Maya SEAFOOD €
(☑971 56 40 35; www.canmaya.com; Carrer d'Elionor Servera 80; mains €11-20; ⊙noon-4pm & 7pm-midnight Tue-Sun Feb-Dec) Dig into shellfish and seafood – such as fried squid, razor clams, grilled monkfish and crayfish rice – on the rustic-feeling glassed-in terrace by the harbour. It's probably the most authentic of Cala Ratjada's seafood restaurants.

🍷 **Drinking**

Café Noah's BAR, CAFE
(www.cafenoahs.com; Avinguda de América 2; ⊙9am-late) The sea views are entrancing from the terrace of this slick lounge bar, straddling as it does the waterfront promenade. It's a prime spot for people-watching and cocktail-sipping. Inside there are comfy leather sofas. DJs get the crowd on their feet every night in summer.

Sa Fonda 74 BAR, CAFE
(www.safonda74.es; Carrer d'Elionor Servera 74; ⊙9.30am-1am) A much-loved sunset spot, Sa Fonda has a classy terrace overlooking the narrow end of the harbour. There's live music (jazz, swing, soul) at 9pm on Saturdays.

DON'T MISS

COASTAL HIKES IN CALA RATJADA

Give the crowds in Cala Ratjada the slip by taking the walking trail that leaves from the far northern end of Cala Agulla and head through the pines of a protected natural area toward the pristine Cala Mesquida, a beach backed with dunes. The round trip is 10km. Along the way, a smaller trail veers off to the right at the signpost for the 'torre', the Talaia de Son Jaume II watchtower. The trail (7km round trip from Cala Agulla) is marked with red dots, and the reward at the end is a spectacular panoramic view.

ⓘ Information

Main tourist office (☑ 971 81 94 67; www.ajcapdepera.net; Carrer de l'Agulla 50, Centre Cap Vermell; ☺ 9am-2pm & 3-9.30pm Mon-Fri) Located in the white town hall building; free wi-fi in the plaza out front. Visit in the morning for English-speaking service.

ⓘ Getting There & Away

Bus 411 links Palma de Mallorca and Cala Ratjada, via Artá, with up to five runs daily in each direction (€11, two hours). From May to October, a daily bus trundles frequently to nearby beaches and sights like Cala Mesquida, Cala Agulla and Coves d'Artà (all €1.85).

From the port, there's a daily hydrofoil to Ciutadella (Menorca).

Coves d'Artà & Platja de Canyamel

The quiet beach resort of Canyamel is a fine alternative to far busier resorts along the eastern seaboard. Apart from the pleasant beach Platja de Canyamel, there's a fine medieval tower, restaurant and a majestic cave complex, which is under far less strain from tourism than other east-coast cave complexes.

Coves d'Artà (www.cuevasdearta.com; Carrer Coves de s'Ermita; adult/child 7-12yr/child under 7yr €13/7/free; ☺ 10am-6pm Apr-Oct, to 7pm Jun-Sep, 10am-5pm Nov-Mar) is an impressive work of nature, a warren of natural burrows into the coast 1km north of Canyamel. Pass through an unassuming fissure in the rock wall that buffers the coast and you'll find yourself in a soaring vestibule, walking along a raised footpath past the 'Queen of Columns', a 22-metre-tall stalagmite, and through rooms including the 'Chamber of Purgatory' and 'Chamber of Hell'. The 40-minute guided tours of the caves in English, German, Spanish and French leave every 30 minutes. Even the walk to get here is spectacular – the caves are halfway up a sheer cliff face and

once served as a refuge for the local inhabitants in times of war and invasion.

Just 3km inland from the beach and signposted off the main coast road, the famed Torre de Canyamel (Carretera Artà–Canyamel Km 5; adult/child under 13yr €3/free; ☺ 10am-3pm & 5-8pm Tue-Sat, 10am-2pm Sun Apr-Oct) – a 23m-high, 13th-century defence tower of Muslim origin – is a rewarding detour.

Opening onto a garden terrace, Porxada de Sa Torre (☑ 971 84 13 10; www.restaurante-porxadadesatorre.com; Carretera Artà–Canyamel Km 5; mains €9-18; ☺ 1-3.30pm & 7-11pm Apr-Oct) is a beacon of Mallorcan cooking, with perfectly cooked *tumbet* (a traditional vegetable dish), roast rabbit with onions, *sobrassada* and *lechona* (suckling pig). You're welcome in the kitchen to see how the dishes are prepared. The stone-and-wood architecture, old farming implements, ancient olive press and friendly service round out a terrific package.

CALA MILLOR TO PORTOCOLOM

For the millions of tourists who descend every year on its sandy beaches, splash in its gentle waves and stay in all-inclusive resorts, the coast from Cala Millor to Portocolom is paradise. But for those who mourn the loss of Mallorca's once-pristine coastline, the overdevelopment is nothing short of an abhorrence. But the crowd-weary don't have to shy away. Stay in one of the cosy rural hotels and drive, cycle or hike to off-the-beaten-path beaches such as Cala Romántica or Cala Varques.

Cala Millor & Around

Along the waterfront at Cala Millor at twilight, when the sun turns the sky violet and the water a soft shade of aquamarine, you can almost imagine that the concrete jungle inland was just a mirage... The saving grace of Cala Millor is that its nearly 2km-long beach, backed by a promenade, is large enough to absorb masses of sun worshippers on all but the busiest summer days.

To escape the crowds, set off for a challenging seaside hike to the **Castell de n'Amer**, which overlooks the sea.

Beyond Cala Millor's sprawl is **Safari-Zoo** (☑971 81 09 09; www.safari-zoo.com; Carretera Portocristo–Son Servera Km 5; adult/child €19/12; ⊙9am-6.30pm Jun-Sep, shorter hours rest of year), where you see wild animals (including rhinos, hippos, zebras, giraffes, baboons, wildebeest and numerous antelope species) from the comfort of your car or an open-sided tourist train. The animals have plenty of space to roam, unlike those in the depressing enclosures in the more traditional zoo that makes up the rest of the park.

The **tourist office** (☑971 58 58 64; www.visitcalamillor.com; Passeig Maritim; ⊙9am-5pm Mon-Fri, to 1pm Sat, shorter hours in winter) occupies a kiosk right on the promenade.

❶ Getting There & Away

Bus lines 441, 446, 447 and others run up and down the east coast, linking Cala Millor with resorts such as Cala d'Or (€8.05, 1¼ hours). Bus 412 heads to Palma (€9.65, 1½ hours, up to 15 daily).

Porto Cristo

POP 7360

Home to Mallorca's grandest caves, Porto Cristo is above all a day-trip destination and attracts would-be spelunkers in their droves to its vast underground caverns. It's true that as a resort it lacks some of the bang of glitzier destinations elsewhere on the coast, but that's no bad thing – what Porto Cristo lacks in glamour it makes up for in quiet charm.

⊙ Sights

★ Coves del Drac
CAVE

(Dragon's Caves; www.cuevasdeldrach.com; Carretera Cuevas; adult/child €14/7; ⊙10am-5pm Apr-Oct, 10.45am-3.30pm Nov-Mar) Mallorca has some wonderful cave complexes, but none surpasses the utterly bewitching Coves del Drac. A 1.2km shuffle with the inevitable crowd, accompanied by a multilingual commentary, leads to a vast amphitheatre and lake, where you'll enjoy a brief classical-music recital. One-hour tours of the caves leave on the hour. It's difficult to truly convey the magic of this place – it's at times like a vast underground cathedral complete with organ pipes, at others like a petrified forest.

The breathtakingly beautiful (and cleverly exploited) chambers, theatrically lit in bright colours, are adorned with impressive stalactites and stalagmites. The tour delves into the most beautiful parts of the 2km-long limestone tunnel and a short boat ride on the lake is possible after the concert.

Passeig de la Sirena
BEACH

Most of the town's activity crowds alongside the Passeig de la Sirena and the harbour, where a small crowded beach provides the perfect place to observe the comings and goings of fishing boats and yachts in the marina. Alongside the beach you'll find the modest Coves Blanques, a handful of small caves that were inhabited during the Talayotic period and were later used by fishers for shelter.

TRANQUIL COVES AROUND CALA RATJADA

Heading north from Cala Ratjada, you'll find a wonderfully undeveloped stretch of coastline flecked with beaches. Long-time favourites of nudists, these out-of-the-way coves are no secret, but their lack of development has kept them calm and pristine.

Cala Mesquida, surrounded by sand dunes and a small housing development, is the most accessible, with free parking and a regular bus service (bus 471) from Cala Ratjada (25 minutes, up to 15 daily).

It requires more determination to access the undeveloped coves due west. **Cala Torta**, **Cala Mitjana** and the beachless **Cala Estreta** are all found at the end of a narrow road that ventures through the hills from Artà, yet a more interesting way to arrive is via the one-hour walking path from Cala Mesquida.

Further west, and following a 20-minute trek along the coast from Cala Estreta, **Cala Matzoc** comes into view. The spacious sandy beach backs onto a hill where you'll find the ruins of a *talayot* (watchtower), once used to guard the coast from pirates.

Coves dels Hams CAVE
(www.cuevas-hams.com; Carretera Ma4020 Manacor–Portocristo Km 11; adult/child 5-12yr/ under 5yr €21/10.50/free; ☺10am-5pm) On the northern side of town on the road to Manacor, this underground labyrinth is not as impressive as the Coves del Drac, but it does have some fine stalactite formations. Having said that, it is overpriced and some of our readers have left feeling ripped off. The Jules Verne video presentation and projections complete with Mozart music and dummies in a boat are also pretty bizarre.

And one final thing: the massive signs all over town to the 'Caves' are slightly misleading – they lead here, so study the signs carefully if your desired destination is the Coves del Drac.

🏃 Activities

**Skualo Adventure Sports &
Dive Centre** DIVING
(☑971 81 50 94; www.mallorcadiving.com; Passeig del Cap d'Es Toll 11; 1/2 dives €40/74, equipment €24; ☺9am-6pm Mon-Sat Easter-Oct) This first-rate dive centre offers scuba 'baptisms' (€90) for novices, plus a wide array of other PADI courses. It also offers snorkelling (€45) and two-hour sea-kayaking excursions (€38), as well as kayak rental (€10/18 per hour for a single/double kayak).

Illa Balear BOAT TOUR
(☑971 81 06 00; www.illabalear.com; Carrer del Moll; per person €18-24, 1 way to Cala Ratjada €15; ☺8.30am-5.30pm) Boat excursions (most in glass-bottomed catamarans) between Porto Cristo and other east-coast resorts such as Cala Ratjada, Cala Romántica and Cala Millor. Up to four times daily in summer.

🎉 Festivals & Events

Festes de Sant Antoni RELIGIOUS
On 16 and 17 January, Porto Cristo goes all out with a bonfire and 'dance of the devils' for the eve of Sant Antoni, the traditional blessing of animals.

Verge del Carme RELIGIOUS
The feast day of the patroness of fisherfolk is celebrated with great cheer along the coast on 16 July.

🍴 Eating

★ Sa Sal MEDITERRANEAN €€
(☑971 82 20 49; www.restaurantesasal.com; Carrer la Tramuntana 11; mains €18-29; ☺6.30-11.30pm Tue-Sun) Sa Sal stands head and shoulders above most restaurants in town, with its refined service, inventive menu and candlelit patio. The interior brings a modern aesthetic to the Mallorcan house's original beams and stone. Follow robustly flavoured starters, like seafood soup with vanilla, mango and ravioli, with mains like filet of veal with polenta, Menorcan cheese and truffle sauce.

La Magrana CAFE €
(☑971 55 69 74; Plaça del Carme 15; snacks €4-8.50; ☺9am-11pm Wed-Mon) This button-cute cafe has a boho vibe, with its appealing jumble of vintage knick-knacks, pot plants, wicker chairs, art and bold colours. Take a seat on the terrace on the plaza facing the church, or in the courtyard for fresh juices, ice creams and light bites like *pa amb oli* (bread with oil) with Serrano ham and tangy apple-vegetable salad.

ℹ Information

Tourist office (☑662 350882, 971 84 91 26; www.visitmanacor.com; Carrer del Moll; ☺9am-3.30pm Mon-Fri) At the end of the wharf.

ℹ Getting There & Away

A dozen bus lines serve Porto Cristo, among them lines 412 and 414 to Palma (one way/return €9.25/16, 1½ hours, three to eight daily) via Manacor (€1.90); lines 441, 442 and 443 connect to the east-coast resorts (varied prices, scores of buses). You'll also find services to Cala Ratjada (€4.30, 30 minutes, three to 11 daily) and a Wednesday service to Sineu (€5.50, 40 minutes).

Portocolom

POP 3880

A relatively sleepy place as far as east-coast holiday resorts go, Portocolom has resisted the tourist onslaught with dignity. It cradles a natural harbour (one of the few on the island) and attracts German, British and Spanish families in equal numbers. Fishing boats, sailing boats and the odd luxury yacht bob in the calm waters of its large horseshoe-shaped bay.

🏖 Beaches

Within reach of Portocolom are some fine beaches, such as the immaculate little cove of **Caló d'en Marçal** and, on the northern end of town, **Cala s'Arenal**, the locals' preferred beach. On the eastern headland at

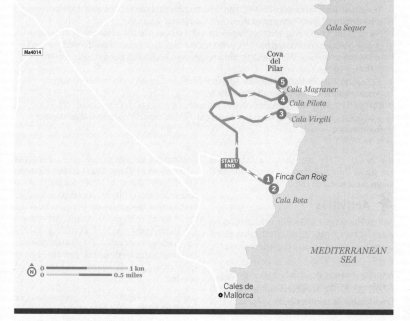

Walking Tour
Four Coves

START/END FINCA CAN ROIG
LENGTH 13KM; 3½ HOURS

Just north of Cales de Mallorca the chaos of the resorts falls away and nature takes over. Over the 6km between Cales de Mallorca and Cala Romántica, there's only pine-specked rocky coves, pitted cliff faces and the aquamarine of the Mediterranean. The walk begins at **1 Finca Can Roig**, a rural estate. To get here, take the Carretera Porto Cristo–Portocolom (Ma4014) and at Km 6 turn east toward Cales de Mallorca. Continue 2.2km and then veer left; after 200m you'll reach the entrance to Can Roig.

Leave your car here and strike out along the wide, rocky track that parallels the coast. After about 15 minutes, a slightly narrower path turns off to the right. Follow it alongside a small gully and through patches of trees to reach **2 Cala Bota**, a sheltered cove with a small sandy beach. A steep trail meanders around and above the cove, giving a bird's-eye view of its beauty.

From Cala Bota, retrace your steps and take the second right toward the next cove, **3 Cala Virgili**. The track brings you to a smaller trail that heads off right down to this narrow, cliff-flanked cove, with limpid water for a refreshing dip. (The walk down takes about 10 minutes.) Return to the main trail and follow it. You'll pass a small trail on your right, but keep straight until you come upon a second path. Take it towards the **4 Cala Pilota**, a lovely cove backed by cave-pocked cliffs. The water is brilliantly turquoise.

Head back to the main trail and continue. Ignore the first right and instead take the second, which rolls down to the final cove, **5 Cala Magraner**, the grandest of the bunch both in size and beauty. The trail is wide at first but stops in a clearing; another, narrower trail leads you the last few minutes. After splashing in the crystalline waters and exploring the small caves that dot the rock, walk the main trail back to Finca Can Roig.

SECLUDED COVES SOUTH OF PORTO CRISTO

The coast running south of Porto Cristo is textured with a series of beautiful, unspoilt coves, many of them signposted from the Ma4014 highway linking Porto Cristo and Portocolom. The largest and most developed of the bunch is **Cala Romántica**, a wedge of pale golden sand flanked by cliffs, with shallow turquoise water. A few hotels form one of the island's more serene resorts and a rough promenade has been hewn out of the rock face by the sea.

Beyond Cala Romántica you can seek out coves and caves such as **Cala Varques** (known for the cave on the cliff above the cove), **Cala Sequer**, **Cova del Pilar** or **Cala Magraner**, a wild and secluded cove at the foot of a gorge and pockmarked cliffs that are popular with climbers. None has direct car access; plan on walking at least the last few minutes.

the mouth of the bay, there's a lighthouse, **Far de sa Punta de ses Crestes**, with good views back towards the town.

🏃 Activities

Ask at the tourist office for information on glass-bottom boats (€19 to €27, two to six hours) to **Cala d'Or** and elsewhere along the coast.

Bahia Azul Dive Center   DIVING
(📞971 82 52 80; www.bahia-azul.de; Ronda de Creuer Balear 78; per dive €27-39; ⊙Apr-Oct) This dive centre in the Hostal Bahia Azul offers courses, try dives and equipment rental.

Skualo Adventure
Sports Centre   DIVING, KAYAKING
(📞971 83 41 97; www.mallorcadiving.com; Carrer de Llampuga; per dive €39; ⊙Apr-Oct) Another well-respected dive centre, with snorkelling (€30 to €38) and sea kayaking (two- to three-hour excursion €38).

🍴 Eating

⭐**Restaurant Sa Llotja**   SPANISH €€
(📞971 82 51 65; www.restaurantsallotjaportocolom. com; Carrer dels Pescadors; mains €15-33.50, menu €35; ⊙1-3.30pm & 7-10.30pm Tue-Sun) A slick, glass-fronted restaurant with a wonderful terrace overlooking the harbour, Sa Llotja tempts with dishes like monkfish, lobster stew, roast Mallorcan lamb and the odd intriguing combination such as tuna tartar with mango sorbet. It's all fresh, attractively presented and uniformly delicious. The three-course menu includes wine, water and coffee and is terrific value.

Restaurant Sa Sinia   SEAFOOD €€
(📞971 82 43 23; Carrer dels Pescadors 25; mains €15-25; ⊙1-3.30pm & 7-11pm Tue-Sun) With menus designed by artist Miquel Barceló and chairs marked with plaques bearing the names of famous people who have sat there, this vaulted maritime eatery has bags of character. Fresh fish, paellas and homemade desserts are the house specialities, as is warm, old-fashioned service.

Restaurante HPC   INTERNATIONAL €€
(📞971 82 53 23; www.restaurantehpc.com; Carrer de Cristòfol Colom 5; mains €10-25; ⊙9am-4pm & 6.30-11pm) This contemporary, high-ceilinged restaurant has a backlit 1st-floor cocktail bar done out in cool whites and blues. It's all in the mix in the kitchen – from suckling pig to pizza to Thai curry – but somehow it works. The atmosphere's classy but never stuffy, especially at the outdoor tables with breezy sea views.

ℹ️ Information

Tourist office (📞971 82 60 84; www.visitfelan-itx.es; Avinguda de Cala Marçal 15; ⊙9am-2pm Mon-Fri, plus 5-7pm Tue & Thu, 9.30am-12.30pm Sat) At the southern end of town, on the road to Cala Marçal.

ℹ️ Getting There & Away

Ten bus lines service Portocolom, including the coastal routes 441, 442 and 443 (varied prices, dozens daily). Up to seven buses link with Palma (€6.90, 1½ hours).

Southern Mallorca

Best Places to Eat

➡ Yacht Club Cala d'Or
(p165)

➡ Alchemy (p162)

➡ Sal de Coco (p159)

➡ Casa Manolo (p161)

➡ Aventura (p164)

Best Places to Stay

➡ Hotel Ca'n Bonico (p180)

➡ Ca'n Bessol (p180)

➡ Can Canals (p179)

➡ Hotel Cala Santanyí (p180)

➡ Hostal Colonial (p179)

Why Go?

The fortresslike coastal geography between the Badia de Palma (Bay of Palma) and Colònia de Sant Jordi has preserved this area as one of the least developed of the island. Much of the coast is buffered by tall, nearly impenetrable cliffs splashed with the sapphire blue waters of the Mediterranean. They may not always be very accessible, but their untamed, raw beauty is hypnotising.

Beyond the cliffs are intimate coves and long beaches, true marvels of nature. Whether enclosed tightly by fjord-like cliffs, or silky sweeps of sand backed by pines and junipers, these are some of Mallorca's best beaches. And best of all, the existence of parks and natural areas, and the proliferation of working farms and rural estates, has, for the most part, kept this part of the island free from the worst excesses of overdevelopment. In other words, this is how all of Mallorca's coast once looked.

When to Go

Mallorca's southern beaches live for the summer, to the extent that you won't find much going on if you arrive before Easter or after October. That's not to say you can't visit at other times: if you do you're likely to have the place to yourself, including some eerily quiet resort towns with just a handful of restaurants, hotels and shops open. But summer is undoubtedly the best time and you'll enjoy it most if you seek out southern Mallorca's resort-free stretches of coastline.

Southern Mallorca Highlights

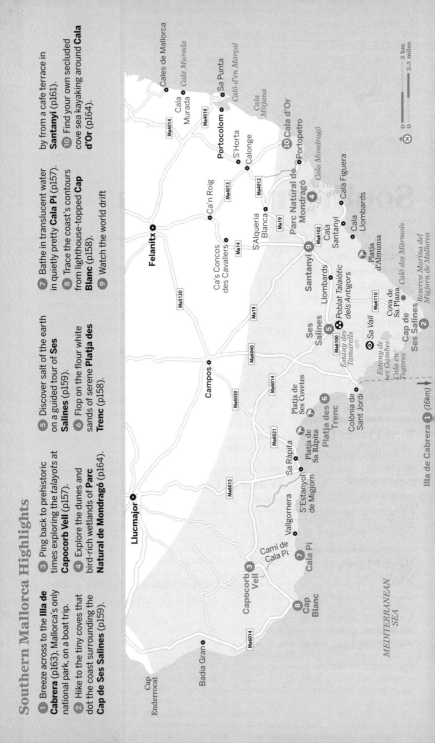

① Breeze across to the **Illa de Cabrera** (p163), Mallorca's only national park, on a boat trip.

② Hike to the tiny coves that dot the coast surrounding the **Cap de Ses Salines** (p159).

③ Ping back to prehistoric times exploring the *talayots* at **Capocorb Vell** (p157).

④ Explore the dunes and bird-rich wetlands of **Parc Natural de Mondragó** (p164).

⑤ Discover salt of the earth on a guided tour of **Ses Salines** (p159).

⑥ Flop on the flour white sands of serene **Platja des Trenc** (p158).

⑦ Bathe in translucent water in quietly pretty **Cala Pi** (p157).

⑧ Trace the coast's contours from lighthouse-topped **Cap Blanc** (p158).

⑨ Watch the world drift by from a cafe terrace in **Santanyí** (p161).

⑩ Find your own secluded cove sea kayaking around **Cala d'Or** (p164).

CAP ENDERROCAT TO SA RÀPITA

The lonely stretch of coastline running along the island's southernmost flank is unspoilt, a reminder of what the Mallorcan coast must have looked like before the tourist onslaught. Its survival in such a pristine state is all the more refreshing considering its location, squeezed between the high-rise hotels on the east coast and the high-speed activity of the Badia de Palma.

Cala Pi & Around

An agreeably low-key resort, Cala Pi overlooks a gorgeous white-sand, pine-flanked sliver of a beach. On the coast, a circular 17th-century defence tower pays homage to the Mallorca of ages past, when pirate threats were constant.

◉ Sights

Cala Pi   BEACH
Reached via a steep staircase (follow the signs along Camí de la Cala Pi), the beach is only 50m wide but it is a beauty: stretching more than 100m inland and flanked on either side by craggy cliffs that ensure the startlingly turquoise water in the inlet stays as still as bathwater. There are no facilities at beach level so bring any provisions you're likely to need.

Capocorb Vell   ARCHAEOLOGICAL SITE
(www.talaiotscapocorbvell.com; Carretera Arenal–Cap Blanc Km 23; admission €2; ⊙10am-5pm Fri-Wed) At this sprawling prehistoric village, you can wander along stony pathways and beside rough stone structures that date to 1000 BC. The site, which includes 28 dwellings and five *talayots* (watchtowers made with stone and, in the case of Capocorb Vell, no mortar) was probably used through Roman times.

✕ Eating

Restaurante Miguel   SPANISH €€
(☑971 12 30 00; www.restaurante-miguel.com; Torre de Cala Pi 13; mains €9-26; ⊙11am-11pm Tue-Sun Mar-Oct) A Mallorcan-style farmhouse with a huge patio, Restaurante Miguel is warmly recommended, and cooks up excellent seafood dishes like paella, mussels in marinara sauce and grouper with lemon sauce, as well as heartier Mallorcan specialities like rabbit with mushrooms. There's a snack menu for grazers too.

❶ Getting There & Away

Bus 520 links Cala Pi and Palma once in the morning and once in the evening (€5.50, 1½ hours).

Sa Ràpita & Around

The main settlement along this stretch of coast, Sa Ràpita is a sleepy seaside village whose rocky shoreline, harangued by waves, provides a scenic diversion from the rest of the nondescript town. Neighbouring Vallgornera has the longest cave on the island.

◉ Sights

Platja de Ses Covetes   BEACH
This sweep of long, silky sand and gin-clear water forms part of the **Reserva Marina del Migjorn de Mallorca** (a protected marine reserve), so no buildings mar its backdrop of dunes and pines. It's unspoilt but not uncrowded. Walking east along the shore, you'll come upon Platja des Trenc. Platja de Ses Covetes is past Sa Ràpita and off the Ma6030 highway. You can park in Sa Rapita.

Cova des Pas de Vallgornera   CAVES
FREE In Vallgornera (3km east of Cala Pi), half a dozen caves burrow their way through the rock underfoot. Some are truly impressive, with underground rivers and lakes or spectacular stalactites and stalagmites. The most famous cave here, Cova des Pas de Vallgornera, is also the Balearics' longest, at 6435m. Sadly it is off limits to all but expert geologists and speleologists.

❶ Getting There & Away

Bus 515 runs to and from Palma (€5.30, one hour, up to five times daily).

COLÒNIA DE SANT JORDI & AROUND

West of the family resort, Colònia de Sant Jordi stretches the 7km of the unspoilt Platja des Trenc, while to the southeast a vast nature reserve protects a long swath of rocky coastline softened by pristine beaches. Offshore sits the Balearics' only national park, the Parc Nacional Marítim-Terrestre de

CAP BLANC

If you're travelling the coast road from Palma to Capocorb Vell and Cala Pi, detour to this wonderfully secluded spot. Take the Ma6014 highway south from S'Arenal and turn right at the sign pointing to 'Cap Blanc'. You'll soon come across a lighthouse and desolate-seeming military compound. Park beside the fence.

You can't reach the lighthouse, but a trail setting off from the fence leads you on a five-minute walk through scrubby bushes and over pitted rocks to a sheer cliff. The views of the Mediterranean are nothing short of majestic with ruddy-coloured cliffs running up the coast and fishing birds circling overhead. Breezy and sunny, this is a fabulous picnic spot, but be careful with kids or dogs; there is no fence and the drop is abrupt.

l'Arxipèlag de Cabrera, while inland a smattering of preserved Talayotic sites interrupt a serene, pastoral landscape.

Colònia de Sant Jordi

POP 2900

The biggest beach resort of the southern coast, Colònia de Sant Jordi has long been the summertime spot of choice for Palma residents. A prim town whose well-laid-out streets form a chequerboard across the hilly landscape, the Colònia is a family-friendly place surrounded by some of the best and least developed beaches in Mallorca. But we like it best as the jumping-off point for the offshore Illa de Cabrera (p163).

◉ Sights

Colònia de Sant Jordi's main attractions are its wonderful beaches and seafront promenade. Best known is the Platja des Trenc, a 20-minute walk from the northwestern end of town.

Platja des Trenc BEACH

The largest undeveloped beach in Mallorca, runs 3km northwest from the southern edge of Colònia de Sant Jordi. With long stretches of frost white sand, azure water and a restful setting among pine trees and rolling dunes, des Trenc proves just how pretty the Mallorcan coast was before development got out of hand. Officially a nudist beach, des Trenc draws a mixed clothed and unclothed crowd.

To reach the parking lot, take the signed turn-off west off Ma6040. The narrow, paved road passes mounds of yellowed salt at the Salines de Llevant salt fields then winds its way alongside fields sprinkled with wildflowers to reach the low-lying marsh area near the beach.

**Centro de Visitantes
Ses Salines** AQUARIUM

(cnr Carrer de Gabriel Roca & Plaça del Dolç; adult/child €6/3; ◷10am-noon & 3-11pm) **FREE** At the northeastern end of town, a block back from the Platja Es Port, this stone-and-glass swirl of a building is part aquarium, part interpretation centre for the offshore marine environs of the Parc Nacional Marítim-Terrestre de l'Arxipèlag de Cabrera. The visit ends with a climb up a spiral ramp that wraps around an extraordinary mural by Miguel Mansanet, based on 16th-century Mallorcan maps of the Mediterranean.

🏃 Activities

Team Double J BICYCLE RENTAL

(☑971 65 57 65; www.teamdoublej.com; Avinguda de la Primavera 9; per day from €7.50-15, per week €35-120; ◷9.30am-1pm & 4-7pm Feb-Oct) Rent bikes here; the team can also give you a map and information on area routes.

Piraguas Mix KAYAKING

(☑971 65 24 74; www.piraguasmixkayaks.com; S'Alqueria Rotje, Campos; sea kayaks per day from €30, guided excursions per person €30; ◷9am-9pm) One of the most respected sea-kayaking outfits on the island.

🍴 Eating

Marisol INTERNATIONAL €€

(☑971 65 50 70; www.restaurantemarisol.eu; Carrer de l'Enginier Gabriel Roca; mains €12-26; ◷12.30-10.30pm; 🛜🚸) Opt for pasta, pizza, fish and shellfish, rice dishes or stews at a table on the spacious covered terrace by the water. The food is fairly standard portside fare, but the setting is pleasant enough.

★ Sal de Coco MEDITERRANEAN €€€

(☑971 65 52 25; www.restaurantsaldecoco.com; Carrer Carreró 47; menus €25-33; ☺1-3pm & 6-11pm Wed-Sun Mar-Oct) This slick, art-strewn bistro takes its name from the sea salt gathered on the rocks around Colònia de Sant Jordi. Marta Rosselló puts an original take on Mediterranean flavours in dishes like homemade fish and spinach ravioli with shrimp sauce, cuttlefish and mushroom risotto and just-right steak tartare – all beautifully presented and revealing true depth of flavour.

ⓘ Information

Tourist office (☑971 65 60 73; www.mallorcainfo.com; Carrer Gabriel Roca; ☺10am-2pm & 4-9pm Wed-Mon Jun-Sep, 10am-1pm & 4-6pm Wed-Mon Feb-Apr & Oct) Located right in the port.

ⓘ Getting There & Away

Bus 502 links the town to Palma (€6.35, up to eight times a day, 1¼ hours).

Ses Salines

Used as a source of salt since the days of the Romans, Ses Salines (the Salt Pans) is an unassuming agricultural centre that's rapidly garnering a reputation as one of southern Mallorca's most agreeable inland towns. With cool bar-restaurants and shops selling the cleverly marketed local salt, it has transformed itself from a rural waystation to a destination in its own right. It stands on the border of some lovely country – replete with walking and cycling trails.

⊙ Sights

The town's attractions are quite spread out and you'll need a car to reach them.

Cap de Ses Salines LIGHTHOUSE

(Carretera de Cap de Ses Salines) Follow the Ma6110 highway 9km south of Llombards to reach the Cap de Ses Salines, a beautiful bluff on Mallorca's southernmost tip with a lighthouse dating back to 1863. There's not much here at the cape, but stretching out along either side of it are wonderfully unspoilt beaches protected by the Reserva Marina del Migjorn de Mallorca.

The eastern beaches are hewn out of the coastal cliffs that run up towards exquisitely beautiful coves like Caló des Màrmols, beaches like the Platja d'Almunia and caves

like Cova de Sa Plana. A rugged coastal path links them all in an 8km trail.

Botanicactus GARDENS

(www.botanicactus.com; Carretera Ses Salines-Santanyí; adult/child €9.50/4.50; ☺9am-7.30pm) Just outside town is Botanicactus, which claims to be Europe's largest botanical garden, bristling with palms, bamboo groves, cypress, carob and orange trees and 12,000 cacti. Come to wander among its 1000-plus species of Mediterranean, exotic and wetland plants.

Poblat Talaiòtic dels Antigors ARCHAEOLOGICAL SITE

FREE One kilometre out of Ses Salines, heading towards Colònia de Sant Jordi (follow the signposts), is this neglected archaeological site. There's no visitors centre, the gate is always open, and only virtually illegible plaques remain, so use your imagination to see how these low stone walls would have once constituted a prehistoric settlement.

☆ Activities

Artestruz Mallorca FARM

(☑971 65 05 62; www.artestruzmallorca.com; Ma6014; adult/child €5/2; ☺10am-2pm & 5-8pm) Signposted off the Ma6014, 3km northwest of Ses Salines, this ostrich farm is certainly different. The main attraction is the chance to see, stroke and feed the ostriches, which kids will love. Meals (featuring ostrich meat, ostrich eggs and Mallorcan wine) are available with advance notice, and there's also a shop on-site, selling ostrich-leather products such as bags and even computer cleaners made from ostrich feathers.

Salines des Trenc GUIDED TOUR

(www.salinasdelevante.com; Carretera Colònia de Sant Jordi-Campos Km 10) If you fancy getting the inside scoop on des Trenc's famous *flor de sal* (hand-harvested sea salt), you can join

SOUTHERN MALLORCA'S TOP BEACHES

- ➡ **Platja des Trenc** (p158)
- ➡ **Sa Plageta** and **S'Espalmador** (Illa de Cabrera; p163)
- ➡ **Cala Mondragó** (p164)
- ➡ **Cala Pi** (p157)
- ➡ **Cala Santanyí** (p161)
- ➡ **Cala Llombards** (p162)

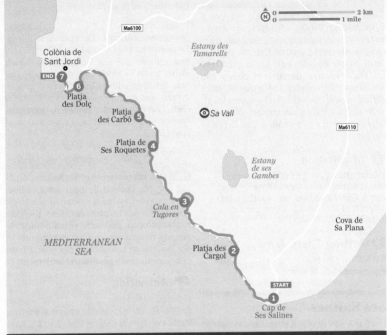

Walking Tour
Cap de Ses Salines to Colònia de Sant Jordi

START CAP DE SES SALINES
END COLÒNIA DE SANT JORDI
LENGTH 9KM; 3 HOURS

Pristine coastline can be hard to come by in Mallorca, but this walk has it in abundance. A coastal trail between Cap de Ses Salines and Colònia de Sant Jordi, it's a flat but rocky trek across battered coastal rock outcroppings and forgotten sandy beaches perfect for swimming. Be sure to take plenty of water; there are no fresh water sources and very little shade along the way. Plants you'll see along the trail include wild asparagus and leafy *azucena de mar* (sea purslane), the fragrant white flowers of which appear in July and August.

Leave your car on the shoulder of the road at ❶ **Cap de Ses Salines**, which is signposted from the main highway. From here, head towards the sea and turn right (west). You'll see the Mediterranean glistening to your left, the Illa de Cabrera in the distance and the private Sa Vall estate, owned by the March family, bordering the walk on your right.

After 30 minutes of a fairly flat walk over the ruddy-coloured rocks that dominate the coast here (the same ones as those used in Palma's Catedral), you'll come upon the first 'virgin' beach of the walk, ❷ **Platja des Cargol**, which is protected by a natural rock pier. In summer it can get quite crowded on land and at sea.

Continue along the coast to reach other coves and beaches, like ❸ **Cala en Tugores** (one hour further on), ❹ **Platja de Ses Roquetes**, ❺ **Platja des Carbó** (after 2¼ hours) and finally ❻ **Platja des Dolç** (after three hours). The beaches, with their fine-as-flour sand and gentle waves the colour of turquoise, are simply gorgeous. Even with summer crowds, the idyllic setting amid juniper trees and squawking seagulls ensures that it always feels like an escape.

When you get to the town of ❼ **Colònia de Sant Jordi**, you've reached the end of the walk.

a 90-minute tour of the salt pans, which are available in Spanish, English and German. The tours give you plenty of background on the salt production process and its history, as well as insights into local birdlife. They set off at 10.30am, noon, 4.30pm and 5.30pm from April to October from the Salines des Trenc office.

✖ Eating

Cassai INTERNATIONAL €
(☎ 971 64 97 21; Carrer de Sitjar 5; mains €13-23.50; ☺ 11am-11pm) A beguiling yet understated designer space, Cassai has the ambience of an Ibiza chill-out cafe for grown-ups. It also runs a designer homewares store in town and it shows in its rustic-sophisticated decor. Dishes include lamb cutlets with *tumbet* (a traditional vegetable dish), red tuna curry, and a well-priced express lunch (€8.50).

★ Casa Manolo MALLORCAN €€
(☎ 971 64 91 30; www.bodegabarahona.com; Plaça Sant Bartomeu 2; mains €16-27; ☺ 11am-4pm & 7-11pm Tue-Sun) With its photo-plastered walls and ceilings strung with Serrano hams, this corner bar looks much as it did when it first opened in 1945. The secret to its staying power is the rice, seafood and fish dishes. Try lobster stew or *arròs notari,* a rice dish overflowing with seafood and a rich squid-ink sauce.

Asador Es Teatre GRILL €€
(☎ 971 64 95 40; www.asadoresteatre.com; Plaça Sant Bartomeu 4; mains €12-22; ☺ 11am-11pm Thu-Tue) Asador Es Teatre specialises in roast lamb, T-bone steaks and other fine cuts of meat. The building dates to the 19th century, but the outdoor terrace is the place to be.

🍷 Drinking

Bodega Llum de Sal BAR, CAFE
(www.llumdesal.es; Carrer Burguera Mut 14; ☺ 9am-midnight) Artworks jazz up the walls of this stone-and-wood, split-level bodega on the main drag – one of the loveliest in this corner of the island. As well as doing a fine line in coffee and cocktails, it sells gourmet food products including local salt and ready-made herb combinations for fish, meats and even wok cooking.

🛍 Shopping

Cassai Gourmet FOOD, WINE
(Plaça Sant Bartomeu 9; ☺ 10am-1.15pm & 5-9.30pm) The official sales point for Flor de Sal d'Es Trenc, the salt you'll see for sale all over Mallorca, this shops sells the natural variety (€17 per kilo), as well as those scented with Mediterranean, hibiscus and black olive herbs among others. It also sells wines, olive oils and other local goodies.

ℹ️ Getting There & Away

The easiest way to arrive here is with your own wheels, not least because you'll need them to explore the surrounding attractions. Infrequent buses run to/from Campos and Santanyí.

SANTANYÍ TO CALA D'OR

The resorts that cling to the island's eastern flank have grown into a more or less continuous stream of hotels, seafood restaurants and umbrella-packed beaches. The only merciful exception to the sprawl in the busiest part of southern Mallorca is the Parc Natural de Mondragó, a bit of fresh air in the form of immaculate beaches rimmed with ruddy cliffs and junipers.

Santanyí

Wedged between the Parc Natural de Mondragó and Ses Salines, Santanyí is having something of a moment. People are slowly waking up to the allure of this easygoing inland town, where honey-coloured houses shelter a fine array of boho cafes, boutiques, galleries, ceramic shops and restaurants.

Most of the action spirals around the church-dotted Plaça Major, especially on market days (Wednesdays and Saturdays) when the stalls fill with produce from nearby farms. The square is fringed by cafes and bars where you can watch the world go languidly by over drinks and tapas.

◎ Sights

Cala Santanyí BEACH
Cala Santanyí's popular but not overcrowded beach is the star in a scenic show that also includes a gorgeous, cliff-lined cove and impossibly cobalt-coloured waters. The beach sits at the bottom of a ravine of sorts where there is a car park (it's a stiff walk or cycle ride back to the resort centre). A small path leads along the coast, where the natural rock arch **El Pontàs** rises out of the surf. This is a popular spot to snorkel.

VISITING ILLA DE CABRERA

Nineteen uninhabited islands and islets make up the only national park in the Balearic Islands, the **Parc Nacional Marítim-Terrestre de l'Arxipèlag de Cabrera** (☑971 72 50 10; ☺Easter-Oct), an archipelago with dry, hilly islands that are known for their birdlife, rich marine environment and abundant lizard populations. The Illa de Cabrera, the largest island of the archipelago and the only one you can visit, sits just 16km off the coast of Colònia de Sant Jordi. Other islands are used for wildlife research. Only 200 people per day (300 in August) are allowed to visit this highly protected natural area, so reserve your place at least a day ahead. Although private boats can come to Cabrera if they've requested navigation and anchoring permits in advance from the park administration, nearly all visitors arrive on the organised cruises. **Excursions a Cabrera** (☑971 64 90 34; www.excursionsa-cabrera.es; Porto de Colònia de Sant Jordi; adult/child boat €40/25, speedboat €42/27) runs both slow boats and speedboats from Colònia de Sant Jordi; **Mar Cabrera** (☑971 65 64 03; www.marcabrera.com; Avinguda Gabriel Roca 18; adult/child from €35/20; ☺9am-1pm & 4-9pm) operates a speedboat service.

During the day you're pretty much on your own. Many people simply enjoy the wonderfully calm beaches, **Sa Plageta** and **S'Espalmador**. At times, the park can seem overprotected – there are few hiking trails open to the public, and for most of them you'll either need to tag along with a guide or request permission from the park office – but this is an extremely fragile ecosystem.

The best-known walking route heads up to a restored **14th-century castle**, a fortress once used to keep pirates off the island. It was later converted into a prison for French soldiers, more than 5000 of whom died after being abandoned in 1809 towards the end of

---

Cala Llombards
BEACH

A petite cove defined by rough rock walls topped with pines, Cala Llombards is a truly beautiful place. A beach-hut bar and sun loungers shaded by palm-leaf umbrellas constitute the extent of human intervention. The view is soul-satisfying – turquoise waters, a sandy beach and the reddish rocks of the cliffs that lead like a promenade towards the sea.

To reach Cala Llombards, follow the sign off the Ma6102 down a stone-walled road bordered by meadows of grazing sheep.

✗ Eating

★**Alchemy**
MALLORCAN €€

(☑971 65 39 57; Carrer de Aljub 10; ☺1-4pm & 7pm-2am Mon-Fri, 7pm-2am Sat, 7pm-midnight Sun) Despite the name, this is nothing to do with molecular gastronomy or other culinary dalliances. With its pretty courtyard, slick bistro interior and warm welcome, Alchemy keeps its look, feel and food refreshingly simple. You might begin with, say, goat's cheese salad or baby squid, followed by a perfect filet of steak or grilled fish.

Es Molí de Santanyí
TAPAS €€

(☑971 65 36 29; Carrer Consolació 19; tapas €5-19; ☺1-11pm mid-Feb–mid-Nov) Look for the windmill, slip into the garden patio shaded by palms and rubber trees and take a seat at one of the marble tables. On the menu are imaginative, well-executed tapas for assembling your own little feast, from tuna sashimi to spicy blood sausage wontons and roasted quail with lentils.

❶ Information

Parc Natural de Mondragò Office (☑971 64 20 67; Carrer de Can Llaneres 8; ☺9am-4pm) Information on visiting this coastal protected area.

❶ Getting There & Away

Up to six buses head to Palma (€6.50, 1½ hours) daily.

Cala Figuera

If you could see Cala Figuera from the air, it would look like a snake with its jaws open wide, biting into the pine trees and low buildings of the resort. Although the town itself is nothing special, the romantic, restaurant-lined port is one of the prettiest on the east coast. A few yachts and pleasure cruisers line up beside the painted fishing boats, but Cala Figuera retains its air of

the Peninsular War. The 30-minute walk to the castle meanders along the northern side of the island before taking you to the 80m-high bluff where the castle looms.

Guides also sometimes lead the 20-minute walk to **Es Celler**, a farmhouse owned by the Feliu family, who owned the entire island in the early 20th century. It's now a small museum with history and culture exhibits. Nearby stands a monument to the French prisoners who died on Cabrera.

Other possible routes lead to the **N'Ensiola lighthouse** (four hours, permission required), the southern sierra of **Serra de Ses Figueres** (2½ hours, permission required), or the highest point of the island, the 172m **Picamosques** (three hours, permission required).

The island is a wonderful place for snorkelling. While you need special permission to dive here, you can snorkel off the beach. Or, in July and August, sign up for the guided snorkelling excursions offered by park rangers.

This is prime territory for birdwatching: marine birds, birds of prey and migrating birds all call Cabrera home at least part of the year. Common species include the fisher eagle, the endangered Balearic shearwater, Audouin's gull, Cory's shearwater, shags, ospreys, Eleonora's falcon and peregrine falcons.

Wildlife is also abundant. The Balearic lizard is the best-known species on Cabrera. This small lizard has few enemies on the archipelago and 80% of the species population lives on the island.

On the cruise back to Colònia de Sant Jordi, the boat stops in **Sa Cova Blava** (Blue Cave), a gorgeous cave with crystalline waters where passengers can take a dip. Speedboats also stop here.

old-world authenticity. Local fishers really still fish here, threading their way down the winding inlet before dawn and returning to the port to mend their nets.

🏃 Activities

Red Star Tours   BOAT TOUR
(☑ 664 243464; www.redstartours.com; Port de Cala Figuera) Hop aboard for a 15-minute tour of the port (adult/child €10/7), a 30-minute trip to surrounding bays including Cala Santanyí (€15/11), or a one-hour nature tour (€25/17) taking in a string of little-known coves.

🍴 Eating

Restaurante Petite Iglesia   FRENCH €
(☑ 971 64 50 09; www.la-petite-iglesia.com; Carrer de la Marina 11; mains €13.50-21, menus €19.90-39.50; ⊙6-11pm Apr-Oct; ﭏ) Situated two blocks up the hill from the water, it may not have sea views but it's nonetheless close to being the most atmospheric setting in town. Inhabiting the shell of a little sandstone church, with outdoor tables under the trees, this place serves up French home cooking with Provençal beef stew and tender lamb shanks infused with rosemary.

Mistral Restaurante   MEDITERRANEAN €
(☑ 971 64 51 18; www.mistral-restaurante.com; Carrer de la Verge del Carme 42; mains €15-18.50; ⊙6.30-11pm mid-Apr–Oct; ﭏ) Choose between tasty, typical tapas or more elaborate dishes such as grilled sole fish with fresh parsley paste, or *tumbet* with meat or fish at this stylish spot just up from the port.

L'Arcada   MALLORCAN, INTERNATIONAL €
(☑ 971 64 50 32; Carrer de la Verge del Carme 80; mains €13.50-26.50; ⊙12.30-10.30pm Apr-Oct) At this elevated restaurant you can watch the boats blink in the port while you eat winningly fresh seafood (from grilled calamari to Mallorcan prawns), paellas and island-wide faves like pork loin with *tumbet*. Pizza is also on offer here if you must.

🍷 Drinking

Bon Bar   BAR, CAFE
(Carrer de la Verge del Carme 27; ⊙9.30am-2am) Views – that's what this place is all about. High above the main body of the inlet and with uninterrupted vistas, this is the place to nurse a cocktail, although it also sells snacks and ice creams.

PARC NATURAL DE MONDRAGÓ

A natural park encompassing beaches, dunes, wetlands, coastal cliffs and inland agricultural land, the 766-hectare Parc Natural de Mondragó is a beautiful area for swimming or hiking, but is best known as a birdwatching destination. Most people who head this way come to take a dip in the lovely **Cala Mondragó**, one of the most attractive coves on the east coast. Sheltered by large rocky outcrops and fringed by pine trees, it's formed by a string of three protected sandy beaches connected by rocky footpaths.

Birdwatchers have a ball with the varied species found in the area, which include falcons and turtledoves. Among those species that nest here are peregrine falcons and Audouin's gulls. Taking one of the walking trails that criss-cross the park will give you plenty of birdwatching opportunities. Also keep an eye out for Algerian hedgehogs, Hermann's tortoises and the Balearic toad.

Cala Mondragó is 2km south of Portopetro. Bus 507 links Mondragó with Cala d'Or (€1.85, 30 minutes, seven times daily Monday through Friday) and a few other seaside resorts.

❶ Getting There & Away

Bus 502 makes the trip from Palma (€7, 1½ hours) via Colònia de Sant Jordi and Santanyí no more than three times a day, Monday through Saturday.

❶ Information

Park office (☑971 64 20 67, 971 18 10 22; Carretera de Cala Mondragó; ⊙9am-4pm) The small park office by the car park has maps with walking suggestions. There's another branch in Santanyí.

Portopetro

There's something in the air in Portopetro. This intimate fishing port's slow pace and laid-back style is immediately apparent as you stroll its steep, shady streets and look out over the protected natural inlet that originally made this town such a hit with fishers.

🏃 Activities

Petro Divers   DIVING
(☑971 65 98 46; www.petro-divers.eu; Calo d'es Moix 8; ⊙9am-6.30pm; ⛴) This diving outlet offers the full array of PADI courses, from intro and children's dives to Open Water Diving certifications. A single dive will set you back €39; the more you book, the cheaper it gets. It also rents out diving gear.

🍴 Eating

★ Aventura   MALLORCAN €€
(☑971 65 71 67; Carrer de sa Punta Mitjana 11; mains €9.50-17; ⊙noon-3.30pm & 6-11pm) Breezy harbour views, friendly service and freshly caught fish make Aventura the pick of the waterfront bunch. Go for mixed tapas for two (€22) with a bottle of *tinto* (red wine), or spot-on mains like hake with clams or grilled John Dory.

La Caracola   MALLORCAN, INTERNATIONAL €€
(☑971 65 70 13; Avinguda del Port 40; 2-course lunch menu €8.50, mains €7-23; ⊙1-3.30pm & 7.30-11pm; ⛴) Besides the usual paella and pasta, this enduringly popular place has been pleasing diners with plates of *calamares rellenos* (stuffed squid), *lechona* (suckling pig) and *tumbet* for 20 years. Not the flashiest place in town, though it's usually the most crowded.

Restaurante Marítimo   MALLORCAN €€
(☑971 65 80 50; Calo d'en Moix; mains €12.50-28; ⊙noon-4pm & 7-11.30pm Tue-Sun; ⛴) Next to the dive school, this unassuming restaurant has a bougainvillea-draped terrace where you can look out across the harbour. Fish is the big deal, with everything from grilled monkfish to crustacean-studded paellas.

❶ Getting There & Away

Up to five buses a day head from Portopetro to Palma (€8.40, 1½ hours) and Cala d'Or (€1.50, 10 minutes).

Cala d'Or

POP 4220

Although the pretty cove beaches and calm, azure waters are still here, they can be hard to find amid this flashy, overgrown resort. Each *cala* (cove) has its own main drag, where pubs, restaurants and souvenir shops flourish, making it very difficult to get a handle on the place.

Cala d'Or's real claim to fame is its yacht marina, **Port Petit**, one of the most glamorous in Mallorca and the main reason why this corner of Cala d'Or is earning a reputation as a stylish, live-large kind of place.

🏃 Activities

Nemar Kayaks KAYAKING
(📞656 851267; http://nemarkayaks.weebly.com; Avinguda de sa Cala Gran 8; kayak rental per day €30-50, 2hr excursions €30-40) Rent a kayak to paddle around to sheltered south-coast bays at your own steam or join one of the excursions to learn from the pros. The excursions include a beach-hop around Cala d'Or, cave combing around the Parc Natural de Mondragó and a trip to Cala Santanyí via the natural rock arch of Es Pontàs.

Xplore Mallorca OUTDOORS
(📞971 65 90 07; www.xploremallorca.com; Carrer de Alga; ⊗May-Oct) Mountain biking (€18), hiking (€15), cycling (€19), and sea kayaking (€18) excursions of varying duration. Children pay half-price.

Sea Riders BOAT TOUR
(📞615 998732; www.searidersweb.com; Cala Llonga; tours adult/child from €21/16; ⊗Apr-Oct) Sea Riders, in Cala Llonga, offers a kid-friendly boat ride as well as a faster 'adrenaline' ride (€42) with up to three departures daily in July and August.

Moto Sprint BICYCLE RENTAL, MOTORBIKE RENTAL
(📞971 65 90 07; www.moto-sprint.com; Carrer d'en Perico Pomar 5; bike rental per day €7.50-16, motorbike rental €29-93; ⊗8am-1pm & 4.30-8pm) Rent a bike and cycling equipment, or a scooter.

🍴 Eating

⭐**Yacht Club Cala d'Or** MEDITERRANEAN €€
(📞971 64 82 03; www.yccalador.com; Avinguda de Cala Llonga; snacks €5-9.50, mains €14-25; ⊗9am-midnight Mar-Oct) You don't need to be a millionaire yachtie to eat in style at this glass-fronted harbour restaurant, where tables overlook a tantalising infinity pool. The menu is Mallorcan with the lightest of international touches, with dishes as simple as Sóller prawn tartare

ⓘ GET YOUR BEARINGS

Cala d'Or's main *calas* (coves) from west to east are **Cala Egos**, where there's a tiny, overcrowded beach; **Cala Llonga** (Port Petit), home to the marina; **Cala d'Or** (Cala Petita), with its tree-lined shores; **Cala Gran** (Big Cove), with the widest beach of the lot; **Cala Esmeralda**, considered the prettiest cove; and **Cala Ferrera**, a busy, long beach backed by hotels.

on avocado, wild sea bass grilled in orange sauce and filet of steak.

Acuarius SPANISH €€
(📞971 65 98 76; www.restauranteacuarius.com; Port Petit 308; mains €11-27, 3-course menu €15; ⊗9.30am-midnight Feb-Nov) A cracking location overlooking the yacht port, chilled music and friendly service makes Acuarius stand out. Snag a spot on the terrace for fresh fish and shellfish or a mean *frit Mallorquí* (Mallorcan-style fried lamb).

Port Petit MEDITERRANEAN €€€
(📞971 64 30 39; www.portpetit.com; Avinguda de Cala Llonga; lunch menus €21.50, mains €19-29.50, dinner menus €39.50-59.50; ⊗1-3.30pm & 7-11pm Wed-Mon Apr-Oct) One of Cala d'Or's top tables, Port Petit puts an innovative spin on local seafood and produce, served on its sleek, covered upstairs terrace looking down over the yacht port. Service is attentive and the cooking assured, with dishes like fresh lobster sautéed in lime butter and roast lamb slow-cooked in its own juices and Mediterranean herbs catching our eye.

ⓘ Information

Tourist office (📞971 82 60 84; Avinguda de Cala Llonga; ⊗9am-2pm Mon-Fri) On the road from the town centre down to Port Petit.

ⓘ Getting There & Away

Bus 501 heads to Portopetro (€1.50, 10 minutes, five times a day), then on to Palma (€8.40, one hour 20 minutes, up to six times a day). Bus 441 runs along the eastern coast, stopping at all the major resorts.

Accommodation

Best Places to Stay

➡ Can Cera (p168)

➡ Es Petit Hotel de Valldemossa (p171)

➡ Can Busquets (p171)

➡ Hotel Formentor (p176)

Best Rural Hotels

➡ Cases de Son Barbassa (p178)

➡ Ca N'Aí (p173)

➡ Alqueria Blanca (p174)

➡ Es Castell (p177)

Best Budget Options

➡ Hostal Dragonera (p170)

➡ Hostal Nadal (p173)

➡ Hostal Villaverde (p172)

➡ Hostal Pons (p169)

Where to Stay

Mallorca's not all about anonymous megaresorts. Plan ahead and you can snag a room with a designer edge or a retreat that will give you a taste of the island long before the dawn of the package holiday. Up and down the coast you'll find charismatic lodgings, from back-to-nature *fincas* (farm-stays) resting in olive groves to town mansions with boutique credentials and hilltop monasteries with stirring views over mountains and sea. Choosing where to stay is much more than finding a bed for the night.

Ultimately the decision is a matter of taste: the west is great for coastal drama, hill towns and hiking; the hinterland for rural relaxation; the east and south for their fine sandy beaches, ideal for families; the north for a dash of everything. If culture, food and shopping are high on your list, Palma is perfect – and you can easily day-trip to great beaches nearby.

Advance booking is always a good idea, especially in high season (May to September) when beds are like gold dust. Increasingly, Palma is becoming a weekend short-break destination, which means that even in low season it can be an idea to at least call ahead. Prices can skyrocket in high season (doubling, sometimes even tripling), while there are usually cracking deals to be had out of season.

From November to Easter, the vast majority of hotels close in coastal resorts. Palma is a year-round option, and you'll also find a sprinkling of places open in towns like Pollença and Sóller.

Pricing

The following price categories relate to a double room with private bathroom:

CATEGORY	COST
$ budget	less than €75
$$ midrange	€75-200
$$$ top end	more than €200

Accommodation Types

Camping & Youth Hostels

There are no official camping grounds on the island, although it is possible to pitch a tent at the Monestir de Lluc. There is one *albergue juvenil* (youth hostel) in Cap des Pinar in the north. For more information, check out www.reaj.com, the official website for Spain's network of youth hostels.

Hotels & Hostales

A *hostal* (sometimes called a *pensión*) is a small-scale budget hotel, usually family run. The better ones can be bright, spotless and characterful. Hotels cover the entire spectrum, from no-frills digs through to design-focused boutique hotels and luxury hotels.

At the budget end, prices vary according to whether the room has a *lavabo* (washbasin), *ducha* (shower) or *baño completo* (full bathroom). At the top end you may pay more for a room with a *balcón* (balcony) or sea view, and you can fork out more for additional comfort in a suite.

Useful resources for booking hotels and *hostales:*

➧ **Mallorca Hotel Guide** (www. mallorcahotelguide.com) Hotel-booking engine run by the island's main hoteliers association.

➧ **Asociación Hotelera de Palma** (p76) For Palma hotels.

➧ **Reis de Mallorca** (www.reisdemallorca. com) Hotels with character.

➧ **Hostal en Mallorca** (www. hostalenmallorca.com) An array of budget places.

➧ **First Sun Mallorca** (www.firstsunmallorca. com) Hotels around Cala Ratjada and Canyamel.

Refugis

Refugis (simple hikers' huts) are mostly scattered about the Serra de Tramuntana, and are a cheap alternative to hotels when hiking. Some are strategically placed on popular hiking routes. Many are run by the **Consell de Mallorca's environment department** (☑971 17 37 00; www.conselldemallorca.net/refugis), while others are run by the **Institut Balear de la Naturalesa** (Ibanat; ☑971 17 76 52; www.caib.es; ☺book 10am-2pm Mon-Fri). Dorm beds generally cost around €12; some also have a couple of doubles and meal service. Call ahead, as more often than not you'll find them closed if you just turn up.

Rural Properties

Whether it's a serene *finca* (farm-stay), a B&B in a manor high in the Tramuntana or a sea-facing villa, Mallorca's rural properties are hands down the most atmospheric places to stay. Many are historic, stylish country estates with outstanding facilities, including swimming pools, romantic restaurants, and organised activities and excursions.

The local tourism authorities subdivide them into three categories: *agroturisme* (working farms), *turisme de interior* (country mansions converted into boutique hotels) and *hotel rural* (a country estate converted into a luxury hotel).

To book rural properties online, check out the following:

Agroturismo en Mallorca (www.agroturismoenmallorca.com)

Associació Agroturisme Balear (☑971 72 15 08; www.rusticbooking.com)

Finca Mallorca (www.fincamallorca.de)

Fincas 4 You (www.fincas4you.com)

Mallorca Farmhouses (☑in UK 0845 800 8080; www.mfh.co.uk)

Rustic Rent (www.rusticrent.com)

Secret Places (www.secretplaces.com)

Top Rural (www.toprural.com)

PALMA DE MALLORCA

Old Palma and Es Puig de Sant Pere charm with their boutique hotels gathered around stately *patis* (patios) and design-focused digs, as well as the occasional family-run hostel. Stay near the Passeig d'es Born or the Plaça Major to be in the thick of the city's shopping and dining scene. Sea view? Head to the Passeig Marítim or Es Portitxol.

Old Palma

Hotel Santa Clara   BOUTIQUE HOTEL €€
(Map p56; ☑971 72 92 31; www.santaclarahotel. es; Carrer de Sant Alonso 16, Palma de Mallorca; d €104-225, ste €168-360; ❉@☎) Boutique meets antique in this historic mansion, converted with respect, where subdued greys, steely silvers and cream blend harmoniously with the warm stone walls, ample spaces and high ceilings of the original structure.

GET THEE TO A MONASTERY

Seeking a meditative retreat? Mallorca has a handful of monasteries (technically hermitages, as their inmates were hermits and not monks) offering basic digs in converted cells, blissful silence and often spectacular views. Kids are more than welcome, but they might have to keep the noise down. Four favourites:

Santuari de la Mare de Déu des Puig (🖉 971 18 41 32; Puig de Maria, Pollença; s €10-14, d €17-22; 🛜🏠) Take in the full sweep of the north coast from this captivating hilltop hermitage in Pollença, where goat bells are your alarm call. Staying here is an ascetic, tranquil experience. First-floor rooms have the edge. Guests can use the refectory and barbecue areas, or you can order food (the paella is terrific).

Petit Hotel Hostatgería Sant Salvador (🖉 971 58 19 52; www.santsalvadorhotel.com; Santuari de Sant Salvador, Sant Salvador; s/d €45/69, 6-bed apt €117-142; ⊙ Feb-Oct; 🏠) High above the plains in the fortresslike monastery of Sant Salvador, the monks have long since gone, but their former cells have been converted into simple, spruce rooms, each with an outstanding panoramic view and private bathroom.

Hospedería del Santuari de Lluc (🖉 971 87 15 25; www.lluc.net; Plaça dels Peregrins, Escora; s €31-36, d €41-62; 🏠) Popular with school groups, walkers and pilgrims, the Santuari de Lluc's rooms vary in size and facilities (some have kitchen access); some look over the courtyard, but those with mountain views are best, while the downstairs rooms are dark and best avoided. It's a magical spot in the Tramuntana.

Ermita de la Victòria (🖉 971 54 99 12; www.lavictoriahotel.com; Carretera Cap des Pinar, Cap des Pinar; s/d €45/69, breakfast €8; 🏠) A side road just east of the bay of S'Illot winds up high to a magnificent viewpoint and this early-15th-century hermitage. The 13 renovated rooms have a crisp feel, all white walls and cream linen with timber window shutters and beams. The massive stone walls and terracotta floors lend it Mediterranean grace and the position is just wow.

There's an intimate spa in which to unwind. Palma is reduced to postcard format from the decked roof terrace, ideal for a sunbathe or a sundowner.

Palma Suites
APARTMENT €€

(Map p56; 🖉 971 72 79 00; www.palma-suites.com; Plaça Mercadal 8, Palma de Mallorca; ste €137–250; 🖩🛜🏊🏠) This stylish newcomer twins hotel luxury with home-style independence. Playful artworks and splashes of bold colour lend character to sizeable, slickly designed apartments, with smart TVs and well-equipped kitchens with Nespresso machines. The triplex suites have bags of room for families. For surround views of Palma's skyline, step up to the roof terrace. There's a minimum three-night stay.

Hotel Dalt Murada
HISTORIC HOTEL €€

(Map p56; 🖉 971 42 53 00; www.daltmurada.com; Carrer de l'Almudaina 6A, Palma de Mallorca; s €105, d €99-170, ste €199, breakfast €7.50; 🖩🛜) Gathered around a medieval courtyard, this carefully restored old town house, dating from 1500, has 14 rooms with antique furnishings (including chandeliers and canopied beds) and art belonging to the family who run the place. That said, mattresses are too springy for some tastes and street-facing rooms can be noisy. The 21st-century penthouse suite has incomparable cathedral views.

★ Can Cera
BOUTIQUE HOTEL €€€

(Map p56; 🖉 971 71 50 12; http://cancerahotel.com; Carrer del Convent de Sant Francesc 8, Palma de Mallorca; r €165-495; 🖩🛜🏠) Welcome to one of Palma's most romantic boutique boltholes, entered via an inner courtyard, where cobbles have been worn smooth over 700 years and a wrought-iron staircase sweeps up to guest rooms that manage the delicate act of combining history with modern design flourishes. The decor is stylish but never overblown, with high ceilings, period furnishings and richly detailed throws.

A terrace with broad views across old Palma, an ornate library, a spa for exclusive use (just say when) and a proper concierge service all add to Can Cera's unique appeal.

Boutique Hotel Calatrava
BOUTIQUE HOTEL €€€

(Map p56; 🖉 971 72 81 10; www.boutiquehotelcalatrava.com; Plaça de Llorenç Villallonga 8, Palma de

Mallorca; r €180-495; ✹ @ 🛜 📶) This new boutique stunner sits right on the old city walls, with dazzling sea views. The rooms combine 19th-century features with minimalist streamlining, rich fabrics and contemporary art, plus welcome touches like smart TVs and minibars with free water. The sun deck will make you want to linger over breakfast, with eggs to order and fresh-pressed juice.

In tune with the discreet vibe, the downstairs spa can be booked for individual use, which means you get onto the whirlpool, sauna and relaxation area all to yourself. The service, too, sets this hotel apart – nothing is too much trouble.

Hotel Palacio
Ca Sa Galesa HISTORIC HOTEL €€€
(Map p56; ✐ 971 71 54 00; www.palaciocasagalesa.com; Carrer del Miramar 8, Palma de Mallorca; s €199-300, d €219-349, ste €299-488; ✹ @ 🛜 ✹)
Rooms in this enchanting 16th-century mansion are arranged around a cool patio garden. A genteel air wafts through the elegant bedrooms, each named after a famous composer and furnished with antiques, artwork and silk throws. Swim below the vaults in the Roman-style subterranean spa or peer across to the cathedral from a cabana bed on the roof terrace.

Plaça Major & Around

Misión de San Miguel BOUTIQUE HOTEL €€
(Map p62; ✐ 971 21 48 48; www.urhotels.com; Carrer de Can Maçanet 1, Palma de Mallorca; r €75-163, ste €115-203; P ✹ @ 🛜) This 32-room boutique hotel is an astounding deal with stylish designer rooms; it does the little things well with firm mattresses and rain showers, although some rooms open onto public areas and can be a tad noisy. Its restaurant, Misa Braseria, is part of the Fosh group. Service is friendly and professional.

Hotel Born HISTORIC HOTEL €€
(Map p56; ✐ 971 71 29 42; www.hotelborn.com; Carrer de Sant Jaume 3, Palma de Mallorca; s incl breakfast €66, d incl breakfast €91-126.50; ✹ @ 🛜) Stepping into this 16th-century Ca'n Maroto manor house wings you back in time. From the palatial reception area, take the spiral staircase to a red-carpeted hallway where carved wooden doors creak open to reveal simply furnished rooms, the high ceilings of which dwarf antique, slightly careworn furniture.

Convent de la Missió BOUTIQUE HOTEL €€
(Map p62; ✐ 971 22 73 47; www.conventdelamissio.com; Carrer de la Missió 7, Palma de Mallorca; s €105-185, d €115-225, ste €200-250; ✹ ✹) In a district that's as busy as a beehive, this is your saving grace. A functioning convent from the 1600s until 2003, it exudes a Zen-like calm created by all-white rooms and airy spaces. There is a romantic Arab-style hot tub and sauna in the stone-walled cellar. Or relax on the rooftop terrace or in the artfully designed reading room.

Es Puig de Sant Pere

Hostal Pons GUESTHOUSE €
(Map p56; ✐ 971 72 26 58; www.hostalpons.com; Carrer del Vi 8, Palma de Mallorca; s €30, d €60-70, tr €85; 🛜 📶) Bang in the heart of old Palma, this is a sweet, simple family-run guesthouse. Downstairs a cat slumbers in a plant-filled patio, upstairs you'll find a book-lined lounge and rooms with rickety bedsteads and tiled floors. Cheaper rooms share communal bathrooms. The roof terrace offers peaceful respite.

Hostal Apuntadores HOSTAL €
(Map p56; ✐ 971 71 34 91; www.palma-hostales.com; Carrer dels Apuntadors 8, Palma de Mallorca; s €40-58, d €50-68; ✹ @ 🛜 📶) Just off the main drag (bring earplugs), this unfussy spot makes up for its smallish rooms and lumpy beds with balconies in some rooms overlooking Plaça de la Reina, lots of sunlight and a rooftop terrace that overlooks a cathedral and serves drinks. Staff can squeeze a cot in if you ask.

Puro Oasis Urbano DESIGN HOTEL €€
(Map p56; ✐ 971 42 54 50; www.purohotel.com; Carrer de Montenegro 12, Palma de Mallorca; s €98-134, d €113-168, ste €167-239; ✹ @ 🛜 ✹) Achingly chic with a decor that crosses Ibiza-style minimalism with Marrakesh flair, this 14th-century-palace-turned-design-hotel has 26 rooms done in monochrome hues, with enormous flat-screen TVs and iPod docks. By day, lounge on the canopy beds, take a dip in the plunge pool or head to Puro beach club; by night join a fashionable crowd for cocktails in the bar.

Hotel Palau Sa Font HOTEL €€
(Map p56; ✐ 971 71 22 77; www.palausafont.com; Carrer dels Apuntadors 38, Palma de Mallorca; s incl breakfast €72-95, d incl breakfast €123-185;

ACCOMMODATION PLAÇA MAJOR & AROUND

✿ @ 🛜 🖼 📶) Slip down a quiet side street to this former 16th-century palace, with 19 rooms decorated in a sparse, minimalist style. Wrought-iron beds, exposed-stone columns and a few splashes of colour – a pale-green headboard or a simple red chair – give the rooms a feeling of almost monastic calm wedded to contemporary Mediterranean style.

★Hotel Tres   BOUTIQUE HOTEL €€€

(Map p56; ✆ 971 71 73 33; www.hoteltres.com; Carrer dels Apuntadors 3, Palma de Mallorca; s €160-280, d €170-290, ste €313-544; ✿ @ 🛜 🖼) Hotel Tres swings joyously between 16th-century town palace and fresh-faced Scandinavian design. Centred on a courtyard with a single palm, the rooms are cool and minimalist, with cowhide benches, anatomy-inspired prints and nice details like rollaway desks and Durance aromatherapy cosmetics. Head up to the roof terrace at sunset for a steam and swim as the cathedral begins to twinkle.

If you want a terrace, request room 101, 201 or 206. Young, friendly staff amp up the cool factor.

Hotel San Lorenzo   HISTORIC HOTEL €€€

(Map p56; ✆ 971 72 82 00; www.hotelsanlorenzo. com; Carrer de Sant Llorenç 14, Palma de Mallorca; s €160-205, d €172-215, ste €270; ✿ 🛜 🖼) Tucked inside the old quarter, this hotel resides in a beautifully restored 17th-century building. It has a fragrant Mallorcan courtyard, its own bar, a rooftop terrace with cathedral views and a bijou garden with swimming pool. Rooms come in a range of styles, from antique wooden furniture and tiled bathrooms to warm-toned rooms with Mallorcan fabrics.

Passeig Marítim & Western Palma

Hotel Mirador   HOTEL €€

(Map p66; ✆ 971 73 20 46; www.hotelmirador.es; Passeig Marítim 10, Palma de Mallorca; d €81-134, f €132-174; P ✿ @ 🛜 🖼) The Mirador's revamped rooms have a stripped-back aesthetic that emphasises clean lines, charcoal-and-white tones and marble floors. There's a small gym and a spa with a heated pool, jets, sauna and *hammam*, as well as a terrace with harbour views. The road outside can be pretty busy, so the double glazing is a plus. It's a 20-minute walk from the centre.

Es Portitxol, Es Molinar & Ciutat Jardí

Hotel Portixol   BOUTIQUE HOTEL €€€

(Map p52; ✆ 971 27 18 00; www.portixol.com; Carrer de la Sirena 27, Palma de Mallorca; s €135-165, d €185-365, ste €330-450; ✿ @ 🛜 🖼) The hip, harbour-front Hotel Portixol has a soothing fusion of Mediterranean and Scandinavian styles. Rooms are bright and breezy, with minimalist decor and home-style comforts like iPod docks, Nespresso coffee machines and DVD players. Most have sea views. There's also an outdoor pool, gym and full array of spa treatments, as well as one of Palma's best restaurants.

WESTERN MALLORCA

Port d'Andratx & Sant Elm

Hostal Dragonera   B&B €

(✆ 971 23 90 86; http://hostaldragonera.es; Avinguda del Rei Jaume I 5, Sant Elm; s €46-50, d €58-68; ⊙ Feb-Oct; ✿ 🛜) Hostal Dragonera sits right by the sea in Sant Elm. It's a friendly, spotless pick, with great views and a nicely chilled vibe. Rooms are smallish and spartan but clean and light; you'll get the most out of staying here if you take a room with a balcony for sea views (the outlay is about €10 extra).

Hostal-Residencia Catalina Vera   GUESTHOUSE €

(✆ 971 67 19 18; www.hostalcatalinavera.es; Carrer Isaac Peral 63, Port d'Andratx; s €60-65, d €65-85; P 🛜) Pablo and his family are welcoming hosts at this family-run abode, a block back from the water in Port d'Andratx. The rooms are simple but immaculate, with occasional antique furnishings and balconies or terraces – some with sea views. Filled with cacti and jasmine, the garden is a quiet escape in this busy summer port.

Estellencs

★Petit Hotel Sa Plana   HOTEL €€

(✆ 971 61 86 66; www.saplana.com; Carrer de Eusebi Pascual, Estellencs; d incl breakfast €95-125; ⊙ mid-Jan–Nov; ✿ 🛜 🖼) Each of the five rooms at this lovely old stone house is named after a Mediterranean wind and individually designed, but all are turned out with terracotta-tiled floors and wood furnishings. The family-run atmosphere is welcoming, the house wine a treat and the tousled garden a shady delight. It's at the western entrance to town, secluded above the main road.

Finca S'Olivar   RURAL HOTEL €€
(✍971 61 85 93, 629 266035; www.fincaolivar.org; Carretera C-710 Km 93.5, Estellencs; r €102-134, d €102-120, tr €130-154; P ✹ @ ☎ ⛱ ♨) What a view! Sprinkled across olive, almond and fig groves, this cluster of renovated stone hermitages has soul-stirring views across terraced slopes down to the sea. Rooms are rustic and simple, with wood-burning stoves or fireplaces and serene terraces, and the edge-of-the-world infinity pool is something else. The farm's olives and tangy jams are a treat.

Banyalbufar

Hotel Sa Baronia   HISTORIC HOTEL €
(✍971 61 81 46; www.hbaronia.com; Carrer de Baronia 16, Banyalbufar; s/d/tr €55/72/95, half board €65/94/135; ☺Easter-Oct; ☎ ⛱ ♨) A rambling building with a real cliffhanger of a swimming pool, family-run Baronia is built in the ruins of a Muslim-era fort (part of the tower remains). The rooms are simple with old-school decor – more 1950s Spanish grandmother than baronial – but the views from most of the balconies are exceptional; some face the sea, others the village.

Son Borguny   HISTORIC HOTEL €€
(✍971 14 87 06; www.sonborguny.com; Carrer de Borguny 1, Banyalbufar; s/d €75/95, ste €100-130; ☎) Penny makes you feel at home at this quaint 15th-century town house, a block up from Banyalbufar's main road. The attractive rooms are never overdone and feature occasional stone walls and wooden beams, plus some have partial sea views. Breakfast – a spread of eggs, fresh fruit, cold cuts and juice – will fire you up for a day's hiking.

★**Can Busquets**   B&B €€
(✍971 14 86 24; http://hostalcanbusquets.com; Carrer Miramar 24, Banyalbufar; s €75, d €86-94, ste €98-110; ✹ ☎ ♨) ✐ Can Busquets gets it right on so many levels – a heartfelt welcome, pretty gardens and spirit-lifting mountain views (especially at sunset). The Mallorcan-style rooms sport rustic flour-

ishes like beams and decorative tiles. Breakfasts are a cut above, with homemade jams and cakes, and eggs from the chickens that cluck around the owners' nearby organic farm.

Esporles & the Inland Circuit

La Posada del Marqués   HISTORIC HOTEL €€€
(✍971 61 12 30; www.posada-marques.com; Es Verger, Esporles; s/d/ste €165/210/278; P ✹ @ ☎ ⛱ ♨) Deep in the mountains around Esporles, the spectacularly located La Posada del Marqués is a luxurious retreat from the clamour of the modern world. The views sweep down the valleys to the distant plains, while the 16th-century stone manor conceals rooms with grand baroque interiors. It's not all about the past – there are plasma TVs, DVD players and wi-fi.

★**Gran Hotel Son Net**   LUXURY HOTEL €€€
(✍971 14 70 00; www.sonnet.es; Carrer del Castell de Son Net, Esporles; d €165-595, ste €525-1475; P ✹ @ ☎ ⛱) Romantic without being poncy, this award-winning 17th-century mansion is just sublime, as are the wild Tramuntana views. Everything here screams luxury – from the handmade Mallorcan fabrics in rooms to the four-posters and hot tubs in the suites, the poolside cabanas to the outstanding Mediterranean food served in a grand stone-walled hall. Its modern-art collection contains Warhol and Hockney originals. The *finca* produces its own wines on the estate, which you can sample at a tasting.

Valldemossa

★**Es Petit Hotel de Valldemossa**   BOUTIQUE HOTEL €€
(Map p95; ✍971 61 24 79; www.espetithotel-valldemossa.com; Carrer d'Uetam 1, Valldemosa; s €117-158, d €130-175; ✹ @ ☎) What better way

ACCOMMODATION BANYALBUFAR

to admire Valldemosa than from the rocking chair on your veranda at this family home turned boutique hotel? Five of its eight sunny, high-ceilinged rooms have gorgeous valley views. In the shady garden you could be an island away from the flow of Cartuja visitors outside. Fresh-baked cakes and pastries make breakfast a sweet treat.

Cases de Ca's Garriguer   RURAL HOTEL €€
(☑971 61 23 00; www.casesdecasgarriguer.com; Carretera Valldemossa–Andratx Km2.5, Valldemossa; s €140-150, d €160-200, tr €210-250; ⊙mid-Apr–Oct; [P][✻][🖈][🗢][🏊][🖼]) This lovely stone-built *finca* on an elevated plateau 3km west of Valldemossa has a relaxed vibe and big mountain views. Rooms are large, light and graceful, with beams and stone arches; all have either a balcony or terrace. The pool is just big enough for a quick dip but is gloriously quiet.

Hotel Valldemossa   HISTORIC HOTEL €€€
(☑971 61 26 26; www.valldemossahotel.com; Ctra Vieja de Valldemossa, Valldemossa; r €300-500; [P][✻][@][🗢][🏊]) Composed of two 19th-century stone houses that once belonged to the monastery, this hotel has 12 immaculate rooms. Luxury is the name of the game, with a blend of antique furnishings, artwork and modern comforts. There are four-poster beds, indoor and outdoor pools and a spa. The service is as impeccable as the immaculately manicured gardens.

Deià & Around

Hostal Villaverde   HOSTAL €
(☑971 63 90 37; www.hostalvillaverde.com; Carrer de Ramon Llull 19, Deià; s/d €58/77; [✻][🗢]) This petite *hostal* in Deià's hilly heart offers homey rooms and a splendid Tramuntana panorama from its terrace. A small number of the doubles have their own terraces and superlative views. The public areas are brimful of antiques, while the rooms are simple but well cared for. You'll wake up to the sound of roosters and running water.

★Hostal Miramar   HOTEL €€
(☑971 63 90 84; http://pensionmiramar.com; Carrer de Ca'n Oliver, Deià; r incl breakfast €75-120; ⊙Mar–mid-Nov; [P]) Hidden within lush vegetation and with views across to Deià's hillside church and the sea beyond, this 19th-century stone house with gardens is a

shady retreat with nine rooms. Various artists (you can scarcely see the breakfast-room walls for canvases) have stayed here over the years. The rooms are petite, antique-furnished and as clean as new pins.

S'Hotel des Puig   HISTORIC HOTEL €€
(☑971 63 94 09; www.hoteldespuig.com; Carrer des Puig 4, Deià; s €80-99, d €125-175, ste €199-315; ⊙Feb-Nov; [P][✻][🗢][🏊]) The eight rooms of this gem in the middle of the old town reflect a muted modern taste within ancient stone walls. Out the back are secrets impossible to divine from the street, such as the pool and lovely terrace. The 'House on the Hill' has appeared in a number of books about Mallorca, and even in a Robert Graves short story.

Hotel Costa d'Or   HOTEL €€
(☑971 63 90 25; www.hoposa.com; Lluc Alcari; s/d incl breakfast from €88/158; ⊙Apr-Oct; [P][✻][@][🗢][🏊]) This secluded spot offers designer rooms in a stone building that backs on to woods high above the Mediterranean. Rooms with sea views cost considerably more, but you get the same views from the restaurant, terrace and pool. A 15-minute walk through pine forest takes you down to a little pebbly beach with crystal-clear water.

Sa Pedrissa   HISTORIC HOTEL €€€
(☑971 63 91 11; www.sapedrissa.com; Carretera de Valldemossa-Deià; s €180-350, d €210-350, ste €350-490; [P][✻][@][🗢][🏊]) Sublime. From a high rocky bluff looking down along the coast and inland to Deià, this stunning mansion (which once lorded it over an olive farm and may date back to the 17th century) is a luxurious choice. The service is faultless, the views from the pool terrace and many rooms are glorious, and the rooms are unpretentiously classy.

La Residencia   HOTEL €€€
(☑971 63 90 11; www.hotel-laresidencia.com; Son Canals, Deià; s/d from €316/519; ⊙Apr-Oct; [P][✻][@][🗢][🏊]) 'The Res' to its habitués, this is where the rich and famous rub shoulders. A short stroll from the village centre, this former 16th-century manor house set in 12 hectares of manicured lawns and gardens offers every conceivable luxury – uniquely designed rooms, tennis courts, spa, two outdoor pools, a sculpture garden and superb restaurant, you name it.

Sóller

Hostal Nadal
HOSTAL €

(Map p100; ☑971 63 11 80; Carrer de Romaguera 20, Sóller; s/d/tr €24/37/48, without bathroom €20/29/39; ☜) It may be simple but it's home, and about as cheap as it gets on the island. Rooms are no-frills basic but spotless and there's a courtyard out the back to flop in after a day's hiking.

Ca's Curial
BOUTIQUE HOTEL €€

(☑971 63 33 32; www.cascurial.com; Carrer de La Villalonga 23, Sóller; d €133-189, ste €163-260; P ❄ @ ☎ ☒ ♨) Barely out of Sóller's centre, this idyllically set hotel offers nine rooms and suites, most with own patio or terrace. Loll around in grounds perfumed by orange and lemon trees or take a dip in the pool. It's hard to leave this stone *finca* to go visit anything! The farm's zesty orange juice and preserves are served at breakfast.

Hotel S'Ardeviu
HISTORIC HOTEL €€

(Map p100; ☑971 63 83 26; www.sollernet.com/sardeviu; Carrer de Vives 14, Sóller; s €85-95, d €100-120; ⊘Feb-Nov; ❄ ☎) Hidden down a lane in the old heart of the town, the seven rooms spread out over this 13th-century stone house vary, some with bare stonework, others beamed and whitewashed. A fountain splashes in the palm-dotted garden where breakfast is served – a fine spread of cold cuts, fresh fruit and just-pressed juice.

Ca'n Isabel
HOTEL €€

(Map p100; ☑971 63 80 97; www.canisabel.com; Carrer d'Isabel II 13, Sóller; s €90-120, d €115-145; ⊘mid-Feb–mid-Nov; ❄ @ ☎) With just six rooms, this 19th-century house is a gracefully decorated hideaway, with a fine garden out the back. The decor won't be to everyone's taste, but the owners have retained the period style impeccably: the 'Romantic Room' has a gorgeous free-standing antique bathtub. The best (and dearest) of the rooms come with their own delightful terrace.

Ca'l Bisbe
HOTEL €€

(Map p100; ☑971 63 12 28; www.hotelcalbisbe.com; Carrer del Bisbe Nadal 10, Sóller; d €137-158, ste €160-185; ⊘Mar–mid-Nov; P ❄ @ ☎ ☒) The bishop who once lived here would no doubt appreciate the addition of the pool in this nicely restored 19th-century parish residence. Perhaps he would have snorted at the little gym. The room decor is largely modern, but some grand details (such as the stone arches and fireplaces) remain intact in the public areas. Rooms are spacious and bright.

★Ca N'Aí
RURAL HOTEL €€€

(☑971 63 24 94; www.canai.com; Camí de Son Sales 50, Sóller; ste €150-310; P ❄ @ ☎ ☒ ♨) Nestling among orange groves, family-run Ca N'Aí is a blissful escape, with its serene pools, garden hammocks and turtle-filled ponds. The nine spacious suites play up rural luxury, with high ceilings, Moorish-inspired tiles, antique furnishings and private terraces. The restaurant's candlelit patio is an incredibly romantic setting for a meal that puts a refined twist on *finca* produce.

It's around 2km northwest of the town centre.

Hotel Salvia
LUXURY HOTEL €€€

(Map p100; ☑971 63 49 36; www.hotelsalvia.com; Carrer de la Palma 18, Sóller; ste €160-285; ⊘Apr-Nov; ❄ ☎ ☒) You'll feel at least like minor royalty in this stately 19th-century abode. Patrick and Sasha have restored it with exquisite taste: suites have gorgeous antiques, shutters that throw open to the mountains and opulent bathrooms with free-standing tubs. Your role is to relax, be it in the lantern-lit patio, chandelier-lit salon or by the pool perfumed by jasmine and orange trees.

Port de Sóller

Hotel Citric Sóller
HOTEL €

(☑971 63 13 52; www.citrichotels.com; Camí del Far 15, Port de Sóller; s €29-63, d €31.50-105; ☎) Wake up to see the rising sun flood across the bay into your grandstand room. Not bad for a newly renovated budget hotel on the waterfront at the quieter, southern end of the bay. The simple whitewashed rooms come with lime green splashes of colour; those with sea-facing balconies have the edge. Breakfast costs extra and is mediocre – skip it.

Muleta de Ca S'Hereu
RURAL HOTEL €€

(☑971 18 60 18; www.muletadecashereu.es; Camp de Sa Mar, Port de Sóller; s/d €90/140, ste €165-180, apt €150-280; P ❄ @ ☎ ☒ ♨) Your car will hate you for the 1.8km track of switchbacks, but this lordly country mansion, dating to 1672, will enchant. Eight sprawling rooms and a handful of apartments, some with distant sea glimpses from this mountainside

HOLIDAY RENTALS

Want to explore the island at your own steam, with the freedom to cook whenever you fancy? Apartment and villa rentals are an appealing (and affordable) alternative to hotels if you're travelling with a group of friends or as a family. A minimum seven-night stay is standard. Check out the following websites:

➡ www.ownersdirect.co.uk
➡ www.holidaylettings.co.uk
➡ www.homeaway.co.uk
➡ www.homelidays.co.uk
➡ www.villarenters.com

position, are filled with charm and antiques, and the pool is rimmed by olive groves. You may be woken by donkey braying.

★ **Espléndido Hotel** HOTEL €€€
(☑ 971 63 18 50; www.esplendidohotel.com; Passeig Es Través 5, Port de Sóller; r €170-420, ste €300-750; ✱ 🛜 🌊 🛆) This marvellous 1954 carcass has been reborn as hip waterfront luxury digs, with vintage-chic interiors. Espléndido's best rooms have terraces that open up straight to the sea. Free minibar drinks and Nespresso machines are thoughtful extras that help justify the price tag. Add three pools, a spa, cocktail bar and bistro, and you're looking at one special place to stay.

Fornalutx

Ca'n Reus HISTORIC HOTEL €€
(☑ 971 63 11 74; www.canreushotel.com; Carrer de l'Alba 26, Fornalutx; d €130-160, ste €170; 🅿 ✱ @ 🛜 🌊) This place is a tempting romantic escape. The British-owned country mansion was built in the early 1800s by a Mr Reus, who got rich on the orange trade with France. The eight rooms are all quite different and all have views; each is stunning and has restrained antique furnishings and exposed stonework, with plenty of light throughout. Children under five are not welcome.

Fornalutx Petit Hotel BOUTIQUE HOTEL €€
(☑ 971 63 19 97; www.fornalutxpetithotel.com; Carrer de l'Alba 22, Fornalutx; s €89-123, d €161-184; ⊘ mid-Feb–mid-Nov; ✱ @ 🛜 🌊) A tastefully converted former convent just below the main square, Fornalutx Petit Hotel is as much art gallery as boutique hotel. Each of the eight rooms is named after a contemporary Mallorcan painter and displays their canvases. There's a free guest sauna and hot tub and a wonderful terrace with views over the fertile valley.

Road from Sóller to Alaró

Refugi S'Hostatgeria REFUGE €
(☑ 971 18 21 12; www.castellalaro.cat; Alaró; per adult/child incl breakfast €12/6, incl half board €24/14; ⊘ May-Sep; 🚶) Perfect for acting out medieval knight and damsel fantasies, this refuge at Castell d'Alaró has staggering views. Yes, it's darn simple, but who cares with this panorama and brilliant hiking trails on your doorstep. The dorm rooms are simply fitted out with bunks (bring your sleeping bag).

You can get sandwiches and drinks in the bar, open from 9am to 11pm. Breakfast costs an extra €4, dinner €10.

Hotel Can Xim HOTEL €
(☑ 971 51 86 80; www.canxim.com; Plaça de la Vila 8, Alaró; s €60-80, d €80-100; 🅿 ✱ @ 🛜 🌊) This family-run establishment has an ideal location overlooking the square. Rooms are spacious and light-filled with modern wooden beams, if ever-so-slightly soulless. It's well-priced, however, by Mallorcan standards.

★ **Alqueria Blanca** RURAL HOTEL €€
(☑ 971 14 84 00; www.alqueria-blanca.com; Carretera Palma–Sóller Km 13.6, Bunyola; s €135-145, d €155-165, ste €185-205; ⊘ Jan-Nov; 🅿 ✱ 🌊) A fine country residence, Alqueria Blanca slumbers in grounds shaded by olive and pine, with a pool overlooking the valley. Its six rooms occupy the oldest buildings, which once formed an Arab *alquería* (Muslim-era farmstead). They echo their past with high ceilings, beams and barley-twist bedsteads. A whimsical Modernista building was added in 1906 (now the breakfast room).

The hotel is about 2km west of Bunyola. If travelling north from Palma, the turn-off is at Km 13.6; head 700m further down the trail.

Finca Son Palou RURAL HOTEL €€
(☑ 971 14 82 82; www.sonpalou.com; Plaça de l'Església, Orient; r €126-159, with terrace €165-211, ste €185-230; ⊘ mid-Jan–mid-Dec; 🅿 ✱ @ 🛜 🌊) On its romantic perch above Orient's tightly packed lanes, this country hotel slumbers

among apple orchards. Rooms are traditional without sliding into twee, with terracotta floor tiles, timber furnishings and (in some cases) exposed beams. Home-grown fruit, veggies and olive oil go into meals served in the highly regarded restaurant. The restful pool has beautiful mountain views.

NORTHERN MALLORCA

Pollença

Hotel Desbrull
BOUTIQUE HOTEL €

(Map p114; ☑ 971 53 50 55; www.desbrull.com; Carrer del Marqués Desbrull 7, Pollença; s incl breakfast €71-88, d incl breakfast €77-99; ❋ ☎) The best deal in town, with six pleasantly fresh if coquettishly small doubles in a modernised stone house. White dominates the decor in rooms and bathrooms, offset with splashes of colour, and if you like the contemporary art on the walls, you can buy it. It's run by a friendly brother-sister combination.

★ Posada de Lluc
BOUTIQUE HOTEL €

(Map p114; ☑ 971 53 52 20; www.posadadelluc.com; Carrer del Roser Vell 11, Pollença; s €89-167, d €99-199, with terrace €133-233; P ❋ @ ☎ ☀) This 15th-century, two-storey town house in Pollença was handed over to the brethren of the Monestir de Lluc as a resting place for pilgrims. It's now a fetching inn with a variety of rooms, many of which have original touches like exposed stone and beams. Those overlooking the pool and with their own terrace have more of a wow factor.

L'Hostal
HOTEL €€

(Map p114; ☑ 971 53 52 82; www.hostalpollensa.com; Carrer del Mercat 18, Pollença; s €70-110, d €90-135; ❋ @ ☎) Just steps from the cafe-rimmed Plaça Major lies L'Hostal. Here you'll find six bright doubles with exposed stone, white tiled floors, bursts of bold colour and modern art on the walls. It's a comfortable, well-priced option in the heart of town.

Hotel Son Sant Jordi
HOTEL €€

(Map p114; ☑ 971 53 03 89; www.hotelsonsantjordi.com; Carrer de Sant Jordi 29, Pollença; s €68, d €72-270, ste €108-270; P ❋ @ ☎ ☀) Occupying a fine old house and sharing a bit of square with the 16th-century Oratori de Sant Jordi chapel, this hotel has elegant rooms with high ceilings, terracotta floors, canopied beds, antique rocking chairs and plenty of light. Out back, a surprisingly expansive garden frames a curvaceous pool. Singles are only available in low season.

Cala Sant Vincenç

★ Hostal Los Pinos
HOSTAL €

(☑ 971 53 12 10; www.hostal-lospinos.com; Urbanització Can Botana, Cala Sant Vicenç; s €33-46, d €66-88, f €98-114, all incl breakfast; ☉ May–mid-Oct; P ❋ ☀ ♿) Set back from the road between Cala Molins and Cala Carbó, Hostal Los Pinos comprises two gleaming white villas sitting in a pine glade. Superior doubles have partial sea views and are wonderfully large with separate lounge areas and balconies. The smaller singles have old-style Mallorcan decor. It's relaxed and peaceful, yet only a short walk from the beach.

Port de Pollença

★ Pensión Bellavista
PENSIÓN €

(☑ 699 549376, 971 86 46 00; www.pensionbellavista.com; Carrer Monges 14, Port de Pollença; s €35-45, d €55-65, tr €75, q €80; ☎ ♿) Bellavista occupies a rambling house that has welcomed guests since 1931. A spiral staircase twists up to simple rooms jazzed up with one-of-a-kind marine-life illustrations and lamps. You'll soon click into the boho groove on the chill-out terrace and in the fig-tree-shaded garden where breakfast (€6) is served. Resident cats, dogs and turtles add to the familiar vibe.

Hotel Sis Pins
HOTEL €€

(☑ 971 86 70 50; www.hotelsispins.com; Passeig d'Anglada Camarasa 77, Port de Pollença; s €33-66, d €56-144; ☉ Feb-Oct; ❋ @ ☎) Going strong since 1952, this monument to the early days of Spain's coastal-tourism boom has old-school grace and service. The rooms are fairly standard, but well priced and those facing the sea are the best.

Hostal Bahia
HOTEL €€

(☑ 971 86 65 62; www.hoposa.es; Passeig Voramar 29, Port de Pollença; d €67-121, with sea view €91-158; ☉ Apr-Oct; ❋ @ ☎ ♿) A 19th-century villa converted into a hotel, the Bahia occupies a terrific waterfront spot along Pollenca's pine-shaded esplanade. A top-to-toe makeover in 2013 has spruced up the rooms, with splashes of blue and turquoise; the best have balconies with sea views. Staff bend over backwards to please and the location – peaceful but close to the action – is perfect.

Cap de Formentor

★**Hotel Formentor** HISTORIC HOTEL €€€
(☑971 89 91 00; www.barceloformentor.com; Platja de Formentor 3, Cap de Formentor; d €225-525, ste €575-900; ☺mid-Apr–Oct; P❄@☎☲⛵) Ever since this ritzy hotel opened its doors in 1929, Hotel Formentor has been a Mallorca classic. The beachfront digs have played host to the likes of Grace Kelly, Winston Churchill, Mikhail Gorbachev, John Wayne and the Dalai Lama. Rooms are pleasing without being the latest in grand luxury, and the seaside doubles and suites are a taste of paradise.

Tennis courts, pools and flowery garden walkways aside, the hotel is so popular because of its location – it has the fabulous Formentor beach all to itself.

Alcúdia

★**Can Tem** BOUTIQUE HOTEL €€
(Map p122; ☑971 54 82 73; www.hotelcantem. com; Carrer de l'Església 14, Alcúdia; s €75-80, d €90-125; ❄☎⛵) Lodged in a 17th-century town house, Can Tem is a boutique delight. Designed with flair, its light-flooded, white-walled rooms manage the delicate act of combining original features like beams and wood-carved bedsteads with contemporary artworks and slick bathrooms. Fresh pastries and homemade cake bring a sweet touch to breakfast, served in a pretty cobbled courtyard.

Petit Hotel Ca'n Simó BOUTIQUE HOTEL €€
(Map p122; ☑971 54 92 60; www.cansimo.com; Carrer de Sant Jaume 1, Alcúdia; s €75-80, d €98-128; ❄@☎☲) Big on rustic charm, this stylish hotel occupies a renovated 19th-century manor house. Each of the seven doubles has its own character, with exposed beams, wrought-iron furnishings and stone feature walls; some notch up the romance with whirlpool tubs and four-poster beds. And it's wondrous how they managed to squeeze in a little indoor pool, spa bath and fitness room.

Ca'n Pere BOUTIQUE HOTEL €€
(Map p122; ☑971 54 52 43; www.hotelcanpere.com; Carrer d'en Serra 12, Alcúdia; s €70-75, d €90-105, d with spa bath & terrace €110-120; ❄☎) A fine boutique option hidden in the old town, Ca'n Pere has all-stone walls and all-white furnishings; some rooms also have the modern equivalent of four-poster beds. Those with the spa bath and private balcony rank among northern Mallorca's best bargains.

Port d'Alcúdia

Botel Alcúdia Mar RESORT €€€
(☑971 89 72 15; www.botelalcudiamar.es; Passeig Marítim 1, Port d'Alcúdia; s €92-208, d €123-277; ☺Mar-Oct; P❄@☎☲⛵) It's not often that we feature resort-style accommodation – there's a sameness to so many – but this place pips the competition with its privileged location away from the crowds yet in the centre of town, and for its gardens, pools, spa and terraces with sea views. The rooms themselves are nothing special, but the overall atmosphere caught our eye.

THE INTERIOR

Santa Maria del Camí

★**Read's Hotel** LUXURY HOTEL €€€
(☑971 14 02 61; www.readshotel.com; Ca'n Moragues, Santa Maria; d from €225, ste €260-460; P❄@☎☲) Northeast of Santa Maria is one of Mallorca's most exquisite country-manor getaways. Set in immaculate gardens with thick palm trees, this warm stone mansion has 23 rooms and suites with terraces. No expense has been spared with the fittings – expect Bang & Olufsen TVs and jacuzzi bathtubs. Indoor and outdoor pools and a spa invite relaxation.

Wines from the estate's own vineyards pair nicely with dishes in the Blues Brasserie, housed in an 18th-century olive press. The owner, Mr Read, and his dog, Mr Brown, are fine hosts too.

Santa Eugènia

Sa Torre RURAL HOTEL, APARTMENT €€
(☑971 14 40 11; www.sa-torre.com; Ma3020 Santa Maria–Sencelles Km 7, Santa Eugènia; apt €140, breakfast €13; P❄@☎☲) This wonderful haven rests on the edge of the tiny hamlet Ses Alqueries. This grand *finca* has been in the same family since 1560 and offers five spacious self-catering apartments, two bliss-

fully calm pools and a highly regarded cellar restaurant. Some of the apartments look onto a stand of almond trees – a treat when they're in blossom.

Around Inca

★ Es Castell
RURAL HOTEL €€

(📞971 87 51 54; www.fincaescastell.com; Carrer de Binibona, Binibona; s €110-120, d €130-180, ste €170-200; 🅿✳@🛜≋) 🏊 If you've come to Binibona for peace and quiet, go a little further beyond the town for utter tranquillity. The Es Castell is an 11th-century farm estate, set out on a ledge by itself in the shadow of the mountains. It encompasses a muddle of sturdy stone houses and 300 hectares of olive groves, and makes the perfect rural escape.

The gentle hum of cicadas and clang of sheep bells are your soundtrack at this adorable *finca*. The rooms are appealingly rustic, with terracotta floors, timber furniture and marble-topped chests of drawers. In keeping with the hotel's ecofriendly approach, the vast majority of the food served is home-grown or market-sourced.

Agroturisme Monnàber Vell
RURAL HOTEL €€

(📞971 51 61 31; www.monnabervell.com; Campanet; s €107-133, d €114-166, ste €141-206; ✉mid-Feb–mid-Dec; 🅿✳@🛜≋) With the Tramuntana as its backdrop, this country estate soothes the soul with its setting among fig, almond and carob trees. The standard doubles are comfortable if a trifle bland, but the suites have bags of character, with exposed stone, beams and antiques. The infinity pool and spa area are incredibly peaceful. For an extra €26, dinner is included.

Agroturisme Monnàber Vell is 3.5km north of Campanet, at the end of a track that winds through the fields and woods; see the website for detailed directions.

Finca Hotel Albellons Parc Natural
GUESTHOUSE €€

(📞971 87 50 69; www.albellons.es; Caimari, Binibona; s €120, d €160-200, ste €220-240; ✉mid-Feb–mid-Nov; 🅿✳@🛜≋🍴) Panoramic views of the Tramuntana and a pool rimmed by olive trees are yours for the savouring at this low-key farmhouse escape, set in the hills 1km north of Binibona. The 12 rooms (half with own terrace) have terracotta floors, timber ceilings and rustic antique furnishings. The home cooking makes half board worth the additional €27 per night.

Hotel Can Furiós
RURAL HOTEL €€€

(📞971 51 57 51; www.can-furios.com; Camí Vell de Binibona 11, Binibona; s €132-180, d €165-225, ste €190-310; ✳🛜≋) Adrian and Suzy are your kind hosts at this renovated 16th-century mansion, which consistently gets rave reviews. It's a romantic bolthole, with bougainvillea-draped gardens, a quiet pool and a restaurant in a converted 17th-century olive press. Stone walls, beams and the odd antique lend an authentic feel to the rooms and suites, some of which have four-poster beds and terraces.

Sineu

Hotel León de Sineu
HOTEL €€

(📞971 52 02 11; www.hotel-leondesineu.com; Carrer dels Bous 129, Sineu; d €90-150; ✳🛜≋) Set in a 15th-century house that was once a wine cellar, León de Sineu retains much of its traditional look; the uneven tiled floors add to the appeal. Out back, the gardens fall away down several levels, stuffed with fountains, palms and huge sunflowers, leading to the pool. Friendly service and a thoughtfully presented breakfast round out a great package.

Can Joan Capo Hotel
BOUTIQUE HOTEL €€

(📞971 85 50 75; www.canjoancapo.com; Carrer de Degà Joan Rotger 4, Sineu; d €120-170, ste €190-220, f €220-250; ✳🛜≋🍴) Sineu's slickest hotel has eight rooms, each with its own style – furnishings range from wood-heavy decor to light wrought-iron frames, while beamed ceilings are a recurring theme. The public areas are a study in converting an old stone building into an intimate designer space, with strategically placed antique farm tools, soothing alcoves, pleasing archways and a decked pool area.

Algaida

Possessió Binicomprat
BOUTIQUE HOTEL €€

(📞971 12 50 28; http://fincabinicomprat.com; Cami de Ses Vinyes, Algaida; d €138-149, ste €150-158, apt €160-278; 🅿✳≋🍴) Looking back on a history that extends to the 1229 Christian reconquest, this *finca* has been in the Moragues family's hands since 1511. It's all you'd expect a country escape to be, with an oak-tree-fringed pool, own chapel, cellar, vineyards and vegetable patch. Rooms subtly blend rustic with boutique chic, while suites and apartments have lounges with fireplaces.

Manacor

La Reserva Rotana
BOUTIQUE HOTEL €€€
(☑ 971 84 56 85; www.reservarotana.com; Camí de Bendris Km 3, Manacor; d €150-255; ☺ mid-Nov–mid-Feb; P @ ❀ ☒ ⴹ) This luxurious *finca* sits in splendid isolation in 500 acres of beautifully tended grounds, 6km north of Manacor. A nine-hole private golf course, tennis court, pool, gym, sauna, own vineyard and fabulous restaurant mean there's no need to leave if you don't want to. Rooms in the 17th-century manor house are grand, with countrified decor and the odd antique.

EASTERN MALLORCA

Artà

Hotel Casal d'Artà
HOTEL €
(Map p144; ☑ 971 82 91 63; www.casaldarta.de; Carrer de Rafael Blanes 19, Artà; s incl breakfast €57-75, d incl breakfast €88-96; ❀ ❀) Hotel Casal d'Artà is a wonderful old mansion in the heart of town. The decor may be old-fashioned, but a sense of light and space pervades this place. Rooms are full of individual charm, some with four-poster beds, others with sunken bathtubs. There's a flower-filled roof terrace, with a bubbling fountain and incomparable views over the village.

★ Jardi d'Artà
BOUTIQUE HOTEL €€
(Map p144; ☑ 971 83 52 30; www.hotel-arta.com; Carrer de l'Abeurador 21, Artà; d €125-165, ste €180-375; ❀ ❀ ☒) A welcome newcomer, Jardi d'Artà hit the ground running when it reopened in 2013 following a total makeover. Richly hued fabrics add a dash of glamour to sleek, lime-washed rooms. Among our favourites are the Chapel Room, embedded in the 800-year walls of a former chapel, and the Terrace Room, opening to gardens fragrant with lime and orange trees.

Jardi d'Artà enchants with its flowery gardens and romantic nooks. There is a gym, *hammam* and pool, and a restaurant where the chef Mika Drouin playfully mixes Mediterranean and Asian flavours.

Hotel Sant Salvador
BOUTIQUE HOTEL €
(Map p144; ☑ 971 82 95 55; www.santsalvador. com; Carrer del Pou Nou 26, Artà; d €99-209; P ❀ @ ❀ ☒) The eight rooms of this luxurious boutique hotel echo the dignified character of this restored manor house, with canopied beds, rich fabrics, contemporary artworks and antique furnishings. The hotel's pride and joy is its curvilinear facade, believed to be the handiwork of Gaudí. Besides a pool and lush garden, the hotel also has a well-regarded restaurant.

Can Moragues
RURAL HOTEL €€
(Map p144; ☑ 971 82 95 09; www.canmoragues. com; Carrer del Pou Nou 12, Artà; s/d €98/135, ste s/d €118/170; P ❀ @ ❀ ☒) A cheery 18th-century country house turned hotel, Can Moragues offers cosy, impeccably clean rooms that respect the house's original architecture, with touches like exposed-stone walls and wood-beam ceilings, and a mixed contemporary-antique look. You can kick back with a small pool and sauna, or ask the friendly owners about arranging activities from horse riding to mountain biking.

Capdepera

★ Cases de Son Barbassa
BOUTIQUE HOTEL €€€
(☑ 971 56 57 76; www.sonbarbassa.com; Camí de Son Barbassa, Capdepera; s €126-231, d €168-298; ☺ Feb-Nov; P ❀ @ ❀ ☒) Presided over by a 16th-century stone tower and set amid almond, olive and carob trees, this is a gorgeous country estate with a touch of the sublime. The rooms play up rural luxury, dressed in local stone and wood, while suites come with jetted tubs. Lazy days here revolve around the pool lined with cabana beds and open-air whirlpool.

A cosy nook with a fireplace, an outstanding restaurant with a mountain-view terrace and gardens fragrant with herbs, lavender and roses make this a great escape from the coast's madding crowds.

The hotel is located just off the road to Cala Mesquida, and signposted off the main Artà–Cala Ratjada road.

Cala Ratjada

Residence – The Sea Club
HOTEL, GUESTHOUSE €€
(Map p148; ☑ 971 56 33 10; www.theseaclub.es; Avinguda de América 27, Cala Ratjada; s €55-82, d €115-175, f €155-195; ☺ Apr-Oct; ❀ ☒ ⴹ) This British-run place is a real treat along the waterfront promenade. The 17 rooms in this old colonial home have been lovingly renovated, and have crisp linen and soothing col-

our schemes. It's the sort of place – unusual in Mallorca – that allows you to have a beach holiday without the depersonalised service experienced at some resorts.

Hotel Cala Gat
HOTEL €€

(☑971 56 31 66; www.hotelcalagat.com; Carretera del Faro, Cala Ratjada; s €58-88, d €86-136; ☺Apr-Oct; ☀@) Set amid dense woodlands on the road to the lighthouse and thus removed from the clamour of downtown, Hotel Cala Gat has a lovely small beach almost to itself and pleasant if uninspiring modern rooms. Overall it's a terrific package for its mix of peace and comfort. Of all the beach hotels, this is probably the one we'd choose.

Petit Hotel Ses Rotges
BOUTIQUE HOTEL €€

(Map p148; ☑971 56 31 08; www.sesrotges.com; Carrer de Rafael Blanes 21, Cala Ratjada; r €85-150, breakfast €20; ☺Apr-Oct; ☀@) This character-ful 18th-century mansion has a more person-al touch than elsewhere in town. The rooms are in keeping with the hotel's history, with antiques, beams and tiled floors. The whirl-pool, roof terrace and bougainvillea-draped patio keep the mood intimate, and there's a well-regarded restaurant. Breakfast is worth the extra, with eggs to order, smoked salm-on, fresh pastries and fruit.

Porto Cristo & Around

Es Picot
RURAL HOTEL €€

(☑637 737943; www.espicot.com; Camí de Sa Mola Km 3.6, Cales de Mallorca; r €92-126; P☀☎⊠) Out on its rural lonesome, with views across wooded hills and down to the sea, Es Picot is a lovely *finca* with a pool and gardens al-most quiet enough to hear an olive plop. The simply decorated rooms, with rustic features like beams and stone walls, have terraces or balconies. Home-grown fruit and eggs land on the breakfast table. It's 5km northwest of Cales de Mallorca off the PM401.

Son Mas
RURAL HOTEL €€€

(☑971 55 87 55; www.sonmas.com; Carrer Porto Cristo–Portocolom, Camí de Son Mas; s €225-273, d €260-320) A fine romance of a *finca*, this 17th-century farmhouse is a step up from Porto Cristo's anonymous package-tour hotels, yet it's just five minutes' drive from the resort. Vaulted corridors, subtly stylish rooms with features like beams and four-posters, a pool for summer lounging, fireplaces for winter snuggling, spa treatments – this is intimate luxury all the way.

Portocolom

Hostal Porto Colom
HOSTAL €€

(☑971 82 53 23; www.hostalportocolom.com; Car-rer d'en Cristòfol Colom 5, Portocolom; s €43-65, d €60-112; ☀☎) Right on the waterfront, Hos-tal Porto Colom has breezy rooms decked out in bright yellows and blues (which might get to you after a while), with parquet floors and big beds. They're decent but nothing flash. Its restaurant and cool cocktail bar command sea views.

SOUTHERN MALLORCA

Cala Pi & Around

Sa Bassa Plana
RURAL HOTEL €€

(☑971 12 30 03; www.sabassaplana.com; Carretera Cap Blanc Km 25.4, Cala Pi; s €58-74, d €71-99, ste €106-135; P☀☎) Set on a working farm, Sa Bassa Plana has 10 double rooms and 12 suites (with kitchenette). They're not luxu-rious, but they are large and comfortable; some are outfitted with antique furniture, evoking an old-world elegance. Half board is available and 90% of the food here is grown on the premises.

Sa Ràpita & Around

★Can Canals
RURAL HOTEL €€

(☑971 64 07 57; www.cancanals.es; Carretera Campos–Sa Ràpita Km 7, Ses Covetes; s €86-124, d €146-198; ☺Feb-Dec; P☀☎⊠♦) A stunning rustic guesthouse near Ses Covetes, Can Ca-nals has 12 well-appointed rooms, which are located inside a lovely farmhouse and sim-ply ooze with rural Mallorcan charm. Every room is different, but stone walls and terra-cotta floors recur. There's a spa and wellness centre on site, as well as salt- and freshwater pools.

Colònia de Sant Jordi

Hostal Colonial
GUESTHOUSE €

(☑971 65 52 78; www.hostal-colonial.com; Carrer de l'Enginier Gabriel Roca 9, Colònia de Sant Jordi; s €35-48, d €66-92, apt €60-110; ☺mid-Mar-Oct; ☀@☎♦) Just 50m from the beach lies this sweet and simple family-run hotel. Its hand-ful of tidy, modern rooms and apartments are done out in crisp blues and whites and come with small balconies or terraces. It also has a famed gelateria, and bikes are available for guests.

Ses Salines

★Hotel Ca'n Bonico HISTORIC HOTEL €€
(☎971 64 90 22; www.hotelcanbonico.com; Plaça Sant Bartomeu 2, Ses Salines; s €124-139, d €168-198; ⊙Feb-Oct; ❄@📶🏊) This fine old townhouse dates back to the 13th century, which is still visible in its architecture, such as the defence tower (now a library) and a former jail; the family who run it also descend from the original owners. There is a peaceful pool and the rooms seamlessly blend whitewashed minimalism with historic features like beams and antique furnishings.

Santanyí

Hotel Cala Santanyí HOTEL €€
(☎971 16 55 05; www.hotelcalasantanyi.com; Carrer de Sa Costa dels Etics, Santanyí; s €115-132, d €160-204, ste €190-230, apt €116-240; ⊙mid-Apr–early Nov; ❄@📶🏊👪) From the outside, this place seems like so many other coastal Mallorcan hotels, but there's much to recommend it. For a start, it's a family-run place, something which shows in the warmth of the welcome and the attention to detail. Rooms and the terrace have wonderful views of the pretty cove; the apartments across the road have lesser views.

Cala Figuera

Hostal Mar Blau HOSTAL €
(☎971 64 52 27; www.marblau.eu; Carrer de la Iglesia 24, Cala Figuera; s €29-37, d €38-46, apt €84-104; ⊙Apr-Oct; ❄📶) Barely 300m from the port of Cala Figuera, Hostal Mar Blau is a friendly, particularly well-priced option. Rooms (the more expensive ones have air-con and a fridge) are clean as a new pin. For greater independence, go for one of the fully equipped apartments (minimum stay three days), some of which have sea views.

Hotel Villa Sirena HOTEL €€
(☎971 64 53 03; www.hotelvillasirena.com; Carrer de la Verge del Carme 37, Cala Figuera; s/d €63/83, 2-/4-person apt €86/135; ⊙hotel Apr-Oct, apt year-round; ❄🏊) Perched on a bluff at the edge of the resort, this pleasant two-star hotel has enviable views of the sea. Rooms aren't fancy, but extras like a breezy seaside terrace make this a great choice. The well-priced apartments across the road are ideal if you're settling in for a longer stay.

Portopetro

Blau PortoPetro HOTEL €€€
(☎971 64 82 82; www.blau-hotels.com; Avinguda des Far 12, Portopetro; s €150-250, d €200-330; ⊙Mar-Nov; P❄@📶🏊👪) The only five-star hotel in the vicinity, the Blau made a real splash when it opened in 2005. A chic spa and hotel, this is no intimate boutique hotel, but its 300-plus rooms are stylish and every imaginable activity is on offer – from private sailing lessons to windsurfing. It's probably the pick of such places along Mallorca's southern coast.

Cala d'Or

★Ca'n Bessol RURAL HOTEL €€
(☎639 694910; www.canbessol.com; Carrer de la Sisena Volta 287, Cala d'Or; s €76-116, d €94-112, apt €118-178; ⊙Feb-Nov; P❄@📶🏊) This family-run *finca* is like a breath of fresh air in Cala d'Or in high season. Four romantic rooms with antique furnishings and rustic beams overlook a pool and palm-dotted gardens, where only the hum of cicadas and the cockerel crowing interrupt the silence. Find it off the highway linking S'Horta with Cala Ferrera, on the outskirts of Cala d'Or.

Hotel Cala D'Or HOTEL €€
(☎971 65 72 49; www.hotelcalador.com; Avinguda de Bélgica 49, Cala d'Or; s €56.50-114, d €91-195; ⊙Apr-Oct; ❄@📶🏊) Built in 1932 and later used as a military barracks, the four-star D'Or has returned to life as a 95-room hotel overlooking the rocky Cala d'Or. The tidy rooms have balconies and garden or sea views – the latter definitely have the edge. A minimum seven-night stay applies in peak season.

Understand
Mallorca

Mallorca Today

Things are looking up for Mallorca. The island has weathered the storm of the financial crisis better than many other parts of Spain and even the corruption scandals of late have not managed to dent its increasingly buoyant mood. Around 22.7 million passengers touch down in Palma each year, winter tourism continues to rise, new hotels (Mallorca Rocks for one) are popping up all the time and the island's gorgeous coast never goes out of fashion with yachting celebs.

Best on Film

Woman of Straw (1963) Stars Sean Connery with Artà as the backdrop.

The Magus (1968) Features Anthony Quinn, Michael Caine and Candice Bergen with Mallorca standing in for a Greek island.

A Winter in Mallorca (1969) Relives Chopin and George Sand's ill-fated stay on the island.

Presence of Mind (*El Celo*, 2000) Stars Sadie Frost, Harvey Keitel and Lauren Bacall; a private tutor comes to the island to educate two orphaned children.

Best in Print

Mañana Mañana (Peter Kerr) The pick of the books about trying to live like a Mallorquin.

Bread and Oil: Majorcan Culture's Last Stand (Tomás Graves) Food-dominated book centred on traditional Mallorca's greatest passions.

British Travellers in Mallorca in the Nineteenth Century (eds Brian J Dendle and Shelby Thacker) An intriguing anthology of Mallorcan travellers' tales.

A Bull on the Beach (Anna Nicholas) One of several lively yarns by the same author about the life of an expat in rural Mallorca.

Economic Storms & Forest Fires

Though Spain may still be in the slackening grip of recession, silver linings show that business has been excellent in Mallorca and is expected to continue this way. Unemployment has been steadily dropping recently and the economic outlook is slowly improving. That's not to say the crisis hasn't hit the island hard: Radio One Mallorca recently revealed that 85% of over-45s have lost their jobs since the recession started, the property bubble has burst and house prices are tumbling – all of which is, according to the *Majorca Daily Bulletin*, giving locals sleepless nights and mounting stress levels.

While Mallorca has been battling economic storms, forest fires over recent summers have put considerable pressure on the environment and emergency services. Once again in 2013, they swept through Peguera and through the Tramuntana north of Andratx, reducing some 1800 hectares of forest to cinders. A Balearic Nature Institute reforestation program is now underway.

Corruption Scandals & Brits Abroad

Mallorca has had a rocky ride in the press recently. The antics of Jaume Matas, the former president of the Balearics, and former Spanish environment minister, have been splashed across front pages. He was sentenced to nine months in prison for fraud and influence peddling in 2013. Even more high profile is the so-called 'Palma Arena' case, in which Iñaki Urdangarín, duke of Palma and the Spanish king's son-in-law, allegedly exploited his status to embezzle millions of euros in public money through fraudulent deals. Urdangarín's Icarus-like fall from grace has been compounded by a recent leak of his bawdy emails to

Spanish newspaper *El Mundo*. The case was ongoing at the time of writing.

Tabloids and TV program never seen to tire of Magaluf's tales of bawdy, boozed-up shenanigans. While Calvià has been doing its utmost to overhaul its image, with improved facilities and a growing emphasis on outdoor activities, the southwestern municipality took several blows in the press in 2013. In January the BBC aired *The Truth about Magaluf*, exposing binge drinking, brawls, lewd behaviour and the dangerous craze of 'balconing' in the island's wild-child resort. In June, Germany's *Bild am Sonntag* ran a feature entitled 'Mallorca's Darkest Summer', painting the Badia de Palma as a place of cheap prostitutes, drugs and pickpockets. Local mayor Manu Onieva was none too pleased with what he saw as 'sensationalist reporting' that was one-sided in nature.

An Image Change

Though they stem from just one or two resorts, it is reports like these that have tarnished Mallorca's reputation over the years. But if Manu Onieva and other tourism officials are successful, this clichéd image is on its way out. They point to the positive examples of new developments such as Mallorca Rocks, where the crème of Europe's DJs play to a relaxed but controlled crowd. They highlight that €3 million is being poured into a major makeover of Platja de Palma, with plans to introduce a 24-hour public-drinking ban, spruce up facilities and upgrade hotels to attract a richer, well-behaved clientele. According to Álvaro Gijón, deputy mayor of Palma, booze tourism is on its last legs; in July 2013 the *Independent* quoted him as saying: 'People vomiting and heeding calls of nature in public is not on.'

Winter tourism is another big focus, with more hotels opening earlier and closing later every year to cater for growing numbers of hikers, cyclists and birdwatchers – precisely the kind of holidaymaker the island is so keen to attract. And it is working: more and more operators are adding outdoor-focused holidays to their portfolio. Magaluf still casts the occasional shadow, but the horizons are looking bright. And while the party is far from over, future visitors will have to behave themselves and keep the noise down.

POPULATION: **859,340**

GDP PER HEAD: **€21,151**

UNEMPLOYMENT RATE (BALEARIC ISLANDS): **17.2%**

NUMBER OF PASSENGERS THROUGH MALLORCA'S AIRPORT (2012): **22.8 MILLION**

if Mallorca were 100 people

78 would be Mallorquin
10 would be Other
9 would be from mainland Spain
3 would be German

belief systems
(% of population)

95
Roman Catholic

5
Other

population per sq km

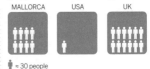

MALLORCA   USA   UK

≈ 30 people

History

Mallorca's position in the heart of Europe's most fought-over sea has placed it in the path of the great sweeps of Mediterranean history and these events have radically transformed the island time and again. And yet, for all its experience of invasion, war, prosperity and hunger, Mallorca has rarely been at the heart of great European affairs.

Mallorca's Talayotic Sites

Ses Païsses, Artà

Capocorb Vell, Cala Pi

Necròpolis de Son Real, Ca'n Picafort

Museu Arqueològic de Son Fornés, Montuïri

Es Figueral de Son Real, Ca'n Picafort

Illot dels Porros, Ca'n Picafort

Mallorca's story begins with a series of unsolved mysteries, with a culture whose *talayots* (watchtowers) are among the few signposts to their presence on the island; these stone towers continue to intrigue archaeologists. The Talayotic people had the island to themselves until the arrival of the Romans in the 2nd century BC. Roman Mallorca remained largely peaceful until the Vandals swept all before them in AD 426, before yielding to the Byzantines a century later. But it was the Muslim armies who brought the gifts of prosperity and religious coexistence to the island, ruling for over 300 years from the early 9th century. In 1229, Jaume I seized the island and it has been in Christian (and, most often, Catalan) hands ever since. Over the centuries that followed, life was often pretty grim for Mallorca's rural poor, living at the whim of absentee landlords, and Mallorca also found itself buffeted by the winds of change blowing from the Spanish mainland, from the grand questions of royal succession to the devastating Spanish Civil War in the 1930s.

Following the Civil War, particularly from the 1960s, Mallorca was transformed beyond recognition by the mass tourism which has yanked the island from centuries of provincial doldrums and propelled it to newfound wealth and somewhat forced cosmopolitanism.

The Talayotic Period

The Balearic Islands were separated from the Spanish continent a mere eight million years ago. They were inhabited by a variety of animal life that carried on in splendid isolation until around 9000 to 10,000 years ago, when the first groups of Epipaleolithic people set out from the Spanish coast in rudimentary vessels and bumped into Mallorca.

TIMELINE	7200 BC	c 1200 BC	c 500 BC
	Archaeologists date the first human settlements in Mallorca to this time, based on carbon-dated findings in the southwest of the island in Cova de Canet, a cave near Esplores.	Warrior tribes invade Mallorca, Menorca, Corsica and Sardinia. Those in Mallorca and Menorca are known today as the Talayotic people because of the stone towers they built.	Phoenician traders install themselves around the coast, extending their influence across Mallorca. Balearic warriors serve as mercenaries in Carthaginian armies.

The earliest signs of human presence on the island date to around 7200 BC. In the following 6000 years the population, made up of disparate groups or tribes, largely lived in caves or other natural shelters as hunter-gatherers. About 2000 BC they started building megalithic funerary monuments, but the island was certainly not at the epicentre of advanced ancient civilisation. (In Egypt they were creating the pyramids at this time.)

Things were shaken up with the arrival of warrior tribes in Mallorca and Menorca around 1200 BC, probably from Asia Minor, which overwhelmed the local populace. They are known today as the Talayotic people, because of the buildings and villages they left behind. The *talayots* are their call sign to posterity. The circular (and sometimes square-based or ship's hull–shaped) stone edifices are testimony to an organised and hierarchical society. The most common were the circular *talayots,* which could reach a height of 6m and had two floors. Their purpose is a matter of conjecture. Were they symbolic of the power of local chieftains, or burial places for them? Were they used for storage or defence? Were they religious sites? There were at least 200 Talayotic villages across the island. Simple ceramics, along with artefacts in bronze (swords, axes, necklaces), have been found on these sites.

The ancients knew Mallorca and Menorca as the Gymnesias Islands, from a word meaning 'naked' (it appears that at least some of the islanders got about with a minimum of covering). Talayotic society seems to have been divided into a ruling elite, a broad subsistence farming underclass and slaves. It is not known if they had a written language.

Contact with the outside world came through Greek and Phoenician traders. The Carthaginians attempted to establish a foothold in Mallorca but failed. They did, however, enrol Mallorquins as mercenaries. Balearic men were gifted with slingshots. These Mallorquin and Menorcan slingshot warriors (*foners* in Catalan) called themselves Balears (possibly derived from an ancient Greek word meaning 'to throw'), and so their island homes also came to be known as the Balearics. These men weren't averse to payment and developed a reputation as slings for hire. In Carthaginian armies, they would launch salvos of 4cm to 6cm oval-shaped projectiles on the enemy before the infantry went in. They also carried daggers or short swords for hand-to-hand combat but wore virtually no protection. They were present in the Carthaginian victory over the Greeks in Sicily in the 5th century BC and again in the Punic Wars against Rome.

Some historians claim the funny white, green and red clay figurine-whistles known as *siurells* were introduced to Mallorca by the Phoenicians and may have represented ancient deities. Classic figures include bulls, horse-riders and dog-headed men.

HISTORY ROMANS, VANDALS & BYZANTINES

DEITIES

Romans, Vandals & Byzantines

When the Roman Consul Quintus Cecilius Metelus approached the shores of Mallorca in 123 BC, possibly around Platja des Trenc in the south, he did not come unprepared. Knowing that the island warriors were capable of slinging heavy stones at his ships' waterline and sinking them, he had

123 BC	AD 426	534	707
On the pretext of ending Balearic piracy, the Roman general Quintus Cecilius Metelus, later dubbed Balearicus, storms ashore and in a short time takes control of Mallorca and Menorca.	Raids on Mallorca by the Vandals, central European barbarian tribes that had pillaged their way across Europe to North Africa, lead to the destruction of the Roman city of Pol·lentia.	Belisarius takes control of the Balearic Islands in the name of Byzantine Emperor Justinian, who until his death in 565 attempted to reestablish the Roman Empire across the Mediterranean.	Muslim Arabs in North Africa raid Mallorca for the first time. Four years later they would begin the conquest of the Spanish mainland.

come up with a novel idea. Using heavy skins and leather, he effectively invented the first armoured vessels. Stunned by their incapacity to inflict serious damage, the Mallorquin warriors fled inland before the advance of Metelus' men. Within two years the island had been pacified.

Metelus had 3000 settlers brought over from mainland Iberia and founded two military camps in the usual Roman style (with the intersecting main streets of the *decumanus* and *cardus maximus*). Known as Palmeria or Palma and Pol·lentia, they soon developed into Mallorca's main towns. Pol·lentia, neatly situated between the two northeast bays of Pollença and Alcúdia, was the senior of the two.

At the same time as Pol·lentia was embellished with fine buildings, temples, a theatre and more (Pol·lentia has Mallorca's most extensive Roman remains), some Roman citizens opted for the rural life and built grand country villas. Nothing remains today but it is tempting to see them as the precursor to the Arab *alquerías* (farmsteads) and Mallorcan *possessions* (country estates).

The indigenous population slowly adopted the Roman language and customs but continued to live in its own villages. Plinius the Elder reported that Mallorcan wine was as good as in Italy, and the island's wheat and snails were also appreciated.

Archaeological evidence, such as the remains of the 5th-century early-Christian basilica at Son Peretó, shows that Christianity had arrived in the island by the 4th century AD. By then storm clouds were gathering, and in the 5th century they broke as barbarian tribes launched assaults on the Roman Empire. The Balearic Islands felt the scourge of the Vandals (an East Germanic tribe that plundered their way into Roman territory) in 426. Forty years later, having crashed across Spain to establish their base in North Africa, they returned to take the islands.

The Vandals got their comeuppance when Byzantine Emperor Justinian decided to try to rebuild the Roman Empire. His tireless general, Belisarius, vanquished the Vandals in North Africa in 533 and the following year took the Balearic Islands. After Justinian's death in 565, Byzantine control over territories in the western Mediterranean quickly waned. By the time the Muslims swept across North Africa in the first years of the 8th century, the Balearic Islands were an independent Christian enclave.

The Islamic Centuries

An Arab noble from Al-Andalus (Muslim Spain), Isam al-Jaulani, was forced by bad weather to take shelter in the port of Palma in 902. During his stay he became convinced that the town could and should be taken, along with Mallorca and the rest of the Balearic Islands, and incorporated into the Caliphate of Córdoba. On his return to Córdoba the Caliph

One way in which Mallorquins have asserted their fidelity to their roots and cultural independence is through language: Mallorquin, a dialect of Catalan, has evolved since the conquest in 1229. Their tongue was edged out of the public realm under Franco, but it has returned as a badge of pride for many Mallorquins.

For a comprehensive history of the ancient, pre-Roman world in Mallorca, Spanish readers should look no further than *Guía Arqueológica de Mallorca*, by Javier Arambau, Carlos Garrido and Vicenç Sastre.

869

Norman raiders sack Mallorca's population centres, just 21 years after an Arab raid from Muslim Spain, which Mallorca's leaders had agreed to in return for being left in peace.

903

Muslim forces take control of Mallorca in the name of the Caliph of Córdoba in Spain. Local Christian warriors resist for another eight years in redoubts across the island.

1075

Mallorca becomes an independent *taifa* (small kingdom) in the wake of the civil conflicts that shattered the Caliphate of Córdoba into a series of *taifas* across Spain.

SIMON GREENWOOD/GETTY IMAGES ©

→ Norman re-enactment

Abdallah entrusted him with the task and Al-Jaulani returned with a landing party in 902 or 903.

The port town fell easily but Al-Jaulani, who was made *wāli* (governor) of what the Arabs dubbed the Eastern Islands of Al-Andalus, remained engaged in guerrilla-style warfare against pockets of Christian resistance on the islands for eight years. By the time he died in 913, the islands had been pacified and he had begun work to expand and improve the archipelago's only city, now called Medina Mayurka (City of Mallorca).

The Muslims divided the island into 12 districts and in the ensuing century Mallorca thrived. They brought advanced irrigation methods and

THE JEWS IN MALLORCA

The first Jews appear to have arrived in Mallorca in AD 70, the same year the Romans largely destroyed Jerusalem and its temple. Under Muslim rule, a small Jewish minority thrived in Medina Mayurka (the name the Moors gave to Mallorca). Christian Mallorca, after the 1229 conquest, was not so kind.

Although barred from most professions and public office, Mallorca's Jews were esteemed for their learning and business sense. Jewish doctors, astronomers, bankers and traders, generally fluent in Catalan and/or Spanish, Latin, Hebrew and Arabic, often played key roles.

By the end of the century, there were perhaps 2000 to 3000 Jews in Ciutat (Palma). They were evicted from the area around the Palau de l'Almudaina and moved to the Call (Catalan equivalent of a ghetto) in the eastern part of Sa Calatrava, in the streets around Carrer de Monti-Sion. They were locked in at night and obliged to wear a red and yellow circular patch during the day. In 1315 their synagogue was converted into the Església de Monti-Sion and they would not have another until 1373. In 1391, rioting farmers killed some 300 Jews in an anti-Semitic pogrom.

In 1435 the bulk of the island's Jews were forced to convert to Christianity and their synagogues were converted into churches. At the beginning of the 16th century they were forced to move from the Call Major to the Call Menor, centred on Carrer de Colom. They were now Christians but were under suspicion of secretly practising Jewish rites; they were a particular target for the Inquisition and the last auto-da-fé (trial by fire) of such so-called *judaizantes* took place in 1691, when three citizens were burned at the stake.

Known as *xuetes* (from *xua*, a derogatory term referring to pork meat), they were shunned by the rest of the Christian populace much as they had been before and it was not until the 19th century that they were finally able to breathe easier. A veritable flurry of 19th-century writers and poets came from *xueta* families. During WWII, when the Nazis asked Mallorca to surrender its Jewish population, the religious authorities purportedly refused the Nazi request. Today the descendants of these families (who even in the mid-20th century were shunned by many other Mallorquins) are estimated to number between 15,000 and 20,000.

1114–15	1148	1185	1203
A Catalan-Pisan crusading force arrives to end the piracy that is damaging Mediterranean trade. They take Medina Mayurka in 1115 and free 30,000 Christian slaves before leaving the island.	Mallorca signs a trade agreement with the Italian cities of Genoa and Pisa, opening Mallorcan markets to the Italians and reducing the threat of further Christian assaults on the island.	The Muslim governor of the island, Wāli Ishaq, dies, ending a period of unprecedented prosperity. His rule represents the high point of Almoravid control over Mallorca.	The Almohads in peninsular Spain defeat the Almoravid regime in Medina Mayurka and take control of the island, although life continues largely unchanged for most of Mallorca's inhabitants.

the *alqueries,* the farms they established, flourished. Medina Mayurka became one of Europe's most cosmopolitan cities. By the end of the 12th century, the city had a population of 35,000, putting it on a par with Barcelona and London. The *al-qasr* (castle-palace; Palau de l'Almudaina) was built over a Roman fort and the grand mosque was built where Palma Catedral now stands. With the raising of walls around the new Rabad al-Jadid quarter (roughly Es Puig de Sant Pere), the city reached the extents it would maintain until the late 19th century. It was a typical medieval Muslim city, a medina like Marrakech or Fez. Few of those narrow streets that made up its labyrinth, now called *estrets* (narrows), remain. Medina Mayurka enjoyed close relations with the rest of the Muslim world in the western Mediterranean, although by 1075 the emirs (princes) of the Eastern Islands were independent of mainland jurisdiction.

Al-Jaulani's successors dedicated considerable energy to piracy, which by the opening of the 12th century was the islands' principal source of revenue, although such activities aroused the wrath of Christian merchant powers. In 1114, 500 vessels carrying a reported 65,000 Pisan and Catalan troops landed on Mallorca and launched a bloody campaign. In April the following year they entered Medina Mayurka. Exhausted after 10 months' fighting, they left Mallorca laden with booty, prisoners and freed Christian slaves when news came that a Muslim relief fleet was on the way from North Africa.

In 1116 a new era dawned in Mallorca, as the Almoravids (a Berber tribe from Morocco) from mainland Spain took control. The Balearics reached new heights in prosperity, particularly under the Wāli Ishaq, who ruled from 1152 to 1185. In 1203 Mallorca fell under the sway of the Almohads who had taken control of Al-Andalus.

No doubt all this internecine strife between Muslim factions had not gone unnoticed in Christian Spain, where the Reconquista (the reconquest of Muslim-held territory by the Christian kingdoms) had taken on new impetus after the rout of Almohad armies in the Battle of Las Navas de Tolosa in 1212. By 1250 the Christians would take Valencia, Extremadura, Córdoba and Seville, and the last Muslims would be expelled from Portugal. In such a context it is hardly surprising that a plan should be hatched to take the Balearic Islands too, especially as Mallorca continued to be a major source of piracy that seriously hindered Christian sea trade.

Jewish cartographers, led by the Mallorquin Cresques family, achieved the height of fame for their extraordinary maps, which were used by adventurers from all over Europe. Abraham Cresques (c 1325–87) and his son Jafuda (c 1350–1410) created one of the best-known such maps in 1375 (now in the national library in Paris).

El Conqueridor

On 5 September 1229, 155 vessels bearing 1500 knights on horseback and 15,000 infantry weighed anchor in the Catalan ports of Barcelona, Tarragona and Salou and set sail for Mallorca. Jaume I (1208–76), the energetic 21-year-old king of Aragón and Catalonia, vowed to take the Balearic Islands and end Muslim piracy in the process. Jaume I, later

September 1229	December 1229	1267	1276
Under Jaume I, king of the Crown of Aragón, Catalan troops land at Santa Ponça in Mallorca, defeat the Muslims and camp before the walls of Medina Mayurka.	Jaume I enters the city, which his troops sack, leaving it in such a state that a plague the following Easter kills many of the inhabitants and invading soldiers.	Ramon Llull, Mallorquin icon and would-be saint, has a series of visions that will ultimately transform him into one of the most important Catalan cultural figures in history.	Jaume I dies, almost 50 years after bringing Christian rule to Mallorca. The territories under his rule are divided between his two sons, prompting decades of internecine conflict.

dubbed El Conqueridor (The Conqueror), landed at Santa Ponça and, after two swift skirmishes, marched on Medina Mayurka, to which he laid siege. Finally, on 31 December, Christian troops breached the defences and poured into the city, pillaging mercilessly. In the following months, Jaume I pursued enemy troops across the island but resistance was feeble.

With the conquest of Mallorca complete, Jaume I proceeded to divide it up among his lieutenants and allies. The Arab *alqueries, rafals* (hamlets) and villages were handed over to their new *senyors* (masters). Many changed name but a good number retained their Arab nomenclature. Places beginning with Bini (Sons of) are Arab hangovers. Many took on the names of their new lord, preceded by the possessive particle *son* or *sa* (loosely translated as 'that which is of...'). Jaume I codified this division of the spoils in his *Llibre del Repartiment*.

Among Jaume's early priorities was a rapid program of church-building, Christianisation of the local populace and the sending of settlers from Catalonia (mostly from around the city of Girona). For the first century after the conquest, Ciutat (the city) held the bulk of the island's population. The Part Forana ('Part Outside' Ciutat) was divided into 14 districts but all power in Mallorca was concentrated in Ciutat. Beneath the king, day-to-day government was carried out by six *jurats* (magistrates).

The Christian Catalan settlers basically imposed their religion, tongue and customs on the island and the bulk of the Muslim population was reduced to slavery. Those that did not flee or accept this destiny had only one real choice: to renounce Islam. The Jewish population would also have a roller-coaster time of it.

In the Part Forana the farmsteads came to be known as *possessions* and were the focal point of the agricultural economy upon which the island would largely come to depend. The *possessions* were run by local managers faithful to their (frequently absentee) noble overlords and were often well-off farmers themselves. They employed *missatges* (permanent farm labour) and *jornalers* (day wage labourers), both of whom generally lived on the edge of misery. Small farm holders frequently failed to make ends meet, ceded their holdings to the more important *possessions* and became *jornalers*.

Mallorca's connection to the seafaring trade routes of the Mediterranean ensured that it was particularly vulnerable to the ravages of the plague, which hit the island repeatedly, decimating the population in the process.

Crown of Aragón

On Jaume I's death in 1276, his territories were divided between his two sons, Jaume II and Pere II; in the years that followed Mallorca was tossed between the two, a process continued under their heirs. By 1349, the previously independent kingdom of Mallorca was tied into the Crown of Aragón, although it retained a high degree of autonomy.

1343	1382	1391	1488
Pere III of the Crown of Aragón invades Mallorca and seizes the crown from Jaume III, who would die six years later in the Battle of Llucmajor trying to get it back.	Sac i Sort (Bag and Luck) is introduced whereby the names of six candidates to be named *jurats* (magistrates) for the following 12 months were pulled out of four bags.	Hundreds of Jews die in a pogrom as farmers and labourers sack the Jewish quarter of Palma. Months later, those involved are released without sentence for fear of causing greater unrest.	The Inquisition, which had operated from the mainland, is formally established in Mallorca. In the following decades hundreds would die, burned at the stake as heretics.

Catalan painter Santiago Rusiñol's *Mallorca, L'Illa de la Calma* (Mallorca, the Island of Calm; 1922) is one of the most beautiful descriptions written of the island. In the book he takes a critical look at the rough rural life of many Mallorquins.

The fortunes of Mallorca, and in particular Palma, closely followed those of Barcelona, the Catalan headquarters of the Crown of Aragón and merchant trading hub. In the middle of the 15th century, both cities (despite setbacks such as outbreaks of the plague) were among the most prosperous in the Mediterranean. Palma had some 35 consulates and trade representatives sprinkled around the Med. The city's trade community had a merchant fleet of 400 vessels and the medieval Bourse, Sa Llotja, was an animated focal point of business.

Not all was rosy. In the Part Forana farm labourers lived on the edge of starvation and crops failed to such an extent in 1374 that people were dropping dead in the streets. Frequent localised revolts, such as that of 1391 (the same year that furious workers sacked the Call in Ciutat), were stamped out mercilessly by the army. A much greater shock to the ruling classes was the 1521 Germania revolt, an urban working-class uprising provoked largely by crushing taxes extracted from the lower classes. They forced the viceroy (by now Mallorca was part of a united Spain under Emperor Carlos V) to flee. In October 1522 Carlos V sent in the army, which only reestablished control the following March.

By then Mallorca's commercial star had declined and the coast was constant prey to the attacks of North African pirates. The building of *talayots* around the island (many still stand) is eloquent historical testimony to the problem. Some of Mallorca's most colourful traditional

THE EVANGELISING CATALAN SHAKESPEARE

Born in Ciutat (ie Palma) de Mallorca, Ramon Llull (1232–1316), the mystic, theologian and all-round Renaissance man before his time, started off on a worldly trajectory. After entering Jaume I's court as a page, Ramon was elevated to major-domo of Jaume II, the future king of Mallorca. Ramon lived it up, writing love ditties and enjoying (apparently) a wild sex life.

Then, in 1267, he saw five visions of Christ crucified and everything changed. His next years were consumed with profound theological, moral and linguistic training (in Arabic and Hebrew). He founded a monastery (with Jaume II's backing) at Miramar for the teaching of theology and Eastern languages to future evangelists. His burning desire was the conversion of Jews and Muslims and he began to travel throughout Europe, the Near East and North Africa to preach. At the same time he wrote countless tracts in Catalan and Arabic and is considered the father of Catalan as a literary language. In 1295 he joined the Franciscans and in 1307 risked the ire of Muslims by preaching outside North African mosques. Some say he was lynched in Tunisia by an angry mob while others affirm he died while en route to his native Mallorca in 1316. He is buried in the Basílica de Sant Francesc in Palma. His beatification was confirmed by Pope John Paul II and the long, uncertain process of canonisation began in 2007.

1521	1706	1773	1809
Armed workers and farm labourers rise up in the beginning of the Germania revolt against the nobles. In October 1522, Carlos V sends troops to Alcúdia to quell the revolt.	The Austrian pretender to the Spanish throne in the War of the Spanish Succession (1702–15) takes control of Mallorca. Nine years later, Mallorca is defeated by Felipe V.	King Carlos III orders that the Jews of Palma be allowed to live wherever they wish and that all forms of discrimination and mistreatment of the Jewish population be punished.	Thousands of French troops captured in battle in mainland Spain are sent to Illa de Cabrera, where they live in appalling conditions. The survivors would not be released until 1814.

festivals, such as Moros i Cristians in Pollença and Es Firó in Sóller date to these times. As Spain's fortunes also declined from the 17th century, Mallorca slid into provincial obscurity. Backing the Habsburgs in the War of the Spanish Succession (1703–15) didn't endear Mallorca to the finally victorious Bourbon monarch, Felipe V, who in 1716 abolished all the island's privileges and autonomy.

Pirate attacks forced Mallorca to be on its guard throughout much of the 18th century until the island received permission to retaliate without punishment in 1785. At the same time, Mallorcan Franciscan friar Fray Junípero Serra was in California, founding missions (now major cities) such as San Francisco and San Diego.

The Napoleonic Wars in the early 19th century had repercussions for Mallorca – waves of Catalan refugees flooded the island, provoking economic and social unrest. The second half of the century saw the rise of the bourgeoisie, an increase in agricultural activity and, in 1875, the opening of the first railway between Palma and Inca.

Mallorca in the Civil War

The 1931 nationwide elections brought unprecedented results: the Republicans and Socialists together won an absolute majority in Palma, in line with the results in Madrid. The Confederatión Espanola de Derechas Autónomous (Spanish Confederation of the Autonomous Right) won the national elections in 1933 and all the left-wing mayors in Mallorca were sacked by early 1934. They were back again in a euphoric mood after the dramatic elections of 1936 again gave a landslide victory to the left.

For many generals this was the last straw. Their ringleader, General Francisco Franco, launched an uprising against the central Republican government in July 1936. In Mallorca the insurrection found little resistance. On 19 July rebel soldiers and right-wing Falange militants burst into Cort (the town hall) and arrested the left-wing mayor, Emili Darder (he and other politicians would be executed in February 1937). They quickly occupied strategic points across Palma with barely a shot fired. More resistance came from towns in the Part Forana, but was soon bloodily squashed.

By mid-August battalions of Italian troops and warplanes sent by Franco's ally, the dictator Benito Mussolini, were pouring into Mallorca. The island became the main base for Italian air operations and it was from here that raids were carried out against Barcelona with increasing intensity as the Civil War wore on.

On 9 August 1936 a Catalan-Valencian force (apparently without approval from central command) retook Ibiza from Franco and then landed at Porto Cristo on the 16th. So taken aback were they by the lack of resistance that they failed to press home the advantage of surprise.

Between 16 and 18 March 1938, Italian air-force bombers based in Mallorca launched 17 raids on Barcelona, killing about 1300 people. Apparently Mussolini ordered the raids, without the knowledge of the Spanish Nationalist high command.

HISTORY MALLORCA IN THE CIVIL WAR

1837	April 1912	June 1922	19 July 1936
A passenger steamer between Barcelona and Palma begins service, creating a regular link to the mainland. Among its first passengers were George Sand and Frédéric Chopin, in 1838.	The train line linking Palma with Sóller opens; until then, poor mountain roads had made it easier for the people of Sóller to travel north by sea to France than south by land to Palma.	The first postal service flight takes place between Barcelona and Palma. The service would use flying boats parked in hangars at Es Jonquet in Palma.	The army and right-wing militias take control of Mallorca for General Franco as he launches his military uprising against the Republican government in Madrid.

A Nationalist counterattack begun on 3 September, backed by Italian planes, pushed the hapless (and ill-equipped) invaders back into the sea. Soon thereafter the Republicans also abandoned Ibiza and Formentera. Of the Balearic Islands, only Menorca remained loyal to the Republic throughout the war.

With Franco's victory in 1939, life in Mallorca followed that of the mainland: use of Catalan in public announcements, signs, education and so on was banned. Rationing was introduced in 1940 and stayed in place until 1952. Of the nine mayors the city had from 1936 to 1976, four were military men and the others conservative.

Boom Times

In 1950 the first charter flight landed on a small airstrip in Mallorca. No one could have perceived the implications. By 1955 central Palma had a dozen hotels and others stretched along the waterfront towards Cala Major.

The 1960s and 1970s brought an extraordinary urban revolution as mass tourism took off. The barely controlled high-rise expansion around the bay in both directions, and later behind other beaches around the coast, was the result of a deliberate policy by Franco's central government to encourage tourism in coastal areas. Many of the more awful hotels built in this period have since been closed or recycled as apartment or office blocks.

The islanders now enjoyed – by some estimates – the highest standard of living in Spain, but 80% of their economy was (and still is) based on tourism. For decades this led to thoughtless construction on the island and frequent anxiety attacks whenever a season didn't meet expectations. The term *balearización* was coined to illustrate this short-termism and wanton destruction of the area's prime resource – its beautiful coastlines.

A Change of Image

In recent years, however, Mallorca's tourism weathervane has slowly been changing direction, with an increasing focus on sustainability, eco-awareness and year-round activities. The island is waking up to the fact that thoughtless construction and anonymous package-holiday hotels are the past, not the future. Mallorca is starting to shrug off its reputation for boozy resorts and cheap-as-chips English breakfasts – and not before time, some would add.

Agritourism has shown that it is more than just a passing fad, and more and more *fincas* (working farms) are opening their doors to visitors, with charmingly rustic accommodation, peaceful locations and meals that make the most of home-grown organic produce. In towns

History Tour

Bronze Age/ Talayotic: Ses Païsses, Artà

Roman: Pol·lentia, Alcúdia

Moorish: Banys Àrabs, Palma

Medieval: Alcúdia's walled old town

Gothic: Catedral, Palma

Renaissance/ baroque: Palma's mansions and patios

1 April 1939	1952	1960	1983
Franco claims victory in a nationally televised radio speech, three days after Madrid had fallen to Nationalist troops and bringing to an end almost three years of conflict.	After almost 12 years, post–Civil War rationing finally ends on the island. Although many Mallorquins continue to live subsistence lives, the tourism boom will soon transform the island forever.	An estimated 500,000 tourists visit the island, marking the beginning of mass tourism on the island. These figures would increase 50 times over during the decades that followed.	The autonomy statute for the Balearic Islands region (together with those of other Spanish regions) is approved eight years after Franco's death.

A RIGHT ROYAL DILETTANTE

As the first battles of the Italian campaign raged in 1915, Archduke Luis Salvador sat frustrated in Brandeis Castle in Bohemia, writing furiously but impeded by the fighting from returning to his beloved Balearic Islands. He died in October that year of blood poisoning after an operation on his leg.

Luis had been born in 1847 in Florence, the fourth son of Grand Duke Leopold II. He was soon travelling, studying and visiting cities all over Europe. From the outset he wrote of what he saw. His first books were published one year after his first visit to the Balearic Islands in 1867. He returned to Mallorca in 1871 and the following year bought Miramar. He decided to make Mallorca his main base – a lifestyle choice that many northern Europeans would seek to imitate over a century later.

Salvador was an insatiable traveller. In his private steam-driven yacht *Nixe* (and its successors) and other forms of transport, he visited places as far apart as Cyprus and Tasmania. Hardly a year passed in which he didn't publish a book on his travels and studies, possibly the best known of which are his weighty tomes on *Die Balearen* (The Balearics). His love remained Mallorca (where royals and other VIPs visited him regularly) and, in 1877, local deputies awarded him the title of Adopted Son of the Balearic Islands. Four years later he was made an honorary member of the Royal Geographic Society in London.

and cities, manor houses are being sensitively restored as boutique hotels. All of which is helping to change the image of tourism in Mallorca, by placing the emphasis on authentic local experiences and cultural immersion.

Though many resorts still go into winter hibernation, some hotels in towns and villages are now staying open in the low season, mostly to cater for a growing number of travellers who come for the island's outdoor activities. Bradley Wiggins regularly trains for the Tour de France in the Tramuntana, and recent press coverage has helped publicise just how fantastic Mallorca is for outdoor pursuits. Adventure-sports companies offering everything from guided hikes and mountain biking to canyoning, caving and coasteering are rising in number. Their message? Look beyond the beach. The word is spreading that Mallorca has year-round appeal.

For an island that is banging the drum about its sustainable tourism, unique landscapes and outdoor activities, the Serra de Tramuntana's inscription on the Unesco World Heritage List of Cultural Landscapes in 2011 was the icing on the cake – these wild mountains are now even more of a draw to tourists and for all the right reasons.

An asteroid discovered by Mallorcan astronomers in 1997 was named 9900 Ramon Llull after the island's great medieval philosopher, writer and evangelist.

May 2007	2009	May 2011	June 2011
Mallorcan Socialist Francesc Antich ends right-wing Partido Popular (PP) rule after regional elections by forming a coalition government with promises to put a brake on construction projects.	The Basque separatist group ETA detonates a series of bombs, killing two policemen and causing havoc at the height of Mallorca's July and August summer tourist seasons.	The conservative Partido Popular storms back into power, winning an absolute majority in regional elections. The kingmakers in 2007, the Unió Mallorquina, loses all its seats.	The Serra de Tramuntana is inscribed as a Cultural Landscape on the Unesco World Heritage List.

Landscape & Wildlife

All of the Balearics are beautiful, but Mother Nature really pulled out the stops for Mallorca. Whether you're slow-touring the wild west, where limestone cliffs drop suddenly to curvaceous bays and water 50 shades of blue; rambling through the hinterland, where hills rise steep and wooded above meadows cloaked in wildflowers, olive groves and citrus orchards; or lounging on flour white beaches on the south coast, you can't help but feel that Mallorca's loveliness is often underrated. Trust us – it's stunning.

Mallorca's Geography Stats

....

Area: 3636 sq km

....

Coastline: 550km

....

Closest distance to mainland Spain: 175km

....

Highest point: Puig Major de Son Torrella (1445m)

....

Highest accessible point: Puig de Massanella (1365m)

Mallorca's Landscape

Mallorca, shaped like a rough trapezoid, is the largest island of the Balearic archipelago. Technically. The island chain is an extension of mainland Spain's Sistema Penibético (Beltic mountain range), which dips close to 1.5km below the Mediterranean and peeks up again to form the islands of Mallorca, Menorca, Ibiza and Formentera. The stretch of water between the archipelago and the mainland is called the Balearic Sea.

The Coast

Mallorca's coastline is punctuated for the most part by small coves, save for three major bays. The Badia de Palma in the south is the most densely populated corner of the island. The two large, shell-shaped bays of the north, the Badia de Pollença and Badia d'Alcúdia, are enclosed by a series of dramatic headlands, Cap de Formentor, Cap des Pinar and Cap Ferrutx.

A series of plunging cliffs interspersed with calm bays marks the south, which is where you'll also find Mallorca's two main island networks: the Illa de Sa Dragonera (offshore from Sant Elm) and the 19-island Parc Nacional Marítim-Terrestre de l'Arxipèlag de Cabrera (from Colònia de Sant Jordi).

Mountains

The island's defining geographic feature is the 90km-long Serra de Tramuntana, a Unesco World Heritage Cultural Landscape since 2011. Spectacularly buckled and contorted, this range of peaks, gullies and cliffs begins close to Andratx in the southwest and reaches its dramatic finale in the northern Cap de Formentor. The highest summits are in the centre of the range, northeast of Sóller, but the steep-sided western flanks that rise abruptly from the Mediterranean shore and shelter numerous villages give the appearance of being higher than they really are. The range is for the most part characterised by forested hillsides (terraced with agriculture in some areas) and bald limestone peaks. A number of tributary ranges, such as the Serra d'Alfabia and Els Cornadors, both close to Sóller, are sometimes named separately.

On the other side of the island, the less-dramatic Serra de Llevant extends from Cap Ferrutx in the north to Cap de Ses Salines in the south; the offshore Illa de Cabrera is considered an extension of the range. Its highest point is the easily accessible Santuari de Sant Salvador (509m), while the range dominates the Parc Natural de la Península de Llevant, north of Artà.

Between the two, in the centre of the island, extends the vast fertile plain known as Es Pla.

Caves

Mallorca, particularly along its eastern and southern coasts, is drilled with caves created by erosion, waves or water drainage. The caves range from tiny well-like dugouts to vast kilometres-long tunnels replete with lakes, rivers and astounding shapes sculptured by the elements. Although underground, most of the caves actually sit above sea level. The best-known are the Coves del Drac and Coves dels Hams, both outside Porto Cristo; Coves d'Artà in Platja de Canyamel; Coves de Campanet in Campanet; and Coves de Gènova, which are close to Palma.

Wildlife

Mallorca's animal population is fairly modest in both numbers and variety, but this is more than compensated for by the abundant birdlife which makes the island a major Mediterranean destination for twitchers.

Land Animals

The most charismatic (and easily visible) of Mallorca's land species is the Mallorcan wild goat *(Capra ageagrus hircus)*, which survives in reasonable numbers only in the Serra de Tramuntana, Cap des Pinar and Parc Natural de la Península de Llevant.

Other mammals include feral cats (a serious threat to bird populations), ferrets, rabbits and hedgehogs. Lizards, turtles, frogs and bats make up the bulk of the native populations. Lizards thrive on Mallorca's islands due to the lack of human population and introduced species, particularly on the Illa de Sa Dragonera, where they have the run of the island, and the Illa de Cabrera; the latter provides a refuge for 80% of the last surviving Balearic lizards *(Podarcis lilfordi)*.

You'll also find spiders, more than 300 moth species and 30 kinds of butterflies.

Among the most complete guides available to Mallorca's caves are the *Cuadernos de Espeleología I and II* (Speology Notebooks I & II), by José Bermejo.

MALLORCA'S PARKS

The creation of protected wildlife areas has helped stabilise Mallorca's wildlife and make it accessible to visitors. Now a full 40% of the island falls under some form of official environmental protection.

PARK	FEATURES	ACTIVITIES	WHEN TO VISIT
Parc Nacional Marítim-Terrestre de l'Arxipèlag de Cabrera	Archipelago of 19 islands and islets; home to 130 bird species and diverse marine life	Birdwatching, hiking, scuba diving, snorkelling, swimming	Easter–Oct
Parc Natural de S'Albufera	Vital wetland sheltering 400 plants and 230 species of bird, many of them on migration paths between Europe and Africa	Birdwatching (including 80% of the birds recorded on the Balearic Islands), cycling	Spring and autumn
Parc Natural de Mondragó	Rolling dunes, juniper groves, vibrant wetlands and unspoilt beaches close to east-coast resorts	Hiking, picnicking, swimming	May–Sep
Parc Natural de la Península de Llevant	Flora and fauna	Walking, birdwatching	May–Sep
Parc Natural de Sa Dragonera	Two small islets and the 4km-long Illa de Sa Dragonera; endangered gull population	Snorkelling, scuba diving	May–Sep

BIRDWATCHING SITES

Just about anywhere on the island is good for birdwatching, but the northern, eastern and southern coasts are prime territory for twitchers.

Parc Natural de S'Albufera A marshy birdwatchers' paradise where some 230 species, including moustached warblers and shoveler ducks, vie for your attention. The park is home to no less than two-thirds of the species that live permanently or winter in Mallorca and is a Ramsar Wetland of International Importance.

Parc Nacional Marítim-Terrestre de l'Arxipèlag de Cabrera These protected offshore islands draw marine birds, migrants and birds of prey, including fisher eagles, endangered Balearic shearwaters, Audouin's gulls, Cory's shearwaters, shags, ospreys, Eleonora's falcons and peregrine falcons.

Parc Natural de la Península de Llevant Watch for cormorants and Audouin's gulls in this rugged promontory north of Artà.

Parc Natural de Mondragó Falcons, turtle doves and coastal species are the major draws here.

Embassament de Cúber In the shadow of the Puig Major de Son Torrella, watch for raptors and other mountain species.

Vall de Bóquer Near Port Pollença, this rocky valley is home to warblers, Eurasian Scops owls, red-legged partridges, peregrine falcons, and other predominantly mountain and migratory species.

Cap de Formentor Species on this dramatic peninsula include all manner of warblers, blue rock thrushes, crag martins, Eleonora's falcons, pallid swifts, migrating raptors and, if you're lucky, the Balearic shearwater.

Marine Mammals

Sperm whales, pilot whales and finback whales feed not far offshore. Also swimming here are bottlenose dolphins, white-sided dolphins and other species. Scuba divers often spot barracuda, octopuses, moray eels, grouper, cardinal fish, damsel fish, starfish, sea urchins, sponges and corals.

Birds

As a natural resting point between Europe and Africa, and as one of the few Mediterranean islands with considerable wetlands, Mallorca is a wonderful birdwatching destination, and coastal regions in particular draw hundreds of resident and migratory species, especially during the migration periods in spring and autumn.

With more than 200 species it's all but impossible to predict what you'll see. The birds can be divided into three categories: sedentary (those that live on the island year-round), seasonal (those that migrate south after hatching chicks or to escape the cold winters in northern Europe) and migratory (those that rest briefly in Mallorca before continuing their journey).

The web forum www.birdforum. net has an extensive listing of Balearic birdwatching sites. Also good is Birding in Spain (www.birdingin-spain.com); click on 'Birding Mallorca' for links to organised tours as well as a list of bird species at major birdwatching sites around the island.

Endangered Species

The populations of Mallorca's threatened species of Mediterranean birds, tortoises and toads are recovering thanks to the conservation and controlled breeding efforts of Mallorca's parks and natural areas.

Endangered species here include the spur-thighed tortoise and Hermann's tortoise, the only two tortoises found in Spain, and bird species such as the red kite.

Among the programs showing results, the endemic Mallorcan midwife toad's status was in 2006 changed to 'vulnerable' from 'critically endangered' on the IUCN Red List of Threatened Species. But there's not such good news about the Balearic shearwater, a waterbird that has suffered greatly because of feral cats; IUCN listed it as 'critically endangered' in its 2013 report.

Plants

The Balearic Islands claim more than 100 endemic species and provide a fertile home to countless more.

Mountains & Plains

On the peaks of the Serra de Tramuntana, Mallorca's hardy mountain flora survives harsh sun and wind. Thriving species tend to be ground-huggers or cliff species such as *Scabiosa cretica* (with exotic-looking lilac blooms), which burrow into rock fissures to keep their roots well drained and cool.

On Mallorca's rocky hillsides and flat plains, where oak forests once grew before being burned or destroyed to create farmland, drought-resistant scrubland flora now thrives. Expect to see evergreen shrubs like wild olives and dwarf fan palms, as well as herbs like rosemary, thyme and lavender. Other plants include heather, broom, prickly pear (which can be made into jam) and 60 species of orchid.

Endemic plants include the lovely *Paeonia cambessedesii,* a pink peony that lives in the shade of some Serra de Tramuntana gullies, and *Naufraga balearica,* a cloverlike plant found on shady Tramuntana slopes.

Forests & Ferns

Where evergreen oak forests have managed to survive you'll find holly oaks, kermes oaks and holm oaks growing alongside smaller, less noticeable species like violets, heather and butcher's broom. Most interesting to botanists are endangered endemic species like the shiny-leaved box *(Buxux balearica)* and the needled yew *(Taxus baccata),* a perennial tree that can grow for hundreds of years. A specimen in Esporles is thought to be more than 2000 years old.

Humidity-seeking ferns (more than 40 species) have found marvellous habitats near Mallorca's caves, gorges and streams. In other damp areas, clusters of poplars, elms and ash trees, all introduced species, form small forests.

Coastal Species

Along the shore, plants have had to adapt to constant sea spray, salt deposits and strong winds. One of Mallorca's most beloved coastal species is samphire *(fonoll marí),* a leafy coastal herb that was given to sailors as a source of scurvy-preventing vitamin C. These days it's marinated and used in salads. Other common species are the spiny cushionlike *Launaea cervicornis,* and *Senecio rodriguezii,* whose purple, daisylike flowers earned it the nickname of *margalideta de la mar* (little daisy of the sea).

In the wetlands, marshes and dunes of Mallorca, a variety of coastal freshwater flora prosper. Duckweed is one of the most common plants here, though it is often kept company by bulrush, yellow flag iris, sedge and mint. These sand-dwelling species often have white or pale-green leaves and an extensive root system that helps keep them anchored in the shifting sands.

Try birdwatching field guides such as *A Field Guide to the Birds of Britain and Europe* (Peterson Field Guides), by Roger Tory Peterson, Guy Mountfort and P.A.D. Hollum, or the slimmer *Collins Bird Guide: The Most Complete Guide to the Birds of Britain & Europe,* by Lars Svensson et al.

The *Plants of the Balearic Islands,* by Anthony Bonner, is the definitive guide to Mallorca's flora and the ideal companion for budding botanists who plan to spend lots of time hiking.

LANDSCAPE & WILDLIFE PLANTS

THE FUTURE IS GREEN

You need only take one look at Mallorca to see the island's potential for producing renewable energy. The island has an average of 300 days of sunshine a year, and steady winds prevail on the coast. Yet until fairly recently the island was dragging its heels when it came to clean energy, despite its natural resources.

Things are slowly changing, as in 2011 Siemens set a precedent by introducing a high-voltage direct current (HVDC) in the form of a 244km submarine cable between Palma and Valencia. The HVDC provides renewable energy from the Spanish mainland. Thought it is early days yet, it is hoped that in the near future the island will derive the vast majority of its power from renewable sources, including wind, solar and hydroelectric power.

Poseidon's Grass

Beach lovers in northern Mallorca are occasionally put off by beaches with great rafts of what many mistake for algae. This is sea grass (poseidon grass or *poseidonia*), vital for the hindering of erosion on the seabed. The oxygen it gives off helps clean the water, attracts abundant sealife and slows global warming by absorbing carbon dioxide. Thick layers on some beaches actually help keep them intact. It can give off an unpleasant odour, but its presence is nonetheless good for the maritime environment.

Environmental Threats

The uninhibited construction that began in the 1960s and 1970s has influenced everything from birds' nesting habits to plant habitats, rainwater runoff and water shortages. Although the government is more environmentally aware than in decades past, the relationship between development and environmental protection remains uneasy.

One of the most pressing concerns for environmentalists is the prevalence of invasive plant species. Many destructive species were first introduced in local gardens but have found such a good home in Mallorca that they're crowding out endemic species. A good example is *Carpobrotus edulis,* called 'sour fig' in England and locally dubbed *patata frita* (french fry) or *dent de león* (lion's tooth) because of its long, slender leaves. A robust low-lying plant, it chokes native species wherever it goes.

Mallorcan Architecture

For an overview of Mallorca's architectural spectrum, a visit to Palma should be high on your list. You'll glimpse Arab baths and Renaissance mansions where Mallorcan aristocrats once swanned around, baroque *patis* (patios) and Modernista mansions, not to mention that whopper of a Gothic cathedral where the city meets the sea. The next chapter is still to be written: the wave of innovation sweeping contemporary Spanish architectural circles has largely passed Mallorca by.

First Beginnings

Remains of the *talayots* (Bronze Age watchtowers) of the Balearic peoples are found at a few archaeological sites around the island, although little is known about the purpose of these structures and the wider lives of those who inhabited the towns. Most settlements of these Talayotic cultures were encircled by high stone walls, within which were numerous dwellings and the towers, which were built of stone, usually without the use of mortar; it is thought that some of the towers served as watchtowers, others tombs. Although these cultures survived roughly until the Roman arrival on the island in 123 BC, many of the structures seen today date back to 1000 BC. The best preserved Talayotic sites are at Ses Païsses and Capocorb Vell.

Despite ruling over Mallorca for more than two centuries and despite their reputation as mighty builders, the Romans left behind surprisingly few signposts to their presence. This dearth of Roman ruins in Mallorca is most likely attributable to the fact that the Romans, unlike their predecessors, occupied the prime patches of coastal real estate, which was later built over by subsequent civilisations. The only meaningful extant Roman site in Mallorca – Pol·lentia, in Alcúdia in the island's north – is also believed to have been its largest city.

ARCHITECTURAL INSIGHT

Patis Flit back to Renaissance times in the *patis* (patios) in Palma's historic centre.

Museu Regional d'Artà Brush up on your knowledge of *talayots* (watchtowers) here.

Palma Cathedral The goliath of Gothic, with its flying buttresses, soaring pinnacles and one of the world's largest rose windows.

Ses Païsses Close to Artà, this is one of Mallorca's most impressive Talayotic sites.

Banys Àrabs Palma's Arab baths are the most important remaining monument to Muslim domination of the island.

Castell d'Alaró The enigmatic ruins of a medieval fortress.

Ca'n Prunera A classic example of a Modernista mansion in Sóller.

Es Baluard This contemporary, skylit gallery seamlessly merges with Palma's Renaissance seaward walls.

Old Alcúdia Here the medieval walls are among the island's best preserved.

Muslim Mallorca

Mallorca has remarkably little to show for its three centuries of Muslim rule, not least because the mosques they built were invariably occupied by conquering Christian armies in the 13th century, and were subsequently converted into churches. Palma's Catedral and Església de Sant Miquel are two such examples; no evidence of their original purpose survives. And mosques were not the only buildings to be appropriated by the new Christian rulers and transformed beyond recognition – Palau de l'Almudaina was first built by the Romans, adapted by a succession of Muslim governors before becoming the seat of royal (Christian) power on the island.

Defensive fortresses on strategically sited hilltops were another feature of the Islamic occupation, but again most were taken over and much modified by Christian forces in the centuries that followed. Castell de Capdepera is perhaps the most impressive example.

Buildings of Muslim Mallorca

Banys Àrabs, Palma

Jardins d'Alfàbia, road from Sóller to Alaró

Remnants of 12th-century Arab wall, Palma

Castell de Santueri, Felanitx

Mallorcan Gothic

The Catalan slant on the Gothic style, with its broad, low-slung, vaulting church entrances and sober adornment, predominated in Catalan-conquered Mallorca. Guillem Sagrera (c 1380–1456), a Catalan architect and sculptor who had previously worked in Perpignan (today in France), moved to Mallorca in 1420 to take over the direction of work on Palma's Catedral, the island's foremost Gothic structure. Sagrera is considered to be the greatest architect and sculptor of the period in Mallorca. He designed one of the Catedral's chapels and the Gothic chapter house, and, more importantly, he raised Sa Llotja, Mallorca's other stand-out Gothic monument.

As in other parts of Spain, Islamic influences were evident in some aspects of building through the Gothic period. In Mallorca this Mudéjar style is not immediately evident in external facades, but a handful of beautiful *artesonados* (coffered wood ceilings) remain. Those in Palma's Palau de l'Almudaina are outstanding. The beautiful *artesonado* in the manor house at Palma's Jardins d'Alfàbia appears to be an Islamic relic.

Renaissance & Baroque

Renaissance building had a rational impulse founded on the architecture of classical antiquity, but it seems to have largely passed Mallorca by. Some exceptions confirm the rule, such as the (later remodelled) main entrance to Palma's Catedral, Palma's Consolat de Mar building and the mostly Renaissance-era sea walls. Although decorated in baroque fashion, the Monestir de Lluc is basically late Renaissance, and was designed by sculptor and architect Jaume Blanquer (c 1578–1636).

The more curvaceous and, many would say, less attractive successor to the Renaissance was a moderate, islandwide baroque that rarely reached the florid extremes that one encounters elsewhere in Europe. It is most often manifest in the large churches that dominate inland towns. In many of the churches, existing Gothic structures received a serious reworking, evident in such elements as barrel vaulting, circular windows, and bloated and curvaceous pillars and columns. Church exteriors are in the main sober (with the occasional gaudy facade). An exception can be found in the *retablos* (*retaules* in Catalan), the grand sculptural altarpieces in most churches. Often gilt and swirling with ornament, this was where baroque sculptors could let their imaginations run wild.

Yet perhaps the most pleasing examples of Mallorca's interpretation of the baroque style comes in the *patis* that grace old Palma's mansions. Drawing on Islamic/Andalusian and Roman influences, dictated by a warm Mediterranean climate, these courtyards represent one of Spain's most subtle baroque forms. Although baroque is the predominant form,

While you can peer into many of Palma's *patis*, architecture buffs will want to be in Palma during Corpus Christi when many of the otherwise-closed courtyards are opened to the public. Or hook onto the 'Courtyards and Palaces' walking tour of Palma with Mallorca Rutes.

VILLAGE ARCHITECTURE

Deià, Fornalutx, Biniaraix, Valldemossa, Banyalbufar, Orient – you'll tick off villages like rosary beads on the roads that loop through the Serra de Tramuntana in western Mallorca. Each one is seemingly prettier than the last, with many clinging to hillsides that rear above the glinting sea or cupped in valleys framed by terraced olive groves and citrus orchards.

They are a striking counterpoint to the concrete monstrosities that too often predominate in the resort towns of the south and east. That's primarily because the villages are built using the soft-hued local stone that is burnished in the warm Mediterranean light.

a handful of noble Palma houses betray Renaissance influences, such as the facade of the Cal Marquès del Palmer; standing in front of this building, you might think yourself transported to Medici Florence.

Modernisme

Towards the end of the 19th century, the Catalan version of art nouveau was all the rage in Barcelona, and whatever was happening in the Catalan capital at the time was sure to influence architectural styles in Mallorca. Symbolised by Antoni Gaudí, who worked on the renovation of Palma's Catedral and was the man behind Barcelona's La Sagrada Família, the eclectic style soon had its adepts, both local and Catalan, in Mallorca. They sought inspiration in nature and the past (especially Gothic and Mudéjar influences), and developed a new freedom and individual creativity.

Palma

Like most islandwide phenomena, Palma is the centrepiece of Mallorca's Modernista period. A contemporary of Gaudí, Lluís Domènech i Montaner (1850–1923) was another great Catalan Modernista architect who left his mark on the magnificent former Grand Hotel, now the CaixaForum.

The undulating facade of Can Casasayas, built for the wealthy Casasayas family known for their historic Confitería Frasquet sweets shop, is a typical feature of Modernisme. Half of the building is residential and the other houses offices. In the original design they were to be joined by a bridge.

Another influential figure in the history of Mallorcan Modernisme was Gaspar Bennàssar (1869–1933). Unlike many other other Catalan architects who worked on the island, Bennàssar was born in Palma and he played with various styles during his long career, including Modernisme. An outstanding example of this is the Almacenes El Águila, built in 1908 at the height of Modernisme's glory. Each of the three floors is different and the generous use of wrought iron in the main facade is a herald of the style. Next door the use of *trencadís* (ceramic shards) in the Can Forteza Rey facade is classic Gaudí-esque. Can Corbella, on the other hand, dates from roughly the same period but is dominated by a neo-Mudéjar look.

The seat of the Balearic Islands Parliament is located in the Círculo Mallorquin, a high-society club on Carrer del Conquistador that local Modernista architect Miquel Madorell i Rius (1869–1936) renovated in 1913.

Sóller

Provincial Sóller can't rival Palma for the breadth of its Modernista buildings, but it does have some outstanding examples of the genre. Most of it is attributable to Joan Rubió, an acolyte of Antoni Gaudí, and the most eye-catching example is his unusual early-20th-century Modernist facade grafted onto the 18th-century Església de Sant Bartomeu. The adjacent and extravagant Banco de Sóller is a typically bold example of his approach. Nearby, the Ca'n Prunera – Museu Modernista sports a typically delicate stone facade with muted wrought ironwork; it's also unusual in Mallorca in that it allows you to step beyond the Modernist facade and see the genre's influence upon early-20th-century interiors.

The return to Christian rule in 1229 came too late for the implementation in Mallorca of a Romanesque architectural style. Enthusiasts will see one sample in the Palau de l'Almudaina, Palma.

Arts & Crafts

Mallorca has provided a constant source of inspiration for artists over the centuries – Joan Miró loved the luminosity of the light he so eloquently captured on canvas, while local legend Miquel Barceló has added a vibrant splash of colour to galleries across the island. Travel the island today and you will still encounter deep-rooted arts and crafts traditions, be it in the upbeat ballads sung at *festes* (festivals) or the leather-making factories in Inca, where funky footwear label Camper took its first steps.

In 1936, inspired by a stay in the then little-known town of Pollença, Agatha Christie wrote the short crime thriller *Problem at Pollensa Bay*, which would later be the title for a volume of eight short crime mysteries.

Literature

For centuries, Mallorca's writers have not only strived for literary excellence, but have sought to deploy such excellence in promoting Catalan or Mallorquin as powerful forms of cultural expression. Many of the works have now been translated, and reading just a few will initiate you into a rich literary scene little known beyond the Catalan-speaking world.

Those curious to find out more about authors writing in Catalan, in Mallorca and elsewhere in the Catalan-speaking world, should check out www.escriptors.cat, the website of the Association of Catalan Language Writers.

The Early Centuries

In one sense Mallorcan literature began with the island's medieval conqueror, Jaume I (1208–76), who recorded his daring deeds in *El Llibre dels Fets* (The Book of Deeds). He wrote in Catalan, a language that the Palma-born poet and visionary evangeliser Ramon Llull (1232–1316) would elevate to a powerful literary tool. A controversial figure, who many feel should be declared a saint (he has only made it to beatification), Llull has long been regarded as the father of the literary Catalan tongue.

Few Mallorquins grapple with Llull's medieval texts but most know at least one poem by Miquel Costa i Llobera (1854–1922), a theologian and poet. His *El Pi de Fomentor* (The Formentor Pinetree, 1907), which eulogises Mallorcan landscapes through a pine on the Formentor peninsula, is *the* Mallorcan poem.

The 20th Century

One of the island's greatest poets was the reclusive Miquel Bauçà (1940–2005). His *Una Bella Història* (1962–85) is a major anthology. Llorenç Villalonga (1897–1980), born into an elite Palma family and trained in medicine, was one of Mallorca's top 20th-century novelists. Many of his works, including his most successful novel, *Bearn* (1952), portray the decay of the island's landed nobility.

Baltasar Porcel (b 1937, Andratx) is the doyen of contemporary Mallorcan literature. *L'Emperador o l'Ull del Vent* (The Emperor or the Eye of the Wind, 2001) is a dramatic tale about the imprisonment of thousands of Napoleon's soldiers on Illa de Cabrera.

Carme Riera (b 1948, Palma) has churned out an impressive series of novels, short stories, scripts and more. Her latest novel, *L'Estiu de l'Anglès* (The English Summer, 2006), tells of a frustrated Barcelona estate agent's decision to spend a month learning English in a middle-of-nowhere UK town.

Guillem Frontera (b 1945, Ariany) has produced some engaging crime novels, particularly the 1980 *La Ruta dels Cangurs* (The Kangaroo Route), in which the murder of the detective's ex-girlfriend muddies his Mallorca holiday plans.

Music

Folk Music

Mallorca, like any other part of Spain, has a rich heritage in folk songs and ballads sung in Mallorquin. At many traditional *festes* (festivals) in Mallorcan towns you'll hear the sounds of the *xeremiers,* a duo of ambling musicians, one of whom plays the *xeremia* (similar to the bagpipes) and the other a *flabiol* (a high-pitched pipe). Younger bands sometimes give these Mallorcan songs a bit of a rough-edged rock sound.

Contemporary Music

Los Valldemossa, who sang Mallorcan folk songs with a jazz feel in Palma's clubs, had some success overseas – they wound up playing the London circuit and, in 1969, won the Eurovision Song Contest, which back then actually meant something. They stopped playing in 2001 but their CDs still abound.

The island's best-known singer-songwriter is Palma's Maria del Mar Bonet i Verdaguer (b 1947). She moved to Barcelona at the age of 20 to join the Nova Cançó Catalana movement, which promoted singers and bands working in Catalan. Bonet became an international success and is known for her interpretations of Mediterranean folk music, French *chanson* (Jacques Brel and company) and experiments with jazz and Brazilian music.

Anaïs Nin set an erotic short story, 'Mallorca', in Deià. It appeared in the volume *Delta of Venus* and deals with a local girl who gets into an erotic tangle with a pair of foreigners and pays a high price. Nin stayed in Deià for a year in 1941.

ARTS & CRAFTS MUSIC

WRITINGS ABOUT MALLORCA

Mallorca has long inspired foreign writers, both in providing a place in which to write and yielding up rich subject matter for the stories themselves.

➡ *A Lizard in my Luggage* (2006), *Goats from a Small Island* (2009), *Donkeys on my Doorstep* (2010), *A Bull on the Beach* (2012), by Anna Nicholas.

➡ *Snowball Oranges* (2000), *Mañana Mañana* (2001), *Viva Mallorca* (2004) and *A Basketful of Snowflakes* (2007), by Peter Kerr.

➡ *Rafael's Wings: A Novel of Mallorca* (2006), by Sian Mackay.

➡ *Tuning Up At Dawn* (2004) and *Bread and Oil: Majorcan Culture's Last Stand* (2006), by Robert Graves' son, Tomás.

➡ *Wild Olives: Life in Majorca With Robert Graves* (2001), by William Graves.

➡ *Un Hiver à Mallorque* (A Winter in Mallorca, 1839), by the 19th-century French novelist George Sand (actually Amandine-Aurore-Lucille Dupin).

➡ *Jogging Around Mallorca* (1929), by Gordon West.

➡ *British Travellers in Mallorca in the Nineteenth Century* (2006), edited by Brian J Dendle and Shelby Thacker.

➡ *Letters From Mallorca* (1887), by Charles W Wood.

➡ *Die Insel des Zweiten Gesichts* (The Island of the Second Vision, 1953), by German writer Albert Vigoleis Thelen (1903–89).

An altogether different performer is Concha Buika. Of Equatorial Guinean origins, she was born in Palma in 1972 and rose through the Palma club circuit with her very personal brand of music, ranging from hip hop to flamenco to soul. Her second CD, *Mi Niña Lola,* came out in 2007, followed by *Niña de Fuego* a year later, and in 2009 *El Ultimo Trago,* a collaboration with Chucho Valdés, the renowned Cuban jazz pianist.

Argentine-born, Mallorca-based starlet Chenoa got her break when she stunned all in the TV talent show *Operación Triunfo.* Since 2002 she has churned out four albums and has become one of the most popular voices in Spanish-Latin pop.

Painting & Sculpture

The Early Centuries

Subsumed after the 1229 conquest into the Catalan world of the Crown of Aragón, Mallorca lay at a strategic point on sea routes. This fostered the movement of artists and not a few were attracted from the mainland, particularly Valencia, to Mallorca.

The earliest works from this revival of Catalan culture, transmitted by Catalan artists, were influenced by the Gothic art of the Sienese school in Italy. Later, International Gothic began to filter through, notably under the influence of the Valencian artist Francesc Comes, who was at work in Mallorca from 1390 to 1415.

Important artists around the mid-15th century include Rafel Mòger (c 1424–70) and Frenchman Pere Niçard, who worked in Mallorca from 1468 to 1470. They created one of the era's most important works, *Sant Jordi,* now housed in Palma's Museu Diocesà. The outstanding sculptor of this time was Guillem Sagrera, who did much of the detail work on Sa Llotja.

Pere Terrencs (active c 1479–1528) returned from a study stint in Valencia with the technique of oil painting – the death knell for egg-based pigments. His was a transitional style between late Gothic and the Renaissance. In a similar category was Córdoba-born Mateu López (d 1581), who trained in the prestigious Valencia workshops of father and son Vicent Macip and Joan de Joanes (aka Joan Vicent Macip, 1523–79), both signal artists. In 1544 López landed in Mallorca where he and his son became senior painters.

Gaspar Oms (c 1540–1614) was Mallorca's most outstanding late-Renaissance painter. The Oms clan, from Valencia, dominated the Mallorcan art scene throughout the 17th and 18th centuries.

Miquel Bestard (1592–1633) created major baroque canvases for churches, such as the Convento de Santa Clara and the Església de Monte-Sion, in Palma. Guillem Mesquida Munar (1675–1747) concentrated on religious motifs and scenes from classical mythology.

19th- & 20th-Century Mallorcan Art

The 19th century brought a wave of landscape artists to Mallorca. Many came from mainland Spain, particularly Catalonia, but the island produced its own painters too. More than half a dozen notables were born and raised in Palma. Joan O'Neille Rosiñol (1828–1907) is considered the founder of the island's landscape movement. He and his younger contemporaries Ricard Anckermann Riera (1842–1907) and Antoni Ribas Oliver (1845–1911), both from Palma, were among the first to cast their artistic eyes over the island and infuse it with romantic lyricism. The latter two concentrated on coastal scenes.

From 1890 a flood of Modernista artists from Catalonia 'discovered' Mallorca and brought new influences to the island. Some of them, such as Santiago Rusiñol (1861–1931), had spent time in Paris, which was then

For those who thought Ibiza was the exclusive Mediterranean home of club sounds, Daniel Vulic (DJ and German radio director in Mallorca) brought out *Cool Vibes Vol 1,* a compilation of strictly Mallorcan chill-out and club music in 2007.

CLUB MUSIC

MIRÓ & MALLORCA

Joan Miró grew up and spent most of his life in Barcelona, but Mallorca was his spiritual home and it became his permanent abode when he moved here in the mid-1950s. The island was an endless source of inspiration to the artist – the horizons, the 'eloquent silence', the pure brilliance of the light, and the vivid blues of the sea that were reflected in works such as *Bleu I, II, III* (1961), a three-part series of intensely hued paintings.

The bustle of Santa Catalina market, the crescent-shaped patterns of the Moors and Mallorcan folk art (baskets, pottery and the ceramic peasant whistles called *siurells*) inspired his increasingly expressive and abstract work.

Here Miró could walk through the streets and listen to the organist in the cathedral unnoticed, and he relished in this anonymity. His studio on the outskirts of the city gave him ample breathing space to fully immerse himself in his art. 'I invent nothing, it's all here! That is why I have to live here!' he enthused. And live here he did until his death in 1983 aged 90.

the hotbed of the art world. Locals enthusiastically joined in the Modernista movement. Palma-born Antoni Gelabert Massot (1877–1932) became a key figure, depicting his home city in paintings such as *Murada i Catedral a Entrada de Fosc* (1902–04). Other artists caught up in this wave were Joan Fuster Bonnín (1870–1943) and Llorenç Cerdà i Bispal (1862–1955), born in Pollença.

Meanwhile Llorenç Rosselló (1867–1902) was shaping up to be the island's most prominent sculptor until his early death. A handful of Rosselló's bronzes as well as a selection of works by many of the painters mentioned here can be seen in Es Baluard in Palma.

By the 1910s and 1920s symbolism began to creep into local artists' vocabulary. Two important names in Mallorcan painting from this period are Joan Antoni Fuster Valiente (1892–1964) and Ramón Nadal (1913–99), both from Palma.

Contemporary

Towering above everyone else in modern Mallorcan art is local hero and art icon, Miquel Barceló (b 1957, Felanitx). His profile has been especially sharp in his island home after the unveiling in 2007 of one of his more controversial masterpieces, a ceramic depiction of the miracle of the loaves and fishes housed in Palma's Catedral. The artist, who divides his time between Paris and Mali's Dogon Country, has a studio in Naples and was a rising star by the age of 25. Although he is best known as a painter, Barceló has worked with ceramics since the late 1990s. However, the commission for the Catedral was on a hitherto unimagined scale for the artist.

Less well known but nonetheless prolific is Palma-born Ferran García Sevilla (b 1949), whose canvases are frequently full of primal colour and strong shapes and images. Since the early 1980s he has exhibited in galleries throughout Europe. Joan Costa (b 1961, Palma) is one of the island's key contemporary sculptors, who also indulges in occasional brushwork.

One cannot leave out 20th-century Catalan icon Joan Miró (1893–1983). His mother came from Sóller and he lived the last 27 years of his life in Cala Major, just outside Palma, where his former home is now a museum, the Fundació Pilar i Joan Miró. Working there in a huge studio, he maintained a prolific turn-out of canvases, ceramics, statuary, textiles and more, faithful to his particular motifs of women, birds and the cosmos.

Best Niche Galleries

Es Baluard, Palma

Casa-Museu Dionís Bennàssar, Pollença

Ca'n Prunera – Museu Modernista, Sóller

Crafts

Tourism may have led to the overdevelopment of the Mallorcan coast, but it has enabled the revival of many traditional crafts and artisan workshops, among them those working with metal, ceramics, paper, glass, leather and jewellery.

The Consell de Mallorca tourist office, its airport branch and some municipal tourist offices around the island have a fine little brochure entitled *Map of Arts & Crafts in Majorca,* pinpointing 21 artisan producers working in a range of materials.

Glasswork

Glasswork was first produced on the island way back in the 2nd century BC and its artisans were part of a network of glass production and trade with its centre on Murano, in Venice. Mallorcan glass manufacturing reached its high point in the 18th century, whereafter the industry fell into decline. But one family, the Gordiolas who first entered the industry back in the 18th century, were almost single-handedly responsible for glassmaking's revival in the mid- to late 20th century. Although you'll find smaller artisans working with glass, the Museu de Gordiola near Algaida is the largest producer and here you can watch traditional glass-blowing techniques.

Leatherwork

Thanks to its world-famous shoe manufacturers like Camper, Mallorca's leather-making industries have become renowned worldwide for their quality. Although smaller traditional manufacturers tend to get drowned out by the larger companies, there's no denying that this industry has become a stunning Mallorcan success story. Inca is the capital of Mallorcan shoe-making with a host of factories and outlets; the latter are open to the public.

Well aware of its pulling power, the industry has produced two useful brochures which you may find in some tourist offices around the island: *Mallorca Mapa Turístico – Ruta de Calzado* (Mallorca Tourist Map – Shoe Route) and *Industry Tour of Majorcan Footwear – Guide to Footwear Manufacturers.*

Top Craft Shops

Arte Artesania, Sóller

Estel@rt, Estellencs

Oliv-Art, Manacor

Teixits Vicens, Pollença

Típika, Palma

Survival Guide

Directory A–Z

Customs Regulations

➡ There are no duty-free allowances for travel between EU countries and no restrictions on the import of duty-paid items into Spain from other EU countries for personal use.

➡ VAT-free articles can be bought at airport shops when travelling between EU countries.

➡ Duty-free allowances for travellers entering Spain from outside the EU include 2L of wine (or 1L of wine and 1L of spirits) and 200 cigarettes or 50 cigars or 250g of tobacco.

Discount Cards

Students, seniors (over 65s), families and young people get discounts of 20% to 50% at many sights. Museum entry is often free for under 12s.

Senior cards Reduced prices at museums and attractions (sometimes restricted to EU citizens only) and occasionally reduced costs on transport.

Student cards An International Student Identity Card (ISIC; www.isic.org) gains up to 50% off stays, attractions and more.

Youth Card Travel, sights and youth-hostel discounts with the European Youth Card (Carnet Joven in Spain; www.euro26.org).

Electricity

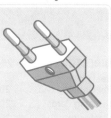

230V/50Hz

Gay & Lesbian Travellers

Homosexuality is legal in Spain. In 2005 the Socialist president of Spain, José Luis Rodríguez Zapatero, gave the conservative Catholic foundations of the country a shake with the legalisation of same-sex marriages. In Mallorca the bulk of the gay scene takes place in and around Palma.

Useful resources and organisations:

➡ **Ben Amics** (Map p56; ☑971 71 56 70; www.benamics.

com; Carrer del Conquistador 2; ⊙9am-3pm) The island's umbrella association for gays, lesbians and transsexuals.

➡ **Gay Mallorca** (www.gay-mallorca.blogspot.com) Weekly events listings.

➡ **Guía Gay de España** (guia.universogay.com/palmademallorca) More useful listings of cafes, saunas, nightclubs and restaurants.

➡ **Mallorca Gay Map** (www.mallorcagaymap.com) A handy guide to gay-friendly attractions (restaurants, hotels, clubs etc); a printed version is available from some municipal tourist offices in Palma.

Health

Mallorca doesn't present any health dangers – your main gripes are likely to be sunburn, insect bites, mild stomach problems and hangovers. Tap water is safe to drink, but is often unpalatable because of high sodium or chlorine levels; bottled water is cheap to buy.

Before You Go
INSURANCE

➡ If you're an EU citizen, a European Health Insurance Card (EHIC), available from health centres or, in the UK, post offices, covers you for most medical care. It will not cover you for nonemergencies or emergency repatriation.

➡ Citizens from other countries should find out if there is a reciprocal arrangement for free medical care between their country and Spain.

RECOMMENDED VACCINATIONS

No jabs are necessary for Mallorca but the World Health Organization recommends that all travellers be covered for diphtheria, tetanus, measles, mumps, rubella and polio, regardless of their destination.

In Mallorca
AVAILABILITY OF HEALTH CARE

➡ If you need an ambulance, call ☑061.

➡ For emergency treatment go straight to the *urgencias* (casualty) section of the nearest hospital. The island's main hospital is Palma's **Hospital Universitari Son Espases** (☑871 205000; www.hospitalsonespases.es; Carretera de Valldemossa 79), but other important ones are based in Inca and Manacor.

➡ At the main coastal tourist resorts you will generally find clinics with English- and German-speaking staff.

➡ *Farmacias* (pharmacies) offer advice and sell over-the-counter medication, and when a pharmacy is closed it posts the name of the nearest *farmacia de guardia* (duty pharmacies) on the door.

HEALTH RISKS

➡ Heat exhaustion occurs following excessive fluid loss. Symptoms include headache, dizziness and tiredness. Treat by drinking plenty of water and/or juice.

➡ Heat stroke is much more serious, resulting in irrational and hyperactive behaviour and eventually loss of consciousness and death. Rapid cooling by spraying the

Climate
Palma

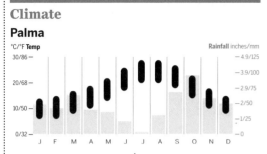

➡ If you have a severe allergy to bee or wasp stings, carry an EpiPen or similar adrenalin injection.

➡ In forested areas watch out for the hairy reddish-brown caterpillars of the pine processionary moth. Touching the caterpillars' hairs sets off a severely irritating allergic skin reaction.

➡ Some Spanish centipedes have a very nasty but nonfatal sting. The ones to watch out for are those with clearly defined segments, for instance, black and yellow stripes.

➡ In summer, waves of stingers (jellyfish) can wash up on the island's beaches. Vinegar, ice and Epsom salts can soothe the pain of a sting. If unavailable, rub in salt water; fresh water can stimulate the sting. Head to a Red Cross stand (usually present on the main beaches) if you are stung.

➡ Sandflies are found on many Mallorcan beaches. They usually cause only a nasty itchy bite but can carry occasionally a rare skin disorder called cutaneous leishmaniasis, a raised lesion at the site of the bite which can leave atrophic scarring.

Insurance

➡ Comprehensive travel insurance to cover theft, loss, medical problems and cancellations is highly

➡ Read the fine print, as some policies exclude 'high risk' activities like scuba diving and canyoning.

➡ EU citizens are entitled to health care in public hospitals (present your EHIC).

➡ Check that the policy covers ambulances or an emergency flight home.

➡ Keep all documents and bills if you have to make a claim.

➡ Worldwide travel insurance is available at lonelyplanet. com/travel-insurance. You can buy, extend and claim online anytime – even if you're already on the road.

➡ For car insurance, see p217.

Internet Access

➡ Numerous cafes and bars have free wireless internet (wi-fi). You may need to ask for the password when ordering.

➡ Most hotels have wi-fi, but in some cases the signal doesn't extend beyond the lobby.

➡ Internet cafes are always opening and closing. Ask at the tourist office for the nearest place. Typical rates are €1.50 to €3 per hour.

Language Courses

Palma is the main place to learn Spanish, but Sóller is an appealing alternative. The

➡ **Dialog** (Map p62; 971 71 99 94; www.dialog-palma.com; Carrer del Carme 14; 2-week course €395; 9.30am-2pm & 4.30-8.30pm Mon-Fri, 10am-2pm Sat)

➡ **Die Akademie** (Map p56; 971 71 82 90; www.dieakademie.com; Carrer d'en Morei 8; per week €140-285; 9am-1.30pm & 5-7.30pm Mon-Fri)

➡ **Estudi Lul·lià de Mallorca** (Map p56; 971 71 19 88; www.estudigeneral.com; Carrer de Sant Roc 4; from €400)

➡ **Lengua Sóller** (Map p100; 674 216677; http://lenguas-soller.es; Carrer de Vives 5; 11am-1pm & 5-8pm Mon-Fri)

Legal Matters

➡ By law you are expected to carry some form of photographic identification at all times, such as a passport, national ID card or driving licence.

➡ The blood alcohol limit in Spain is 0.05%. There are stiff fines (up to €1000) for anyone caught exceeding this limit.

➡ Cannabis is legal but only for personal use and in very small quantities. Public consumption of any drug is illegal.

➡ If arrested, you will be allotted the free services of a duty solicitor (abogado de oficio), who may speak only Spanish (and Mallorquin). You're entitled to make a phone call.

➡ If you end up in court, the authorities are obliged to provide a translator.

Maps

Island Maps

Among the better and clearer island maps:

➡ Freytag and Berndt's Mallorca (1:100,000)

➡ Michelin's No 579 Balears/Balearics (1:140,000)

➡ Marco Polo's Mallorca (1:125,000)

Walking Maps

➡ Walking maps need to be scaled at least at 1:25,000. Anything bigger is near useless.

➡ Alpina Editorial produces three such maps of the Serra de Tramuntana range (Mallorca Tramuntana Sud, Mallorca Tramuntana Central and Mallorca Tramuntana Nord). These come with detailed walk descriptions in a solid booklet. The third is in Catalan and German only.

➡ The Kompass Wanderführer 5910 Mallorca (in German), by Wolfgang Heizmann, comes with detailed walking maps.

➡ Walk! Mallorca (North & Mountains), by Charles Davis, is packed with walks, basic maps and GPS aid. You'll need to buy additional maps though.

➡ Spain's **Centro Nacional de Información Geográfica** (CNIG; www.cnig.es) covers a good part of the island in 1:25,000 scale sheets.

➡ Some of these maps are available in Palma at **La Casa del Mapa** (Map p56; Carrer de Sant Domingo 11; 9.30am-2pm Mon, to 7pm Tue-Fri), while some map specialists in other countries, such as **Stanfords** (020-7836 1321; www.stanfords.co.uk; 12-14 Long Acre, Covent Garden, London, WC2E 9LP, UK) in the UK, have a good range.

Money

Spain's currency is the euro. For exchange rates, see p17.

ATMs

➡ Many debit and credit cards, such as Visa, MasterCard and Cirrus, can be used to withdraw cash from cajeros automáticos (ATMs).

➡ ATMS are ubiquitous in towns and major resorts, and accessible 24/7.

➡ Remember that there is usually a charge (around 1.5% to 2%) on ATM cash withdrawals abroad.

Cash

Most banks exchange major foreign currencies and offer the best rates. Ask about commissions and take your passport. Exchange bureaux (look for the sign 'cambio') tend to open longer hours but can charge outrageous commissions.

Credit & Debit Cards

Cards can be used to pay for most purchases. You'll often be asked to show your passport or some other form of photo ID. Among the most widely accepted are Visa, MasterCard, American Express (Amex), Cirrus, Maestro, Plus, Diners Club and JCB. Report lost and stolen cards by contacting **American Express** (900 814500), **Diners Club** (901 101011), **MasterCard** (900 971231) or **Visa** (900 991124).

Taxes & Refunds

➡ Visitors are entitled to a refund of the 21% IVA (the Spanish equivalent of VAT) on purchases costing more than €90 from any shop if they are taking them out of the EU within three months.

➡ Ask the shop for a cash back (or similar) refund form showing the price and IVA paid for each item.

➡ Present the refund form to the customs booth for IVA refunds at the airport, port or border when you leave the EU. For more information, see www.globalblue.com.

Tipping

Menu prices include a service charge. Most people leave some small change if they're satisfied: 5% is normally fine and 10% extremely generous. Porters will generally be happy with €1. Taxi drivers don't have to be tipped but a little rounding up won't go unappreciated.

Travellers Cheques

Travellers cheques are a dying breed in an age of network-linked ATMs. If you do take them, you'll be charged commission at banks and currency exchange offices. Take along your ID when cashing travellers cheques.

Opening Hours

Opening hours vary throughout the year. We've provided high-season opening hours; hours will generally decrease in the shoulder and low seasons. Bear in mind that most resort restaurants and hotels close from mid-October to Easter.

Banks 8.30am to 2pm Monday to Friday; some also 4pm to 7pm Thursday and 9am to 1pm Saturday

Bars 7pm to 3am

Cafes 11am to 1am

Clubs midnight to 6am

Post offices 8.30am to 9.30pm Monday to Friday, 8.30am to 2pm Saturday

Restaurants Lunch is generally 1pm to 3.30pm; dinner, 7.30pm to 11pm

Shops 10am to 2pm & 4.30pm to 7.30pm (or 5pm to 8pm) Monday to Saturday; big supermarkets and department stores generally open 10am to 9pm Monday to Saturday

Post

The Spanish postal system, **Correos** (☎902 190197; www.correos.es), is generally reliable, if a little slow at times.

Postal Rates

Sellos (stamps) are sold at most *estancos* (tobacconists' shops with 'Tabacos' in yellow letters on a maroon background), as well as post offices. A postcard or letter weighing up to 20g costs €0.75 from Spain to other European countries, and €0.90 to the rest of the world. For a full list of prices for *certificado* (certified) and *urgente* (express post), check the 'Fee Calculator' on the website.

Sending Mail

Delivery times are erratic but ordinary mail to other western European countries can take up to a week; to North America up to 10 days; and to Australia or New Zealand between 10 days and three weeks.

Public Holidays

The two main periods when Spaniards (and Mallorquins are no real exception) go on holiday are Semana Santa (the week leading up to Easter Sunday) and August, at precisely the same moment when half of Europe descends on Mallorca. Accommodation can be hard to find and transport is put under strain.

There are 14 official holidays a year, to which most towns add at least one to mark their patron saint's day. Some places have several traditional feast days, not all of which are official holidays, but which are often a reason for partying. The main island-wide public holidays:

Cap d'Any (New Year's Day) 1 January

Epifania del Senyor (Epiphany) 6 January – in Palma a landing of the Three Wise Men (Reis Mags) is staged in the port, followed by a procession

Dia de les Illes Balears (Balearic Islands Day) 1 March

Dijous Santa (Holy Thursday) March/April

Divendres Sant (Good Friday) March/April

Diumenge de Pasqua (Easter Sunday) March/April

Festa del Treball (Labour Day) 1 May

L'Assumpció (Feast of the Assumption) 15 August

Festa Nacional d'Espanya (Spanish National Day) 12 October

Tots Sants (All Saints) 1 November

Dia de la Constitució (Constitution Day) 6 December

PRACTICALITIES

➡ **DVDs** Spain is in region code 2.

➡ **Newspapers** English- and German-language dailies are widely available in resorts. Major Spanish newspapers include centre-left *El País* (http://elpais.com) and centre-right *El Mundo* (www.elmundo.es). For Mallorcan news, try *Diario de Mallorca* (www.diariodemallorca.es), *Ultima Hora* (http://ultimahora.es) or English-language *Majorca Daily Bulletin* (http://majorcadailybulletin.com).

➡ **Radio** Regional stations include Radio Balear (www.radiobalear.net) and English-speaking Radio One Mallorca (www.radioonemallorca.com).

➡ **Smoking** Banned in all enclosed public places.

➡ **Weights & measures** Metric system.

➡ **Women's clothing** A Spanish size 36 is a UK size 8 and a US size 4, then increases in twos, making size 38 a UK size 10 and a US size 6.

L'Immacula da Concepció (Feast of the Immaculate Conception) 8 December

Nadal (Christmas) 25 December

Segona Festa de Nadal (Boxing Day) 26 December

Safe Travel

Mallorca is safe. The main thing to be wary of is petty theft. Most visitors to Mallorca never feel remotely threatened, but that's no reason not to exercise the usual caution.

Theft & Scams

➡ Theft is mostly a risk in the busier resort areas and Palma. Take care when dragging around luggage to or from your hotel.

➡ Watch for pickpockets and bag snatchers and for an old classic: ladies offering flowers (the so-called *claveleras*, because they usually offer *claveles*, ie carnations) for good luck. We don't know how they do it, but if you get too involved in a friendly chat, your pockets always wind up empty.

➡ Keep a firm grip on daypacks and bags at all times. Anything left on the beach can disappear in a flash when your back is turned.

➡ Never leave any valuables in rental cars.

➡ Report thefts to the national police. It is unlikely that you will recover your goods but you need to make a formal *denuncia* for insurance purposes. To avoid endless queues at the police station, you can make the report by phone (🖉902 102112) in various languages or on the web at www.policia. es (click on 'Denuncias').

Telephone

Blue payphones are easy to use for international and domestic calls. They accept coins, *tarjetas telefónicas* (phonecards issued by the national phone company Tel-

efónica) and, in some cases, credit cards. Calling using an internet-based service such as Skype is generally the cheapest option.

Area Codes

All telephone numbers in Mallorca (including for mobiles) have nine digits. Almost all fixed-line telephone numbers in Mallorca begin with 🖉971, although a small number begin with 🖉871. Numbers starting with a '6' are for mobile phones.

Numbers starting with 🖉900 are national toll-free numbers, while those starting 🖉901 to 🖉905 come with varying costs. A common one is 🖉902, which is a national standard-rate number, but which can only be dialled from within Spain. In a similar category are numbers starting with 🖉800, 🖉803, 🖉806 and 🖉807.

It is possible to dial an operator in your country of residence at no cost to make a reverse-charge call (*una llamada a cobro revertido*) – pick up the number before you leave home. You can usually get an English-speaking Spanish international operator on 🖉1008 (for calls within Europe) or 🖉1005 (rest of the world).

Mobile Phones

Spain uses GSM 900/1800, which is compatible with the rest of Europe and Australia but not with the North American GSM 1900 or the system used in Japan. If your phone is tri- or quadriband, you will probably be fine. Shops on every high street sell *teléfonos móviles* with prepaid cards from around €80 for the most basic models.

Phonecards

Cut-rate phonecards from private companies can be good value for international calls. They can be bought from *estancos*, newsstands and *locutorios* (call centres), especially in Palma and coastal resorts – compare rates if possible.

Time

Mallorca runs on central European time (GMT/UTC plus one hour). Daylight saving time begins on the last Sunday in March and ends on the last Sunday in October.

UK, Ireland, Portugal & Canary Islands One hour behind mainland Spain.

USA Spanish time is USA Eastern Time plus six hours and USA Pacific Time plus nine hours.

Australia During the Australian winter (Spanish summer), subtract eight hours from Australian Eastern Standard Time to get Spanish time; during the Australian summer, subtract 10 hours.

Toilets

Toilets are of the sit-down variety, although public toilets are rare to nonexistant across the island. If you find yourself in need of the facilities, remember that most bars and restaurants will expect you to purchase something before or after you use the toilet, though the busier the place, the less likely you are to be detected.

Tourist Information

➡ Almost every town and resort in Mallorca has a walk-tourist office (*oficina de turismo* or *oficina de información turística*) for local maps and information.

➡ Tourist offices in coastal areas usually open from Easter or May until October and keep surprisingly short hours. If you do find them open, they're usually helpful and overflowing with useful brochures.

➡ In Palma you'll find municipal tourist offices which focus on Palma and the immediate surrounds. There's also the **Consell de Mallorca tourist office** (Map p56; 🖉971 71 22 16; www. infomallorca.net; Plaça de la

Reina 2; ☺8am-8pm Mon-Fri, 9am-2pm Sat), which covers the whole island.

➜ For general information about the Balearic Islands, visit www.illesbalears.es.

Travellers with Disabilities

➜ Mallorca is a long way from being barrier free, but things are slowly improving. Disabled access to some museums, official buildings and hotels represents something of a sea change in local thinking. You need to be circumspect about hotels advertising themselves as disabled friendly, as this can mean as little as wide doors to rooms and bathrooms, a ramp into reception or other token efforts.

➜ Cobbled streets and flights of steps in hill towns can make getting around difficult.

➜ Palma city buses are equipped for wheelchair access, as are some of those that travel around the island. Some taxi companies run adapted taxis – they must be booked in advance.

Organisations

➜ **Accessible Travel & Leisure** (☏01452-729739; www.accessibletravel.co.uk) Claims to be the biggest UK travel agent dealing with travel for the disabled and encourages the disabled to travel independently.

➜ **Associació Balear de Persones amb Discapacitat Física** (Asprom; Map p52; ☏971 28 90 52; www.asprom.net; Carrer de Pasqual Ribot 6) The island's disabled persons' organisation is more of a lobby group than a source of practical holiday information.

➜ **Discount Mobility** (☏966 44 58 12; www.mobilitymallorca.com) Hires out mobility scooters for the disabled.

➜ **Easy Rider** (☏606 543099, 971 54 50 57; www.easyridermobilityhire.com) A

Port d'Alcúdia–based outfit hiring out mobility scooters.

➜ **Mobility Scooters** (☏971 13 25 38; www.mobilityscootersmallorca.com) Delivers mobility scooters for hire to customers around the island.

Visas

Spain is one of 26 member countries of the Schengen Convention, under which 22 EU countries (all but Bulgaria, Cyprus, Ireland, Romania and the UK) plus Iceland, Norway and Switzerland have abolished checks at common borders.

The visa situation for entering Spain is as follows:

Citizens or residents of EU & Schengen countries No visa required.

Citizens or residents of Australia, Canada, Israel, Japan, New Zealand and the USA No visa required for tourist visits of up to 90 days.

Other countries Check with a Spanish embassy or consulate.

To work or study in Spain A special visa may be required; contact a Spanish embassy or consulate before travel.

Extensions & Residence

➜ You can apply for no more than two visas in any 12-month period and they are not renewable once in Spain.

➜ Nationals of EU countries, Iceland, Norway and Switzerland can enter and leave Spain at will and don't need to apply for a *tarjeta de residencia* (residence card), although they are supposed to apply for residence papers.

➜ People of other nationalities who want to stay in Spain longer than 90 days require a residence card; getting one can be a drawn-out process, starting with an appropriate visa issued by a Spanish consulate in their country of residence. Start the process well in advance.

Volunteering

Most volunteering opportunities in Spain are on the mainland, but it is worth checking **Go Abroad** (www.goabroad.com) for projects in Mallorca. For *fincas* (farms) and families offering work and board on a voluntary basis, see **Work Away** (www.workaway.info).

Women Travellers

Travelling in Mallorca is largely as easy as travelling anywhere else in the Western world. However, you may still occasionally find yourself the object of staring, catcalls and unnecessary comments. Simply ignoring them is sufficient. Remember that eye-to-eye contact and flirting is part of daily Spanish life and need not be offensive.

Spanish women generally have a highly developed sense of style and put considerable effort into looking their best. While topless bathing and skimpy clothes are in fashion at the coastal resorts, people tend to dress more modestly in the towns and inland.

Work

Nationals of EU countries, Switzerland, Norway and Iceland may work freely in Mallorca. Virtually everyone else needs to obtain, from a Spanish consulate in their country of residence, a work permit and (for stays of more than 90 days) a residence visa.

Many bars (especially of the UK and Irish persuasion), restaurants and other businesses are run by foreigners and look for temporary staff in summer. Check any local press in foreign languages, which carry ads for waiters, nannies, chefs, babysitters, cleaners and the like.

Translating and interpreting could be an option if you are fluent both in Spanish and a language in demand. You can start a job search at **Think Spain** (www.thinkspain.com).

Transport

GETTING THERE & AWAY

Most visitors to Mallorca fly into Palma's international airport, though it's possible to arrive by ferry from points along the Spanish coast (Alicante, Barcelona, Denia and Valencia). The neighbouring islands of Ibiza and Menorca are also linked to Mallorca by air and ferry. Flights and tours can be booked online at lonelyplanet.com/bookings.

Entering Mallorca

Passport

Citizens of most of the 28 European Union member states and Switzerland can travel to Spain with their national identity card. Citizens of countries that don't issue ID cards, such as the UK, need a full passport. All other nationalities must have a full valid passport.

If applying for a visa, check that your passport's expiry date is at least six months away. Non-EU citizens must fill out a landing card.

By law you are supposed to carry your passport or ID card with you at all times.

Air

Airports

Palma de Mallorca Airport (PMI; ☑902 404704; www.aena-aeropuertos.es) is 8km east of Palma de Mallorca. In summer especially, masses of charter and regular flights form an air bridge to Palma from around Europe, among them many low-cost airlines. In 2012 the airport received 22.7 million incoming passengers, making it one of the busiest in Europe.

The arrivals hall is on the ground floor of the main terminal building, where you'll find a tourist information office, money-exchange offices, car hire, tour operators and hotel-booking stands. Departures are on the 2nd floor.

Airlines

Nearly every European airline serves Mallorca, along with the majority of budget carriers. Airlines flying to the island include the following:

➡ **Air Berlin** (www.airberlin.com) From London (Stansted), dozens of cities all over Germany and elsewhere in mainland Europe.

➡ **British Airways** (www.britishairways.com) From London.

➡ **EasyJet** (www.easyjet.com) From 13 UK airports and nine in mainland Europe.

➡ **Germanwings** (www.germanwings.com) From dozens of UK and mainland Europe airports.

CLIMATE CHANGE & TRAVEL

Every form of transport that relies on carbon-based fuel generates CO_2, the main cause of human-induced climate change. Modern travel is dependent on aeroplanes, which might use less fuel per kilometre per person than most cars but travel much greater distances. The altitude at which aircraft emit gases (including CO_2) and particles also contributes to their climate change impact. Many websites offer 'carbon calculators' that allow people to estimate the carbon emissions generated by their journey and, for those who wish to do so, to offset the impact of the greenhouse gases emitted with contributions to portfolios of climate-friendly initiatives throughout the world. Lonely Planet offsets the carbon footprint of all staff and author travel.

⇒ **Iberia** (www.iberia.es) With its subsidiary Air Nostrum, flies from many mainland Spanish cities.

⇒ **Jet2** (www.jet2.com) From Belfast, Leeds, Edinburgh and Newcastle.

⇒ **Lufthansa** (www.lufthansa.com) From numerous central European cities.

⇒ **Monarch** (www.flymonarch.com) Scheduled and charter flights from London (Luton), Edinburgh, Birmingham and Manchester.

⇒ **Niki** (www.flyniki.com) From dozens of Spanish and European cities.

⇒ **Ryanair** (www.ryanair.com) From numerous UK and mainland European airports.

⇒ **Thomson Fly** (www.thomsonfly.com) From many UK cities.

⇒ **Vueling** (www.vueling.com) Dozens of flights from mainland Spain and further afield.

Tickets

For the best deals on airfares, choose your timing carefully – fares go through the roof during school holidays. You'll get the best deals by booking early and travelling at nonpeak times (midweek, low season and early morning/late at night).

⇒ Check airline websites for last-minute deals. You can cost compare flights on websites such as www.skyscanner.net, www.kayak.com, www.gocompare.com or www.travelocity.com.

⇒ Full-time students and people under 26 can sometimes get discounted fares.

Sea

Ferry services connect Mallorca to the Spanish mainland and to Menorca, Ibiza and Formentera. Most services operate only from Easter to late October, and those services that con-

tinue into the winter reduce their departure times. Most ferry companies allow you to transport vehicles on longer routes and have car holds (this incurs an additional fee and advance bookings are essential). If you are travelling with your own vehicle, be sure to arrive at the port in good time for boarding. Prices vary widely according to season; those given in the table on p216 are just a guide.

A good place to start is to check routes and compare prices at **Direct Ferries** (www.directferries.com).

Ferry companies that operate to and from Mallorca include the following:

⇒ **Acciona Trasmediterránea** (☑902 454645; www.trasmediterranea.es)

⇒ **Baleària** (☑902 160180; www.balearia.com)

⇒ **Entre Islas y Canales** (☑902 100444; www.entreislasycanales.com)

⇒ **Iscomar** (☑902 119128; www.iscomar.com)

Tours

Joining an organised tour to Mallorca is certainly not necessary – it's an easy destination for independent travel. But some companies offer specialist tours that make it so much easier to indulge your passions.

⇒ **Balearic Discovery** (☑971 87 53 95; www.balearicdiscovery.com) Choose from tailor-made trips that allow you to build your own itinerary to a set-activities trip where you can choose activities from sailing to horse riding.

⇒ **Cycle Mallorca** (www.cyclemallorca.co.uk) Well-organised road-cycling holidays.

⇒ **Inntravel** (www.inntravel.co.uk) A slow-tour specialist offering walking and cycling holidays.

⇒ **Mallorca Muntanya** (☑639 713212; www.mallorcamuntanya.com) Trekking tours, mostly in the Serra de Tramuntana.

⇒ **Mar y Roc** (☑678 196821; www.mallorca-wandern.de) Group hiking tours in Mallorca.

⇒ **Naturetrek** (☑in UK 01962 733051; www.naturetrek.co.uk) Eight-day birdwatching tour.

⇒ **Unicorn Trails** (☑in UK 01767 600 606; www.unicorntrails.com) Two week-long horse-riding tours to choose from.

GETTING AROUND

Bicycle

British Tour de France winner Bradley Wiggins and co have really put Mallorca on the map for cycling in recent years, and the island has become one of Europe's most popular destinations for road cycling. Although the uphill slog can be tough in mountainous areas, particularly along the island's western and northwestern coasts, much of the island is reasonably flat and can be easily explored by bike. You can take your own or hire one once you arrive.

For an overview of cycling on the island, visit www.illesbalears.es and click on 'Sport Tourism'. It has numerous routes across the island. Another recommended website with routes graded according to difficulty is http://mallorcacycling.co.uk.

Signposts have been put up across much of rural Mallorca indicating cycling routes (usually secondary roads between towns and villages).

Hire

Bike-hire places are scattered around the main resorts of the island, including Palma, and are usually highly professional. Prices vary widely, but on average you can reckon on paying between €10 and €15 per day for a city bike, and €15 to €30 per day for a mountain bike. The longer you hire the bike, the cheaper daily rates get.

Bus

The island is roughly divided into five zones radiating from Palma.

Bus-line numbers in the 100s cover the southwest, the 200s the west (as far as Sóller), the 300s the north and much of the centre, the 400s a wedge of the centre and east coast and the 500s the south. These services are run by a phalanx of small bus companies, but you can get route and timetable information for all by contacting **Transport de les Illes Balears** (TIB; ☎971 17 77 77; www.tib.org).

Most of the island is accessible by bus from Palma.

All buses depart from (or near) Palma's **Estació Intermodal** (Map p62; ☎971 17 77 77; www.tib.org; Plaça d'Espanya). Not all lines are especially frequent, and services slow to a trickle on weekends. Frequency to many coastal areas also drops from November to April and some lines are cut altogether (such as those between Ca'n Picafort and Sa Calobra or Sóller).

Although services in most parts of the island are adequate, out-of-the-way places can be tedious to reach and getting around the Serra de Tramuntana by bus, while possible, isn't always easy. Bus 200 from Palma runs to Estellencs via Banyalbufar for example, while bus 210 runs to Valldemossa and then, less frequently, on to Deià and Sóller. Nothing makes the connection between Estellencs and Valldemossa and all but the Palma–Valldemossa run are infrequent.

Distances are usually short, with very few services taking longer than two hours to reach their destinations. For fares, consult the Getting There & Away information in the On the Road chapters.

Car & Motorcycle

Mallorca's roads are generally excellent, though there are a few coastal hair-raisers in the north and west of the island that are not for fainthearted drivers (Sa Calobra and Formentor to name two). The narrow roads on these cliff-flanked coasts and the country roads that thread through the interior are ideal for motorbike touring.

The island's main artery is the Ma13 motorway, which slices through the island diagonally, linking Palma in the west with Alcúdia in the north. The Ma1 loops southwest of Palma to Andratx.

While you can get about much of the island by bus and train, especially in high

FERRY SERVICES

TO	FROM	COMPANY	PRICE	FREQUENCY	DURATION (HR)	SLEEPER BERTH
Palma	Barcelona	Acciona Trasmediterránea, Baleària	seat from €49, sleeper from €109	1-2 daily	7	yes
Palma	Denia	Baleària	seat from €49, sleeper €109	2 daily	2-5	yes
Palma	Ibiza (Ibiza City)	Acciona Trasmediterránea, Baleària	seat from €35	Fri & Sat	4	yes
Palma	Maó (Menorca)	Acciona Trasmediterránea	seat from €31	Sun	3½	yes
Palma	Valencia	Acciona Trasmediterránea, Baleària	seat from €49, sleeper from €109	1 daily	8	yes
Port d'Alcúdia	Barcelona	Baleària	seat from €49, sleeper from €115	1 daily	7	yes
Port d'Alcúdia	Ciutadella (Menorca)	Baleària	seat from €21.50	2 daily	1-2	no

season, having a car will give you far greater freedom. With your own wheels you can seek out the nature parks, secluded coves and mountain retreats away from the crowds.

If your car is not equipped with satnav, it's worth investing in a decent road map to negotiate the island's more offbeat corners. Marco Polo produce a decent one at a 1:125,000 scale.

Automobile Associations

The **Real Automóvil Club de España** (RACE; ☑900 100992; www.race.es; Calle de Eloy Gonzalo 32, Madrid) is the national automobile club. It may well come to assist you in case of breakdown, but in any event you should obtain an emergency telephone number for Spain from your own insurer.

Bring Your Own Vehicle

Always carry proof of ownership of a private vehicle.

Every vehicle should display a nationality plate of its country of registration. It is compulsory in Spain to carry a warning triangle (to be used in case of breakdown) and a reflective jacket. Recommended accessories include a first-aid kit, spare-bulb kit and fire extinguisher.

Driving Licences

EU driving licences are recognised throughout Europe. Those with a non-EU licence are supposed to obtain a 12-month International Driver's Permit (IDP) from their home automobile association to accompany their national licence. In practice, national licences from countries such as Australia, Canada, New Zealand and the USA are usually accepted.

Fuel

You'll find *gasolineras* (petrol stations) in major towns and cities and most large resorts. Make sure you have a full tank if you're exploring rural areas off the beaten track. Choose between *sin plomo* (lead-free; 95 octane) and *gasóleo* (diesel). Petrol prices are on a par with the rest of Europe.

You can pay with major credit cards at most service stations.

Hire

Car-hire rates vary, but you should be able to get an economy vehicle for between €30 and €60 per day; bear in mind that compact cars can be a tight fit for families. Additional drivers and one-way hire can bump up the cost. Extras like child seats (around €10 per day) should be reserved at the time of booking.

To rent a car you have to have a licence, be aged 21 or over and, for the major companies at least, have a credit card. A word of advice: some agencies try to make even more money by charging a €90 fee for fuel, instead of asking you to bring it back with a full tank. Always read the fine print carefully before signing off.

All the major car-hire companies are represented on the island. It can pay to shop around, and you might want to check a cost-comparison site like www.travelsupermarket.com before going down the tried-and-trusted route. Branches at the airport include the following:

➡ **Avis** (☑902 110261; www.avis.com)

➡ **Europcar** (☑902 105055; www.europcar.com)

➡ **Gold Car** (☑902 119726; www.goldcar.es)

➡ **Hertz** (☑971 789 670; www.hertz.com)

➡ **Sixt** (☑902 491616; www.sixt.com)

Insurance

➡ Ask your insurer for a European Accident Statement form, which can simplify matters in the event of an accident.

➡ A European breakdown-assistance policy such as the AA Five Star Service or RAC European Breakdown Cover is a good investment.

➡ Third-party liability insurance is a minimum requirement in Spain and throughout Europe.

➡ Car-hire companies provide this minimum insurance, but be careful to understand what your liabilities and excess are, and what waivers you're entitled to in case of an accident or damage to the hire vehicle.

➡ Insurance that covers damage to the vehicle – Collision Damage Waiver (CDW) – usually costs extra, but driving without it is not recommended.

➡ Car-hire multiday or annual excess insurance can be cheaper online; try www.icarhireinsurance.com or http://insurance4carhire.com.

Road Rules

Blood-alcohol limit 0.05%. If found to be over the limit you can be judged, fined and deprived of your licence within 24 hours. Fines range up to around €1000 for serious offences. Nonresident foreigners will be required to pay up on the spot (at 30% off the full fine).

Legal driving age For cars, 18; for motorcycles and scooters, 16 (80cc and over) or 14 (50cc and under). A licence is required in all cases.

Motorcyclists Must use headlights at all times and wear a helmet if riding a bike of 125cc or more.

Overtaking Spanish truck drivers often have the courtesy to turn on their right indicator to show that the way ahead of them is clear for overtaking (and the left one if it is not and you are attempting this manoeuvre).

Roundabouts (traffic circles) Vehicles already in the circle have the right of way.

Side of the road Drive on the right.

Speed limits In built-up areas, 50km/h; increases to 100km/h on major roads and up to 110km/h on the four-lane highways leading out of Palma.

Local Transport

Palma is the only centre with its own local transport system, **EMT** (☑971 21 44 44; www.emtpalma.es). Buses are the main way around, although a metro line (probably of more interest to commuters in the suburbs than to visitors) runs from the centre to the university.

It's easy to get around Palma (especially the old centre) by bicycle, although cycling lanes are limited (the main one runs along the shoreline).

Palma is well supplied with taxis, and there are several stands around the city. Elsewhere on the island, you may not necessarily find them waiting when you need them, but generally they're fairly easy to order by phone; ask at your hotel or at the local tourist office.

Train

Two train lines run from Plaça d'Espanya in Palma de Mallorca; **Transport de les Illes Balears** (TIB; ☑971 17 77 77; www.tib.org) has details.

One heads north to Sóller and is a panoramic excursion in an antique wooden train, and is one of Palma's most popular day trips.

The other line heads inland to Inca, where the line splits to serve Sa Pobla and Manacor. Prices are generally cheaper than buses and departures are frequent throughout the day. There are plans underway to extend the line from Manacor to Artà, although no one could tell us when the extension would be completed.

Language

Mallorca is a bilingual island, at least on paper. Since the Balearic Islands received their autonomy statute in the 1980s, the islanders' native Catalan (*català*) has recovered its official status alongside Spanish. This said, it would be pushing a point to say that Catalan, or its local dialect, *mallorquí*, had again become the primary language of Mallorca or the rest of the Balearic Islands. Today Spanish remains the lingua franca, especially between Mallorquins and other Spaniards or foreigners.

Spanish pronunciation is straightforward as most Spanish sounds are pronounced the same as their English counterparts. Note that the kh in our pronunciation guides is a guttural sound (like the 'ch' in the Scottish *loch*), ly is pronounced as the 'lli' in 'million', ny as the 'ni' in 'onion', th is pronounced with a lisp, and r is strongly rolled. In our pronunciation guides, the stressed syllables are in italics. If you follow our pronunciation guides given with each phrase in this chapter, you'll be understood just fine.

Spanish nouns (and the adjectives that go with them) are marked for gender – feminine nouns generally end with -*a* and masculine ones with -*o*. Where necessary, both forms are given for the words and phrases in this chapter, separated by a slash and with the masculine form first, eg *perdido/a* (m/f).

Also note that Spanish has two words for the English 'you': when talking to people familiar to you or younger than you, use the informal form, *tú*, rather than the polite form *Usted*. The polite form is used in the phrases provided in this chapter; where both options are given, they are indicated by the abbreviations 'pol' and 'inf'.

WANT MORE?

For in-depth language information and handy phrases, check out Lonely Planet's *Spanish Phrasebook*. You'll find it at **shop.lonelyplanet.com**, or you can buy Lonely Planet's iPhone phrasebooks at the Apple App Store.

BASICS

Hello./Goodbye.	*Hola./Adiós.*	o·la/a·*dyos*
How are you?	*¿Qué tal?*	ke tal
Fine, thanks.	*Bien, gracias.*	byen *gra*·thyas
Excuse me.	*Perdón.*	per·*don*
Sorry.	*Lo siento.*	lo *syen*·to
Yes./No.	*Sí./No.*	see/no
Please.	*Por favor.*	por fa·*vor*
Thank you.	*Gracias.*	*gra*·thyas
You're welcome.	*De nada.*	de *na*·da

My name is ...
Me llamo ...   me *lya*·mo ...

What's your name?
¿Cómo se llama Usted? ko·mo se *lya*·ma oo·*ste*

Do you speak (English)?
¿Habla (inglés)?   a·bla (een·*gles*)

I (don't) understand.
Yo (no) entiendo.   yo (no) en·*tyen*·do

ACCOMMODATION

I'd like to book a room.
Quisiera reservar una habitación.   kee·*sye*·ra re·ser·*var* oo·na a·bee·ta·*thyon*

How much is it per night/person?
¿Cuánto cuesta por noche/persona?   *kwan*·to *kwes*·ta por no·che/per·*so*·na

air-con	*aire acondicionado*	ai·re a·kon·dee·thyo·*na*·do
bathroom	*baño*	ba·nyo
bed	*cama*	*ka*·ma
campsite	*terreno de cámping*	te·*re*·no de *kam*·peeng
double room	*habitación doble*	a·bee·ta·*thyon* *do*·ble
guesthouse	*pensión*	pen·*syon*
hotel	*hotel*	o·*tel*

single room	habitación individual	a·bee·ta·thyon een·dee·vee·dwal
window	ventana	ven·ta·na
youth hostel	albergue juvenil	al·ber·ge khoo·ve·neel

DIRECTIONS

Where's ...?
¿Dónde está ...?   don·de es·ta ...

What's the address?
¿Cuál es la dirección?   kwal es la dee·rek·thyon

Could you please write it down?
¿Puede escribirlo,   pwe·de es·kree·beer·lo
por favor?   por fa·vor

Can you show me (on the map)?
¿Me lo puede indicar   me lo pwe·de een·dee·kar
(en el mapa)?   (en el ma·pa)

behind ...	detrás de ...	de·tras de ...
far away	lejos	le·khos
in front of ...	enfrente de ...	en·fren·te de ...
left	izquierda	eeth·kyer·da
near	cerca	ther·ka
next to ...	al lado de ...	al la·do de ...
opposite ...	frente a ...	fren·te a ...
right	derecha	de·re·cha

EATING & DRINKING

'd like to book a table.
Quisiera reservar   kee·sye·ra re·ser·var
una mesa.   oo·na me·sa

What would you recommend?
¿Qué recomienda?   ke re·ko·myen·da

What's in that dish?
¿Que lleva ese plato?   ke lye·va e·se pla·to

I don't eat ...
No como ...   no ko·mo ...

That was delicious!
¡Estaba buenísimo!   es·ta·ba bwe·nee·see·mo

Please bring the bill.
Por favor nos trae   por fa·vor nos tra·e
la cuenta.   la kwen·ta

Cheers!
¡Salud!   sa·loo

Key Words

appetisers	aperitivos	a·pe·ree·tee·vos
bar	bar	bar
bottle	botella	bo·te·lya
breakfast	desayuno	de·sa·yoo·no
cafe	café	ka·fe

KEY PATTERNS

To get by in Spanish, mix and match these simple patterns with words of your choice:

When's (the next flight)?
¿Cuándo sale   kwan·do sa·le
(el próximo vuelo)?   (el prok·see·mo vwe·lo)

Where's (the station)?
¿Dónde está   don·de es·ta
(la estación)?   (la es·ta·thyon)

Where can I (buy a ticket)?
¿Dónde puedo   don·de pwe·do
(comprar   (kom·prar
un billete)?   oon bee·lye·te)

Do you have (a map)?
¿Tiene (un mapa)?   tye·ne (oon ma·pa)

Is there (a toilet)?
¿Hay (servicios)?   ai (ser·vee·thyos)

I'd like (a coffee).
Quisiera (un café).   kee·sye·ra (oon ka·fe)

Could you please (help me)?
¿Puede (ayudarme),   pwe·de (a·yoo·dar·me)
por favor?   por fa·vor

children's menu	menú infantil	me·noo een·fan·teel
cold	frío	free·o
dinner	cena	the·na
food	comida	ko·mee·da
fork	tenedor	te·ne·dor
glass	vaso	va·so
highchair	trona	tro·na
hot (warm)	caliente	ka·lyen·te
knife	cuchillo	koo·chee·lyo
lunch	comida	ko·mee·da
main course	segundo plato	se·goon·do pla·to
market	mercado	mer·ka·do
menu (in English)	menú (en inglés)	me·noo (en een·gles)
plate	plato	pla·to
restaurant	restaurante	res·tow·ran·te
spoon	cuchara	koo·cha·ra
supermarket	supermercado	soo·per·mer·ka·do
with/without	con/sin	kon/seen
vegetarian food	comida vegetariana	ko·mee·da ve·khe·ta·rya·na

Meat & Fish

beef	carne de vaca	kar·ne de va·ka
chicken	pollo	po·lyo
duck	pato	pa·to

spinach	espinacas	es·pee·na·kas
strawberry	fresa	fre·sa
tomato	tomate	to·ma·te
vegetable	verdura	ver·doo·ra
watermelon	sandía	san·dee·a

Signs

Abierto	Open
Cerrado	Closed
Entrada	Entrance
Hombres	Men
Mujeres	Women
Prohibido	Prohibited
Salida	Exit
Servicios/Aseos	Toilets

fish	pescado	pes·ka·do
lamb	cordero	kor·de·ro
pork	cerdo	ther·do
turkey	pavo	pa·vo
veal	ternera	ter·ne·ra

Fruit & Vegetables

apple	manzana	man·tha·na
apricot	albaricoque	al·ba·ree·ko·ke
artichoke	alcachofa	al·ka·cho·fa
asparagus	espárragos	es·pa·ra·gos
banana	plátano	pla·ta·no
beans	judías	khoo·dee·as
beetroot	remolacha	re·mo·la·cha
cabbage	col	kol
carrot	zanahoria	tha·na·o·rya
cherry	cereza	the·re·tha
corn	maíz	ma·eeth
cucumber	pepino	pe·pee·no
fruit	fruta	froo·ta
grape	uvas	oo·vas
lemon	limón	lee·mon
lentils	lentejas	len·te·khas
lettuce	lechuga	le·choo·ga
mushroom	champiñón	cham·pee·nyon
nuts	nueces	nwe·thes
onion	cebolla	the·bo·lya
orange	naranja	na·ran·kha
peach	melocotón	me·lo·ko·ton
peas	guisantes	gee·san·tes
(red/green) pepper	pimiento (rojo/verde)	pee·myen·to (ro·kho/ver·de)
pineapple	piña	pee·nya
plum	ciruela	theer·we·la
potato	patata	pa·ta·ta
pumpkin	calabaza	ka·la·ba·tha

Other

bread	pan	pan
butter	mantequilla	man·te·kee·lya
cheese	queso	ke·so
egg	huevo	we·vo
honey	miel	myel
jam	mermelada	mer·me·la·da
oil	aceite	a·they·te
pepper	pimienta	pee·myen·ta
rice	arroz	a·roth
salt	sal	sal
sugar	azúcar	a·thoo·kar
vinegar	vinagre	vee·na·gre

Drinks

beer	cerveza	ther·ve·tha
coffee	café	ka·fe
(orange) juice	zumo (de naranja)	thoo·mo (de na·ran·kha)
milk	leche	le·che
tea	té	te
(mineral) water	agua (mineral)	a·gwa (mee·ne·ral)
(red) wine	vino (tinto)	vee·no (teen·to)
(white) wine	vino (blanco)	vee·no (blan·ko)

EMERGENCIES

Help!
¡Socorro! · so·ko·ro

Go away!
¡Vete! · ve·te

Call a doctor!
¡Llame a un médico! · lya·me a oon me·dee·ko

Call the police!
¡Llame a la policía! · lya·me a la po·lee·thee·a

I'm lost.
Estoy perdido/a. · es·toy per·dee·do/a (m/f)

I'm ill.
Estoy enfermo/a. · es·toy en·fer·mo/a (m/f)

Where are the toilets?
¿Dónde están los baños? · don·de es·tan los ba·nyos

NUMBERS

1	uno	oo·no
2	dos	dos
3	tres	tres
4	cuatro	kwa·tro
5	cinco	theen·ko
6	seis	seys
7	siete	sye·te
8	ocho	o·cho
9	nueve	nwe·ve
10	diez	dyeth
20	veinte	veyn·te
30	treinta	treyn·ta
40	cuarenta	kwa·ren·ta
50	cincuenta	theen·kwen·ta
60	sesenta	se·sen·ta
70	setenta	se·ten·ta
80	ochenta	o·chen·ta
90	noventa	no·ven·ta
100	cien	thyen
1000	mil	meel

SHOPPING & SERVICES

I'd like to buy ...
Quisiera comprar ...   kee·sye·ra kom·prar ...

May I look at it?
¿Puedo verlo?   pwe·do ver·lo

How much is it?
¿Cuánto cuesta?   kwan·to kwes·ta

That's too/very expensive.
Es muy caro.   es mooy ka·ro

Can you lower the price?
¿Podría bajar un   po·dree·a ba·khar oon
poco el precio?   po·ko el pre·thyo

There's a mistake in the bill.
Hay un error en la cuenta.   ai oon e·ror en la kwen·ta

Catalan – Basics		
Good morning.	Bon dia.	bon dee·a
Good afternoon.	Bona tarda.	bo·na tar·da
Good evening.	Bon vespre.	bon bes·pra
Goodbye.	Adéu.	a·the·oo
Please.	Sisplau.	sees·pla·oo
Thank you.	Gràcies.	gra·see·a
You're welcome.	De res.	de res
Excuse me.	Perdoni.	par·tho·nee
I'm sorry.	Ho sento.	oo sen·to
How are you?	Com estàs?	kom as·tas
(Very) Well.	(Molt) Bé.	(mol) be

ATM	cajero	ka·khe·ro
	automático	ow·to·ma·tee·ko
credit card	tarjeta de	tar·khe·ta de
	crédito	kre·dee·to
post office	correos	ko·re·os
tourist office	oficina	o·fee·thee·na
	de turismo	de too·rees·mo

TIME & DATES

What time is it?
¿Qué hora es?   ke o·ra es

It's (10) o'clock.
Son (las diez).   son (las dyeth)

Half past (one).
Es (la una) y media.   es (la oo·na) ee me·dya

morning	mañana	ma·nya·na
afternoon	tarde	tar·de
evening	noche	no·che
yesterday	ayer	a·yer
today	hoy	oy
tomorrow	mañana	ma·nya·na
Monday	lunes	loo·nes
Tuesday	martes	mar·tes
Wednesday	miércoles	myer·ko·les
Thursday	jueves	khwe·bes
Friday	viernes	vyer·nes
Saturday	sábado	sa·ba·do
Sunday	domingo	do·meen·go

TRANSPORT

I want to go to ...
Quisiera ir a ...   kee·sye·ra eer a ...

What time does it arrive/leave?
¿A qué hora llega/sale?   a ke o·ra lye·ga/sa·le

I want to get off here.
Quiero bajarme aquí.   kye·ro ba·khar·me a·kee

1st-class	primera clase	pree·me·ra kla·se
2nd-class	segunda clase	se·goon·da kla·se
bicycle	bicicleta	bee·thee·kle·ta
boat	barco	bar·ko
bus	autobús	ow·to·boos
car	coche	ko·che
cancelled	cancelado	kan·the·la·do
delayed	retrasado	re·tra·sa·do
motorcycle	moto	mo·to
one-way	ida	ee·da
plane	avión	a·vyon
return	ida y vuelta	ee·da ee vwel·ta
ticket	billete	bee·lye·te
ticket office	taquilla	ta·kee·lya
timetable	horario	o·ra·ryo
train	tren	tren

GLOSSARY

Most of the following terms are in Castilian Spanish which is fully understood around the island. A handful of specialised terms in Catalan (C) also appear. No distinction has been made for any Mallorcan dialect variations.

agroturisme (C) – rural tourism

ajuntament (C) – city or town hall

alquería – Muslim-era farmstead

avenida – avenue

avinguda (C) – see *avenida*

baño completo – full bathroom with toilet, shower and/or bath

bodega – cellar (especially wine cellar)

bomberos – fire brigade

cala – cove

call (C) – Jewish quarter in Palma, Inca and some other Mallorcan towns

cambio – change; also currency exchange

caña – small glass of beer

canguro – babysitter

capilla – chapel

carrer (C) – street

carretera – highway

carta – menu

castell (C) – castle

castellano – Castilian; used in preference to '*Español*' to describe the national language

català – Catalan language; a native of Catalonia. The Mallorcan dialect is Mallorquin

celler – (C) wine cellars turned into restaurants

cervecería – beer bar

comisaría – police station

conquistador – conqueror

converso – Jew who converted to Christianity in medieval Spain

correos – post office

cortado – short black coffee with a little milk

costa – coast

cuenta – bill, cheque

ensaïmada (C) – Mallorcan pastry

entrada – entrance, ticket

ermita – small hermitage or country chapel

església (C) – see *iglesia*

estació (C) – see *estación*

estación – station

estanco – tobacconist shop

farmacia – pharmacy

faro – lighthouse

fiesta – festival, public holiday or party

finca – farmhouse

gasolina – petrol

guardía civil – military police

habitaciones libres – literally 'rooms available'

hostal – see *pensión*

iglesia – church

IVA – *impuesto sobre el valor añadido,* or value-added tax

lavabo – washbasin

librería – bookshop

lista de correos – poste restante

locutorio – telephone centre

marisquería – seafood eatery

menú del día – menu of the day

mercat (C) – market

mirador – lookout point

Modernisme – the Catalan version of the art nouveau architectural and artistic style

monestir (C) – monastery

museo – museum

museu (C) – see *museo*

objetos perdidos – lost-and-found

oficina de turismo – tourist office; also *oficina de información turística*

palacio – palace, grand mansion or noble house

palau (C) – see *palacio*

pensión – small family-run hotel

plaça (C) – see *plaza*

platja (C) – see *playa*

playa – beach

plaza – square

port (C) – see *puerto*

possessió (C) – typical Mallorcan farmhouse

PP – Partido Popular (People's Party)

puente – bridge

puerto – port

puig (C) – mountain peak

rambla – avenue or riverbed

refugis (C) – hikers' huts

retablo – altarpiece

retaule (C) – see *retablo*

robes de llengües (C) – traditional striped Mallorcan fabrics

santuari (C) – shrine or sanctuary, hermitage

según precio del mercado – on menus, 'according to market price' (often written 'spm')

Semana Santa – Holy Week

serra (C) – mountain range

servicios – toilets

tafona (C) – traditional oil press found on most Mallorcan farms

talayot (C) – ancient watchtower

tarjeta de crédito – credit card

tarjeta de residencia – residence card

tarjeta telefónica – phonecard

terraza – terrace; pavement cafe

torre – tower

turismo – tourism or saloon car

urgencia – emergency

Behind the Scenes

SEND US YOUR FEEDBACK

We love to hear from travellers – your comments keep us on our toes and help make our books better. Our well-travelled team reads every word on what you loved or loathed about this book. Although we cannot reply individually to your submissions, we always guarantee that your feedback goes straight to the appropriate authors, in time for the next edition. Each person who sends us information is thanked in the next edition – the most useful submissions are rewarded with a selection of digital PDF chapters.

Visit **lonelyplanet.com/contact** to submit your updates and suggestions or to ask for help. Our award-winning website also features inspirational travel stories, news and discussions.

Note: We may edit, reproduce and incorporate your comments in Lonely Planet products such as guidebooks, websites and digital products, so let us know if you don't want your comments reproduced or your name acknowledged. For a copy of our privacy policy visit lonelyplanet.com/privacy.

OUR READERS

Many thanks to the travellers who used the last edition and wrote to us with helpful hints, useful advice and interesting anecdotes: Anton Krivtsun, Frank Jansen, Helen Gallivan, Katrin Flatscher, Libya Charleson, Monika Zaboklicka, Pauline La Fleur, Peter Tasker, Phil Gillette, Romy Schwäbe, Samantha Rennie, Steven and Linda Alderson, Torsten Kempa.

ACKNOWLEDGMENTS

Climate map data adapted from Peel MC, Finlayson BL & McMahon TA (2007) 'Updated World Map of the Köppen-Geiger Climate Classification', Hydrology and Earth System Sciences, 11, 1633–44.

Cover photograph: Valldemossa, Mallorca, Michele Falzone/AWL.

AUTHOR THANKS

Kerry Christiani

A heartfelt *gràcies* to all the Mallorquins who helped out, in particular tourism pros and the folk at TIB. Warm thanks to Antonia for the apartment in Pollença, Carmen Vila Altimir for tips and good times, and my interviewees: Kai and Julia at Kite and Bike, master chef Marc Fosh and Mallorca Rutes guide Mateu. Last but never least, a big thank you to my husband, Andy, for being a great travel companion, a savvy map-reader and skilful mountain driver.

THIS BOOK

This 3rd edition of Lonely Planet's *Mallorca* guidebook was researched and written by Kerry Christiani. The 2nd edition was written by Anthony Ham, and the 1st edition was written by Damien Simonis and Sarah Andrews, with contributions from Sally Schafer. This guidebook was commissioned in Lonely Planet's London office, and produced by the following:

Destination Editors Dora Whitaker, Joanna Cooke
Product Editor Briohny Hooper
Senior Cartographer Anthony Phelan
Book Designer Wendy Wright
Managing Editor Angela Tinson
Senior Editors Claire Naylor, Karyn Noble
Assisting Editors Lauren Hunt, Kellie Langdon,

Charlotte Orr, Erin Richards, Gabrielle Stefanos
Assisting Cartographer James Leversha
Cover Research Naomi Parker
Language Content Branislava Vladisavljevic

Thanks to Anita Banh, Joe Bindloss, Ryan Evans, Larissa Frost, Genesys India, Jouve India, Kate Mathews, Catherine Naghten, Martine Power, Ellie Simpson

Index

Map Legend

Sights

- Beach
- Bird Sanctuary
- Buddhist
- Castle/Palace
- Christian
- Confucian
- Hindu
- Islamic
- Jain
- Jewish
- Monument
- Museum/Gallery/Historic Building
- Ruin
- Sento Hot Baths/Onsen
- Shinto
- Sikh
- Taoist
- Winery/Vineyard
- Zoo/Wildlife Sanctuary
- Other Sight

Activities, Courses & Tours

- Bodysurfing
- Diving
- Canoeing/Kayaking
- Course/Tour
- Skiing
- Snorkelling
- Surfing
- Swimming/Pool
- Walking
- Windsurfing
- Other Activity

Sleeping

- Sleeping
- Camping

Eating

- Eating

Drinking & Nightlife

- Drinking & Nightlife
- Cafe

Entertainment

- Entertainment

Shopping

- Shopping

Information

- Bank
- Embassy/Consulate
- Hospital/Medical
- Internet
- Police
- Post Office
- Telephone
- Toilet
- Tourist Information
- Other Information

Geographic

- Beach
- Hut/Shelter
- Lighthouse
- Lookout
- Mountain/Volcano
- Oasis
- Park
- Pass
- Picnic Area
- Waterfall

Population

- Capital (National)
- Capital (State/Province)
- City/Large Town
- Town/Village

Transport

- Airport
- Border crossing
- Bus
- Cable car/Funicular
- Cycling
- Ferry
- Metro station
- Monorail
- Parking
- Petrol station
- S-Bahn/S-train/Subway station
- Taxi
- T-bane/Tunnelbana station
- Train station/Railway
- Tram
- Tube station
- U-Bahn/Underground station
- Other Transport

Note: Not all symbols displayed above appear on the maps in this book

Routes

- Tollway
- Freeway
- Primary
- Secondary
- Tertiary
- Lane
- Unsealed road
- Road under construction
- Plaza/Mall
- Steps
- Tunnel
- Pedestrian overpass
- Walking Tour
- Walking Tour detour
- Path/Walking Trail

Boundaries

- International
- State/Province
- Disputed
- Regional/Suburb
- Marine Park
- Cliff
- Wall

Hydrography

- River, Creek
- Intermittent River
- Canal
- Water
- Dry/Salt/Intermittent Lake
- Reef

Areas

- Airport/Runway
- Beach/Desert
- Cemetery (Christian)
- Cemetery (Other)
- Glacier
- Mudflat
- Park/Forest
- Sight (Building)
- Sportsground
- Swamp/Mangrove

OUR STORY

A beat-up old car, a few dollars in the pocket and a sense of adventure. In 1972 that's all Tony and Maureen Wheeler needed for the trip of a lifetime – across Europe and Asia overland to Australia. It took several months, and at the end – broke but inspired – they sat at their kitchen table writing and stapling together their first travel guide, *Across Asia on the Cheap*. Within a week they'd sold 1500 copies. Lonely Planet was born.

Today, Lonely Planet has offices in Franklin, London, Melbourne, Oakland, Beijing and Delhi, with more than 600 staff and writers. We share Tony's belief that 'a great guidebook should do three things: inform, educate and amuse'.

OUR WRITER

Kerry Christiani

Kerry's love affair with Mallorca began as a child, but she really fell head over heels with the island when she met her now-husband, Andy, while working there in the summer of 1999 (ah, happy days!). Luckily, he too was just as enthralled with the island's mountain hikes, coastal trails and middle-of-nowhere monasteries as she was. Kerry has spent stints living in and around Pollença, and returned there again this year for a whole glorious summer. Kerry studied Spanish to MA level and has authored some 20 guidebooks, including numerous Lonely Planet titles. She contributes frequently to magazines and websites such as bbc.com/travel and *Lonely Planet Traveller*. Kerry tweets about her adventures @kerrychristiani

Read more about Kerry at:
lonelyplanet.com/members/kerrychristiani

Published by Lonely Planet Publications Pty Ltd
ABN 36 005 607 983
3rd edition – Jul 2014
ISBN 978 1 74220 750 6
© Lonely Planet 2014   Photographs © as indicated 2014
10 9 8 7 6 5 4 3 2 1
Printed in Singapore